YOU CAN'T GO TO WAR WITHOUT SONG

YOU CAN'T GO TO WAR WITHOUT SONG

Performance and Community Mobilization in South Africa

—ⱄⱄ—

OMOTAYO JOLAOSHO

INDIANA UNIVERSITY PRESS

This book is a publication of

Indiana University Press
Office of Scholarly Publishing
Herman B Wells Library 350
1320 East 10th Street
Bloomington, Indiana 47405 USA

iupress.org

Manufactured in the United States of America

First printing 2022

Library of Congress Cataloging-in-Publication Data

Names: Jolaosho, Omotayo, author.
Title: You can't go to war without song : performance and community mobilization in South Africa / Omotayo Jolaosho.
Description: First printing. | Bloomington, Indiana : Indiana University Press, 2022. | Includes bibliographical references and index.
Identifiers: LCCN 2022021477 (print) | LCCN 2022021478 (ebook) | ISBN 9780253063205 (hardcover) | ISBN 9780253063212 (paperback) | ISBN 9780253063229 (pdf)
Subjects: LCSH: Protest movements—South Africa. | Political activists—South Africa. | Community activists—South Africa. | Protest songs—South Africa. | Performing arts—Social aspects—South Africa.
Classification: LCC HN801.A8 J66 2022 (print) | LCC HN801.A8 (ebook) | DDC 303.48/40968—dc23/eng/20220503
LC record available at https://lccn.loc.gov/2022021477
LC ebook record available at https://lccn.loc.gov/2022021478

"For our dead, not a moment's silence, but a lifetime of struggle"

CONTENTS

Editor's Note ix

Acknowledgments xi

Maps xv

Introduction 1
Activist Portrait: Ma Patrycja 35
1. Emergence 41
2. Routinization 69
   Activist Portrait: Kanelo 99
3. Efflorescence 106
   Activist Portrait: Lebo 136
4. Ruptures 144
   Activist Portrait: Willeen 172
5. Countermobilization 177
6. Redemption 210
   Conclusion 243
   Epilogue: Wesley 253

Bibliography 257

Index 277

EDITOR'S NOTE

OMOTAYO (TAYO) JOLAOSHO PASSED AWAY on October 22, 2021, in Tampa, Florida, at the age of thirty-six, just a few months after submitting the final version of this book. They were a gifted anthropologist, an award-winning playwright and performer, a full-stack software engineer, a yoga instructor, and much more. In 2020, at the height of racial justice protests amid the COVID-19 pandemic, they founded a nonprofit organization dedicated to promoting healing and collective recovery for multiple marginalized individuals and communities.

I had the honor of serving as Tayo's PhD adviser at Rutgers University and was their friend and mentor ever since. After their death, I asked their family and Indiana University Press if I could oversee the last stages of the book's publication in honor of their legacy and that of their interlocutors and friends in South Africa. Our writing styles are very different, so I have tried to honor their style as I reviewed copyedits. Since I did not have access to their field notes, interview transcripts, or other research materials, I could not verify quotes, dates, or other information.

Tayo was a warm, fierce, brave, joyful soul who used their gifts and skills to try to understand the deep disparities of the world and do whatever they could to bring about justice and change, whether through their writing, teaching, singing, yoga, or activism. They were much loved and are deeply missed.

Dorothy Hodgson
Dean of Arts and Sciences and
Professor of Anthropology
Brandeis University

ACKNOWLEDGMENTS

MY GRATITUDE MUST BEGIN WITH members of the Anti-Privatisation Forum (APF) and other activists, who gave their time and energy to share their lives, their views, and their political strivings with me. Although many activists declined the protection of anonymity, insisting that they were not afraid of any repercussions resulting from their views, I decided not to include their names on these pages for ethical reasons. While I may not be able to thank them by name, I express my gratitude nonetheless, and I hope to keep offering my thanks in direct communication with them.

I would like to thank Indiana University Press and its editorial staff, especially Dee Mortensen, Gary Dunham, and Ashante Thomas, for their support in making this book a reality. Earlier versions of some chapters appeared in *African Studies Review, Journal of Material Culture,* and *Signs: Journal of Women in Culture and Society*; I am grateful to the editors of those journals for allowing me to reproduce material here. Thanks to Benjamin Mittler for the great maps accompanying this project. I would like to especially thank the anonymous reviewers who read the manuscript and offered critical feedback that vastly improved the work. I maintain responsibility for its partiality and shortcomings.

The critical approach to theory and ethnography of the Rutgers University Program in Cultural Anthropology set my foundation as a scholar committed to socially engaged research. I am especially grateful to Dorothy Hodgson, who served as a dedicated adviser throughout my graduate training and remains my appointed adviser-for-life. She has been a mentor, advocate, and ardent supporter fostering my personal and intellectual growth. Words are inadequate to express my thanks for her consistent engagement, guidance, and encouragement. Laura Ahearn, Angelique Haugerud, Fran Mascia-Lees, and

Catherine Besteman also offered dedicated feedback on the dissertation that forms the basis of this book. They have each gone above and beyond the call of duty in ways I cannot hope to repay, but for which I remain eternally grateful. I thank Ousseina Alidou, Abena Busia, Barbara Cooper, Renee DeLancey, Teresa Delcorso-Ellmann, Allen Howard, and Rick Schroeder for the warmth and engagement that has enriched my sense of scholarly belonging.

At the University of South Florida, I have benefited from being in community with colleagues in Africana studies, the School of Interdisciplinary Global Studies, and those in other departments, including anthropology, sociology, and women's and gender studies. For university comradeship through the years, special thanks to Cheryl Rodriguez, David Ponton III, Laurie Lahey, Edward Kissi, Kersuze Simeon-Jones, Cheryl Hall, Scott Solomon, Steven Tauber, Bernd Reiter, Peter Funke, Kiki Caruson, Elizabeth Hordge-Freeman, Dillon Mahoney, Kevin Yelvington, Ylce Irizarry, and Tangela Serls.

A Foreign Language and Area Studies Fellowship, awarded by Indiana University's Center for African Studies, and a Fulbright-Hays Zulu Group Project Abroad supported the language training needed for this research. Fellowship support from the US Department of Education (Fulbright-Hays DDRA), the National Science Foundation (NSF-GRF & NSF-DDRIG), and the Social Science Research Council (IDRF) enabled me to conduct long-term fieldwork in South Africa. Additional support from the Humanities Institute and the College of Arts and Sciences at the USF allowed me to return to South Africa for follow-up research on multiple occasions.

During my fieldwork in Johannesburg, I was affiliated with the Department of Anthropology at the University of the Witwatersrand (Wits University). Achille Mbembe was the first to invite me to seek affiliation at Wits University; his suggestion led me to a thriving community. In addition to Achille Mbembe, I would like to thank Kelly Gillespie, David Coplan, Julia Hornberger, Molefi Trinity Makola, Leigh-Ann Naidoo, Prishani Naidoo, and Eric Worby. It was through the Sawyer Seminar held at Wits University that I met Micaela Alicia Smith, who has since become a dear friend and comrade. Kelly Gillespie and Leigh-Ann Naidoo hosted me in their home during my final months in South Africa. In so doing, they facilitated the completion of my fieldwork and eventual return to the United States.

Neo Lekgotla Laga Ramoupi eased my transition into the field by hosting me in his home during the first few months of fieldwork. I am grateful for the boundless generosity he, his family, and his friends have extended toward me. He drove me to my research sites when I had yet to secure a car; he even taught me how to drive with a manual transmission. He displayed lasting patience in those moments of which I am certainly undeserving, but for which I am eternally grateful. Neo's niece, Tshepiso Nomathamsanqa Zungu, along with Sehlisiwe Sibanda and Thabo Molefe provided invaluable research assistance throughout fieldwork, and I am grateful for their support, friendship, and insights into cultural and linguistic undercurrents in events and interviews.

Along with several activists who became close friends, I am grateful for the camaraderie shared in Johannesburg with Dawu Sehlaphi Sibanda, Lilian Smit, Maki Mareiza Mokone, Carin Runciman, Dale McKinley, Tonderai Chiyindiko, Thapelo Lekgowa, and Nompumelelo Mathabela. These friendships and mutual support continue to enrich my scholarly and personal life. Charlotte Schaer, who has sadly passed away, taught me how to sculpt and showed me why molding clay mattered for justice. She held me together in the field, and my grief is remembering that she is no longer just a phone call away.

A Smithsonian Institution summer fellowship allowed me to conduct archival research and interviews in Washington, DC, on the circulation of South African freedom songs in the United States. At the Smithsonian, I would especially like to thank James Early, Diana Baird N'Diaye, and Atesh Sonneborne. I am grateful to Ysaye Maria Barnwell, Bernice Johnson Reagon, and Pam Rogers, for letting me interview them during my time at the Smithsonian.

I started my academic explorations at Simon's Rock College of Bard. My scholarly life is a result of the intellectual and personal foundation laid by the Simon's Rock community. For their investment in me, I especially need to thank (in some cases honor the memory of) Mary-King Austin, Lesley Banks, Karen Beaumont, Jennifer Browdy de Hernandez, Veronica Chambers, Jason Clampet, Dana Cummings, Emmanuel Dongala, Pauline Dongala, Audrey Kerr, James Sterling King, Beth Moser, Okey Ndibe, Victoria Paxton-Hill, Krishna Raghunath, Bernard Rodgers Jr., Beth Sack, Wendy Shifrin, and Larry Wallach.

I have received helpful feedback from discussants, fellow participants, and audience members from numerous conferences and seminars at which I presented this work over the years. I am especially grateful to colleagues I met while completing a postdoctoral fellowship at the University of California, Merced's Center for the Humanities, including Nigel Hatton, Robin Maria DeLugan, Susan Amussen, Jayson Beaster-Jones, Katherine Steele Brokaw, Gregg Camfield, Kevin Dawson, Tanya Golash-Boza, and Ruth Mostern. Dialoguing with and supporting me have also been Jeffrey Juris, Scott Matter, John Burdick, Nayanika Mookherjee, Kerry Chance, Mhoze Chikowero, Cajetan Iheka, Bianca Williams, Jesse Weaver Shipley, Gabriel (of the) Peoples, Chérie Rivers Ndaliko, Samuel Anderson, Thomas F. DeFrantz, Deborah Thomas, John L. Jackson, and Deniz Daser. Thank you to Christen Smith, particularly for sharing insight on red ants as antagonizers across the African diaspora. Gabriel Dattatreyan and Jessica Johnson have been constant coconspirators and were joined in recent years by Jennie Burnet and Rebecca Peters. I am thankful for these partnerships that have broadened my perspective, affirmed my dedication, and offered sanctuary.

Academic colleagues, close friends, and family have been generous throughout the research and writing process. To the Association of Black Anthropologists and the Black Performance Theory network, I remain steadfastly committed. I am particularly indebted to Nancy Moinde and my godchildren, Ninette Diogene, and Gabrielle Morris, who balanced my writing focus with family visits and video calls. I am grateful as well to Emma Alabaster (febrile creativity), Emma Arogundade, Carlton Rounds, Riaan Oppelt ("I have come to take you home"), Chaunetta Jones, Fatimah Williams, Benjamin Greene, Liz Caplan, Lisa Wilson, Jessica Lynne Trese, Michael Johnson, Ingrid Askew, Abosede George, Faisal Garba, Ruth Hearns, Josiah Houston, Baba Ifaluyi Oguname, Jill Kelly, Corbin Laedlein, Josh Lutter, Kissangwa Mbouta Jr., Yolanda Covington-Ward, Xavier Livermon, Kamela S. Heyward-Rotimi, Rachel Watkins, Austin Okigbo, Oghenetoja Okoh, N. Fadeke Castor, Nick Smith, Adryan Wallace, and the countless individuals whose love, support, shared laughter, and even tears made this book possible.

Finally, I never would have made it without my grandmother's prayers, my grandfather's dreams, my mother's persistence, or the breaths of the ancestors. I would therefore like to honor my family, Omolara Bello, Dare Bello, Dupe Bello, the Bellos, the Bedus, and the Odetolas, who constitute the foundation on which I mindfully stand.

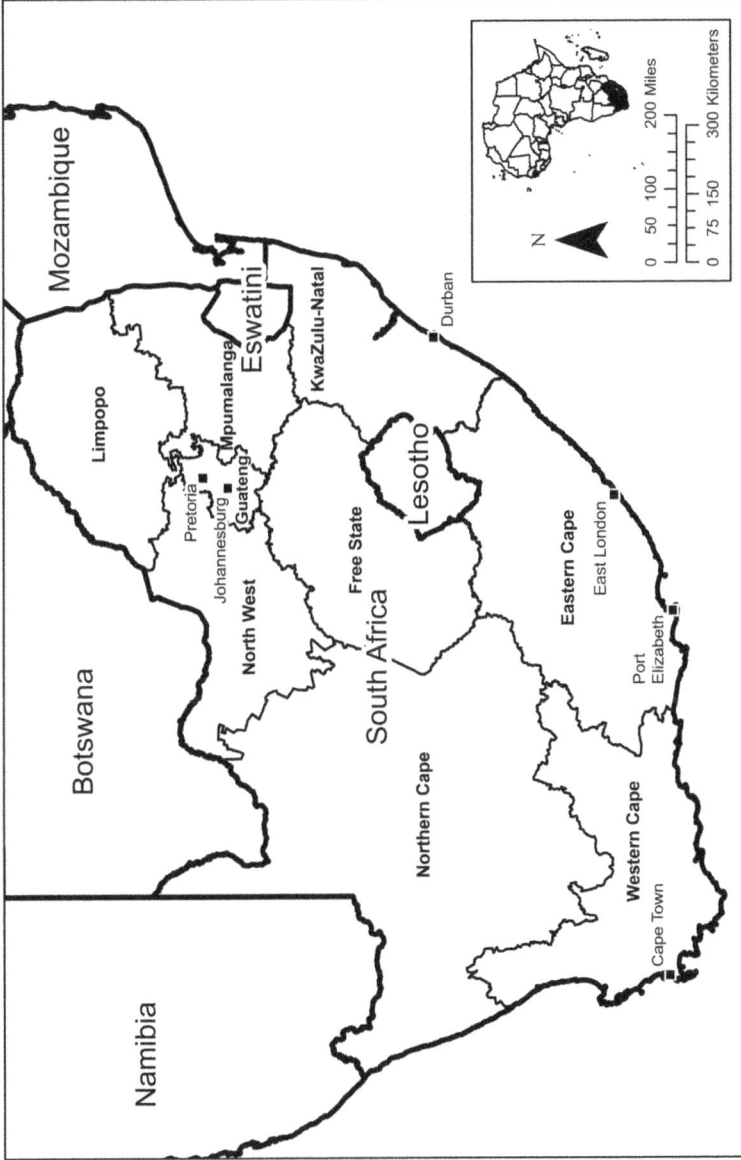

Map 0.1. Map of South Africa: Benjamin Mittler, Center for Digital Heritage, University of South Florida Libraries. *South Africa*. 1:11,250,000

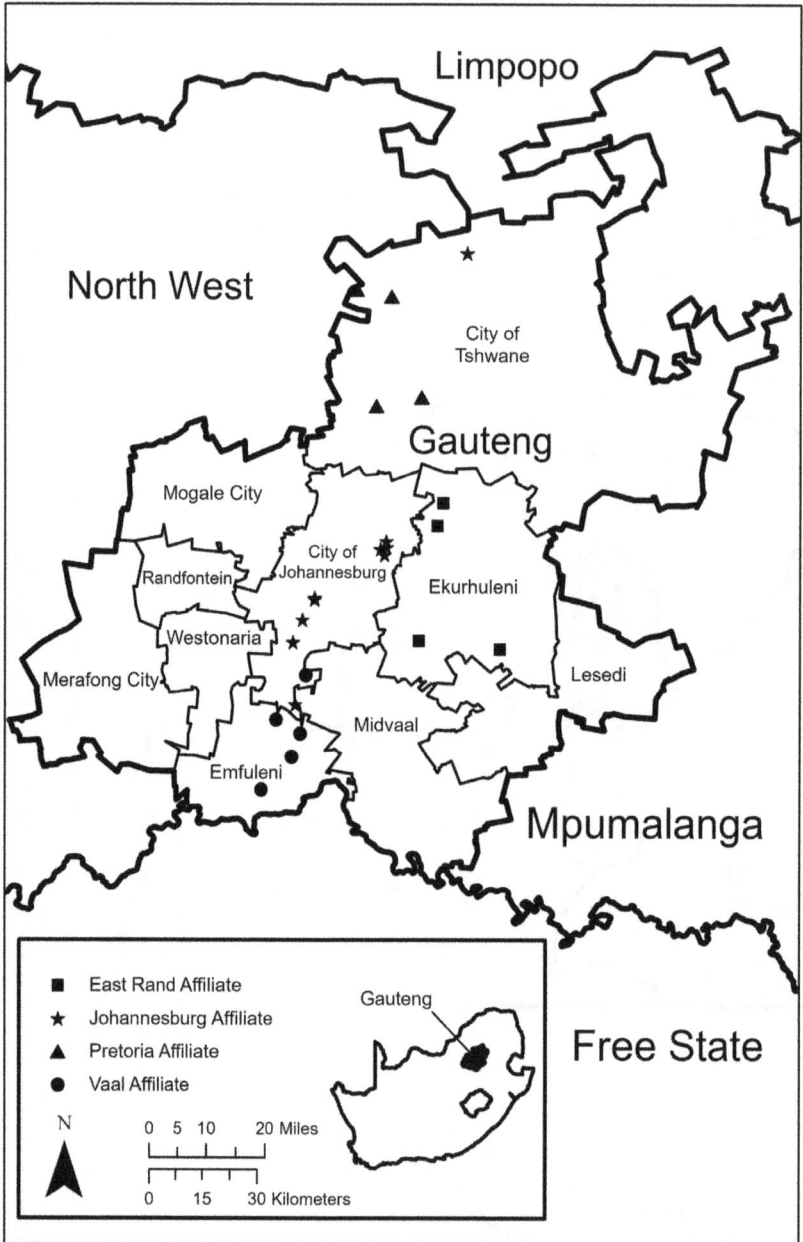

Map 0.2. Map of Gauteng Province indicating location of some APF affiliate organizations: Benjamin Mittler, Center for Digital Heritage, University of South Florida Libraries. *Gauteng Province Affiliates*. 1:1,500,000

YOU CAN'T GO TO
WAR WITHOUT SONG

INTRODUCTION

SHE REALLY DID NOT KNOW how it started. Her feet were sore, and she could not walk properly. "When you go to the hospital, they always give you Panado [a pain and fever reliever] and not take you seriously," Ma Lindi explained.[1] Without access to better health care, Ma Lindi's condition deteriorated. "I was told that my body was not able to drain water, my heart had enlarged, I had so many problems," she said. When I met Ma Lindi at a women's activist workshop in May 2010, she used a cane to support her weight as she trod slowly, but she had not surrendered to her health problems. She refused to accept help from anyone unless absolutely necessary. Even when she had to get assistance, she insisted on her own pace.

I was drawn to Ma Lindi when workshop facilitators observed she had made remarkable progress since becoming involved with the activist group, a group she had initially sought to avoid. When the workshop series began, about a year and a half before I met her, Ma Lindi had been reluctant to attend because of her health challenges: "I just could not walk, and I didn't want to be exposed or come into contact with new people because I saw pity in their faces." But her engagement with the group transformed her. During the overnight workshop where I met her, Ma Lindi described her desire to "grab at" all the collective offered. "There is so much energy and talent in me that I still want to impart," she declared. "I do have so much to give, and I feel I cannot stay at home."

The story of a social movement begins well before demonstrators capture the media's gaze. Movements begin in domestic spaces, catalyzed by individual bodies attending to material, environmental, and social needs. They begin in homes such as Ma Lindi's. Her transformation from a self-conscious recluse to an engaged and eager participant in collective action illuminates the more

1

robust examination of activism I urge throughout this book. That examination entails moving beyond the surface images of social movements encapsulated in media depictions of mass marches and street demonstrations. Those depictions establish the dominant trope of South African social movements as the mass protest: thousands of demonstrators taking to the streets, wearing matching T-shirts, brandishing placards, singing freedom songs accompanied by highly kinetic stomps. Beginning this book with an account of such a demonstration would contribute to public focus, in discussions of collective politics, on big events designed to capture media attention and amplify visibility—a focus that overlooks nuances in the constitution of these mass gatherings.

The story of an individual like Ma Lindi reveals the bodily labor of collective politics. Before leaving the house on any morning, Ma Lindi had to deliberately rally her body through a lengthy routine designed to relieve her organs and drain fluid. The prolonged rallying of her body and assuaging of her organs to face the day and gather with others is precisely the work of mobilization that encapsulates activism. A movement is the coming together of individuals, each with her own inner life and domestic travails, whether visible on the body or not. Each individual must be motivated toward coordinated, collective action on the basis of her own internal logic, unique perspectives, distinct needs, and sensory perceptions. This book focuses attention on the accounts of the individuals—the activists who constitute the collective movement—who have for too long been disregarded even within the historical and socioeconomic configurations of their own lives. In doing so, it offers necessarily fragmented and incomplete—but no less evocative and abundant—considerations of the embodied day-to-day activities of individual and collective political formation in South Africa.

Ma Lindi's eagerness to avoid pity offers the first testament of many to the striving for dignity inherent in activist endeavors. The decisions made in service to that concern, including Ma Lindi's original decision to stay home, highlight the primacy of activists' bodily conditions in their movement toward or shying away from political collectivity. Who gets to show up to activist events and public demonstrations is already preconditioned by sensory and corporeal undercurrents. Bodily conditions, as they drive politics, often present themselves to experiential awareness through sensations, including pain, that manifest in quotidian routines and specialized rituals, and even more so in the heightened expressiveness of performance. Hence, unsurprisingly, those with whom I worked (including Ma Lindi) prioritized performance as a crucial motivator for their activism. The prominence of freedom songs, dances, visual representations, and other displays of creative expression in protests, workshops, and organizational events reveal the intrinsic ties between protest and embodied performance in the practice of many South African activist communities. This link holds for performance in all its dimensions—not only artistic or creative expression but also daily actions and interactions such as performing a lengthy wellness routine to prepare the body for the day or performing one's membership role in an activist group. In its many intersections with collective politics, dynamically embodied performance is not epiphenomenal to activism; rather, it constitutes the very basis through which demands for justice occur.

I met Ma Lindi through the Anti-Privatisation Forum (APF), the organization that provides this book's vantage point for understanding the role of performance in the constitution of the activist community. The APF was one of many social movements that emerged in the wake of South Africa's democratic transition. It served as an umbrella body that coordinated the activist efforts of a fluctuating number of organizations in about thirty-four communities in the Johannesburg metropolitan area. Founded in July 2000, the organization flourished for years but was essentially defunct by 2012. Typical of the many shifting responses to the challenges that arose in the wake of the country's adoption of neoliberal economic policies, APF members adapted anti-apartheid songs and created new expressive forms to inform and comment on their struggles for access to water, electricity, housing, education, and health facilities, the costs of which have been made prohibitive by privatization. During sixteen months of fieldwork in 2009 and 2010, involving participant observation in activists' events, interviews, and archival research, I investigated the APF's adaptations of anti-apartheid performances to the shifting social dynamics governing activists' relationships with the state, articulation of racial and gender issues, emerging class consciousness, and intergenerational linkages.

In this analysis, I consider performance in its multiple dimensions, ranging from routine enactments that secure, sustain, or weaken political outcomes and commitments to more practiced creative expression. I show how routine negotiations and artistic displays shaped the APF's collective identity. Furthermore, through an integrative bodily approach to the examination of political performances, I consider sensory experiences and their mediation, revealing how these experiences influenced the mobilization activities activists pursued. Particularly in moments of creative expression, sensory experiences generated positive associations that made collective political struggle desirable. Ma Lindi is instructive here. Gender at Work, the collective she participated in, emphasized sensory experiences such as drawing on sense memory in collective dialogues and creative writing exercises and practicing tai chi. (I describe the rationale for this process more fully in chapter 5.) In addition to these group activities, Ma Lindi practiced specific exercises recommended by the group's facilitators at home. These exercises helped her regain a sense of control over her body, particularly her internal organs. With that reconnection to her body, she was able to heal emotionally and spiritually and was thereby empowered to seek further connection with others through the group.

Ma Lindi's transformation is intriguing because it exemplifies mobilization as sensorial, embodied, social, and relational. In contrast to Ma Lindi's positive association of mobilization with sensorial embodiment, sensory experience also yielded aversions for some activists: combativeness in the APF generated stress, eroded solidarity, and alienated many members. By considering these varied effects, I provide an expansive analysis of mobilization, emphasizing the role of dynamically embodied performance in the conduct of collective politics. The APF's story provides fertile ground for examining the emergence of collective activism and the resulting processes of formation, maintenance, and dissipation, exploring how collectives are sustained and how and why they stop working.

Although this book does not address the causes of the APF's eventual demise (as I was not present for those events), the movement's decline provides a backdrop for my analyses. The members I met held a nostalgic yearning for past glory and their varied frustrations became entangled with the APF's makeup in its latter years. That nostalgia was evident in a conversation with two youth members during my first research visit with APF members, in a community called Bophelong in the Vaal region. Tshepang, twenty-four, described how the APF had been immediately recognizable in the past: "When you wear a red T-shirt, people would know that this is APF." As if to demonstrate the APF's ubiquity in the region, as we were driving to Sharpeville from Bophelong that day, we saw a woman pedestrian wearing the APF T-shirt with its readily recognizable logo. However, Tshepang expressed concern that the organization's performances were no longer as frequent or as prominent as they had been in the past. A fellow activist and youth member, Prudence, nineteen, offered hope: "We could revise that." In response, Tshepang, already attentive to the APF's bureaucratic constraints, asked, "Where is the budget for that?" Tshepang's question evoked an essential conflict experienced by APF activists, who were caught in many ways between collective spirit and the strictures of organizational form. This book presents their challenges, describing how those conflicts were mirrored in the unfolding of APF performances over the movement's life course.

PERFORMANCE: ESSENTIAL CONTESTATIONS IN ACTIVIST COLLECTIVITY AND KNOWLEDGE PRODUCTION

Months after my conversation with Tshepang and Prudence in Bophelong, I stood outside the gates of Soweto's iconic Regina Mundi church waiting for a

friend to arrive. Buyisiwe, a thirty-four-year-old APF activist, who, with rever-
ence, had installed custom subwoofers in his car (so as to really "feel" the music,
he said). The pounding house beats announced his arrival before he came into
sight, music blasting as he pulled into the church parking lot for our meeting,
windows down, sunglasses on, the epitome of effortless cool.

Unsurprisingly, given his facility for customizing his automobile, Buyisiwe's chosen metaphor for the role of performance in activist struggles was
vehicular functionality. As we took in the church's depictions of anti-apartheid
struggle scenes and heroic figures in stained glass splendor, Buyisiwe offered
his perspective: for a car to have good performance, he said, two different
components—the engine and the gearbox—had to function well together.
Performance in community activism, he continued, required a similar efficacy:
an engine, the collective spirit powering a movement; and a gearbox, leadership
to set the orientation and pace of the movement.

This recognition of dual functions for performance is not unusual. Often
theorized as "an essentially contested concept" (Strine et al. 1990: 183; Gallie
1964: 187–88; Carlson 2004: 1–5), *performance* can refer both to heightened,
specialized displays and to the unmarked, everyday behavior constituting the
mundane. And, as Buyisiwe points out, the term can also reference the capabilities of vehicles and other machines or of workers in achieving specified
targets. Through contestation, scholars and laypeople have advanced the term's
relevance for multiple usages. In that process, contradiction in meaning has
become constructive. Reconciliation of these differences is not a preeminent
concern; rather, differences provide valuable spaces in which to expand and
enrich the concept.

Conceiving performance as an essentially contested concept suggests a ri-
valrous relationship among its multiple manifestations, or it at least implies
that these manifestations operate independently of and in contrast to one another. But as Buyisiwe indicates, performance works within social movements
through a mutually constitutive relationship in which the multiple elements of
the phenomenon reveal and reinforce one another. These multiple elements include at least three manifestations of performance. Freedom songs and protest
dances, as culturally specific display, exemplify the first manifestation of performance. The second manifestation involves iterative acts whose effects con-
geal over time (a process identified in the term *performative*) such as Ma Lindi's
deliberate practice of a daily bodily routine, her developing self-identification
as an activist, and her contribution to Gender at Work's collective identity.
The final manifestation involves acts completed in accordance with shared
standards which are therefore subjected to evaluation. Buyisiwe's definition
of a movement's efficacy as dependent on successful coordination between a

movement's membership and its leaders is an example of the possible evaluations to which performance acts can be subjected. Below I briefly trace each of these three strands as they manifest in the book.

Performance and Culturally Specific Display

The phrase *cultural performances* refers to organized events or activities "with a set of performers, an audience, and a place and occasion of performance" (Singer 1955: 27). They are discrete, observable, direct experiences that for anthropologists have historically provided the "most concrete observable units of [a] cultural structure" (Singer 1959: xiii).[2] Taking place within culturally specific "performance frames" (Bauman 1975), these expressive conventions provide access for contemporary anthropologists not to a unitary collective voice but to variations within collectivities (Burdick 1995; Gilbert 2005).[3]

In impoverished communities, the heightened display of cultural performances matters not only for what it reflects of shared values but also as a vital resource for political dissent in the face of material deprivation. These performances can reinforce an existing social order or incite change by offering "licensed criticism," a term Leroy Vail and Landeg White used to describe the frank expression that is socially permitted as part of a performance frame (1991: 41).[4] In South Africa during apartheid, freedom songs were cultural performances that allowed for covert critique, as protesters took advantage of language barriers between them and state officials. As the apartheid government caught on, officials adopted ever more repressive measures, but they were unable to stem the flow of political expression through song and dance.[5]

Thus, song, specifically, provides insight into the dynamics of dominion. Songs and other cultural performances are particularly valuable, as historian Shirli Gilbert has noted, in "those communities for whom conventional channels of communication and expression are restricted or proscribed" (2005: 11; see also Conquergood 1991: 189).[6] Cultural performance therefore remains as an important arena for understanding not only creative political dissent but also the very nature of power itself (Ebron 2002: 5). Through their freedom songs and creative expressions, community activists build on a history of culturally sanctioned displays to interrogate existing conditions and mobilize the community toward shared hopes and visions of the world as it could be.

Performance, Performativity, and the Constitution of Community

Performance in this context is much more than a display of artistry. My concern with how performance cultivates an activist community also draws on approaches to performance as constitutive of the everyday. Communities do not come into existence without intervention. Rather, they emerge through repeated acts over time that reinforce and reproduce the reality of being together. As Bruno Latour notes, "If you stop making and remaking groups, you stop having groups" (2005: 35). The cumulative effect of routine interactions is encapsulated by the concept of the *performative*, a term first coined by British philosopher J. L. Austin to distinguish utterances through which, in appropriate circumstances, a speaker performs a particular action. In making a performative utterance, the speaker is not merely describing or reporting an action but is actually performing the act. Examples include "I do take this woman to be my lawfully wedded wife"; "I apologize"; "I promise I will be there tomorrow." These examples perform the act of marrying, apologizing, and promising.[7] Austin recognizes that it is not just these types of verbs that generate action in social life; rather, all language is performative. He asks, "When we issue any utterance whatsoever, are we not 'doing something'?" (1962 [1955]: 92; see also Austin 1979; Ahearn 2012: 164–65).

Judith Butler extends the concept of performativity in her discussion of gender.[8] Building on prior scholarship, Butler argues against a view of gender as a stable identity, asserting instead that gender "is an identity tenuously constituted in time" (1988: 519) created through "a *stylized repetition of acts*" (1988: 519; italics in original). The notion of an abiding gendered self, according to Butler, is an illusion created through this institution of repeated acts. That gender is performative means that "it is real only to the extent that it is [continuously] performed" (1988: 527). It is based on social convention constituted through time by means of the repetition and reproduction of *acts* of gender.[9] These insights into performativity apply not only to the social manifestation of gender but also to the social manifestation of race, class, indigeneity, sexual orientation, nationhood, and other aspects of individual identity and collective formation (Muñoz 2006; Askew 2002; Jackson 2001: 188–89; Johnson 2003: 9; Smith 2016; Huarcaya 2015; Covington-Ward 2018).

Demonstrating how these insights traverse scales—from interpersonal to geopolitical relations—Kelly Askew's *Performing the Nation* (2002) expounds on the performative constitution of Tanzania, a nation-state forged from two separate, distinct countries. Of the unsteadiness of such a forging, Askew notes, "The power entailed in trumpeting one version of reality (e.g., the existence of a Tanzanian nation) over others (e.g., the existence of not one but two nations in Tanzania) requires work, continual reenactment, unremitting performance" (2002: 291). Performativity therefore reveals not the definitiveness of social categories but the fact that these categories are always already in flux, exposed, contestable, and open to renegotiation. Just as importantly, performativity reveals the role of performance in upholding the taken-for-granted categories that constitute the everyday.

The routine negotiations of political sensibilities that took place during the APF's organizational meetings and activist events are performative acts that shape collectivity. The making, remaking, and dissipation of an activist group is performance, the performative effect of which is not only an emergent collective identity but also, for some at least, individual transformation—as was the case with Ma Lindi. This usage honors a distinction between performance as the enactment, the doing itself, and performativity as the effect. Performance and performativity are conjoined elements of social action (Diamond 1996: 4–5; Pollock 2005: 7–8). Such a distinction matters not merely for clarity but also for what it makes analytically available. Performance renders performativity specific and materially discrete. In doing so, matters "of embodiment, of social relations, of ideological interpellations, of emotional and political effects, all become discussable" (Diamond 1996: 5). Conversely, performativity reveals the nonfinite workings of performance (Askew 2002: 23), that a performance reverberates beyond the spatio-temporal specificities of its appearance.

Ma Lindi's bodily lived experience demonstrates that the acts of individual people performatively create political collectives. Ma Lindi, in her laborious and dignified movement, evocatively highlights activism as the internal (rallying her organs in preparation for the day) and external moving body. Her necessarily measured movement and action throws into relief the personal effort involved in coming together with others. Anybody who observed Ma Lindi walking toward an activist meeting (as I did) would see that she did not take her moving body for granted. Her every step was labored and deliberate—revealing in her slow pace the routine bodily effort of every individual who gathers with others in preparation for collective action. This movement, for Ma Lindi as for all activists, is both physical and embedded in the social. Activists must consider themselves in relation to the social world around them. Performativity becomes evident in these individual efforts in two ways: (1) a single person constitutes her activist identity through repeated acts such as attending meetings; and (2) these personal activities converge with the actions of fellow activists in the making of a political collective. So important is the individual to the collective that the effects, decisions, or conditions of a single person influence the overall conditions of possibility within a movement, whether or not this influence is recognized. Ma Lindi was an important aspect of the women's group she attended; without her presence, the group would have lost critical possibilities of what it could be. A consideration of collective movements through the lens of performativity recognizes the real, significant role of individual potential in constituting the collective.

Performance and Standards

In both its prevalent dimensions (specialized displays and mundane behavior), performance is subject to evaluation. As Richard Schechner notes, "'to perform' is to do something up to a standard—to succeed, to excel" (2002: 22). As practice, performance involves movement from the envisaged to the enacted, yielding appraisals of experience and outcomes. The expectations that activists have both of themselves and of their collectivity vary, and the ongoing evaluation of experience in the context of those expectations is revealed in the appraisals I encountered of the APF's decline as a failure of its *performance*.

APF members, including Buyisiwe, who were anxiously aware of the organization's shortcomings, described the APF's decline in terms of performance failure. Buyisiwe drew on his automotive metaphor of engines and gearboxes to offer an assessment of the APF. Despite the organization's past achievements, he said, performance had downshifted and was "now low." The engine and gearbox of the APF's metaphorical vehicle were not linking, halting performance: "Today, I don't see more action and activity and that hype you know, I mean for me the struggle today, eish, drags slow."[10] Buyisiwe's representation of the APF's decline illuminates how performance can be understood in relation to the gap between activist ideals and the inadequacy of their enactment. Such usage was prominent enough to constitute a third dimension of performance practice distinct from but connected to the displayed and the unremarked.

Against Buyisiwe's suggestion that performance only happens when ideals are perfectly executed, with everyone enacting his part in synchrony, I propose that performance constitutes that gap between activists' ethical ideals and the collective's faltering practice. In other words, to suggest that the APF in its decline stopped performing would be misleading. Since performance is practice itself, quotidian and uneven, it must be viewed as an intermediating engagement and not a fixed achievement. A performance analytic therefore remains useful—it is perhaps even more so—in matters of failure.

In calling attention to the gap between activists' ideals and the variable execution of those ideals, I do not intend a definition of performance as the imperfect enactment of linguistic competence (Chomsky 1965), a dichotomy that is problematic for its dismissal of language use in socioculturally specific contexts (see Ahearn 2012: 162–63). Performance in this context is not a question of competence. Nor am I saying that some universal model for activism exists that can hypothetically be rendered perfectly, absent human limitations.

The expectations that activists have both of themselves and of their collectivity vary, but they do have expectations, and they evaluate their experiences.

My formulation of the gap between idealized intentions and lived practice benefits from what Richard Bauman refers to as "the emergent"—that there is an interplay among individuals, their goals, and social contexts such that any performance cannot be accounted for by the sum of its parts (1975: 302; see also Mayr 1982; Williams 1977). Emergence offers a way of considering the uniqueness of each performance act, in that its outcomes cannot be specified ahead of time. This unpredictability or lack of fixity explains the tensions and frustrations activists encounter between their guiding visions and the emergent organizational collectivity. Addressing gaps between activists' intentions and the outcomes of the collective activity, I argue against the sterility of failure, demonstrating instead that an analytic lens attuned to performance and performativity recognizes political activities and their effects even when—especially when—these activities do not live up to expectations. If performance happens in the gaps, failure is a constitutive part of performance, particularly for movements seeking social transformation.

"PROTESTS ARE AN EMOTIONAL POSITION": THE POLITICAL AESTHETICS OF COLLECTIVE POWER

Given the centrality of the body's lived experience to the manifestations of performance in social life, understanding activism through a performance lens—that is, one receptive to the uncertainties that come with practice—requires attunement to the complex interplay of emotion, senses, and sensation. A conversation I had in March 2010 following a community meeting in Orlando East, Soweto, highlights the primacy of emotions in collective politics. Members of the Orlando Residents Association and their surrounding communities had requested a meeting with a Johannesburg municipal official to discuss, among other things, transportation infrastructure in the area. Standing outside the Orlando East community hall at the conclusion of the meeting, I chatted with one of the association's leaders. I mentioned that I had attended one of their protests and asked if the group planned to stage another one. His response highlighted the tensions between collective emotional spontaneity and organizational procedure. "We cannot plan protests," he said. "Protests are an emotional position. We can plan meetings, we can plan gatherings. We can't plan protests because protests will be brought about when the people feel, 'But now this is too much.' Then people protest.... We don't organize protests. The protests are an emotional issue where people now react to something."[11]

In this comment, the association leader presents a view of protest as an extra-legal emotional eruption that ensues when other avenues have been exhausted. Refusing my characterization of protests as "staged," he asserted the intensity of a person's emotions in response to unbearable maltreatment by their governing agents as a marker of a protest's genuineness. For this community leader and other activists, emotions authenticate protests, to the extent that without emotion, protest is not possible.

The logic underlying these views was completely bypassed in foundational social movement scholarship. In fact, scholarship devoted to the emotional dimensions of collective politics only began to flourish in the late 1990s through the early 2000s (e.g., Jasper 1998; Goodwin et al. 2001; Juris 2008b; Gould 2009). Prior scholarship occluded or distorted the role of emotion due to a number of factors, especially the belief in a Cartesian gap that separates emotions from rationality and feeling from analysis (Goodwin et al. 2001: 1–2; Aminzade and McAdam 2001: 23; see also Farnell 1999).[12] New scholarly emphases on framing, collective identity, and the symbolic dimensions of social movements have generated greater receptivity to emotions in more recent work (Goodwin et al. 2001: 9), however, and feminist work has helped delink emotions and irrationality by interrogating the assumptions that would bind them (see Goodwin et al. 2001: 9; Aminzade and McAdam 2001: 23; see also Lutz 1986). Because "emotions can be strategically used by activists *and* be the basis for strategic thought," the empirical task becomes investigating the interaction of emotional dynamics with other dynamics, including cultural, organizational, and strategic ones (Goodwin et al. 2001: 9; italics in original).

The interlinkages of emotional, cognitive, and somatic processes, however commonly unrecognized, are revealed in the common root of the English words *sense, sensibility, sentiment,* and *sensation* (the Latin *sensus,* which, according to the Oxford Dictionary of English, means "the faculty of feeling, thought, and meaning," from the verb *sentire,* "to feel"). The relevance of these interlinkages for collective politics is captured in recent interventions around political aesthetics inspired by French philosopher Jacques Rancière. As Rancière points out, politics becomes possible due to a shared "distribution of the sensible" that bounds a community (1999, 2004: 12). A shared distribution of the sensible "defines what is visible or not in a common space, endowed with a common language, etc." (2004: 12–13).[13] Rancière views aesthetics not just as sensory experience itself (from the Greek *aisthetikós,* meaning "perceptive by feeling") but also as the structural systems through which human sense experience is conditioned and organized.

Through Rancière's views, we can understand that not everything that presents itself to sense experience can be accounted for; not everything is sensible or perceivable (sense-able). There are delimitations between what is intelligible and what is unintelligible to sense experience: between the visible and the invisible, between speech and noise. The distribution of the sensible that a community shares establishes the boundaries of the perceptible. These boundaries in turn define social positions within the shared distribution. This distribution of the sensible "reveals who can have a share in what is common to the community based on what they do and on the time and space in which this activity is performed" (Rancière 2004: 12).[14] Politics, then, is the disruption of common sense and the eruption beyond established patterns of belonging into "previously unthinkable emergences" (Dave 2011: 4). Politics is shaped by aesthetics because aesthetics offer a domain that conditions social life and through which rupturing interventions can occur.

In his concern with the limitations of perceptibility that strip certain people of recognition within the community, Rancière is describing life on the margins of a society. In one ethnographic exemplification of Rancière's insights, Daniel Goldstein found that, despite the proximity of the communities he studied to loci of official power, "invisibility is the critical condition facing marginalized people in urban Bolivia" (2004: 29). The need to counter this invisibility spurred spectacular collective displays of public vigilante justice, the kind of break in the social order that is at the heart of Rancière's definition of politics.[15] Perhaps it is recognition of the power of such a transgressive charge that fueled the Orlando leader's disinclination to plan protests.[16] In these heightened moments of shared emotion, people discover a capacity for political impact they had not known before.

This discovery is often facilitated by dynamically embodied cultural performances. Even with limited material resources, APF members and other contemporary South African protesters could evoke freedom by drawing on age-old singing and movement practices that activists have deployed across decades of political dissent. The heightened attention cultural performances draw, in contrast to the minutiae of everyday life, affords opportunities for such transgression. These performances are also a platform for the evocation of alternative possibilities for what life could be and how social relationships could unfold (see Goldstein 2004: 16; Guss 2000; Mendoza 2000; Turner 1986: 22). The potential for such critique within any performance is both conditioned and enabled by established patterns of interaction. And while aesthetics cannot be reduced to art (though it often is), cultural performances—dynamically embodied practices prevalent in the mundane and spectacular—foreground the aesthetic and its concerns for the sensory and sensible politics of human existence (Hobart and Kapferer 2005).

In addition to offering a performance-based elaboration of the aesthetics of collective politics, this book furthers anthropological inquiry into how marginalized communities claim power through three considerations. First, it enriches Rancière's conceptualization of the convergence of the sensual, sentimental, and sensible through an attentiveness to *hyper*marginality, underscoring the impact of race and gender as compounding factors of activist marginalization. Second, it grapples with durability, addressing the maintenance of collectivity in the aftermath of political eruption, a concern that Rancière's model does not account for. Finally, it enhances Rancière's provocation of aesthetic disruption with more interdependent possibilities through an articulation of the relationship to self and others as the sensory basis for collective action.

Regarding the first consideration, Africa's colonial legacies and the fraught relationships there between blackness and the state compound marginalization despite proximity to recognized centers of power. While class is an important factor in marginality, the state has historically, and across geographic locations, constituted itself *through* racialized, systemically anti-Black violence. Even when Black people occupy municipal and national government positions, the political structure of the nation-state has been established and is often sustained *in contraposition* to blackness (Smith 2016).[17] In South Africa, postapartheid continuities with the brutally repressive apartheid state were made publicly visible when police, agents of the state, fired into a crowd of striking mine workers in Marikana on August 16, 2012. This lethal use of force, which killed thirty-four striking workers and injured seventy-eight by official accounts, has been widely designated the Marikana massacre; it is but one instance of the reification of state power at the expense of Black lives in a contemporary South Africa governed by the African National Congress (ANC), the anti-apartheid liberation movement turned political party. The state violence Marikana laid bare, violence at a level that some had not seen since the country's 1994 transition from apartheid, unfolded for many activists in continuity with their experiences at the hands of state agents.

The APF's emergence, well before the 2012 events at Marikana, was motivated by intentions to disrupt South Africa's adoption of neoliberal economic policies. As the APF came into being in the early 2000s, South Africa's "postapartheid" transition jarred with activists' ideological commitments and direct experiences.[18] The state's alliance with a globally encroaching neoliberalism drove a reframing of the ANC's political vision from its anti-apartheid aspirations. This reframing entailed a shift from the socialist democratic ideals enshrined in the Freedom Charter, a liberation manifesto the ANC and allies adopted in 1955, to neoliberal tenets, including the privatization of basic services. In what might appear to be a deracialization of capitalism, these neoliberal policies and Black Economic Empowerment programs enabled a rising Black elite. But vectors of inequality and spatial exclusion remained largely continuous with those of the racially repressive apartheid regime, as the uneven distribution of resources worsened apartheid-era disenfranchisement for many South African communities. Township struggles to access adequate housing, electricity, water, sanitation, and other basic survival needs, then as well as now, provide particular insight into the partial nature of South Africa's transformation.

Ironically, the reframing of the ANC's political vision also entailed appropriation of the indigenous ideology of *ubuntu*, a concept that identifies interdependency, communality, and mutuality as central to being and becoming human. Ubuntu as an ethical philosophy finds its clearest and most common expression in the isiZulu phrase "umuntu ngumuntu ngabantu" (or "motho ke motho ka batho" in seSotho), which can be translated as "a person is a person through people." One becomes human in collectivity and relationship to others. Ubuntu became of political interest in South Africa's liberation struggle and in the contemporary postcolonial moment as a "narrative of return," restoring dignity to African being in the recovery of indigenous African values (Matolino and Kwindingwi 2013; see also McDonald 2010). As state policy and nationalist rebranding, ubuntu appeared in South Africa's interim constitution (although not in the final constitution), in the documents of the Truth and Reconciliation Commission, and in government documents across functions ranging from foreign policy to agriculture, service delivery, and corrections. Key among these manifestations is the government's service delivery public slogan, *Batho Pele* (people first).

While neoliberal principles would seem to be the antithesis of ubuntu, with its emphasis on communality and interdependence as the basis of human dignity, the ANC's ubuntu-oriented policymaking dovetailed with neoliberal objectives through self-help dictums and campaigns targeting impoverished communities. On assuming power in 1994, the ANC government called for an end to rates boycotts in townships and put in place legislative mechanisms to enable cost recovery and disconnection of unpaid municipal services. By the government's logic, refusing to pay for municipal services such as water, electricity, and sanitation violates the spirit of ubuntu by withholding the individual's fiscal contribution to the whole. The use of ubuntu in this way, to reinforce neoliberal policymaking, recasts national economic transformation as a matter of personal fiscal responsibility, neatly sidestepping the exacerbation of deep structural inequities the economic change has entailed, including the fact that many historically impoverished households could not afford to pay the high prices of basic services and were cut off from life-critical utilities.

The ANC's neoliberal depoliticization of ubuntu demanded ethical counterclaims. As the disillusionment arising from confrontation with these stark postapartheid realities was channeled into individual and collective dissent, including local showdowns over eviction, extralegal electricity and water reconnections, land occupations, and collective protests, impoverished South Africans experienced heavily militarized state repression. Marikana was not a break in South Africa's transformation. Instead, it was a public unveiling of apartheid-era continuities, particularly that the state was again constituting itself through anti-Black violence.

The APF emerged through the convergence of different constituents, among them historically disenfranchised Black township inhabitants who felt especially vulnerable to South Africa's neoliberal transformation. This convergence generated unforeseen political possibilities that APF organizers sought to harness by developing democratic structures that would sustain the newly formed collectivity beyond its inception. My second extension of Rancière's proposition tackles those attempts, asking, if politics is the disruption of existing conditions, can such social transformation be made durable without itself becoming a constraint on disruptors?

With this question, I consider the tension with normalization that accompanies the effort of sustaining a nascent collective beyond its initial emergence. As the APF solidified its structure, as it normalized, it reproduced marginalization in its ranks, particularly along the lines of race and gender, a reproduction I designate as hypermarginalization within the social movement. Hopes of harnessing transgression to generate new forms of democratic participation were dashed. Verbal commentary on membership hierarchies and exclusions included distinctions between "briefcase comrades" and "street comrades" (a reference to the workings of racial and class privilege within the movement that I detail in chapter 4) and recognition among some women activists that success within the APF entailed having "the biggest cock" (further discussed in chapter 5). These colorful comments offer apt internal critiques of the APF from the perspectives of those who felt marginalized and undervalued.

By allowing its analytical gaze to linger beyond a movement's incipience, this book reveals relationship—to self and others, contentious though often affirming—as the sensory undercurrent of collective action. Confronted with the perceived denial of their humanity, not only by state agents but also by fellow activists, hypermarginalized APF members sought redress through claims to dignity that diverged from the viewpoints of the state and those of their more privileged comrades. Their insistence countered the state's distorted ideology of ubuntu, deployed to the detriment of impoverished communities.[19] I recognize these claims as assertions of individuals' inherent significance—of their dignity—independent of their external conditions.

Enriching the consideration of dignity as a focal point in activist practice, I show how the movement's stratification led APF members to emphasize different appreciations of its import. Claims to dignity operate within an aesthetic of relationship—an understanding of how connections to others feed into senses of self to generate and sustain political capacity. To claim dignity when it has been denied is to maintain a self-image that transcends the disdain of those who are not "faithful to our freedom" (Cornell 2002: 2). The relational dimension of political becoming, suggested in Rancière's conception of societal status distributions, is revealed in my formulation of status as premised not only on power but also on a necessary interdependency. Relationships unfold through felt exchanges in which bodily experience retains primacy. Along with dignity, I examine other sensorial practices of relationship as they shape collective action, including the cultivation of care, the stresses of suspicion, and the imaginative work of cross-generational empathy.

EMBODIMENT

Historically, political mobilization has been theorized in ways that reduce it to a matter of calculated interests, resources, or cognitive strategies. This conceptualization creates an unresolved conflict in conventional social movement scholarship, rooted in a Cartesian gap that separates mind from body. That conflict manifests in the analytical inability of prior investigations of social movements to bridge supposed fissures between cognition and embodiment, between the ideal and the real, between the inner life of participation and the outside effects of mobilization, between the means and the end of mobilization. As dance scholar Randy Martin notes of scholarship on social movements limited by this Cartesian gap, "No matter how intimate with actors one became, their social activity was still largely cognitive, disembodied acts spurred on by locally generated common interests" (1998: 9). Relatedly, Rancière's articulation of the politics of sensemaking in communal life is limited in its engagement with the corporeal dimensions of its insightful provocation. The absence of fleshed experience distances the conceptualization of collective politics from the direct experience of activists in their efforts to inaugurate change. Without a clear articulation of embodiment as a primary "mode of presence and engagement in the world" (Csordas 1994: 12), analyses of political aesthetics remain incomplete.

To address these absences, bridge the gaps, and thereby "indicate the practical dynamic between production and product" (Martin 1998: 4), I advance as a corrective an understanding that mobilization is constituted through fleshed kinesthetic movements that consolidate, reproduce, and have the potential to disrupt convention. This approach facilitates the investigation of the "inner life of participation" in social movements (Martin 1998: 9)—the variety of acts and processes that aggregate into collective action in its many forms, be it community meetings, protest marches, or the struggles of a women's group to empower female voices in male-dominated forums. Foregrounding "how bodies are made, how they are assembled and how demands for space produce a space of identifiable demands through a practical activity" (Martin 1998: 4), the dynamics of mobilization can be seen only in the movement of actual bodies in space, a movement that is connected with thought, not separate from it. As Martin writes, and as performance theorists have also recognized, reflection and experience are interconnected moments of the same activity (1998: 5; see also Turner 1982: 105; Pineau 1995: 46).[20]

Although he was concerned with understanding professional dancers' political activity, Martin's critiques were prescriptive for social movement scholars because he did not examine the role of dance in social movements directly. Others working at the intersection of dance and politics have advanced inquiry into the contributions a choreographic lens may offer to the analysis of protest tactics (Foster 2003; Franko 2006; Parviainen 2010).[21] My research furthers these concerns through inquiry into a nonprofessional world in which local communities mobilize by drawing on performance, including dance.

Through this inquiry, I join with ethnographers, including Yolanda Covington-Ward (2018), who attend to the body as a quotidian resource for political transformation. Covington-Ward uses the concept of performative encounters to articulate the body as being (1) central to social processes; (2) the conduit of ideas, values, mores, and ideals; and (3) the catalyst for sociopolitical transformation. While Covington-Ward demonstrates the analytic benefits of attentiveness to the body in everyday use, she does so by willingly foregoing the advances of scholarship on embodiment. By describing her intervention as "shift[ing] the focus in studies of embodiment from affective states and feelings to how bodies are actually used in everyday life" (2018:16), Covington-Ward implicitly exposes a conceptual gap as key to her assessment of embodiment scholarship: that despite advances in articulating the interiority of bodily experience, such scholarship has still remained far from grasping the quotidian. As a scholar who locates the promise of embodiment in its paradigm-shifting attention to the body as the base of knowledge, experience, and capacity for being in the world, I seek to reconcile aesthetically rooted interventions from embodiment scholarship with Covington-Ward's compelling demonstrations of the political significance of the body in everyday use. Such reconciliation urges recognition that analyses of the body need not abandon knowledge *from* the body as articulated through sensory perceptions and affective states in order to grapple with the political significance of corporeality in everyday use.

To foreground the nonspecialist moving body in its political potential, I draw attention to physical *and* psychological processes that occur within and among individuals during commonplace embodied events. These processes include, for example, individuals' attempts to heal themselves by rallying their personal bodies in collective action. Mobilization figures in all identifiable stages of collective action and provides avenues for assessing the transformative impact of such action—especially considering that the most significant impacts might be on individuals themselves. Analyses of mobilization and political aesthetics need therefore to consider the body (Gouws 2005: 227), not just materially but affectively, in terms of relationships of care.

Perhaps there is no better example of mobilization as intimately emotive, sensorially embodied, and relational than the full context of Ma Lindi's participation in the activists' workshops where I met her in 2010. As we sat in her room during that overnight workshop, the stout, middle-aged woman recalled how she came to attend despite her initial reluctance: Nomvula, an APF member who also happened to be her daughter, actively encouraged her. At the workshops, she was introduced to a variety of relaxation exercises. Amelia, the facilitator of the workshop I attended, commented on how delicate Ma Lindi's health had been; the facilitators were worried she would pass away before the workshop series ended. Ma Lindi, however, improved through consistent use of the physical exercises Amelia taught her, as well as through meditation and prayer. She started practicing finger holds, holding one finger at a time for a number of minutes, and noticed that this exercise helped activate her overworked organs and drain the water from her body. Points in the finger correspond with different organs and energy centers in the body, as Amelia, drawing from reflexology, explained to her: "[Amelia] said the small [finger] is the one attached to the heart and the small intestines and then the next one is the spleen, the lungs and then the fourth one is the kidneys and then the big one, the thumb is the big intestines. So by touching all these parts you are reconnecting yourself to the parts of your body in your system and if you were asleep, you are waking up once more." Finger holding became a consistent part of Ma Lindi's daily routine and health practice, replacing the tablets that kept her "in the loo for the whole day" to drain water.

For Ma Lindi, this practice not only facilitated a physical reconnection to herself; it also awakened a spiritual and social reconnection. She explained that her emotions had been broken, making her reclusive, "but as I'm able to drain this water and I'm feeling much better, I can now talk to people." She could attend the Gender at Work workshops and participate more readily. She could also continue her work as a community leader. She still leaned heavily over a cane as she walked, but she insisted on making her own way, however slowly. She still did not want to see pity on the faces of those around her. To participate in the collective, Ma Lindi had to develop a routine of care that improved her sense of well-being more readily than the tablets she had been prescribed, with their side effects. She also had to cultivate her fortitude in confronting responses to her physical challenges.

Social movements cannot take the collective for granted if the individuals who compose it are not well. Ma Lindi was not the only one who sought healing through her participation in the activist workshops. Other women also began to do the physical exercises in their daily lives, sometimes with similarly profound results. Ma Patrycja, who had had kidney cancer for twenty-five years, found that the exercises helped energize her throughout the day: "Since I've been doing these exercises, I can go every day, every day, nothing stops me and I don't feel pains or nothing." She began teaching and practicing the exercises with other women in her community. Ma Lindi and Ma Patrycja's experiences highlight my conception of mobilization as individuals rallying their personal bodies to participate in collective action, as well as the need for what Naisargi Dave calls "affective, cohesive sociality" (2011: 6). Such sociality exemplifies what I frame as an aesthetic of relationship, and it is evident in the impact of Nomvula's encouragement on Ma Lindi's participation. As Deborah Gould notes, "the *movement* in 'social movements' gestures toward the realm of affect; bodily intensities; emotions, feelings, and passions" (2009: 3) that activists cultivate among one another and in seeking audiences beyond themselves.

Performance and Mobilization Revisited

For the activists with whom I worked, the movement of "bodily intensities, emotions, feelings, and passions" involved performance: aesthetics, affect, mobilization, and creative expressions were interrelated dimensions of the same experience.[22] Consider the words of an elder female protester on the role of freedom songs in protest events: "When I sing these songs, I feel pain from inside [*tapping her chest*]. I take out the pain by singing these songs, and even if that person on the street passes by, they would see and feel the same pain through the songs that this person is hurt. And it's going to be easy for them to understand why am I singing those songs." Song became an avenue for this elder woman, alienated from a broader society, as evidenced by her pain (see Scarry 1985; Daniel 1994), to transmit her sentiment to a passerby and overcome an inexpressibility that would leave her in society's margins.

While song was the protester's avenue, for Ma Lindi, the unburdening of her pain-driven alienation came as an effect of the performance of her wellness routines. Transmission for Ma Lindi happened in two ways. First, she was coaxed out of isolation by individual relationships: her daughter convinced her to attend a gathering of fellow women activists, and at that gathering, Amelia worked with her to create a set of daily practices to improve her well-being. Second, as she improved physically, she drew on the collective environment for further healing, becoming less alienated. Within the collective, she "grabbed at . . . the knowledge, the skill, the wisdom and for listening to other people who also had problems and challenges but [were] coming out as strong women." Being with others who shared their pain and problems offered Ma Lindi perspective beyond her own physical limitations. As her fellow participants' emerging strength became evident to Ma Lindi, she further "embraced whatever was happening" to the extent of being able to declare: "I now feel, much as I am not yet able to walk on my own, I have moved on and I am a better person." Performance, in the sense of Ma Lindi's ritualized wellness routines, conducted by herself and with others, moved Ma Lindi from alienation to necessary social connection—as it did the elder protester.

Music, dance, gesture, and other symbolic bodily enactments (ritual) provide the means to transcend (or transgress) boundaries so that marginalized individuals and collectivities can "restructure patterns of inclusion" (Goldstein 2004: 19; Covington-Ward 2018). Both for its transmissive potential and as a preferred mode of sensory experience, performance was a necessary component of the activist events I attended (see Bauman 1975: 299), whether in integrating song, dance, and ephemera at protest events; singing to fill the breaks at organizational meetings; providing an audience for fellow participants' creative outputs during commemorative programs; or practicing bodily wellness routines together. Performance was also a preferred manner of representation. In January 2010, when an Australian media crew sought to film conditions at a squatter camp in Itereleng (on the outskirts of Pretoria), Boipelo, an APF organizer, urgently tried to organize its residents to meet the camera crew singing. When I asked why this display would matter, he responded, "To show that they are in the struggle. That's the international media there, they have to be seen chanting."

What these activists prioritize also anchors my analysis. If, as I argue, performative acts constitute community, then collective solidarity and social identity take shape through a performing body in motion. Performance in this project therefore attends to a variety of embodied and sensory practices (such as wellness routines; protest dances; freedom songs; speechmaking; and the design and display of posters, leaflets, banners, clothing, and other symbolic materials) through which activists engage with one another and thereby produce or disrupt collective bonds. This intersection of performance and activist politics allows me to interweave my abiding concern for embodiment and affect and broader consideration of political aesthetics into a narrative of the internal dynamics of mobilization.

BEING IN THE FIELD

I departed New York for Johannesburg on August 28, 2009, and returned to New York about sixteen months later, on January 12, 2011. Securing permission to proceed with APF research took six long weeks. This delay was caused by some of the cracks in the APF's organizational solidity that would later drive its decline. I had secured my ties with the group's primary organizer during a previous visit, in 2007. By the time I returned in 2009, he and two other key organizers (all male) were embroiled in a legal and disciplinary process that eventually led to their expulsion. Their expulsion not only affected the APF's organizational capacity; it also created divisiveness among its members, which eventually resulted in personal, social, and organizational fallout that hastened the APF's eventual demise. When I arrived in August 2009, I found I had to start over with an already diminishing organization (although I did not know then the extent of the organization's decline). I had to present myself and my work to the organization anew once I was able to secure a meeting with its new officers. The process was frustrating but ultimately productive; it helped to clarify my role in ways I would have missed had I had a more unchallenged transition to the field.

While I was waiting for this meeting, my affiliation with the Department of Anthropology at the University of the Witwatersrand (henceforth Wits) provided support. I met with a scholar-activist in the Department of Sociology

who provided some insight that prefigured my observations. She and her partner had been active in the APF but had begun to feel alienated from the main
organization. While she carried on her work with the community-embedded
Orange Farm Water Crisis Committee, an affiliate of the APF, she viewed the
broader APF's current moment with a long-held and therefore practiced cau-
tiousness.[23] She chronicled the change she had seen from the organization's
beginning, which came, she said, with much energy and activity about "trying
to imagine ourselves differently." At the APF's genesis, the intention was to
depart from old forms and methods of struggle and create something new. Yet
issues with the activities of imagination and representation arose even then,
particularly in the tendency to celebrate without being too critical of internal
contradictions, she said. People who wrote about the new social movement
at its nascence, including herself, perpetuated these forms of representation,
partly because they were thrilled to find alternatives to the past and to the status quo. I examine the evolution of the APF from the effervescence of activist
emergence to organizational decline in chapter 4. For now, it is worth pointing out that I arrived at a moment when APF's activists and intellectuals (not
exclusive terms) were self-reflexively assessing their roles and representations,
and I was able to capture some of these frustrations in my concern with organizational performance.

My research in a sense began with this conversation, as the sociologist referred me to other key figures in tracing the history of the APF's performance
practices. While it seemed my work with performance would be directed at
recovering the remnants of the APF's more active flourishing, I discovered
many ongoing practices that revealed the primacy of these practices among
activists. In addition to Boipelo's insistence that communities "have to be seen
chanting" to demonstrate that "they are in the struggle," several other moments
demonstrated the immediacy with which performance, ritual, and cognate
practices were adapted to shifting politics.

Although securing access was and remains an ongoing challenge, my first
meeting with the APF's office bearers in October 2009 allowed me to integrate into its organizational space. I began by shadowing the APF's part-time
organizers, attending their weekly coordination meetings and other meetings
of office bearers. As these organizers and APF members came to know me,
they invited me to events, including protest marches and meetings in their
communities. I documented thirty-eight such events through photographs
and video recordings and attended many more meetings and protests than I
sought to capture visually. At these events, I tried to understand the dynamics
among gathered actors (movement participants, nonparticipants, bystanders,

and state representatives who had recurrent contact with community activists, including police).

Through these events, I encountered a range of freedom songs and body movements. I witnessed activists deploying these performance forms in a variety of situations, including heated exchanges with the police and rousing meetings at communal halls. I videotaped protests and key organization meetings; such footage became pertinent for the interviews I conducted. Through feedback interviews (Stone and Stone 1981), I solicited responses to past events using the video footage and photographs I collected. My footage, along with field notes, proved useful for capturing event dynamics such as the placement of bodies, their orientation to space, the sound configuration, and other sensory details, and the construction of meaning through these elements. I also conducted intercept surveys (Bernard 2006: 161) at protests, soliciting bystanders' and protesters' interpretations of the unfolding events and their reception of the performances. These surveys took the form of opportunistic conversations that would be impossible to count. They involved the convenience sampling of those present, recruited based on willingness to provide quick responses to questions about the event. Feedback interviews and responses solicited in the immediacy of the moment allowed me to investigate more concretely events that can be quite amorphous.

Seeking, along with other aims, to understand the dynamics of inclusion and exclusion among the APF's potential constituents (Burdick 1995), I conducted forty-six semistructured interviews with current members and nonmembers selected through a combination of judgment and snowball sampling (Bernard 2006: 189–94). As I familiarized myself with the organization, I developed affinity with some participants, including leaders and organizers, whose perspectives I sought. I requested interviews from those involved in events and activities that were key to my research, including protest participants who stood out (whether or not they were APF members), activists who were involved in performance initiatives, and participants in Remmoho, the women's group that cultivated embodied wellness practices among its members. At the conclusion of each interview, I asked interviewees to suggest others whom I could contact who might have insights and experiences relevant to my research.

With APF members, I inquired into the history of their involvement with the APF and with community organizations in general. I also solicited their insights and personal responses to collective protest performances within the coalition. My analytical focus on the internal dynamics of the APF entails a commitment to understanding members' experiences. I therefore draw on interviews with nonmembers only to amplify or clarify the story of the APF.

Many of the nonmembers I interviewed were participants at the protests I attended. In interviews, I sought their interpretations of the significance of collective protest performances. I also inquired into reasons for their nonparticipation in the APF, as well as their historical and contemporary involvement in other forms of collective action. I did not encounter major differences between members and nonmembers' perceptions of collective protest performances. In fact, these performances drew evocative interpretations and responses from members and nonmembers alike.

My ethnographic data are augmented by historical research drawing on the South African History Archive's collection of transcribed oral histories of the APF, as well as ephemera from the movement. The collection is publicly accessible, on registration, through an online exhibition and at the South African History Archive in Johannesburg. As part of the collection, Dale McKinley and Ahmed Veriava, two founding APF activists with whom I interacted during my research tenure, conducted thirty-six oral history interviews of selected APF leaders, past and present. McKinley wrote a final project report that profiled the APF's history and highlighted key themes emerging from the oral history interviews. The historical insights gained from this collection have been invaluable for my analysis, and I am grateful for its availability. Chapters 1 and 4, in particular, draw on these interviews in addition to my own ethnographic data. These interviews, conducted by McKinley and Veriava, are acknowledged as they appear within the text.

In the interest of reciprocity and to facilitate readers' understanding of the partial nature of this work, I must elaborate my inner life of participation. As I write, geographically and temporally removed from the settings I describe, I do so with an awareness that I did not give everything to the movement; I did not let it consume me. I had gone to the field with ideas of kinesthetic apprenticeship (Downey 2002: 497–500) that would facilitate my understanding of the experiences of people I care about. What I found were my own limits as I negotiated physical safety and mental integrity. To be clear, I never confronted physical danger, but these were ongoing considerations. I benefited from a fleeting phenotypic solidarity that marked me as native until I was recognized as an outsider (Jackson 2004)—people meeting me for the first time assumed I was a Black South African until I spoke. I shifted my national categories of belonging in negotiating access and safety. I would emphasize pan-African connections rather than my relative though temporary class privilege as a globally mobile American. Yet concerns about xenophobic attacks in the wake of South Africa's hosting of the 2010 FIFA World Cup led me to deemphasize aspects of my background.

Andile Mngxitama (2010) astutely described the xenophobic dynamics of contemporary South Africa as "afrophobia in disguise." An encounter in the Vaal raised these concerns when a male bystander walked toward me after a protest and pointed at me (I am still not sure whether in address or in reference), saying something to the effect of "After the World Cup, all foreigners must go." To navigate bodily safety given the persistence of such encounters, I began to underplay my Nigerian origin in some contexts and hoped that America, an already problematic ascription, would work for me. As a Nigerian who had lived in the United States for thirteen years (I am now a US citizen), I was not a typical Nigerian in South Africa, if there is such a thing. I did not embody the linguistic or physical accents of other Nigerians whom those I worked with had encountered and with whom they lived in proximity. Such insights reveal how my being in the field was interpreted and consciously rendered.

My concern about xenophobic violence was an instance in which my body was on the line without my choice. Yet there were other instances where, much as it was rationally appealing, I could not place my body on the line. Margaret Thompson Drewal has argued for the primacy of the researcher's embodied participation for fieldwork on performance (1991: 33–35); similarly, I recognized that bodily apprenticeship with my interlocutors would inform my research beyond what I could access solely through observation or verbal account. Yet, in attending protest events where I had initially expected to participate by singing and dancing as my South African co-participants did, I found that it felt insurmountably awkward to inhabit that activist positionality. While I was acting in solidarity, it felt presumptuous even to attempt to bridge the subjective distance that reminded me of my difference from APF activists. My camera, as a bodily appendage, came to facilitate my participation at protest events. It gave me something to do, a platform of belonging that acknowledged the distance and the quality of my proximity to protesters. I usually recorded "from my gut" (see Wilson 2004; Csordas 1999: 184). I am drawing on figurative implications with that phrase, but I also mean that I placed my camera around my lower abdomen rather than using a direct optical viewfinder. This positioning freed my eyes to observe so that I was not solely taken with the camera but could absorb a wider perspective.

I obtained consent from organizers to videotape events in enclosed spaces. In the more public spaces of protests, where consent was impossible to obtain from all present, I turned the camera off or diverted its focus if anyone present indicated reluctance to be captured on screen. Public protests were often videotaped and photographed by news media, event organizers, and the police. The typical assumption was that I was a journalist, and many approached me to share their stories as a result. APF members who knew me vouched for my association, and I made sure to identify myself as a researcher whenever I approached or was approached by anyone present.

The footage and photographs allowed me to refer to specific moments in my feedback interviews. As a result, I was better able to guide interviewees' reflexive awareness and interpretations of their actions. As I listened, I sought to demonstrate my receptivity as people shared the things that profoundly affected them. I expressed receptivity through verbal and embodied affirmation facilitated by what some performance studies scholars call "copresence."[24] The manner of my listening, the phrasing of my questions, the embodied experiences of my own that I offered facilitated intersubjective engagement.

I asked questions about sensory experience: "How do you feel in your body when you are singing these songs?" I asked questions of taste or aesthetic preferences: "Which is your favorite song and why?" In feedback interviews, my interviewees and I probed fleeting moments together and, however partially, attempted to untangle their meanings: "Why did you raise that song at that particular moment?" "What did you sense that called forth that song or made it fitting for what was going on?" "Why did you change the rhythm of your clapping, right there?" These questions yielded insights into aesthetic preferences and distinctions among constituents—like the tempo youth prefer to feel in their bodies as distinct from the tendency of mass gatherings to slow down (chapter 6), or the tension of uttering colorful vulgarity in songs that older participants sought to bar from the mouths of youth, causing one interviewee to note an age restriction on some songs (chapter 3). These questions also yielded insights into concerns that consumed my interviewees, including issues around health and physical integrity (chapter 5); feelings of being inhabited by "spirits within you which nobody else can relate to" (chapter 3); and suspicion of fellow activists as being out to sabotage others' efforts (chapter 4).[25]

STRUCTURE

The interconnections of performance, aesthetics, and politics that lie at the core of this book unfold in counterpoint. Specifically, the main analysis of the APF's organizational trajectory is developed through six chapters interspersed with portraits of individual activists. These portraits frame the activism of the APF's members in the context of their life trajectories; they also demonstrate a reciprocal movement between individual concerns and collective processes that deserves further engagement among activists and scholars. Contrapuntally, they foreshadow and detail at the level of individual experience organizational issues explored in the chapters, elaborating the origination of and motivation toward collective activism, as well as the personal considerations many activists bear, considerations that are often hidden from public view and separated from social movement analysis. I chose particular activists to profile for the ways in which their life histories and perspectives illuminate and augment the analyses of collective politics presented in the chapters. For instance, before tracing the APF's emergence, I begin with a portrait of Ma Patrycja, one of the APF's elder activists. Because she made a life and raised her children under an apartheid regime that rendered access to basic needs laborious, Ma Patrycja's story offers an apt point of entry into a social movement organization that emerged out of South Africa's political transition, in an effort to address what that transition left unreconciled.

Chapter 1, "Emergence," details the APF's origins, including its founders' attempts to inaugurate a new modality of activism that would resolve the shortcomings of apartheid-era mobilizations. APF founders championed an organizational form that sought to prioritize community struggles by recognizing three categories of membership. These attempts at greater inclusivity through recognition of members' heterogeneity nonetheless contributed to a complex imbalance of power that manifested in the organization's internal dynamics. My historical investigation into the exuberance of the APF's origins clarifies the original intentions against which the tensions that led to its decline must be understood. I show how, performatively, structural choices made and reinforced over time to channel the energy of mass demonstrations inaugurated and maintained a mode of organization that forestalled other possibilities for collective action.

Chapter 2, "Routinization," narrates the normative forms and practices that supported the APF's program of action in the years following its emergence. It continues the examination of the APF's performative constitution by elaborating the spatial and temporal rhythms of the APF's main office located in Johannesburg's central business district. It also addresses what is easily overlooked when one identifies a movement solely with its administrative center—the physical environments that not only constituted the daily lives of the APF's target constituents but also elaborated a need for dignity that drove their activism. By showing the routinized spatial practices that both produce and curtail collective dissent—what I call performative geography—the chapter sets the necessary foundation to examine the more visible and audible mass gatherings that are more commonly associated with protest performances.

Contrasting with the preceding two chapters' focus on the performative bureaucratization of mass dissent into organizational structure, chapter 3,

"Efflorescence," more fully examines the role of creative expression within social movements. The APF at its most effective was sustained not merely by organizational procedures but by the communion of singing and moving together in effervescent collective dissent. The chapter throws into relief practices that enable inclusive political participation in ways that make the impact of this participation more immediately and sensorially experienced. I explore the embodied aesthetics of freedom songs in public protest events. In particular, I detail how musical qualities of antiphony, repetitive variation, and embodied rhythm facilitated activists' political interventions. Through these foundational elements, the performances of freedom songs secured a political identity and commitment among activists.

Chapter 4, "Ruptures," details fissures in the activist community that hampered the APF's organizational efficacy and considers the making of community and how activism's everyday practices come to fall short of its ideal. The chapter furthers the analysis of the performative begun in chapter 1's examination of the performative achievement of mobilization in the APF's emergence, turning to an exploration of the underside of that achievement. The chapter demonstrates the role of performance—manifesting here through interactions and the minutiae of everyday life—in the dissipation and loss of collectivity. While this continual dissipation and ongoing loss of collectivity might be interpreted as the failure of mobilization, or an absence of organizational performance, I situate performance instead in the breaks—the ruptures occasioned by the conflicting motivations toward activism inherent in oppositional coalitions. These conflicting motivations are particularly evident with regard to differing understandings of dignity and its role in ethical collectivity.

Performance provides access not only to collective voices but also to variations within collectivities (Burdick 1995; Gilbert 2005); the remaining two chapters explore those variations within the APF by examining performance practices that complicate views of gender and intergenerational relationship. Chapter 5, "Countermobilization," considers gendered approaches to protest performance through Remmoho, the APF women's group that sought to challenge problematic gender roles in the organization. Its members employed what one facilitator described as "radical methodologies" to empower themselves in their homes, communities, and political organizations. These methodologies involved adapting performance techniques (including singing and the construction of rituals) to support their own wellness as well as contesting male domination in collective activist endeavors.

The active engagement of youth has been common to efforts within the APF to use performance as a deliberate organizational tool. Chapter 6,

"Redemption," examines the cultivation of performance practices among youth activists as well as the intergenerational dynamics of community mobilization. It investigates the processes through which young people became involved in their communities' political struggles, thereby challenging portrayals of contemporary South African youth as apolitical and driven more toward enjoyment than toward civic engagement. It advances the notion of an aesthetic of relationship as a way of understanding youth activist commitment and demobilization from activist formations.

Together, the chapters and portraits present an ethnography of the APF through the lens of performance. Considering performance in its multiple dimensions and connections with collective politics, the book presents an expansive analysis of mobilization that foregrounds the inner life of participation among activists.

ON "YOU CAN'T GO TO WAR WITHOUT SONG"

The title of this book is drawn from an encounter in which my interviewee proclaimed that protest was like a battle, and "you can't go to war without song because that's the only thing that will keep you going."[26] While my interviewee was referring to his vulnerability, as a protester, to police hostility, the description of activism as war resonated with other activists' experiences. Ironically, however, the combativeness that prevailed in APF activists' reflections often referred to dynamics internal to the movement, not opposition stances external to the movement. In a meeting that I examine in chapter 4, one APF member described how the suspicion she encountered from a fellow comrade alienated her to the extent that she felt her activism was a war. Against such tensions, performance and allied practices served a variety of mitigating roles—offering refuge, sustenance, and the possible reconfiguration of problematic dynamics in the constitution of activist community.

NOTES

1. In order to protect the confidentiality of the activists with whom I worked, I either withhold names or use pseudonyms except in already published accounts, in oral history interviews I did not conduct, and to maintain continuity with others' interviews that overlap with my accounts. The latter exception usually involves public figures, including organizers and facilitators.

2. Victor Turner also considered performance as a self-conscious expression of culture; he thought cultural performances not only reflect communities'

"central meanings, values, and goals" but also shape behavioral paths (Turner 1982: 122). Anthropologists have extended these nascent views of performance as a totalizing presentation of a society to itself (see Geertz 1973), and some have queried the homogenizing tendency of such an approach. Daniel Goldstein, for example, argues that "to speak of society or the public performing itself for itself [as is suggested by the term *cultural performances*] is to miss the very thing that makes these performances valuable as sites of social analysis: their availability to differentially empowered groups . . . to produce alternative visions of the social world" (2004: 17–18; see also Crapanzano 1986).

3. Bauman (1975) draws on the work of Erving Goffman (1974) and Gregory Bateson (1972) to develop the idea that metacommunicative devices let the audience know that all that is enclosed within such a frame is intended as performance. Bauman notes that performers display communicative competence to an audience, and the audience evaluates that competence. Each community has its own way of distinguishing, or "keying," the performance frame (Bauman 1975: 295–96; see also Ahearn 2012: 172–73; Madison 2005: 153–55).

4. Publishing in the same year as Vail and White, Margaret Thompson Drewal (1991) notes the simultaneous capability of performances to uphold and disrupt social orders. She writes, "Performance is a means by which people reflect on their current conditions, define and/or re-invent themselves and their social world, and either re-enforce, resist, or subvert prevailing social orders. Indeed both subversion and legitimation can emerge in the same utterance or act." For more on the reproductive and transformative potentialities of performance, see also Bakhtin (1984); Erlmann (1996); Gunner (1994); Peterson (2000); McAllister (2006); Madison (2010).

5. While South Africa has a distinct and gripping history of the mobilization of freedom songs and other cultural performances for collective liberation, the country is not unique in this regard. The analyses of activist beliefs and practices I offer is therefore not meant to advance a narrative of South African exceptionalism but rather to afford deeper resonance for understanding activism and activist embodiment through performance in South Africa and across other comparative contexts. Scholarship that offers insight into South Africa's distinct history—discussing antecedents and influences on contemporary protest performances—include Gray (1996); Mthembu (1999); Gunner (2009, 2015); Erlmann (1996); Coplan (2008); James (1999); and McNeill and James (2011), among others. Scholarship on the politics of cultural performance beyond South Africa include examinations of Irish rebel songs, US civil rights movement freedom songs, and liberation music across Zimbabwe's Chimurengas (see Millar 2020; Chikowero 2015; Roy 2010; Teitelbaum 2017; Dillan et al. 2018; Gunner 2019). In earlier work, I show how connections across geographies matter in grasping the significance of these cultural performances as much as the

geopolitical specificities of their originations (Jolaosho 2012; see also Redmond 2014).

6. Conquergood writes, "Through cultural performances, many people both construct and participate in 'public' life. Particularly for poor and marginalized people denied access to middle-class 'public' forums, cultural performance becomes the venue for 'public discussion' of vital issues central to their communities, as well as an arena for gaining visibility and staging their identity" (1991: 189).

7. Austin's student John Searle (1969) expands on this theory of performativity by emphasizing individual intention. Jacques Derrida (1973) takes issue with speech-act theory, Austin and Searle's approach to performativity, arguing that it overlooks the historical and cultural basis of the effects and achievements of utterances.

8. Butler draws on Edmund Husserl, Maurice Merleau-Ponty, and George Herbert Mead, among others, espousing a phenomenological theory that social reality is constituted by the acts, gestures, and other semiotic practices of social agents.

9. Butler distinguishes her insights into gender performance from Erving Goffman's (1959) suggestion of a self "which assumes and exchanges various 'roles' within the complex social expectations of the 'game' of modern life" (Butler 1988: 528). Goffman views performance as a form of impression management in social relationships. His definition of performance as attempts to influence others within situated interaction must be understood within his larger project, as defined by the title of his book, of delineating "the presentation of self in everyday life." For Butler, gender is not an external role assumed by an eternally abiding interior self. Rather, gender is a performative act—created and naturalized through performance. Gender "constructs the social fiction of its own psychological interiority" (Butler 1988: 528); there is no interior self regulating gender's performance. Rather, this self is discursively constituted and fictively interiorized.

10. Interview with the author, June 16, 2010, Johannesburg.

11. Conversation with the author, March 16, 2010, Johannesburg.

12. Goodwin et al. address the distortion of emotions in social movement scholarship, referring back to "classic models" of irrational collective behavior in which emotions either "came directly from crowds," having little to do with individual traits, or were reduced to internal conflicts that individuals sought to alleviate through participation in collectivities (2001: 4). In more recent formulations, like those of resource mobilization theorists who dismissed prior classic models' conceptualization of social movements as irrational, emotions were nevertheless still discounted as "murky, dangerous and pejorative phenomena" (Goodwin et al. 2001: 5) that were hard to analyze and

therefore dismissible in "empirical, scientific, rigorous" approaches (Goodwin et al. 2001: 5). Similarly, Aminzade and McAdam write that "a positivist epistemology of dispassionate investigation that views emotions as distorting observation and impeding knowledge . . . has produced a devaluation of those methods that can provide access to the emotional lives of activists and emotional climates and dimensions of their movements" (Aminzade and McAdam 2001: 24).

13. This shared distribution of the sensible is akin to Kant's *sensus communis* (Kant 1931: 170–71)—a common sense on which any community is premised. Katherine Wolfe writes, "A community itself begins with something in common . . . [and] the commonality upon which a community is founded is *sense*" (Wolfe 2006). This shared sense is twofold—shared logic and shared sensory experiences. Panagia describes the twofold nature of the sensible as "both 'what makes sense' and 'what can be sensed'" (2009: 3). The relationships among our sensory organs and acts of perception reinforce normative orders and "relate our bodies to the world, but also determine the conditions through and by which we might sense the world and those who occupy it; in short, such regimes of perception confer what counts as common sense" (Panagia 2009: 7).

14. Rancière's concern intersects with Clifford Geertz's insight that common sense "represents the world as a familiar world, one everyone can, and should, recognize, and within which everyone stands, or should, on his own feet" (Geertz 1983: 91). João Biehl considers common sense a characteristic of "all solid citizens" that works as a "totalizing frame of thought," justifying "which kinds of lives societies support" and which lives are systematically devalued and neglected (Biehl 2005: 15).

15. Other scholars have also grappled with the liminality between visibility and invisibility, between perceptibility and imperceptibility. In a different ethnography, João Biehl traces one individual's passage from social belonging to ostracization, being rendered invalid and foreclosed from social capability (2005: 11). Understanding her "not as an exception but as a patterned entity" (2005: 13), Biehl asks, "What kind of subjectivity is possible when one is no longer marked by the dynamics of recognition or by temporality?" (2005: 11).

16. I am drawing here on the distinction Dwight Conquergood makes between transcendence and transgression. His construction of performance is relevant for the political potential of heightened emotional encounters more broadly: "Instead of construing performance as *transcendence*, a higher plane that one breaks into, I prefer to think of it as *transgression*, that force which crashes and breaks through sediment meanings and normative traditions and plunges us back into the vortices of political struggle" (Conquergood 1998: 32). Emotional insurgence is transformative as a critical, legitimized expression and experience of collective power. However, the Orlando leader's insistence that protests

are unplanned eruptions belies the often stimulating, sometimes routinized, coordination and staging involved in their manifestation.

17. Keisha-Khan Perry (2013), Christen Smith (2016), and others have elucidated the gendered dimensions of this systemically anti-Black state constitution as it is manifested in Brazil, Jamaica, and the United States, among other circum-Atlantic locations that make up the African diaspora.

18. Echoing activists with whom I worked, I use the polysemic *postapartheid* to indicate the present as a provocation: rather than being viewed as a novelty, or as a disruption of the past, the present offers incitements to act in response to dashed hopes, unfulfilled visions, and outright material urgencies (see Hayem 2017). Because I acknowledge as questionable the premise that the ANC's 1994 election victory brought apartheid's demise, I have tried to limit my use of the term in this book.

19. Social movement scholarship often refers to dignity without significant analytical engagement. Earlier studies of South African contemporary social movements focus on appeals to dignity as they are made to the external targets of the movements, including the ANC government and its municipal representatives, as well as multinational corporations that sought to exploit labor conditions to maximize profit. Among the first studies of postapartheid community struggles, Ashwin Desai's *We Are the Poors* (2002) compellingly invokes these activists' demands as premised on dignity. Similarly, Nigel Gibson's edited collection describes the rapid growth of new social movements as expressing a "quest for a new humanism" in their demands for recognition of basic human needs (2006: 40). However, such studies focus on appeals to dignity made to the external targets of the movements, which constitutes but one aspect of the significance of dignity for activist formations; I argue for more attention to claims of dignity within movements.

20. Martin's work connects with a tradition of anthropological inquiry into the moving body as a way of illuminating larger societal processes. Brenda Farnell (1999) highlights movement as integral to social action. For Farnell, attention to the moving body expands scholars' abilities to understand agency as individuals agentively produce meaning through the physical movement of their bodies. In a masterful study that links historical moments with contemporary practices, Yolanda Covington-Ward (2018) examines movement and gesture as modes of generating and contesting power in the Democratic Republic of Congo.

21. Foster proposes to reconstruct protests, not by conceptualizing them as dances—which would decontextualize the event—but by interrogating them through questions a dance scholar might raise: "What are these bodies doing?; what and how do their motions signify?; what choreography, whether spontaneous or pre-determined, do they enact?; what kind of significance and impact does the collection of bodies make in the midst of its social surround?; how

does the choreography theorize corporeal, individual, and social identity?; how does it construct ethnicity, gender, class, and sexuality?; how have these bodies been trained, and how has that training mastered, cultivated, or facilitated their impulses?; what do they share that allows them to move with one another?; what kind of relationship do they establish with those who are watching their actions?; what kinds of connections can be traced between their daily routines and the special moments of their protest?; how is it possible to reconstruct and translate into words these bodies' vanished actions?; how is the body of the researcher/ writer implicated in the investigation?" (Foster 2003: 396–97).

22. Regarding how performance draws attention to the primacy of embodiment, see, for example, Madison 2010: 7–10. Because it "takes as both its subject matter and method the experiencing body situated in time, place, and history" (Conquergood 1991: 187), the rise of performance within anthropology during the 1980s and 1990s helped ethnographers address a textual bias in social analysis (see Madison 2005: 166–67). Performance ethnographies drew attention to bodily experiences ahead of corresponding paradigmatic shifts toward embodiment that grew with the realization that "bodies cannot be divorced from their lived experiences" (Mascia-Lees 2011: 2; see also Csordas 1994; Van Wolputte 2004).

23. For an illuminating case study of the APF-affiliated Orange Farm Water Crisis Committee, see Naidoo (2010).

24. For example, Conquergood writes of "an ethnography of the ears and heart that reimagines participant observation as coperformative witnessing" and goes on to describe this as a "hermeneutics of experience, relocation, copresence, humility, and vulnerability" (2004: 315). See Spry (2006) for more on copresence.

25. The challenge of articulating one's own experience, as well as that of apprehending another's, persists in making meaning of these research encounters. In light of such a challenge, I turn to my interviewees' responses, as well as my own perceptions, as points of entry in disclosing and evoking the "seemingly impenetrable interiority of experience" (Downey 2002: 487–88). Of language and experience, Csordas notes that "one need conclude neither that language is 'about' nothing other than itself, nor that language wholly constitutes experience, nor that language refers to experience that can be known in no other way. One can instead argue that language gives access to a world of experience in so far as experience comes to, or is brought to, language ... language is itself a modality of being-in-the-world" (Csordas 1994: 11). Language facilitates the sharing of intersubjective experience that attends to the sensory coproduction of the social (Chau 2008) and, inversely, the social production of the sensual (see, for example, Downey 2002).

26. Feedback interview with the author, January 22, 2010, Johannesburg.

—m—

ACTIVIST PORTRAIT

Ma Patrycja

THE HOME LIVES AND DOMESTIC situations of Anti-Privatisation Forum (APF) members offered important insights for understanding their motivations toward activism. Activists' physical habitations are often hard-won and vulnerable to competing claims; they cannot be taken for granted. To provide a personalized background for the history of the APF's emergence as a social movement organization in the next chapter, I would like you to meet one of its members in her own home. This context offers a way to understand motivating conditions that are not readily apparent when activists gather in the urban center for meetings or protest in streets that might be far from their homes I begin with Ma Patrycja to highlight the significance of home in one APF member's life trajectory and to show how the commitment to home can spur political commitment. A concern with dignity lies at the core of Ma Patrycja's story. Indeed, as I will demonstrate throughout this book, activism is a claim to dignity.

"I'VE GOT THIS HATRED IN ME . . ."

Transformation—in terms of both desired societal changes and the reversals the activists already perceived in their own behavior and emotional outlook— was the topic for discussion at a workshop by Remmoho, an APF's women's group, organized on a Saturday in February 2010. We were seated around a flipchart on which were written notes from pair discussions on what we as activists were trying to change within and among ourselves and in our broader society. Self-acceptance, support, and forgiveness were among the qualities listed. "Work on anger," one pair had contributed.

Tumi, picking up on this note, offered, "I remember in the past when in our meetings someone said, 'I've got this hatred in me. . . . I could kill someone.'"

"Yes, wasn't that Ma Patrycja?" Amina chimed in.

"When I left my marriage, I was a very violent person," Ma Patrycja responded, confirming. "If it wasn't for this space, I'd be in Sun City."

"What's in Sun City?" Amina asked.

"Prison," a number of women responded.

The idea that Ma Patrycja could have been prison-bound due to interpersonal violence at any point in her life intrigued me. Within the APF, she was among the most committed elder activists, having been involved in South Africa's anti-apartheid struggle. To me, she seemed unassuming but dedicated. I had to know more.

A SHACK OF HER OWN

Ma Patrycja regretted getting married. As she frequently cautioned her daughter, "Work for yourself, buy yourself a house or rent a flat, buy yourself a car. You mustn't get married, you must just date, you must not be dated." The vision of female autonomy that she tried to impart was rooted in costly experience—her hopes for married life had been dashed years earlier by a neglectful and abusive husband.

"I thought maybe when I am married," she admitted, "life will change now because my husband is working and I'm working. It would be much easier then. I will start helping my mother with bigger things" such as monthly groceries. Her husband, however, "never knew that he must buy food for his own children!" Showing me a picture of her last-born, Ma Patrycja continued, "He never knew what sizes they were wearing, are they going to school or not? He was not even worried to pay the rent." Although as a driver he earned more than she did, she had to cover the entire expenses of her household with income she earned as a laborer—buying food, paying rent, and paying for day care, uniforms, and other expenses to ensure her children's education. Feeling alone in her marriage, she started considering divorce to acknowledge the separate lives she and her husband were leading: "Then I'll know that I'm alone," she said. "I'll have to stand for my kids."

The marriage became a tug-of-war. While she was away working, Ma Patrycja's husband would consume food she had set aside for the children. In response, she became more vigilant. She bought a refrigerator, put a lock on it, and recruited a neighbor to take charge of the key and to retrieve food for her children and the neighbor's children when they were hungry. "The only one that must not eat my food is my husband," she told the neighbor. Seeing that he was no longer being fed, her husband became violent and abusive. Ma Patrycja refused to succumb to the abuse. Instead, she began fighting for herself. She told her husband, "Always when you are starting swearing, making noise, you are drunk. I won't be drunk, I will hit you one day, and you won't believe it!" He did not take her seriously.

The final straw was when he brought a woman he was involved with into her home. Ma Patrycja remembered the exact day—Friday, July 27, 1973—because it was her son's second birthday. She asked a male neighbor to intercede. The neighbor entered the dining room to find Ma Patrycja's husband with a lady who claimed to be his girlfriend.

"Aaron told that woman he doesn't want her anymore," the lady alleged, referring to Ma Patrycja. "Why is she staying here? Why can't she go back to her family's place, her mother and father's house, and stay there? If somebody doesn't want you, he doesn't want you; don't force it!"

The neighbor refused to engage the would-be usurper and instead found two elder women to reason with the husband. The three gathered in Ma Patrycja's home and tried to engage their neighbor, but Ma Patrycja's husband remained silent while his girlfriend responded to their queries. Eventually, the three left and entreated Ma Patrycja to come with them. Ma Patrycja refused: "No, I won't get out of my house for another woman. I won't make that mistake. I was suffering, running up and down pillar to post looking for a house in those hot days, in those rainy days with a baby on my back. I will not just get out of my house!" Instead, she asked one of the neighbors to take her children so as to preserve their happy memories of the day. The children got to have ice cream at the neighbor's house to top off their birthday celebration.

With her children safely out of the house, Ma Patrycja tackled the occupation of her home. She offered her husband opportunities to leave, reminding him at 7:30 p.m. that he and the other woman still had a window to catch a taxi to a nearby hotel before the taxis stopped running at 8:00 p.m. They ignored her. Ma Patrycja bided her time.

At 9:00 p.m., she locked her front gate, her front door, and the back door. She retrieved from her bedroom a knobkerrie—a short stick with a knobbed head that can be used for beatings—and started on her husband, who had been drinking throughout the evening. After hitting him with the knobbed head of the stick, she switched to a beer bottle, which broke on contact. The other woman begged for forgiveness, but those entreaties fell on deaf ears. With broken glass, the knobkerrie, and whatever else was at her disposal, Ma Patrycja fought both of them through the night. The neighbors shouting outside could not get past her locked gate and high fence.

The police arrived at 1:00 a.m. Caught up in the battle for her home, Ma Patrycja did not notice their entry until she turned around and was startled by a sergeant who had jumped the gate and kicked her door open. The police found a mess—Ma Patrycja's husband was on one side, the other woman was on the opposite side, and blood was splattered everywhere.

"Should I call an ambulance?" the sergeant asked.

"Yes, it's your duty to call an ambulance, not me," Ma Patrycja responded. "Call an ambulance because I want to clean my house now."

Ma Patrycja was arrested, but a sympathetic magistrate dismissed her charges. Her husband had lied to the police, claiming that the other woman was his wife and Ma Patrycja was a jealous girlfriend who had attacked them both in their own home. When Ma Patrycja presented her marriage certificate in court, catching her husband in his lie, and detailed the history of domestic abuse, the magistrate released her. Ma Patrycja repeated her request for a divorce, and her husband found accommodation with an aunt before moving into a men's hostel. As the magistrate pointed out, Ma Patrycja's husband did not have much chance of acquiring another home rental. With urban Black home and land ownership prohibited under apartheid, housing choices were restricted to rental allocations from the government, hostels designed to accommodate migrant labor, or illegally constructed shelters in occupied space.

Upon Ma Patrycja's release, her mother entreated her to move back in with her, but Ma Patrycja was adamant in her refusal to give up her home. Even when her mother worried that Ma Patrycja's ex-husband might gather some friends to gang up on her, Ma Patrycja remained defiant. "I won't die alone," she said. She was not going to concede what little space she had claim to without fighting to the end.

When Orange Farm was established as a township in 1989, Ma Patrycja applied for the house she was living in when we met. She ceded her former house in Diepkloof, Soweto, to her children; her second-born was residing there at the time of our interview in 2010. "I wanted a shack of my own," she explained, a home that was not associated in her children's mind with their father but with her own independence.

Ma Patrycja's marriage left an indelible mark on her. "I'm old now," Ma Patrycja told me one afternoon, "but when I just see a man going here, all those things they just start coming back. I'm a man-hater really." As if to confirm that radical self-ascription, she repeated, "I'm a man-hater. Even if I see somebody, maybe they're fighting, and it's a man and a wife, I won't help the man. I'm going to help this lady; even if you can kill this man, I don't care. I don't want to see a man hitting a wife because I am from that life." Thus, her abusive marriage was the root of the rage that her sustained participation in Remmoho helped her confront.

MEANINGS OF HOME

Over the course of Ma Patrycja's life, home was something she had to fight for. Securing a home to rent when she was married entailed bureaucratic struggle, trekking from one government office to another in heat and rain while carrying a baby on her back. She recounted this experience as a suffering she endured for her children's sake, one she did not want to pass on to them. Her husband's effort to subvert her claim to that home and his girlfriend's admonishment that Ma Patrycja to return to her parent's house reveal how romantic entanglements can curtail or broaden a woman's material prospects in South Africa. Her husband's lies and attempts to claim their home highlight the difficulty of urban Black home access under apartheid, legacies of which pervade housing experiences in contemporary South Africa.

In pursuit of independence, Ma Patrycja became a shack dweller. That home brought its own challenges, especially after South Africa's democratic turn, as government neglect continued: "You see my shack now, it's starting to open," she told me. "When it rains then the water comes inside. [The government] thinks nothing about us, but when they want votes, I'm telling you, every day they'll be busy here." Indeed, as Ma Patrycja notes, many in South Africa are not recognized by their political representatives except during election season, when politicians campaign for votes. Then the impoverished are offered food parcels, blankets, and promises of adequate housing.

Nonetheless, Ma Patrycja's shack was the space she claimed, the space she was willing to fight for. That space drove her activist commitments, as she joined with others in her vicinity to improve her living conditions. She became active in the Orange Farm Water Crisis Committee upon its founding and, by extension, the APF. She was also a fierce advocate for women, building on her history of anti-apartheid activism and channeling her experiences toward collective struggle. She continued, as she always had, to share life with her neighbors. She was a trusted confidante for a number of women in her community.

The bulk of APF members live in townships such as hers, in inadequate housing conditions that are animated by interpersonal relationships and marked by interdependence and, sometimes, violation. Townships with their substandard housing are one of the legacies of apartheid-era policies that guide the movement of the following chapters. Chapter 1 details how the APF's formation six years after South Africa's first democratic elections in 1994 was rooted in the inadequacies of South Africa's transformation.

ONE

—ᴍᴍ—

EMERGENCE

During our first days we were just campaigning in the streets, militantly, visibly through direct action. The idea was that we did not want to debate privatisation. We wanted to take action against it. And, at that time privatisation was still a debatable issue. . . . But, those comrades who came together had made up their minds that privatisation was unacceptable. The APF was therefore born as a militant organisation, not a talk-shop.

—Trevor Ngwane (quoted in Naidoo and Veriava 2005: 39)

IN 2000, WHAT WOULD BECOME the Anti-Privatisation Forum (APF) was nothing more than a series of direct-action protests underpinned by performance. By the turn of the twenty-first century, South Africa had held two national democratic elections (in 1994 and 1999). Enough time had passed since the transition to the African National Congress's (ANC) governance of the country for many South Africans (particularly those living in impoverished communities, like Ma Patrycja) to realize that the socialist democratic ideals they had nurtured through anti-apartheid struggles were being abandoned for neoliberal principles. At the urging of the World Bank and other policy experts, the ANC had adopted a neoliberal structural adjustment program known as the Growth, Employment and Redistribution Strategy (GEAR) in 1996. By 2000, the GEAR's impact across societal spheres was still rippling out. No clear civic consensus against the policy had emerged, but for those its effects hit hardest— residents in impoverished communities, workers, and dissenters within the ANC political alliance—there was no debate: the GEAR and its neoliberal economic approach, including the privatization of basic services, had to be stopped. Johannesburg's activist networks, inspired by protests against the World Trade

Organization's 1999 ministerial conference in Seattle, turned to militant disruption, particularly of symbolic events, to mobilize resistance. These mobilizations brought together diverse groups of activists who forged connections among their fragmented groups. The APF emerged from these efforts.

One of these disruptions was of the 2000 Urban Futures conference at Wits University. Activists viewed the conference as a showcase for the privatization designs of Wits University and the Johannesburg City Council and a key battleground to halt the encroachment of neoliberalism into South Africa. Two participants who would become founding members of the APF recalled that as a protest group approached the Great Hall at Wits, they were excited at the sound of singing, which they took as a sign that their comrades (fellow activists from earlier demonstrations) were already at the hall. But they had actually stumbled on a memorial service for a recently deceased member of the National Education, Health and Allied Workers' Union (NEHAWU). Recognizing that the union members were aligned with their aims, the protesters included the union members, bringing more participants to their cause. The combined group proceeded to meet others who had gathered at the Great Hall as planned. Participants shared stories, many of them from an action earlier in the week in Newtown, where a collective had taken over a conference session on water privatization. They laughed when someone asked whether there was food to be seized as there had been in Newtown.

In those inaugural moments of planned disruption, several factors seemed to hinder the group's process and decision-making. First, the group conspicuously lacked a leader, someone to direct the flow of the demonstration. As protesters gathered at the Great Hall, confusion about the next steps prevailed; the session the group had intended to disrupt had already begun. Shut out of the proceedings, activists were left asking, in the words of the two participants, *"Do we just stand here outside and sing quietly while their conference closes or . . . ? And who is supposed to decide?"* (Naidoo and Veriava 2005: 28–29; italics in original). The two participants describe what happened next:

> We bang on the doors, scuffles break out with security guards, and finally the doors are kicked open—[Wits University's vice chancellor] Colin Bundy and neoliberalism's legion of consultants, academics, and policy experts gathered cannot believe their eyes. A motley crew of student activists, academics, workers, unionists and political activists take over the stage as Bundy is hurriedly ushered out to a press conference next door. They are not going to get away with proclaiming that their neoliberal projects are the answers to the needs of the poor. We choose comrades to represent our positions, and over a

loudhailer delegates are reminded of the role they are playing in selling out the lives of the poor. Toyi-toyiing continues. (Naidoo and Veriava 2005: 28–29)

Questions about leadership and execution were overcome through consensus. The assembled protesters divided into smaller groups, then reconvened around a general agreement to force entry into the Great Hall. An activist's suggestion that Colin Bundy be held accountable moved the action from the session the activists had interrupted to a press conference Bundy had been rushed out to lead next door.[1] As the group crashed the press conference, one comrade grabbed Bundy "by the scruff of his neck" as he attempted to leave, a situation that could have escalated irreparably, but violence was averted when another comrade intervened. These abrupt shifts highlight the decidedly impromptu nature of this gathering and the dynamics of a receptive collectivity exploring its own contours.

These early assemblies of those affected by and radically opposed to neoliberalism's advance into South Africa offered fertile ground for the APF's genesis. The performative nature of the APF's emergence is evident in these nascent moments. Cultural performance (the prominence of singing first heard in the distance and then shared in the massed group) served the multiple purposes of claiming space sonically, indicating comradely presence, and mobilizing support from potentially aligned bystanders. In addition, performance allowed a mirthful sense of history to take hold, as prior disruptions, which were essentially political performances, engendered possibilities for further action. By retelling the story of past activity and delighting in the appropriation of conference food for the protesters' nourishment, the budding collective established continuity and drew inspiration from recent successes, extending the buoyant experience of shared vigor across events.

The disruption of the Urban Futures conference worked on many levels as a tactical performance. It was improvised rather than scripted, enabling a range of possibilities for inclusive participation and the recruitment of aligned bystanders. It relied on stoppage for its effectiveness—activists interrupted the conference, capturing attention in a space from which they had been excluded through sheer force of will despite the robust efforts of security guards to keep them at bay. By gaining entry into Wits' Great Hall and taking command of the stage, they shocked conference participants and shut down the session. They interrupted the existing social balance—disrupting the distribution of the sensible, as Rancière would put it—and erupted into undetermined formations that highlighted what pulsing bodies can do—kick down doors and interrupt proceedings. The grabbing of the vice chancellor was not irrational violence but rather an enactment of the underlying message of the protest: the university and the conference organizers were not going to get away with proclaiming neoliberalism as the indisputable future for Johannesburg and, by extension, South Africa. Seized by the scruff of his neck, Colin Bundy, the architect of Wits University's neoliberal designs, was not going to get away. The intervention of the other activists to stop the seizure of Bundy was a bodily dialogue, a reasoning out through action that called to the fore the possibility of going too far.

The protesters' actions had immediate and long-lasting emotional consequences for them. The disruption of the conference generated the possibility of more such performances to contest the planned trajectory for the city and nation, a possibility that was affirmed sensorially. The environment of the university hall, from which the protesters were alienated, was reclaimed bodily, through patterned and eruptive movement and through sound. In this performance of protest, activist potential could be perceived and recovered. The two participants concluded their recollection of that day with a resonant sentiment: *"For the first time in a long while it feels like we're a force again, like there is the possibility for further struggle"* (Naidoo and Veriava 2005: 29; italics in original). The significance of such a sense of possibility cannot be overstated. The country's activist networks had been facing a crisis of relevance due to uncertainty about the ANC's political direction following South Africa's formal transition from apartheid. Providing sensory affirmation that further struggle against the ANC's neoliberal turn was possible—activists *felt* like a force again—the Urban Futures conference disruption planted the seeds for more demonstrations at other key events. From these intermittent mobilizations emerged a durable social movement organization rooted in opposition to the state. That organization was the APF.

The APF's structure as an activist organization was thus forged not through one-off achievements but through events, choices, and practices that became normative over time. The APF's emergence is therefore a story of performativity in the *longue durée*, a temporal scale implied but not often analytically deployed in engagement with the concept of performativity. Scholarship building on Judith Butler's encapsulation of performativity as "acts sedimented over time" (1988: 524) readily emphasizes acts, gestures, routines, rituals, and other discrete units of behavior that solidify categories through repetition. What gets overlooked in this formulation is temporal scale—performativity entails not only repeated acts and citational loops but also, just as importantly, progression or decline *over time*.[2] The history of a social category or political collective is performativity at its fuller scale.

With this understanding in mind, my conception of the emergence of social movements articulates the sociopolitical and historical field that gives rise to activist mobilization while identifying the phases and acts key to that mobilization. This effort requires calling out the emotional and sensorial underpinnings of the movement's formative trajectory to highlight the lived experience and inner life of what was previously unimaginable. I capture this trajectory of performativity through a fourfold process model that begins with *preemergence*—the precursors to collective activism as well as the uncertain political environment that catalyze the union of differently positioned activists in recognition of shared struggle. That union occurs in the second step of emergence, *convergence*, which is facilitated by sensory affirmation of interconnection across geographic distance. This convergence leads to the materialization of a shared predicament that had been invisible and that supports recognition of the feasibility of further collective action. From this recognition comes the third step, *formation*, or the inauguration and assertion of a distinct collective. The fourth and final step is *normalization*—the drive to secure the sustainability of the inaugurated collective by fixing the forms it can assume. Ultimately, however, solidifying practices inevitably opens gaps between intention and experience. What follows, then, is a movement from (1) ambivalence and uncertainty, to (2) convergence built on sensorial evidence, to (3) formation and confident assertion, to, finally, (4) normalization and the delimitation of form.

PREEMERGENCE

Understanding the precursors that contributed to the channeling of political uncertainty into mass action requires reexamining the immediate aftermath of South Africa's postapartheid transition in the mid- to late 1990s. A long history of political opposition to state politics was crucial in securing South Africa's democratic transition. However, the period following the 1994 democratic election that brought the ANC into national governance was a particularly ambiguous one for popular movements that had been dedicated to the demise of apartheid.[3] Former anti-apartheid organizations—previously anti-government—suddenly found themselves allied with the state, under the governance of the newly elected ANC. According to one set of analyses (Ballard et al. 2006), the shift among these organizations from opposition to more collaborative political engagements created a vacuum—few organizations were left to oppose the ANC's government. New social movements emerged to fill this void from the late 1990s onward.

As Marcelle Dawson (2010: 268–69) argues, however, such a view overstates the lack of popular opposition in the immediate postapartheid transition. Although grassroots struggle took a hiatus—as "people held their breath in awe of the dawning of a new era" (Ngwane 2010: 3)—this awed suspension did not last for long. Criticism of the ANC's policies began in the mid-1990s, shortly after the party took power. Activists criticized the government's Reconstruction and Development Programme (RDP) as a dilution of the aims and demands of the liberation struggle. When the government changed its guiding economic policy from the RDP to the more neoliberal GEAR program, criticism came from the ANC's factions as well as from the broader civil society. Still, the ascendance to power of the country's leading anti-apartheid movement did result in some demobilization of activism—although not an utter void in state opposition—as many liberation-era organizations were aligned with the new ruling party (Bond 2006: 115–16).[4]

The unevenness of oppositional activities to shifting political structures during this period is a key characteristic of what Raymond Williams has identified as the emergent. Recognizing that "new practice is not, of course, an isolated process," Williams finds that the ushering in of oppositional forms is "likely to be uneven and is certain to be incomplete" (1977: 124) due to the interaction of nascent forms with more dominant modes. Emergence, then, is not an issue of what is fully reconcilable in the present; rather, "it depends on finding new forms or adaptations of form. Again and again what we have to observe is in effect a *pre-emergence*, active and pressing but not yet fully articulated, rather than the evident emergence which could be confidently named" (Williams 1977: 126; italics in original). Allowing for unevenness in the earliest stages of the APF's performative becoming reveals engagements that were not fully defined, taking place in the interstices of past liberation struggles and the anticipation of a politics that was not yet confidently named.

In interviews, APF activists described the transition as a political moment characterized by both political opportunity and unsteadiness. For Claire Ceruti, an APF founding member, the immediate aftermath of the ANC's ascendance to power enabled further struggle in her activist sphere. For her, the hiatus in mobilization did not come until three years later, in 1997. In a 2010 interview excerpted throughout this chapter, Ceruti discussed how, after South Africa's first election, mainstream political organizations became consumed with governance, creating, in her words, "a vacuum in politics."[5] At the same time, however, new confidence in the impact of collective struggle emboldened communities and strengthened their expectations for change. Since 1987, Ceruti had been a member of the International Socialists of South Africa (ISSA), a Marxist reading group that sought to tie class struggle to more mainstream struggles for national liberation. She describes how, in the moment of transition, ISSA members were able to connect their ideologies to mass-based action:

> The recent history was, we got this far by major struggle and therefore we . . . you know there was a real willingness to just go on the streets sort of thing, you know. So we as this tiny little organisation of fourteen people were able to hold mass meetings in Hillbrow over rent control, for example. There were things like the Spar strike, which I think was a piece of history that still needs to be properly documented, where a couple of workers got fired for going to Mandela's inauguration and there was basically a national strike over this issue. And we related to that and so on, and then especially in Potchefstroom, in particular, where our comrades there were able to actually be quite instrumental in leading a number of struggles over relocations and over services, and this was not long after 1994.

The vacuum in the opposition created by the ANC's ascendance to power presented new possibilities for these activist-intellectuals to connect their political visions, nurtured through long-term intellectual labor, to practical, community-based struggles. For Ceruti, "That was a kind of period where you know you were able to be a revolutionary in a very practical way about very day-to-day issues, to say look we can really push the envelope at the moment, we can win some victories."

These opportunities proved unsteady because the connections made were not sustained or coherently focused around abiding political visions. The communities the ISSA rallied became disillusioned when they encountered opposition from a government they had expected to be on their side, and they stopped responding to calls to protest. The wider movement the ISSA had sought to foster diminished over a span of just three years. Struggle fatigue set in:

> So basically, we got back to that point where we were sort of back down to four people in a room—it is not that all those other people disappeared completely, but a lot of members just got burnt out because it was a really high level of, you know we really were . . . we did nothing else for three years except the struggle. You know there were [sic] just so much happening and so much potential but there didn't seem any point, and then when that stopped getting results then people just . . . you can imagine, people just collapse.[6]

Seeking alternatives, Ceruti and others in her activist circle joined the South African Communist Party (SACP). Participation in the party, however, came to feel constraining. The ISSA subsequently took on the name Keep Left to highlight the ideological commitment its members wanted to promote even as they expanded their participation in more mainstream organizations. Keep Left would later be a founding political group within the APF.

Grassroots protests unrelated to the efforts of Ceruti's group started to take hold in some South African communities in the mid- to late 1990s, as the South African government began harshly enforcing cost-recovery approaches to the provision of basic services. These communities protested electricity cutoffs and the lack of municipal infrastructure; the protests were characterized by a resourceful militancy legitimized by South Africa's political transition. In Tembisa, for example, residents reconnected themselves to the grid after having their electricity disconnected, a tactic that the new social movements that followed would adopt. Elsewhere, people invaded unoccupied land and erected shacks, claiming "a place in the sun and a piece of the pie" (Ngwane 2010: 4) for themselves. Although these "popcorn protests" (Ngwane 2010: 4) were somewhat sporadic and inchoate, they gradually cohered as South African communities responded to the dashing of their hopes for the dawn of democracy.

The advent of South Africa's democracy was thus marked by uneven tendencies. It was a period of hope and investment in the newly elected government, while political freedom assured some grassroots activists that they could agitate for change. The opening of possibilities and the fledging of imaginative militancy in the wake of the ANC's ascent to power were quickly confronted with disillusionment over the government's shifting economic policies and silencing of dissenting views. Activists believed that trade unions—in particular the Congress of South African Trade Unions (COSATU), which was in a tripartite leadership alliance with the ANC—would challenge such policies (Buhlungu 2006). However, dissent within the ruling alliance was stifled, sometimes harshly. Dale McKinley, who was part of the opposition within the tripartite alliance, described the level to which contention was suppressed: "I had been through a huge amount of really rough kind of politics, but I had never experienced a situation where I had been physically prevented from attending meetings and physically threatened because of the stance of opposition that we took. In other words, the politics turned very nasty very quickly for those that had a dissenting voice to this kind of agenda and we lost that battle, as was clear a few years onwards when [GEAR] was unveiled as the official policy of the ANC."[7] McKinley was among those activists whose criticism of the three institutions constituting the alliance (the ANC, the COSATU, and the SACP) resulted in their expulsion from these organizations; he was expelled from the SACP. Trevor Ngwane, a municipal councilor for Pimville in Soweto, who criticized the cost-recovery model because of its negative impact on his constituents, was expelled from the ANC, and he lost his appointment as councilor (2003). John Appolis, who was critical of the CO-SATU's participation in the alliance, lost his job as a union regional secretary. Each of these three became a key founding activist in the APF. Their experiences underscore the harsh constraints and inadequacies of existent political structures in addressing concerns inimical to the government's burgeoning alliance with capital.

The legacy of this preemergent period included tactics such as utility reconnection and land invasion that would be elaborated in the second phase of community mobilization. In the early 2000s, the formation of social movement organizations—including the Treatment Action Campaign, the Anti-Eviction Campaign, Jubilee South Africa, the Landless Peoples Movement, Abahlali baseMjondolo, and the APF—heralded the second phase of postapartheid oppositional mobilization.[8]

CONVERGENCE

Conventionally, convergence entails a coming together from different directions, with the implication that such a meeting will yield a singular union. Common usage of the term also assumes that convergence occurs at a single point in space or time. Departing from these assumptions, I show that while convergence does involve meeting across difference, it is an ongoing process, not an end state. When activists with distinct investments form a coalition, their differences do not simply melt into a singular, uniform alliance. Rather, the differences remain significant; the power dynamics among these different commitments make convergence not a static outcome but an ongoing process happening simultaneously at different intersections.

Because the APF was formed through the convergence of differently located political strivings, it was by no means a monolith. As Dale McKinley described, "I don't set the formation of the APF in July 2000, when it was formally announced; I set the formation of the APF around a bunch of things that came together."[9] One of the APF's formative strengths was that it fostered linkages among geographically dispersed movements, including community-based movements, labor movements, and student movements, to overcome fragmentation and support shared struggle. Differences among the APF's varied constituencies remained a significant factor in efforts to foster these linkages as the organization became established and sought equitable distributions of representation, resources, and responsibilities. A view from one of the communities that came to constitute the APF, a community involved in land invasion, illustrates some of the inequalities that shaped the early moments of the APF's convergence.

The Small Farm Land Invasion

One of the first land invasions in South Africa's transition period took place in anticipation of the 1994 general election that marked the end of apartheid. Backyard dwellers in townships around the Vaal Triangle, a heavily industrialized urban complex south of Johannesburg, decided "as a final nail in the coffin of apartheid" to resettle in an unused open space outside the Small Farm area. Activists within this newly established community would come to affiliate with the APF at its founding. The community's distance of about twenty-seven miles from the Johannesburg city center contributed to the unevenness of the APF's early convergences, as Vaal activists had farther to travel—with more restrictions on those relying on public transportation—to connect with the emerging social movement. These activists were also coming with a distinct regional history of struggle.

Anti-apartheid activism in the Vaal Triangle had been particularly combative. Vaal communities had initiated widespread campaigns, including the "Asinamali" rent boycotts of 1984, which sparked national fervor. Ten years later, backyard dwellers reasoned that additional rent boycotts could lead to violence against them, this time by their Black landlords, the fellow residents whose backyards they leased and in which they built small homes. Emboldened by the transition underway in South Africa, they decided to claim their own land. Thulani was one of those early land claimants. With his patient pastor's voice, he recalled, "We shouted this slogan for, 'Land back to people! Land back to people!' That's what we wanted to say to everyone, to say: 'Now we are free, let's get our land back!'"[10] The land invasion was intended to ensure that the scheduled elections would not be postponed, as Thulani noted: "Because there was this thing of saying, '27th of April will be the elections, now to be postponed.' So our aim was to make sure that they don't postpone this day. So we needed to make sure that there is something happening around here for that day so we invaded this land." The invasion itself was quite chaotic. On April 16, the new residents brought zinc sheets and other materials to the open space and constructed homes, claiming their space as they found it: "You just put your yard here then you stay here, it's your home," said Thulani. The new community defended its claim against apartheid government soldiers and police in the days leading up to the elections. After the elections, when government officials in the new ANC dispensation also tried to remove the residents, citing a lack of essential services in the area, the residents pointed out the continuities with their past experience of the state. According to Thulani, "They said, 'Guys, there is no water here.' We said, 'Yes we've lived here with no water . . . we are okay here, just leave us alone.'"

Finally, in 1997, the ANC government called the community to the negotiating table with the goal to formally demarcate the area; the community was formalized in 1998. When it came time to name the place they had claimed, community leaders chose Kanana, after Canaan, the biblical land of milk and honey. A group of residents, including Thulani, formed the Kanana Community Development Forum (KCDF) in 2000 as a community-based organization independent of any political party, including the ANC. Thulani pointed out the dangers of affiliating with any political organization: "We had a problem that when you demanded something, somebody will say, 'No, Comrade you know, you know using that title [Comrade], you are also a member of the ANC, how could you fight the ANC?'" To avoid such conflict, the residents grounded their claims in the community rather than in political affiliation. When the KCDF eventually affiliated with the APF, that the APF was not a political party but a coalition legitimized by the oppositional claims of Johannesburg-area communities was a particular point of appeal to KCDF members.

Fighting University and Municipal Restructuring at Wits University

In 1999, a year after the ANC government formalized Kanana, one of the legal advisors Thulani had come to know through his community advocacy invited him to "eruptions" taking place at Wits University:

> He said, "Look, there is a meeting at Wits, so will you participate there?"
> I said, "Wits?" He said, "Yes."
> I said, "What time?" He said, "6 o'clock at night."
> I said, "But how am I going to get back home?"
> He said, "Comrade, don't worry, just go."

Thulani went to the meeting, where he met other community-based activists and academics from the Johannesburg metropolitan area, including the East Rand and Soweto, connecting him and the KCDF to the wider network of community activism the APF sought to consolidate.

That meeting, along with other gatherings at Wits that Thulani attended, sought to mobilize activists against a series of neoliberal restructurings the City of Johannesburg Metropolitan Municipality proposed under the iGoli 2002 plan, which would increase the involvement of the private sector in the provision of basic services through outsourcing their management and distribution. City officials believed the introduction of commercial management practices to the delivery system would allow for greater autonomy and flexibility (City of Johannesburg 2001: 32). The driving tenets of the policy included a cost-recovery model of municipal service provision; "the objective [was] to recoup the full cost of production" (McDonald 2002: 18). Distorting the philosophy of ubuntu, the recognition that being human entails interdependence, the policy recast not paying for services, regardless of ability to pay, as antisocial and unneighborly. Contributing to municipal fiscal deficits by not paying, the argument ran, placed the individual over the community (McDonald 2010: 146–47). Because of Johannesburg's significance as a key industrial capital then generating 16 percent of South Africa's economic production (Beauregard et al. 2003), the city's proposed neoliberal restructuring, among the nation's earliest, was seen as a crucial battleground.[11]

The South African Municipal Workers Union (SAMWU) firmly opposed the policy, lodging a formal complaint against the Greater Johannesburg Metropolitan Council in 1999. As both municipal workers and consumers, SAMWU members were doubly vulnerable to the proposed changes, which would result in both increased costs and job losses (especially for municipal workers). SAMWU members reached out to Trevor Ngwane, the ANC municipal councilor who had been expelled for speaking out against the iGoli 2002 plan. The SAMWU invited Ngwane, the only councilor who had publicly opposed the plan, to speak at their marches.

Ngwane and others also created alternative spaces where those affected could engage with the plan, including a workshop organized by the Campaign Against Neoliberalism in South Africa (CANSA). Attendees at that workshop decided to start an Anti-iGoli Forum with the idea of drawing local communities into the workers' struggles "because the government's main argument then was, 'The workers are selfish, this is good for the communities.' And it made sense because the first line of attack was the workers."[12] The importance of linking workers' struggles with the concerns of the communities in which they were embedded cannot be overstated, since social fragmentation is an effect of globalized neoliberal capitalism (Gill 2009; Harvey 2005). Government rhetoric that pitted the interests of workers against those of community residents leveraged such fragmentation, alienating one group from the other and obscuring the "relationships and associational forms" that could shield them all "from the brunt of market forces" (Gill 2009: 668).

Some of the disagreement was genuine. Not everyone was sold on the detriments of neoliberalism, as Ngwane recalled: "Of course you can't believe it now ... but there was debate about whether privatization was a good thing or a bad thing in society." Communities were also ambivalent about opposing the government: "For many people the struggle was against the legacy of apartheid. And so let us all join hands and roll back the legacy of apartheid through reconstruction. The main line was, 'Let us not fight the government, let's be partners with the government!' And the government's idea was, 'Let's privatize.'"

The Anti-iGoli Forum sought to clarify this ambivalence and bridge divides between workers and the broader community as well as between township struggles (for basic services) and forums arising in town. One such forum, the Wits University Crisis Committee, was created at Wits University in response to the university's own restructuring program. In 1999, university administrators announced a strategic plan, Wits 2001, to reposition the university financially and to build financial viability by reorganizing academic departments to promote more market-oriented logics and outsourcing support services, including cleaning, catering, maintenance, grounds, and transport. The outsourcing component of the plan threatened the jobs of the university's support staff. Along with the NEHAWU—the union representing these campus workers—concerned academics, students, and staff mobilized in opposition to Wits 2001. These groups came together to form the Crisis Committee.

Members of the Anti-iGoli Forum supported the campaigns of the Wits University Crisis Committee, as both groups were protesting connected neoliberal onslaughts. The two groups also shared some members. The overlapping of membership in these groups provided activists with integrated perspectives, illuminating the need to build a more inclusive campaign. Ahmed Veriava, a student at the time, described the moment as one when "on campus . . . we kind of realized that it's going to be very difficult for us to win this campaign without broadening it."[13] Thus, the campus protests became a platform for establishing connections between opposition to the iGoli plan and community struggles happening elsewhere. As Veriava recalled, "We saw in these the hopeful possibility of potentially making more kind of real connections with, or kind of establishing something of a broad front against neoliberal privatization."

The Crisis Committee's efforts against Wits 2001 were the subject of that first meeting Thulani attended in town. He was so excited to connect with activists and academics from other locations that he stayed after the meeting for a roundtable discussion on privatization. Thulani described an exchange of ideas rooted in the possibilities of coming together, of uniting as front, and "defending our resources that we have currently." Whether participants were commanding the floor through delivering speeches or actively listening with shifting physical positions, their embodiment animated an exchange that gripped Thulani's attention and flowed well into the night. Afterward, as he had feared, he had no way to get home—the taxis had stopped running to his area. Because he lived farther from the city center, where the meetings and discussions were being held, he did not have the ease of mobility some others at the meeting and roundtable took for granted. This inequality of mobility is a key point of difference among those whose coming together would lead to the formation of the APF. Although Thulani was eager to connect with others in struggle, his limited mobility made it costly for him to do so. That first evening, he was effectively homeless in the city. He slept on a bench at Park Station, Johannesburg's ground transportation hub. As a result, he was already in town the next day when there was a march in support of the Wits workers. After what must have been a long night, Thulani remained eager to show up for others. Rather than return home at his next opportunity, he attended the Wits march. His participation in this and other such marches deepened knowledge of his newfound comrades through bodily confirmation. In his own words, by "toyi-toying with them," marching together unified by song and highly kinetic rhythmic stomps, he "got to know most of the comrades there [at Wits]."

In addition to the sensorial and bodily pull driving connection, Thulani's experience evidences how unequal distributions of personal resources factor into convergence: when community activists, union members, and students come together from different ideological and geographical locations, participation entails greater sacrifice and bodily exposure for some than for others. Although he avoided harm, Thulani willingly put his body on the line to contribute to the political collective that was developing. But not all activists could, or would, make the same choice—further illustration of the uneven stakes among different clusters of activists as they converge toward a social movement.

Thulani's engagement with the KCDF and the Wits Crisis Committee was a movement from being one to becoming more—the essence of convergence. This movement into more raises the possibility of what Judith Butler calls "plural performativity" (2015: 8), a phrase that designates forms of emergence that exceed individual capability and can only happen through coordinated action with others. The movement from "I" to "we" transcends the individual and generates activity that reflects the quality of relationship between and among those gathered, however unequal that relationship might be. Convergence therefore yields to (and can be concurrent with) a third phase of performative becoming, one with greater emphasis on coordination among the discrete entities within a social movement's emerging makeup.

FORMATION

When the Wits University Crisis Committee, the Anti-iGoli Forum, and other similarly invested groups decided to integrate their efforts, they called a joint meeting of their members. At its start, one of the conveners called the meeting a gathering of the "Anti-Privatisation Forum," writing that phrase on the classroom whiteboard. As Trevor Ngwane recalled, "What [else] could he write because it was Wits Crisis Committee, and we were called Anti-iGoli? So he just said this is the Anti-Privatisation Forum for activists; so this is how the APF was formed like an activist forum." With the convener's performative declaration, the APF was born. The forum brought together a wide range of activists, including those from the South African Students Congress (SASCO); the SAMWU; the NEHAWU; the COSATU; the Independent Municipal and Allied Trade Union (IMATU); several "left-wing" groups, including Keep Left, the Democratic Socialist Movement, and the Johannesburg Branch of the SACP; and a number of community organizations, including the Soweto Electricity Crisis Committee (SECC). These organizations formally affiliated with the APF in its initial formation.

Formation refers not only to a movement's composition but also to developmental moments (as in a person's formative years) in which enduring qualities start to take shape. As it pertains to activism and social movements, formation involves the strategic alignment of individuals inhabiting multiple social positionings as they converge across boundaries of ethnicity, race, class, gender, status, and generation in support of a shared purpose. Formation raises questions of inclusion and exclusion, alignment and misalignment, as the budding collective comes into focus. Formation, as an ongoing process, encourages activists to grapple with how to best leverage privilege and varied social capital for shared justice aims. An ideal formation entails centering and supporting the leadership of often-marginalized individuals whose direct experience informs their oppositional standpoints and strategic pursuits.

Emotions matter in this process: the APF's formation was forged through shared feeling generated by direct action. Activists recalled the collective's commitment to direct action as a key bond distinguishing this new coalition from its antecedents. As Ahmed Veriava explained:

> I think what was specific about the APF and what separated it from previous, similar kinds of discussion groups like CANSA, even the Anti-iGoli Forum itself, was that this particular activist forum was orientated towards forms of direct action and building a kind of common, a kind of sense of belonging together as a political entity through actual forms of struggle and that was immediately expressed in its foundational activities. And in my somewhat kind of generous narrative of this, I do somewhat link this also to the presence of a particular group of students, who were keen to kick in doors and those kinds of things.

That "particular group of students" drew to the fore the different capabilities the various groups brought to the APF's formation. Wits students had earlier recognized one advantage of their relative autonomy compared to the union workers they had partnered with. Union workers were required to go through labor mediation processes before they could engage in protest action on campus, and they were limited to lunchtime protests. During the Wits 2001 protests, the student activists, as Veriava recalled, "saw certain opportunities to perhaps use the cover that students had, to undertake somewhat more antagonistic actions." These actions included the occupation of the vice chancellor's office by students, who became leaders in the resistance to the neoliberal program. A proclivity toward direct action that leveraged different capabilities among participant clusters continued in the newly formed APF, and it was critical to the liveliness and keen enthusiasm of participants during the APF's formative moments.

One of the first demonstrations of the new collective was held during the 2000 Urban Futures conference at Wits, described at the beginning of this chapter. Wits University and the Greater Johannesburg Metropolitan Council organized the conference jointly; the collaboration between the two main targets of anti-privatization activism in Johannesburg caused particular concern in the activist community. Activists interpreted the conference as an effort "to showcase the sale of our city and our university" to financial institutions, including the International Monetary Fund (IMF) and the World Bank, both seen as fraternal proponents of neoliberal policies (Ngwane and Dor 2000). The activists thus responded with a sense of urgency, drawing inspiration from anti-globalization initiatives that cohered most notably in the disruptions of the 1999 ministerial conference of the World Trade Organization in Seattle, Washington.[14] APF activists protested the conference over its entire run, from July 10 to July 14, at three different venues—the Wits University campus, the Johannesburg City Hall, and the Newtown Cultural Precinct. Activists successfully disrupted the final conference ceremony, which was to be addressed by Wits vice chancellor Colin Bundy, whose administration was responsible for the retrenchment of support staff under Wits 2001. The APF's immediate success at the Urban Futures conference offered a tentative hope that left-wing activists could be a vibrant force for continued struggle postapartheid.

Activists' uncertainty about how to proceed in the new political landscape is especially understandable in the context of the unevenness of prior attempts at opposition, particularly the burned-out withdrawal from the struggle, described by Claire Ceruti, generated by the failure to create enduring change and the stifling of dissenting voices within the ANC's alliance (see also Buhlungu 2004: 2). In Naidoo and Veriava's narrative, the exhaustion of defeat is palpable.

They recount many losses in the developing struggle. At Wits University, as the privatization plans were implemented in the months leading up to the Urban Futures conference, 613 workers lost their jobs, and only 250 were reemployed under contracts with outsourced service providers, in positions that paid a fraction of their former salaries and offered no access to health insurance or any of the other benefits to which they had been entitled as employees of Wits (Van der Walt et al. 2001). As Naidoo and Veriava noted:

> When the Urban Futures conference came up in July 2000, it presented the perfect opportunity for all those who had begun to feel the effects of the implementation of GEAR (at the university, in the city, in Soweto, in the unions, and in the ANC and Congress-aligned structures such as SASCO, SANCO [South African National Civic Organization] and the SACP)—and *the exhaustion of trying unsuccessfully to fight it from within the ANC Alliance*— to come together in a symbolic show of the willingness to fight privatisation at all costs, whether this meant taking on the ANC Alliance or not. (Naidoo and Veriava 2005: 40; italics mine)

In the face of this exhaustion, the experience of confronting such defeats during the Urban Futures conference was an invigorating affirmation that provided "*a new energy to fight on*" (Naidoo and Veriava 2005: 29; italics in original).

The new energy sprang from and fed back into the newfound formation of the APF. The APF at this stage had joined a long line of attempts to open up political space, and many of Johannesburg's leftist progressives had begun assessing its potential. The Urban Futures disruption presented this new grouping as a hopeful novelty and as a frame to promote a variety of political visions. Veriava's assessment captures the recognition, generated by the action at the Urban Futures conference, of a powerful connection among those previously dispersed:

> I think when it actually happened, when we took over the stage and when there were certain kinds of expressions of collective power, I think it gave people a certain kind of confidence in whatever this formation was and the desire to perpetuate it in some way as well as focus it. But also remember that in its very constituent parts, it brought together at the time the unions, students, the communist party, a range of activists within Johannesburg. So in terms of what it was, it was in itself novel, something that people were quite excited about, and I mean from the kind of people making plans on white boards in a kind of small Trotskyite circles [sic] and those people within that kind of union movement . . . who even coming from those similar kinds of politics also had an experience of mass politics or wanting to build a broad front of what was the watchword there—a kind of neoliberal privatization.

At the center of the new APF formation was a focused target for its opposition, one embedded in its very name. Privatization had become a rallying point in the new assembly of city- and township-based politics in particularly instructive ways. The articulation of the global with the local had made leftists vigilant against the encroachment of privatization on South African shores. The retreat of the nation-state from spheres of social provision did not yet have the same connotations or seismic significance for South Africa that it did for the European or American nations where it had originated. Ahmed described learning about neoliberalism through the ensuing struggles to oppose it: "Our actual giving flesh to those concepts of neoliberalism and privatization actually took place in a mode in which we confronted these things at different levels . . . in various struggles that arose." Through such struggles, the global watchword—*neoliberalism*—attained a deeper meaning and was "given its own particular inflection in our political context."

Township struggles in particular provided insight into the day-to-day impact of neoliberal policies and fed into the energy that was channeled into the APF. When the parastatal electricity agency Eskom cut off Soweto households that could not pay drastically increased electricity bills,[15] many illegally reconnected themselves by bribing Eskom employees. These discreet practices were politicized in the formation of a mass organization, the SECC, that became a founding affiliate of the APF. Regarding these reconnections, Trevor Ngwane recalled: "When we raised the question in mass meetings, it would come as a relief to everyone to find that their neighbors were illegally connected, too—they'd all been hiding it from each other. We turned what was a criminal deed from the point of view of Eskom into an act of defiance. It was good tactics and good politics" (Ngwane 2003: 47).

These reclamation practices established, as Veriava described, what the strategies of resistance to privatization "were to be." For the SECC, and for the APF, coming together meant the articulation of ambivalent practices as acts of definition and defiance, giving organizational solidity to previously hidden (and thereby fragmented) commonality. By identifying privatization as a central point of critique or problematization (Dave 2012: 8; Foucault 1997; Faubion 2001), political potential established its contours and found its name.

The APF's naming was not simply about unifying the constituent parts of this new formation under a common term; naming itself is performative—it calls into being that which is named. It delimits areas of focus and asserts possible trajectories for a movement's growth. It is an affirmation of a life, one for which longevity is hoped. Naming is a rite of passage, indicating the shift from amorphous and ambiguous potential to an assured designation of what is taking shape. With its naming, the APF became a discernable assembly with a banner under which supporters could gather, although the underlying structures and public strategies through which the forum would operate were not yet determined. That is the work of the fourth and final stage of a movement's emergence.

NORMALIZATION

The drive toward normalization challenges early exercises of activist formation, even as new forms are being conceived as radical alternatives to problematic norms. The critical practice of politics is forged in opposition to normalization, and yet, it is also nurtured by it.[16] If, as Rancière argues, politics is the disruption of one community and the inauguration of another, hopefully more inclusive one, then with this inauguration comes another form of delimitation that repartitions the sensible. However, this inevitable containment—"the fixing of potential into certain normative forms" (Dave 2012: 203)—need not be negative; it can be productive rather than restrictive, as critical practices come into being by interrogating and *reshaping* norms. Performative transformation thus relies on the normalization, through diffusion and durability, of what has been reconstituted differently.

In the case of the APF, normalization occurred through popular recognition of the movement's viability, consolidation of its organizational structures, and explicit articulation of the group's goals in a document that would eventually serve as its constitution.

The APF's Founding Conference

The APF held its founding conference in September 2000 on the tenth floor of the COSATU House. Representatives of the coalition of organizations that constituted the forum, including trade unions and student congresses, elected as cochairs Sibongile Radebe of SASCO and John Appolis of the COSATU Wits Region. Thus began the APF's process of normalization.

Normalization entailed resolving ambivalent orientations toward the ANC and establishing the APF's identity in its own right, separate from its constituent organizations. A part of this evolution came in a shakeout in 2001. As the APF cultivated antagonistic opposition to the ANC's policies, maintaining affiliation with the forum became increasingly untenable for those organizations that were part of the ANC's alliance with the SACP and the COSATU. As a result, the COSATU Regional Executive Committee decided to withdraw from the APF, and several other organizations stopped participating without formally withdrawing. Activists affiliated with the COSATU who wanted to maintain their involvement with the APF, including John Appolis, could do so only as individual activists and not as union representatives.

The APF's break with the ANC took a very visible form two years later. The APF had secured a three-year funding award from the UK-based War on Want in 2002 that allowed it to open an office in the COSATU House and hire two full-time employees, an organizer, and an administrator. In June 2003, the APF was evicted from its COSATU premises at the behest of the ANC. The organization eventually found offices at the Khanya College "house of movements." While the APF had maintained its operations in the COSATU House even when the congress withdrew from the APF's coalition, their eventual eviction was an unapologetic break that served to underline and harden the APF's oppositional politics, marking the closure of potential for collaboration with the ANC-aligned labor union.

While the participation of some founding organizations, particularly labor unions, faded, community-based activist groups became more involved. By mid-2001, the number of APF community-based affiliates had increased from the three at the founding conference to eight. These community-based groups were reaching out to one another to establish solidarity in their struggles, evidence of the ongoing, processual nature of convergence. Frequently, that outreach led organizations to the APF, as when an activist with the Lenasia-based Thembelihle Crisis Committee (TCC) received a phone call from an SECC organizer who had heard a radio interview about march the TCC had held. The organizer called to offer recognition of shared struggles and expressed a desire to unite. As a result of that call, the Lenasia-based activists visited the SECC in Soweto, and the two organizations cultivated a relationship. Activists in the SECC eventually introduced the TCC to the APF.

The APF's normalization process also entailed growing popular recognition of the group, evidenced primarily by its mobilization against the World Summit on Sustainable Development (WSSD), a UN conference held in Johannesburg from August 26 to September 4, 2002. The APF was a key organization (under an alliance called the Social Movements Indaba) involved in organizing a march targeting the WSSD. Although the government warned against any disruptions to the summit, oppositional forces like the APF mobilized as many people as possible outside the official routes to participation in the event itself. On August 31, more than twenty thousand protesters took to the streets in a procession that moved from the impoverished township of Alexandra to the far more opulent Sandton, where the summit was held. By numbers, the WSSD march was the APF's largest oppositional gathering to date, and its success marked a turning point in APF activities, motivating more communities and individuals to seek affiliation with the organization.

If the possibilities for struggle had been uncertain before, the march demonstrated the extent of the APF's potential base. As Claire Ceruti reflected, "It showed that there really was a space for organizations outside of those mainstream organizations to do something, to get something together, and I think it also showed that that space was open." The event further affirmed a spirit of common purpose among activists. An activist who later became one of the APF's organizers reflected on the march:

> Seeing a lot of people out there in the streets and everybody joining in singing . . . I think it was electrifying [and] at the same time exciting to say our voices are also going to be heard outside your original movements which were there. It's a memory that someone will carry on for quite a long time, and I think it brought some excitement to say, "Hang on, we are on to something new here, and something is going to develop." Unlike being within your affiliate where you think it's only us and a very few people who have similar sort of outlook to things and how things should be, it is quite a, well, bigger number and a bigger network. That was quite exciting.[17]

As a political performance, the march demonstrated nodal interconnections and a potential for amplification that could be readily perceived in the assemblage of bodies claiming physical and sonic space. Importantly, the new affiliates' recognition was of each other—the march made possible a moment in which they realized they were not alone and became conscious of a moment of conception, an epiphany. Something new was coming into being, organically, and its emergence lent protesters a sense of confidence and a desire to sustain and further define it. Such a desire for definition and sustainability is, in essence, a drive toward normalization.

Constituting the APF as an Organization

The WSSD protest also provided impetus for another step toward normalization—the consolidation of the APF's organizational structure. In its early years, the APF had functioned as a forum, a loosely structured gathering place that nonetheless ensured the autonomy of its affiliated groups. In 2002, those with experience in mass-based organizations argued for a more grassroots-oriented structure. Such a transformation—the cultivation of one possibility over others that were thereby foreclosed—did not come without debate. John Appolis provided a view of this moment and elaborated the importance of organizational development:

I think we sort of decided to harness that mood, that militancy that was displayed at WSSD into a much more stronger, solid organizational form, and hence we started moving in the direction of formalizing the APF. . . . I think there were comrades who were opposed to this kind of internal organizational consolidation and building of organization and wanted to continue with a kind of big event sort of politics. I remember those debates where people used to argue that if you don't take to the streets, you are not struggling. . . . I didn't support that kind of approach to struggle. I mean you can't be in permanent action, you know people get exhausted, you need to consolidate, you need to develop your organization, you need to develop the perspective of the militants, you have to provide certain training and political understandings, you know, for them to sustain the organization and carry the organization through.[18]

Such insights are critical, particularly in light of earlier experiences of post-apartheid mobilization that were not coupled with long-term vision; recall Claire Ceruti's assessment of the struggle fatigue in her political group. Cultivating the APF's structure facilitated the movement's longer-term sustainability and provided a safeguard against loss of cohesion due to exhaustion.

The drive to consolidate was also a moment of creativity, fed by convergence and by the APF's early successes. As APF members gained confirmation of the feasibility of further struggles, they were driven to develop a different conception of activism. Inherent in this formative moment was the possibility of discarding old forms of struggle and the excitement of bringing about something new. In its formation, APF members were imaginatively challenged to do organizational work differently. This drive accounted for compelling evolutions in the APF's organizational structure.

Despite continued wariness toward the bureaucratization that formality would bring, the APF consolidated its structure after the WSSD march. Between 2002 and 2003, it adopted a Memorandum of Association that became the basis for its constitution. By this time, there were twelve to fourteen community-based affiliates; the memorandum established regional structures in an attempt to decentralize the organization and facilitate local connections among these communities.[19] In addition, the memorandum captured a change in organizational structure, recognizing an APF Council composed of representatives from all community affiliates and political groupings as the organization's highest decision-making body. Further, it called for the creation of an executive committee to coordinate the routine practicalities of organizational work and subcommittees to focus on specific issues, such as education and media. Elected offices in the new structure included a chair, secretary, and treasurer.

The memorandum acknowledged three categories of membership: (1) community groups such as the SECC and the TCC; (2) political groups such as Keep Left, the Socialist Group, and the Democratic Socialist Movement (all of which were Trotskyist in orientation), and the Bikisha Media Collective (which was anarchist); and (3) individual unaffiliated activists. When the APF's final constitution was adopted in 2007, the APF council became a coordinating committee, and elected offices included a chairperson, deputy chair, secretary, deputy secretary, treasurer, and campaigns and project coordinator. The executive committee and subcommittees persisted. The constitution outlined the timing of meetings, with general meetings to be held annually and elections every two years. The constitution also clarified the APF's membership structure, including procedures for admitting new affiliates and the rights and obligations of affiliates. The structure outlined in this constitution prioritized community-based organizations, granting them more representational weight than political groups.

The intent of these articulated priorities was to create more representative structures and to promote internal democracy, breaking with the organizational tendencies of South Africa's past liberation movements, which limited avenues for open contestation. The constitution was also designed to counter the dominance of individuals, an imbalance created by the movement's early reliance on those with access to monetary and other resources. Increasing the involvement of members from Johannesburg's impoverished communities by promoting decentralized and nonhierarchical coordination was, as a result, a key challenge. The shift in the APF's structure sought to achieve this purpose through the interplay of established and emerging organizational practices, such as a consideration for linguistic plurality expressed in meetings that were conducted with interchanges and translations between isiZulu, seSotho, English, and other languages. The desired lack of hierarchy was also expressed in other ways; in interactions, for instance, members addressed one another as "comrades." Debate was also critical to the openness the APF sought to foster, and it was prominent in many of the meetings I observed.

However, some unresolved aspects of the APF's stabilization as an organization generated gaps between intentions and outcomes. One of these issues was the perceived delegitimization of political groupings created by the insistence that the struggle be grounded in the experiences of the APF's working-class constituents, rather than ideological commitments. This stance against ideology was an attempt to break with the experiences of many APF activists. Claire Ceruti elaborated the dynamic in play:

The issues of politics were really in some ways more about the ANC and so on than about an organization like Keep Left, but obviously, it did start to come over to say, somehow, any kind of politics is not allowed. So I kind of remember that being one of the . . . big points as things started to kind of settle and to solidify. . . . Should an organization like Keep Left be able to affiliate as a political organization? It wasn't just us; there were other organizations as well. So there was that period where there was a bit of a debate about whether only community organizations were legitimate and what gave you that legitimacy.

This destabilization of legitimacy represented one of the possibilities that was lost in the APF's transformation, prompting Claire Ceruti to lament, "I think it was a shame to lose the activist forum in some ways." For her, political direction and organizational unity felt much more organic; she recalled the forum as "an impromptu front . . . of organizations that were being swept along together . . . in the same general direction."

Formalizing the APF's structures authorized some forms of participation at the expense of others, especially of organizational affiliation over individual participation. Activists participated in the APF as representatives of their affiliates; unaffiliated individuals were held at a further associational remove. This distancing complicated the voicing of perspectives: some affiliated individuals felt their choices were constrained by the organizations they represented, and unaffiliated individuals often felt they lacked a claim to the experiential legitimacy that organizations were granted in the new structure. In Claire Ceruti's perspective: "When we moved towards the sort of representative structure, if you want to call it that way, but without somehow making a way for individual members to also be represented, I think there was, I mean I am speculating quite honestly about other people's motives, because I could always still speak through Keep Left. But I think maybe there was a thing that people maybe then felt unsure about standing up and saying, 'I am arguing my point here as one person,' and that maybe drove a lot of things underground. So that was an issue."

These issues of personal and organizational representation were submerged into "playing politics," elaborated in chapter 4, which focuses on the internal dynamics among APF members. The constraints created by the APF's structural approach were significant enough that when some APF members started a separate women's forum, they designated membership on an individual basis, with each woman participating for herself rather than as a representative of an organization.

While the APF's organizational formation supported its long-term sustainability—the APF withstood the disintegration of several other movements, beginning around 2006—it was also a performative normalization; it established patterned procedures that conditioned the experiences of its members, both positively and negatively, for years to come. When I came to know the APF between 2009 and 2010, the organization had about thirty-four community affiliates and two active political groups. A few individual members who had been key to the APF's formation had faded from the group, and much conflict persisted within the organization. I disentangle this conflict in chapter 4.

The eruption of politics is hardly spontaneous; rather, it is embedded in the ongoing, long-term cultivation of oppositional sensibilities, a reminder of the performative nature of collective activism. Performativity in the longue durée draws attention to potential and actualization as well as unsteadiness, unevenness, and foreclosure with recognition that none of these qualities precludes the others. This discussion considered preemergence, convergence, formation, and normalization separately for analytical ease; however, these stages in performative becoming are not discrete or temporally contained. Rather, these moments are ongoing, iterative processes that overlap in the progression that results in a social movement's emergence.

CONCLUSION

The APF emerged at a period of transition in which a dominant economic system was consolidating as the trajectory for South Africa. The formal culmination of the anti-apartheid struggle heralded a potential for change, but the adoption of neoliberal policies exacerbated already dire living conditions and privileged a market logic that exposed workers and students to greater risk. At the same time, the repression of dissent within the ANC-led tripartite alliance, in many cases through expulsion of contentious members, demonstrated the limits of engagement within established systems. The convergence of efforts by various groups affected by privatization—whether in student organizations, labor unions, or communities—launched a heterogeneous, plural, oppositional formation that cohered first through commitment to concrete direct action in opposition to the encroachment of neoliberalism.

The collective formed in that opposition extended beyond its critique of neoliberalism to envisioning alternatives, "creating the space for the imagining of an alternative society in which basic services are delivered through the direct collective action of people and the reorganization of social life outside of the framework of the market" (Naidoo and Veriava 2005: 45). For the movement, the challenge was to channel the energies of successful mass demonstrations into sustainable organizational structures that transcended the tendencies of earlier formations toward elitism and hierarchy. These attempts at inaugurating new modes of internal democracy necessarily foreclosed other possibilities, including the more expressly horizontal relationships fostered by an activist forum.

While the debate within the APF ultimately prioritized normalization over the looseness of street politics, the APF's life cycle reveals the need for reciprocal development of *both* fixity of structure *and* fluidity of spirit. As opposed to an emphasis on one over the other, a generative nexus of both augments the distinct contributions of each to movement work. This nexus is what sustains a political collective beyond incipience and through the ethical challenges of coalescence. Privileging formalization overlooks what activists found valuable in their coming together—the sensorial evidence of togetherness; an intuitive coordination that felt organic, yielding, unprompted, and unrehearsed; and demonstration of political impact and capability in confrontation with targeted opponents. Yet, without day-to-day coordination and the temporal rhythms of collective production, the big events, the masses taking to the streets, could not occur. Such a recognition of the need for both fixity and fluidity calls for reciprocal development through cycles of planning, implementation, and demonstration that marry the potential of momentous political performances with quotidian acts. Inattention to either element risks diluting collective investment in shared struggle.

The APF was forged through the interlinking of shared struggle, by bringing together the campaigns at Wits University, among labor unions, in Johannesburg, and in the neighboring townships. This foundation is all the more significant because it shows the potential embedded in the APF's formative years to prevail over the social fragmentation created by neoliberal policies that pit the interests of one group against another. Collectives that seek social change critique convention and usher in their critiques with limitless potential. Although this potential for community and recognition of commonality became stunted in the APF's later years, as I will show more fully in chapter 4, the organization's possibilities were open at its inauguration. Choices made and performatively reinforced over time—assertions that the collective needed a structure, and a particular kind of structure—narrowed and normalized what the APF became and defined the avenues for change the organization could recognize.

NOTES

1. Bundy, one of the primary targets of anti-privatization activists' ire, is a historian of South African rural, peasant, and agrarian liberation movements

who studied inequality during apartheid before transitioning into university administration.

2. Even when Judith Butler examines the performativity of coalitions and alliances, as she does in *Notes Toward a Performative Theory of Assembly* (2015), her analysis focuses on transient gatherings because she views transience as critical to the democratic function of popular assemblies. Once these assemblies become institutionalized, "they risk losing their character as the popular will" (7). As it became established following transient events, the APF took on this challenge of institutionalization, demonstrating the importance of reconsidering temporality in the constitution of oppositional social movements.

3. On the myriad contradictions of South Africa's democratic transition in community life, see especially Ashforth (2005), Besteman (2008), Ross (2010), Makhulu (2015), Chance (2018), and Livermon (2020).

4. This demobilization occurred despite the ANC government's intentions to support and cultivate social movements and civil society organizations. According to the 1994 *Reconstruction and Development Programme*, "Social movements and Community-Based Organizations are a major asset in the effort to democratize and develop our society. Attention must be given to enhancing the capacity of such formations to adapt to partially changed roles. Attention must also be given to extending social-movement and CBO structures into areas and sectors where they are weak or non-existent" (African National Congress 1994, chap. 5, quoted in Bond 2006: 116).

5. Oral history interview with Claire Ceruti, conducted by Dale McKinley, February 23, 2010, Johannesburg. All of the quotes attributed to Ceruti in this chapter are from this interview. Interview housed in the Anti-Privatisation Forum collection of the South African History Archive. Minor punctuation adjustments have been made to enhance clarity and readability.

6. This narrative complicates Dawson's characterization of the immediate aftermath of political transition by showing that activity did flourish in some realms. The fatigue described here is different from that of Dawson's portrayal, which was due to the hard-won attainment of political freedom (Dawson 2010: 268). Here, the fatigue is due to sustained activism with few results.

7. Oral history interview of Dale McKinley, conducted by Ahmed Veriava, March 1, 2010, Johannesburg. The quotes and comments from Dale McKinley in this chapter are from this interview. Interview housed in the Anti-Privatisation Forum collection of the South African History Archive. Minor punctuation adjustments have been made to enhance clarity and readability.

8. A significant body of work details the emergence, ideologies, and dynamics of these new movements. See, for example, Ballard et al. (2006), Bond (2006), Desai (2002), Gibson (2006), Naidoo and Veriava (2005).

9. In an oral history interview of Ahmed Veriava, conducted by Dale McKinley, February 19, 2010, Johannesburg. Interview housed in the Anti-Privatisation Forum collection of the South African History Archive.

10. Interview with the author, August 25, 2010, Johannesburg. All quotes attributed to Thulani are from this interview.

11. Oral history interview with Dale McKinley, conducted by Ahmed Veriava, March 1, 2010, Johannesburg. Interview housed in the Anti-Privatisation Forum collection of the South African History Archive.

12. Interview with the author, November 14, 2010, Johannesburg. Subsequent quotations and comments from Trevor Ngwane are from this interview.

13. Oral history interview with Ahmed Veriava, conducted by Dale McKinley, February 19, 2010, Johannesburg. The quotations and comments from Ahmed in this chapter are from this interview, with minor punctuation adjustments to enhance clarity and readability. Interview housed in the Anti-Privatisation Forum collection of the South African History Archive.

14. As Ahmed Veriava recalled, "At least from our side, the targeting of that conference [Urban Futures] owed something to the inspiration of Seattle, a kind of conference bashing, and I think we wanted our own mini-Seattle." Lesley Wood (2012) describes the widespread diffusion of Seattle tactics in the aftermath of the event and analyzes the limits of this diffusion.

15. Under apartheid, payments for services were fixed; under the ANC, Eskom started charging per kilowatt-hour.

16. As Naisargi Dave notes, "[Activist] sociality takes the form of a commons in which the radical, creative possibilities that the commons enables must also, to some extent, be enclosed within itself in order for those possibilities to thrive, thus always reproducing certain disciplinary apparatuses" (Dave 2012: 8–9; see also Dave 2010, 2011; Hodgson and Brooks 2007).

17. Oral history interview with Silumko Radebe, conducted by Dale McKinley, February 23, 2010, Johannesburg. Interview housed in the Anti-Privatisation Forum collection of the South African History Archive. Minor punctuation adjustments have been made to enhance clarity and readability.

18. Oral history interview with John Appolis, conducted by Dale McKinley, March 17, 2010, Johannesburg. Interview housed in the Anti-Privatisation Forum collection of the South African History Archive.

19. The APF's first Annual General Meeting (AGM), held in 2004, was attended by nineteen community-based affiliates.

TWO

—∿—

ROUTINIZATION

AS SOCIAL MOVEMENTS ESTABLISH THEMSELVES, creating stability may require both spectacular disruptive measures and quotidian negotiations, particularly of spatial barriers. These barriers are often the effects of government policies that shape individual and communal experiences of space, for instance, through zoning laws and regulations regarding housing, public assembly, and other aspects of space and spatial deployment. Government decisions in these domains can impose severe restrictions that can divide constituents or create points of shared hardship around which they might agitate for change. Space is therefore an arena contested by governing institutions and their constituents. Space also makes contestation possible. Activists need space to congregate, either intermittently or regularly, whether physically or virtually. They need space to disrupt, to claim visibility, and to assert their presence as a challenge to the status quo. In the scale of their visual display, these spatial disruptions often rise to the level of spectacle. Activists need space to host spectacular disruptions. Just as importantly, activists need space for solidarity—for sharing presence in one another's everyday environments as a demonstration of reciprocal investment.

For many activist organizations, space is not just a means to an end but an end in itself. One outcome of privatization in South Africa, and more globally, has been significant spatial disruption affecting both people's habitation—evictions, battles over title deeds, inadequate access to basic services like water, electricity, and sanitation—and spatial access to public commons. The public sphere has eroded, with city squares replaced by private malls and curtailed access to (as well as increased surveillance in) places traditionally meant to be for the public good, including universities. Reclaiming those spaces is, for many activists, a goal of disruption. When the activists who would eventually form the Anti-Privatisation Forum (APF) disrupted the Urban Futures conference at Wits University in 2000, their anger at having their access to campus restricted by turnstiles and security guards was palpable. Further indignation arose when security guards required those without campus IDs to be photographed before entrance. This anger stemmed from the pain of being restricted from the university, a physical and ideological space they had fought for along with those same security guards: *"In those early days of the 90s, we were together, security guards, workers, academics and students . . . raising our fists and shouting slogans at the helicopters overhead and the police line before us. Our campaign was part of a national campaign under the broad banner, 'The Doors of Learning and Culture Shall Be Open'"* (Naidoo and Veriava 2005: 28; italics in original). For those activists, being made to feel they did not belong in a place they had fought for represented a repudiation of their past struggles, particularly in light of the new struggle to halt the advance of privatization as a governing principle in South Africa.

By 2009, nine years after this seminal event, the APF was itself a more spatially established social movement organization. As part of its normalization, it had formalized structures and practices that defined the organization's movement through routine, in part to challenge spatial circumscription resulting from the government's attempts to limit the APF's reach. The 2003 eviction from COSATU House, at the behest of the African National Congress (ANC), was just one of the government's attempts to restrict the APF by spatially limiting it.

After its eviction from COSATU House, the APF rented offices at Khanya College, a nongovernmental organization (NGO) established in 1986 to provide educational and infrastructural resources to anti-apartheid activists and movements. The linkage proved to be auspicious for the APF. Being at Khanya College allowed the organization to cultivate routines in everything from the rhythm of internal meetings to internally displayed discourses to external displays, such as in public protests and campaigns, and establish itself in space and time.

The routinization of a movement occurs not in isolation from but rather in tension with the counterefforts and routines of state opposition. This chapter explores that dynamic by examining three important terrains. It begins with the spatial and temporal rhythms of the APF's stabilization at its centralized office, highlighting how APF members' quotidian concerns were erased there. The second terrain is the backstage work involved in producing protests in urban areas which entails spatial negotiation and, paradoxically for an oppositional movement, collaboration with state authorities. Finally, the chapter examines struggles centered in Alexandra Township, considering elements of what was easily overlooked at the APF office because of the organization's vertical administrative orientation: the physical environments that constituted the daily lives of the APF's target constituents and underlay the need for dignity that drove their activism.

By focusing on the organization's quotidian distributions, this chapter demonstrates a performative geography—the iterative and constitutive impact of space and placemaking on human subjects. I argue that the APF's spatial orientation toward its administrative center obscured activities and experiences in its affiliates' immediate environments. The verticality of the APF's administrative structure was unidirectional—members and leaders were oriented toward a central administrative space that was distant from many activists' residences. This unidirectionality, and insistence on vertical connections, resulted in ongoing blind spots in the organization's viewpoint that account for deeper ruptures in the solidarity of the organization. Leaders situated at the administrative center were at a remove from on-the-ground experiences and needs of constituent communities.

The APF's spatial orientation toward Johannesburg's city center was born of and reproduced South Africa's spatial distribution under apartheid; thus, the spatial operations of the South African state, in its shifting attempts to regulate dissent and remake activists through neoliberal sensitivities, must be kept in view. Therefore, I elaborate activists' claims to dignity in relation to their indignation about their immediate environments and state-imposed spatial restrictions. I show that song was a readily available resource for self-sovereignty despite material deprivation. Each section thus orients around the configuration of space and time as a central problematic of collective performance. Taken together, these discussions illustrate how space routinizes collective dissent through its production, instrumentalization, and contention. Routinization, in turn, sets the necessary foundation for the mass gatherings more commonly associated with protest performances.

PERFORMATIVE GEOGRAPHY: THE APF'S ADMINISTRATIVE CENTER

After its eviction from COSATU House, the APF moved its offices to the sixth floor of a building dubbed "the house of movements," a location that provided a centralized base for the APF's operations and a gathering place for affiliates. Owned by Khanya College, the house was located in Johannesburg's central business district, its otherwise nondescript entrance marked by glass doors. Attached to the building was a pink-painted halal restaurant and takeaway establishment where APF activists bought hot drinks, snacks, and meals, including "fat cakes" (fried dough) and chips (potato fries), vegan options I indulged in when eating with comrades. On the other side of the building's entrance was a computer and cell phone dealer's shop, which was always useful for cell phone repairs and batteries.

The house of movements had two elevators positioned just beyond the building's foyer; rarely did both elevators function at the same time. If neither was in working order, foot traffic was forced to the stairs. On the sixth floor, a metal gate and a wooden door guarded the entrance to the APF office. The gate served as a security measure, allowing visitors to be screened before they were granted entrance. Those who did not have keys had to be let in by the administrator, who had a buzzer under her desk, or by an APF member already in the office. Visitors had to sign into logs kept by the administrator. These access control measures were not atypical for residential and commercial buildings in Johannesburg's city center; they served to deter unwanted guests and combat theft. They were also evidence of the APF's focused concerns: those who visited the APF's office must have a purpose.

These placemaking routines did not operate in a vacuum; rather, they evolved in the context of historical legacies and the ongoing dynamics of spatial ordering in the South African state. The regulation of access to and of bodily presence in space exemplified by the entrance to the APF's offices echoes a broad system of state regulation of space built on physical enclosure, bureaucratic procedures, and civic surveillance.[1] Such regulation of access is constituted through patterns of spatial control that are replicated across institutions beyond the state, including universities and social movement organizations (recall the reclaiming of Wits's Great Hall by Urban Futures protesters). Especially with the receding of the public sphere under neoliberal dispensations (Harvey 2006), space remains "the physical terrain and symbolic expanse over which contestations of power take place" (Bozzoli 2004: 7). As states seek to delimit the contours of shared civic life through spatial control, political movements constitute themselves by asserting material presence, attempting to reclaim a space in time, not only during transitory protest demonstrations but also through administrative longevity.[2] These spatial strategies contribute to the construction, disruption, and remaking of individual and collective identities.

Assertions of identity as a claiming of space constitute what I mean by *performative geography*, a term that designates the use of space for an intended outcome. While every use of space is consequential to some degree, I am concerned here with the durable effects of spatial maneuvers, especially in changing the status of people, as illuminated by Maurya Wickstrom's (2012) case study of neoliberal Ireland. Wickstrom recounts the Irish state's use of space to rehabilitate citizens for neoliberalism by fixing people in place through the promotion of sedentariness. One illustration of this approach is the housing developments, a key characteristic of new Irish neoliberal subjectivity that changed the landscape of Dublin. Rural areas west of Dublin became crowded with new houses, many of which were second homes for Irish professionals and therefore symbolic markers of middle-class neoliberal success (Wickstrom 2012: 154–55). As more space was claimed for settled Irish, those who had not adapted to or been absorbed by "more flexible and energetic approaches to life and work" (Coulter 2003: 12)—nomadic communities in particular—were actively erased, cast as waste that was "supernumerary to neoliberal processes altogether" (Wickstrom 2012: 25).

Among those most directly and detrimentally affected by the Irish state's spatial maneuvers were Irish Travellers—an indigenous ethnic minority group identified with economic nomadism, who numbered about thirty-three thousand in 2012. The Irish state attempted to halt Travellers' movement through efforts to criminalize nomadism and fix them in place in housing settlements; it also symbolically produced the Travellers as waste by associating the group with improper sanitation and uncollected refuse based on their proximity to dumps and other wastelands. Travellers, in their refusal to assimilate to the state's neoliberal emphasis on settlement, were cast as outsiders to the nation, outside of the state's responsibility and investment. Through iterative acts— building homes, restricting movement using walls and boulders, evicting individuals from occupied land—that established the status of some citizens as normative subjects and others as *unfixable* and justifiably excluded, the Irish government generated a performative geography.

Governments make and remake citizens through performative geography, through spatial practices designed to designate some people as more or less worthy of national belonging than others. Discriminatory policies are enforced through spatial routines that are continually reinforced to stratify and in some cases strip populations of citizenship. For instance, Jim Crow laws in the southern United States, which influenced South Africa's apartheid laws and Germany's Nuremburg laws, limited where Black people could shop, travel, live, eat, and even drink water. But performative spatial maneuvers are not limited to states. Individuals, communities, and coalitional social movements use space to actively produce themselves in ways that can marginalize others. Often, these spatial productions are conditioned by state practices.

Under apartheid and in its wake, space was a key element of political contestation in South Africa. Apartheid structured South Africa's terrain along
ethnicized and racialized lines. Rural "homelands" served as labor reserves for
urban industry, including mines. In the cities themselves, Black mobility and
spatial access were severely confined through ghettoization into townships
(Bozzoli 2004; Wolpe 1972; Christopher 1994; Mabin 1989, 1991; Robinson
1996; Smith 1992). Townships such as Alexandra served to separate Black daily
life from the broader public sphere; the designation of township space provided
daily reminders of residents' subordination (Bozzoli 2004: 22).

These spatial circumscriptions provide the historical foundations for contemporary invisibilities and exclusions. While spatial mobility and access are
ostensibly less restricted after apartheid, the everyday lives of impoverished
Blacks remained bounded by political and socioeconomic barriers, both within
social movements like the APF and in the broader metropolis. Cleanup campaigns to rid city centers of street hawkers and other "undesirables" in advance
of the 2010 World Cup exemplify the linkage between spatial control and the
image of itself—and of the kinds of people who belong in it—a city wants to
project (see Ngonyama 2010: 173). In this context, state spatial interventions,
both historical and contemporary, remain consequential, playing out even
within social movement organizations that seek to advance racial and economic justice. Within the APF, these legacies manifested particularly around
ease of access to the centralized office and reciprocity of presence in activists'
local environments.

Spatial legacies do not persist merely as residues of the past; they are reinforced, negated, or supplanted through ongoing human acts that shape identities. Iteration and space are both key tenets of performativity: groups do not
exist unless they are iteratively acted out in space. Collectives are not ontologi-
cally stable; rather, they hinge on ongoing performance in ways that are often
so conventional as to slip by unnoticed. Such ongoing performances define
the spaces that offer solidity to collectives as they converge. The APF's solidity, its recognition as a social movement organization, was deployed through
citational placemaking practices—for instance, the display of documents and
the configuration of offices and meeting rooms—that imparted a sense of longevity, diligence, and industry to the APF's physical headquarters.

The APF's citational placemaking began in the waiting area that greeted visitors who earned passage beyond the metal gate. The waiting area was equipped
with seats and copies of newsletters, including current and past issues of the
APF newsletter *Struggle Continues*. On the first day I reported to the APF office,
the back page of the issue of *Struggle Continues* I picked up featured an article in

seSotho by the APF's vice president describing her experiences as a female activist and the particularities of women's struggles in contemporary social movements. To the left of the waiting area was the APF's primary meeting room, where most workshops and meetings were held. Space for larger meetings and conferences, which were usually held on the second floor, was negotiated with Khanya. On the other side of the waiting area was the administrator's office, which led into the organizer's office, at least until the organizer was suspended and eventually expelled. The last office, through the organizer's office, was used as a meeting space for the APF's four part-time regional organizers. Each of the regional organizers (who were hired with funding from the Rosa Luxemburg Foundation) served one of the APF's four regions.[3]

The administrator's office was the nexus for some key resources the APF offered activists: the multipurpose printer-photocopier-fax machine and the telephone. When activists mentioned APF resources, they often referred to document services—printing and photocopying flyers and announcements of meetings and protest events. The telephone was another critical resource, and the administrator was often responsible for making phone calls to inform individual activists of scheduled meetings at the office or at particular affiliates.

The notes and documents spread throughout the office symbolized transmuted performances captured in words, documentary evidence of the APF's activities. Posters, flyers, newspaper articles, and other written mementos covered the walls of the meeting rooms, and a list of affiliates and their contact details was posted behind the administrator's desk for ready reference. Participants in workshops or other activist sessions contributed the products of the activity to the offices' walls. For instance, attendees at a women's workshop on activism and sexual violence posted placards to the wall with key messages:

"Men, please stop treating us like 'sex slaves.'"
"Let us break the silen[ce] and come forward to say away with woman and childre[n] abuse, away."
"Police contribute in women abuse, they must stop and care for us, not making us to feel like the world has no mercy for us."

By claiming space on the walls of the APF's conference room, the workshop participants immortalized its gendered interventions, allowing them to address subsequent users of the room, their comrades in resistance.

As these ephemera accumulated over time, some elements repeated across contexts. Signs and placards captured the full range of concerns addressed by the movement and its affiliates. Another workshop on prepaid water meters contributed multiple signs bearing the message "There is no water prepaid metre in heaven for municipalities to buy water and sell to communities. Break the metre and enjoy free water." Some signs also bore intertextual slogans that transmuted written and spoken forms. Spoken chants provided verbal formulas whose subjects were readily interchangeable, appearing on a variety of signs:

"Away with women and children abuse, away."
"Viva women, viva."
"No to water prepaid meters."

These slogans echoed protests, when they would appear as chants that alternated between leaders and protesters, focusing the collective and articulating the message of the demonstration. Repeated on signs, these slogans reinforced and routinized the APF's principal concerns and themes.

Protest discourses and imagery also circulated through newspaper clippings, posted on the walls, which transported kinetic evidence across space and time. In a meeting at an Orlando East community center in December 2009, when I asked the chairperson of the APF affiliate Soweto Concerned Residents (SCR) about the organization's protest performances, she referred me to newspaper clippings on the wall as a stand-in for what she could not immediately demonstrate. "There are [physical] movements," she said. "You know if you can see us [during our protests], we're so crazy there, everybody is like crazy because everything is just getting crazy." As evidence of this "craziness," she pointed to reports posted on the wall that highlighted Soweto protesters' occupation of the entrance of a councilor's home during a militant standoff with police and security guards over water and electricity cutoffs. Another posted story described the occupation of the home of Johannesburg's mayor, Amos Masondo, during which a security guard fired live bullets into the gathered protesters, injuring two. In response, protesters threw stones and smashed the mayor's water meter. Captured in media coverage and featured on the organization's office walls, such demonstrations became ever-present references, indexing a collective disposition to militancy.

The APF's walls, like those of its affiliates, memorialized newsworthy events featuring the organization or its members; headlines included "SECC 'Attack' Jozi FM" and "Mamelo Mayhem." These clippings highlighted the spectacles of dissent created by APF protesters that captured the media's gaze and demonstrated how these spectacles become further sensationalized in journalists' representation. Strewn across the office space, these markers brought bodily coordinations—mass protests—to the fore. Imagery also supported the symbolism of physical presence. An image of protesters in T-shirts prominently featuring the APF logo showed members in formation; their bodily alignment, captured in the photograph, presented a unified front. A different image, presented under the heading "Dance Tunes of the Working Class," showed a single arched line of women, their energy directed not outward but to the middle. They were captured midsong, with bystanders in the background, each woman in a different gestural moment, their kinesthetic engagement with each other and with the protest in evidence.

The items on the walls were not actively curated; new items claimed available surface area, and previous posts were not removed. As APF leaders and administrators added ephemera over time, layers of history intermingled, creating a congealing effect in which past and potential action interweaved with the present, revealing the continuity of the APF's past with the potentialities of its future. These ephemera were not representational—they did not capture a stable, inherent APF collectivity. Rather, they showcased the iterative construction of the collectivity across events; the office walls were just one instance of the performative constitution of an organization. They revealed the depth and vigor of its affiliates' activities, dispersed across space and attuned to a range of concerns.

As the office was not a rapidly changing environment, its walls exuded the familiarity of long-witnessed visual depictions and the assurance of expectation. As members shuffled in and out of meetings, the APF's office walls did not elicit much remark, but the absence of direct engagement did not mean the items on the walls were ignored or not absorbed. References to particular items at opportune moments confirmed activists' awareness of the presence and composition of these materials—as when three APF part-timers (as part-time organizers were often called), conversing among themselves, concluded that South Africa's "capitalist democracy" was worse than apartheid. One of them pointed to a poster featuring Karl Marx on the wall. "There is the man we've been talking about," he said, and their conversation promptly moved on. Thus, although activists would not necessarily stand in front of posted newspaper articles to reminisce, or otherwise linger over posters or flyers, the APF's office environment still registered to particular effect. The covered surfaces of the APF's office were taken-for-granted performances: through accretion on its walls, the office provided a setting that declared particular affiliations, commemorated activities of symbolic significance, and served as a readily available visual referent for members, the absence of which would have been disquieting.

That performativity unfolds not only in the use of space but also in cyclical time is evident in the daily mechanisms of discourse and ritual that build a social movement. In the APF, meetings shaped daily, weekly, monthly, and annual routines. The meetings had a variety of structures, including an annual general meeting (AGM), and office bearers formed a separate committee with its own meetings and also met as part of an extended group that included part-time organizers and regional coordinators. In 2009, the office bearers' meeting was reduced to once a month because of a mandate to cut expenses due to diminished funding.

In their meetings, the office bearers addressed concerns regarding the functioning of the organization; as much as possible, decisions were deferred to other meeting structures, such as the coordinating committee. That committee, which consisted of affiliate delegates and the office bearers, met quarterly; the coordinating committee was the highest decision-making body between AGMs. Executive committee meetings, attended by a representative from each affiliate, office bearers, and subcommittee and region coordinators, were called to set the agenda for coordinating committee meetings and guide APF activities in accordance with committee directives. Subcommittees comprised of representatives from APF affiliates were created to address specific sets of issues, such as media, legal, education, housing, and labor.

Thus, in any given week, the APF office might host leadership meetings, subcommittee meetings, and organizers' meetings. In addition, Johannesburg region leaders would also often meet at the APF office. The APF had affiliates in four regions: the Vaal, Johannesburg and the inner city, Tshwane, and the East Rand.[4] Each region had its own officials, including a regional coordinator who participated in office-bearer meetings; each of the four part-time organizers came from a different region. The organizers received monthly stipends and also participated in office-bearer meetings. These regional structures had their own rhythm of meetings and gatherings.

Although Buhlungu (2004) estimated a "support base" for the APF of about ten thousand in 2004, the lack of a membership database makes it impossible to count the APF's total individual membership as it evolved in the organization's later years. In 2010, the APF comprised thirty-four affiliate organizations based in communities across its four regions, as well as at least two political groups that were not embedded in particular communities. During the April 2010 AGM, when the APF documented attendance by gender, 26 of 34 affiliates sent 95 male and 67 female members, for a total of 162 attendees. According to the APF's constitution, each community-based affiliate could send 10 delegates to the AGM, while political groups could send 5; any participants in excess of those numbers served as observers. Only 4 affiliates sent the full allotment of 10 delegates to the 2010 AGM. The coordinating committee meetings I attended consisted of about 80–90 APF members in addition to the office bearers. An executive committee meeting might number between 30 and 40 attendees.

As much was erased as was displayed in the ephemera on exhibit and in the rhythm of meetings. Although the APF's walls depicted the impact of poverty and the necessity of gender and economic struggles, many APF members found their realities unaccounted for. Silindiwe offers one minor example. As one of the APF's four part-time organizers, Silindiwe, who represented the Vaal region, often needed to be in the office for meetings. When we met once, before an organizers' meeting, Silindiwe greeted me with frustration. The meeting had been pushed back three hours. "Tell me," she said as I walked into a tense room. "My children had to wake up at 6:00 a.m., to get to school so that I could be on time for this meeting [at 9:00 a.m.], and then I get here and find out the meeting won't start until later. Tell me, is that fair?" Silindiwe's frustration was directed not only at the time costs of making it to the office, only to find the meeting delayed, but also at the disruption the delay represented to her daily reality as a mother of young children. Those disruptions, that daily reality, were overlooked when the meeting was delayed without the courtesy of prior notification. Such delays were not uncommon; the APF's specified calendar of meetings hardly proceeded according to intention. Temporally and spatially, routines the organization attempted to establish proved difficult to maintain, at least partially due to the extent to which members' on-the-ground realities were not accounted for.

Transportation and the need for it were central features of those on-the-ground realities. Very few activists drove to meetings in private cars; of those who could afford private transportation, one drove a motorcycle. Most arrived via Johannesburg's formal and informal public transport system. Some came from the immediate metro area, while others traveled one to three hours from the Vaal, Tshwane, and Ekurhuleni. Many attendees at these meetings got there using mini-bus "kombis," Johannesburg's informal transport industry with its unwritten convention of hand signals. Along with kombis, larger-capacity buses also served the road. Some activists, especially those from the Vaal, traveled to the APF by train, which from the Vaal was less expensive than kombis.

During a January 2010 workshop on women and public transportation, Nomvula, Ma Lindi's daughter, regaled us with stories of the unique subcultures peculiar to train travel. The usual order of the APF's conference room had been upended that day, with the central tables moved aside so that about twenty workshop participants sat facing one another in a circle. A soft-spoken soprano, Nomvula commanded our attention as she delved into the results of her self-appointed investigation. Each train car had its dominant group, which she elaborated to much laughter. The first and last cars usually served gamblers. Church congregations also jostled for space and held services during workers' commutes. There were "staff riders"—train surfers who risked riding on top of trains—and "cheeseballs," a term I never got to clarify. But then the conversation became serious, as talk turned to the fact that, on the often-overcrowded trains, riders (particularly women) risked theft and sexual violation. As our expressions sobered with this reminder, the workshop facilitator requested a song to clear the air. Silindiwe responded with a rallying call that harkened back to the 1956 women's march against the imposition of pass laws on Black South African women, "wathinta' bafazi" (you strike the women). "Wathinti' mbokodo" (you strike a rock), we cheered in response. "Wathinta' abafazi," Silindiwe called out, louder this time as she stood up. "Wathinti' mbokodo," we responded, a number of us off our seats. Having roused us to standing, Silindiwe offered her finish, "Basop [watch out] taxi driver!" As the echoes resounded from a past generation of women's struggles, the placards hanging along the conference room walls bore silent but visible witness, conveying the words of earlier groups of women who had met in this very space.

The focus on the office as the hub of activity contributed to the invisibility of some people's struggles with transportation. The APF's centralized spatial practice meant that, along with scheduled meetings, key resources—including the telephone, desktop computers, and printer-scanner-copier-fax machine—were only accessible at the office or through remote requests to the office administrator. As a result, the APF office was a necessary destination for its members who were dispersed across the Gauteng province. Wherever they lived, members relied on the office to conduct regional and local affiliate affairs. This arrangement focused attention away from people's immediate environments and toward the APF's administrative center. Ironically, this situation paralleled South Africa's spatial distribution under apartheid, which, through segregation and control of Black mobility, concentrated civic and business activity in urban centers, relegating a Black underclass to city peripheries. Without deliberate and sustained efforts to upend these marginalizations, many members' day-to-day conditions were rendered invisible and often obscured in the name of shared struggle.

CONDITIONING PROTEST: SPACE AND THE ROUTINIZATION OF DISSENT

While South Africa has anecdotally been declared the protest capital of the world, due to its high number of protests per year, protests in the country are quite often heavily regulated in ways that rob them of political impact. Demonstrations are often isolated events; many take place on outlying township streets and remote arteries that, disruptive as they are meant to be, are shielded from the attention of many fellow South Africans. Under apartheid, ungovernability was the strategic goal driving many township revolts; since then, the regulation of protests in contemporary South Africa has upheld state authority even among social movements formed in opposition to the state. The transition to ANC governance has meant a movement from outright rebellion to routinization, with social movement organizations like the APF operating from a negotiating and collaborative stance in matters of the spatial access needed to stake oppositional claims.

Historically, apartheid segregation was not met with surrender, and collaborators with the regime invited stigma, heavy critique, and sometimes physical retaliation on discovery. The ANC, as a liberation movement, encouraged an anti-apartheid strategy of ungovernability that harbored no compromise—rebellion was the unequivocal township stance toward the state, along with subversion. Black township residents used their spatial exclusion to subversive advantage by cultivating social networks, appropriating physical landmarks, and developing location-specific knowledge and memorial attachments to space that made township life impenetrable to outsiders and to the state (Bozzoli 2004; see also Scott 2009). Belinda Bozzoli's study of a 1986 rebellion in the township of Alexandra, northeast of Johannesburg's city center, shows how the state's regime of spatial control paradoxically became a resource for insurgence, as protesters appropriated meaning and redeployed boundaries in an attempt to purge one township of state authority and shield it from outsider access (2004: 13–15). In the period leading up to the rebellion, invisibility that was intended to be repressive created a space of freedom. Alexandrans used the concealment of the township—its impenetrability to outsiders—to facilitate revolt and wrestle social control from the state. The repertoires of contestation in the Alexandra rebellion were spatial; they evolved from nonviolent measures, such as land occupation and boycotting, to incorporate spectacularly violent attacks, culminating in the 1986 uprising.

Bozzoli characterizes the staging of the revolt as a dramatic statement that erupted from the hidden world of the township to seize public attention (2004: 19; see also Taylor and Van Dyke 2004: 269). Even after the democratic turn of 1994, revolt as a style of dissension remained a patterned part of memory and protest convention. The APF protests called back to this history. These protests ranged from mega demonstrations such as the 2002 World Summit on Sustainable Development (WSSD) march described in chapter 1, which drew more than twenty thousand protesters in a procession from Alexandra to Sandton, to a far more modest 2010 World Cup march, which drew dozens of demonstrators to a gathering that did not overwhelm state forces.[5] Some protests were organized by one APF-affiliated community, while others brought together regional cross sections of activists to emphasize particular contentions. Common to such protests was the coexistent use of space by both activists and state forces, an interaction that often proceeded according to routinized expectation, which led many to question the effectiveness of the protests.

The contours of such routinization of public dissent proceeded from an act passed in the last days of apartheid. Working to develop a performative geography, the transitioning South African state sought to channel dissent and in effect produce neoliberal activist subjectivities conditioned by, rather than disruptive of, the status quo. To accomplish this end, the government passed the Regulation of Gatherings Act of 1993. The act, which was implemented in 1996, established protocols for the peaceful enactment of dissent.[6] Under the act, protest groups larger than fifteen people were required to notify the responsible officer in their local municipal council of their intent to protest at least seven days before the intended gathering. Notification could be accepted as little as forty-eight hours before a protest with an explanation for the delay in notification. The notice had to include such details as the convener of the protest; the number of people expected to gather; the type of protest; the protest route, including the beginning and end points of the march; and the names of the marshals, or protest supervisors. While the act did not specify a required number of marshals, the recommended practice called for one marshal for every ten protesters. On receipt of notification, the responsible officer was required to respond within twenty-four hours, either authorizing the protest to proceed as planned or convening a "section IV meeting" to discuss changes to the protest plan. This meeting, sometimes called the "golden triangle meeting," brought the three factions involved— the protest conveners, the responsible officer from the municipal council, and an authorized member of the police—together to negotiate the terms of the protest.[7]

This process of notification and negotiation challenges popular conceptions regarding the staging of protest and the dynamics among the various factions involved. To the extent that the act established a protocol for the enactment of collective dissent, it complicates the view of protests as spontaneous eruptions of mass indignation. Furthermore, the act requires police officers and protesters, more usually seen as antagonistic parties, to cooperate in the days leading up to a protest event. The ensuing protest thereby becomes an outcome not just of the protesters' intent but also of police planning. In this regard, Duncan (2010: 111) aptly comments, "Gatherings are not spaces entirely of . . . protestors' own making; in fact, they could be described as negotiated spaces for the expression of dissent."

Another element of the routinization of protest was the delivery of memoranda expressing protesters' grievances. Ahead of a protest demonstration or march, conveners would notify intended recipients of their intent to deliver a memorandum of grievances that also, sometimes, set a time frame for the grievances to be addressed to avoid further protests. The delivery of the memorandum would be scheduled with recipients of the memorandum as part of protest planning; sometimes, the scheduling occurred during a section IV meeting. The memorandum would be read aloud at the protest itself, either by protesters or by a representative from the receiving party (often, municipal government officials). The memorandum would then be dated and signed by representatives for the protesters and the receiving party.

By convention, the reading of the memorandum, its delivery, and acknowledgment of receipt often ended a march; protesters would disperse once the memorandum was delivered and signed. In light of this expectation, receiving parties would ask for the memorandum to be delivered early so that protesters could disperse, clearing entrances and pathways and allowing the usual flow of business to resume. Protest conveners, however, seeking to maximize the spatial access and impact of their assembly, would seek to extend the delivery. Performance helped in this regard—before delivery of the memorandum, protesters' assemblies often were constituted in song for as long as desired, and the delivery of the memorandum itself was prolonged by its performance. Memoranda were read out with various levels of flair; the reader might occasionally seek verbalized agreement and acclaim from fellow protesters to create dramatic moments. Appearing in these ways, performance was routinized in the sense that it was a patterned part of protest.

The experience of singing together both supported the protesters' creation of space for themselves and their complaints and transcended the tedium of routinization. The expectation that song would accompany protests remained prevalent throughout the APF's tenure. Recall Boipelo's words in the introduction that for one community in Itereleng to show that they are in the struggle, "they have to be seen chanting." Practiced activists were so familiar with the contours of these performances that, when I conducted interviews in 2010, many commented on protests becoming routine deployments that did not effect change—their disruptive potential had become normalized. Buyisiwe, who lamented the APF's decline as a failure of performance, specifically questioned the effectiveness of marches, saying they yielded no results. "So today," he said, "we can have a lot of noise. They [protesters] can like unveil their souls but nothing will happen. How many marches did we have singing sad songs, songs of happiness, songs of demise, songs of whatever? ... Not even one memorandum is answered, you know."[8]

To be sure, not all protests complied with the Gatherings Act. Activists employed a variety of strategies to express discontent and push the government to address their plight. Road barricades and the occupation of municipal offices and officials' homes, along with some marches and other activist events, bypassed the Gatherings Act protocol altogether. And yet, songs and other performance practices remained ubiquitous in legal and extralegal protests. In key ways, they transcended routinization, as I will demonstrate in chapter 3.

ROUTINES OF EXPOSURE: THE ALEXANDRA RENEWAL PROJECT

The routinization of dissent fostered by the Gatherings Act meant that, despite unlimited strategic possibilities, protests in impoverished communities often proceeded along expected beats. Occasionally, however, activists managed to break out of that rhythm. Among the APF's repertoires of contention, one event stood out precisely because it did not rely on the street-oriented protest display that the Gatherings Act sought to normalize and regulate. Rather, its organizers, the Alexandra Concerned Residents (ACR, one of the community organizations affiliated with the APF), reversed the spatial encounter typical of activists and their publics. Instead of expressing discontent by taking to the streets (e.g., Cohen-Cruz 1998), the ACR convened a "people's inspection" to expose the community's wretched living conditions and garner support for their struggle to hold the government accountable for providing adequate housing. For this event, the activists invited fellow APF members, representatives from the media and nongovernmental organizations, and other interested parties to inspect the community and speak with residents.

> It is not just the loss of being able to afford the basic things of life; it is also the loss of *dignity* that destroys people and their communities.
>
> —FROM "PLATFORM ADOPTED AT RIGHT TO WORK CONFERENCE," UNDATED. APF INTERNAL DOCUMENT; ITALICS IN ORIGINAL

The inspection brought protest not to the streets but into the APF activists' homes in an effort to draw public attention to the government's failure to protect these spaces delineated as private. As exemplified by Ma Patrycja's story, the home is emblematic of the private; it is a site at which material politics are generally shielded from public access.[9] The public sphere nevertheless is never far removed from the home, since housing interconnects both physically and legally with governmental control through land and housing allocation, basic utility infrastructure, and related regulations. Addressing housing needs became part of the routine for the ANC after apartheid, but these efforts often failed, sparking countermeasures like the people's inspection.

The inspection, held November 17–19, 2009, came in the wake of the Alexandra Renewal Project (ARP), a government-funded enterprise to build houses, provide jobs, and improve the lives of the people living in Alexandra Township. The renewal project, scheduled to take seven years, 2001–2008, was planned to involve the participation of local residents. Rather than the envisioned social, economic, and environmental uplift, however, a significant base of the community found the project actually worsened their living conditions. The ACR formed in that period to expose the project's failure and show the extent to which it exacerbated displacement and impoverishment; the people's inspection was a tool to accomplish this exposure.

The 2009 event was not the first people's inspection; the ACR had held that in 2005. In the press release announcing that inspection, the organization noted that the Johannesburg mayor had convened a meeting at which Alexandra residents discussed their concerns. They remarked that although the mayor listened, "we are not sure that the Mayor and his staff truly understand the seriousness of the social, economic, and environmental crises in Alexandra. We want to make sure that the government as well as the people of South Africa and the world understand that the crisis in Alexandra is serious and immediate."[10] The people's inspection, as a vehicle for the understanding Alexandrans demanded, is performative just as protest songs are performative. Both aim for a paralinguistic transmission of emotion that transcends words, and both depend on presence—of protesters and audience in the same space—for their power.

Describing South Africa's liberation struggle, the anti-apartheid activist Sifiso Ntuli once noted, "Song is something that we communicate to the people who otherwise would not have understood where we were coming from. You could give them a long political speech and they would still not understand, but I tell you, when you finish that song, people be like I know where you guys are coming from. Death unto apartheid" (in Hirsch 2002). This statement highlights the need to transcend words, a need to provoke a state of awareness that surpasses verbalization. Song transmits the emotive fervency of experience, one that relies on the presence of listeners to facilitate a deeper connection to and investment in protesters' sung plight. The people's inspection seeks a transmission of understanding that similarly relies on participants' presence. To fully grasp the crisis, as the ACR implicitly argued in hosting the people's inspections, you had to experience it for yourself, directly and physically. The ACR was not alone in this insight; many impoverished communities agitated for a visit from a government official, oftentimes no less senior than the president himself, with the implicit understanding that once he saw residents' living conditions, he would act immediately to correct them.

In a similar vein, many activists valued showing up for each other as a marker of respect: meeting people on their own terrain, without seeking to exploit or extract something from them, accords dignity. A lack of reciprocity in showing up was a frequent complaint among many impoverished activists. They traveled from their communities and homes to stand in solidarity in the broader struggle, they pointed out, and yet, no one visited them in their homes or rallied to their sides when needed.

The Inspection

The 2009 people's inspection focused on the relocated residents of Silver Town Transit Camp, who were among the approximately seven thousand residents relocated within Alexandra and beyond as part of the ARP (see Sinwell 2005; Bonner and Nieftagodien 2008: 402–10). In 2005, to create space for a shopping complex, residents were moved from their houses to the transit camp, which consisted of single-roomed metal containers along the banks of the Jukskei River. The containers, which were made of silver corrugated iron, were rudimentarily fenced in. Within the fencing, they were placed so close together that an individual could not comfortably pass between them. Seven of the ninety-four containers were used for storage because the containers were too small to allow residents to keep all their belongings. The remaining eighty-seven single-roomed containers housed an estimated three hundred people, who shared six communal taps and twelve portable chemical toilets. Families constructed makeshift plastic tents to wash themselves or otherwise found space to wash inside their designated rooms, using basins for their daily ablutions. The community had no designated cooking areas, and the electricity supply was unreliable because the cables were often stolen. The containers easily flooded with sewage when it rained, as the polluted river overflowed its banks.

The living conditions at Silver Town Transit Camp were similar to conditions in refugee camps housing displaced populations. Dwight Conquergood described the liminality of these refugee camps as "zones where people displaced by trauma and crisis—usually war or famine—must try to regroup and salvage what is left of their lives. Their world has been shattered. They are in passage" (1988: 180). His description is also relevant to Alexandra. The residents at Silver Town, and other transit camps created in the wake of the ARP, were economic refugees, displaced not by war but by neoliberal development and "renewal."[11] Their past was bulldozed—shopping malls now stood in place of their former homes—and they faced an uncertain future. They had been told the relocation was only temporary, but in 2009, they were still fighting for more humane, permanent housing. During the inspection, one female resident asked visitors, "How must I live like this? Until when? I don't know." Another woman commented in exasperation, "We were supposed to be the first people to move out into houses, but we are still here. When they took us from the places where we used to live, they said to us you are going to get the houses after six months. Six months now is five years."

Their present hung in a precarious balance. The community was already exposed, vulnerable to ailments stemming from the persistent dampness of their homes, the lack of sanitation, and the frequent floods; any further disruption would be fatal. Yet disruptions came. In May 2010, all twelve mobile toilets were removed from Silver Town without explanation, a development covered by the newspapers—a clip was posted on the APF's office wall. The toilets were eventually replaced, and the residents discovered they had been removed because the supplier's contract with ARP had expired. As untenable as conditions already were, the toilet removal was a reminder that they could worsen. "We have children, old people, and sick people who will not be able to handle such a situation," a community member reported (Lobelo 2010).

Silver Town did not represent the full range of Alexandra residents' experiences, although concerns about overcrowded and poorly constructed spaces, lack of clean water, unreliable electricity, and absent sanitation were persistent. The containers at Marlboro Transit Camp, for example, were constructed of wood, which disintegrated over time, helped along by ants that ate into the structures. Residents lived without electricity and shared six communal toilets and taps. At the Alexandra Transit Camp, the tiny two-room concrete houses cracked over time. Dampness in the buildings caused residents' belongings to rot. While residents had access to running water and prepaid electricity (when they could pay for it), they shared one communal toilet and washing facility for every sixteen houses. During the people's inspection in 2009, the toilets were already leaking, and some were completely blocked. The camp was enclosed in a barbed-wire fence; individuals had to sign in and out at a security post, a surveillance routine that inhibited residents' freedom. At Alexandra Transit Camp, as at Silver Town, the residents were relocated with the assurance they would be back in their homes within a few months, once the homes had been renovated through the ARP. As at Silver Town and Marlboro, these temporary relocations became prolonged, contributing to residents' frustration.

While the transit camps were intended as stopgaps in the drive to renewal, other precarious living conditions in Alexandra arose from the severe housing shortage, which drove people to occupy whatever space they could find. From the mid-1990s, as many businesses fled Alexandra, individuals and associations, including the South African National Civic Organization (SANCO), invaded the factories, warehouses, and office buildings these businesses had abandoned. The grassroots civic associations constructed shacks inside these buildings and charged occupants rent. Some of these one-room structures were only big enough for two people to sleep on the floor. With no space available anywhere else, children would sometimes sleep in the corridors. In the area known as Council House, a sixteen-year-old girl was raped while sleeping in a corridor a week prior to the people's inspection.

At Ghanda Center, a shopping complex whose owners fled in the 1990s during a spate of violence in the run-up to South Africa's first democratic elections, people moved into the burned-out buildings and constructed shacks around them. Residents of Ghanda Center shared one tap, and sewage flowed into the dwellings. Residents connected themselves to electricity and used paraffin stoves, which caused fires. The buildings had burned twice, but they remained occupied. At the Marlboro Warehouses—a collection of fifty-two warehouses distinct from the Marlboro Transit Camp—shacks were precariously constructed on top of each other using wood, plastic, and found materials. At the Wynberg Warehouses, which were located directly behind a mortuary, occupants lived and raised children literally in a space of death (Taussig 1984); the water from the washing of corpses ran through the compound. The Wynberg Warehouses were also close to a chemical storage facility; bags of chemicals were piled illegally in front of the compound. Residents obtained electricity only through illegal connections, and the damp walls of their homes were full of mold. One male occupant told me, "It's bad, bad, bad, bad, bad. Look at me, I am not supposed to stay like this." His emphasis on the atrocity of the conditions echoed that of many others I met, as did his plea for my recognition of his humanity and identification with his indignation.

Embodied Receptivity

From Silver Town to Wynberg, blatant structural and sanitation inadequacies resulted in a variety of bodily concerns. Cooking with paraffin stoves in

enclosed spaces exposed residents to smoke that was slow poison. The dampness in the floors, ceilings, windows, and walls seeped into bodies. As she
explained how she had laid newspaper beneath a thin vinyl carpet to absorb
moisture, Mum Alice, one of the APF's four part-time organizers and a resident
of Silver Town, mentioned her constant bouts of colds and infections. This link
between impoverished living conditions and bodily ailments resonates with
Bertolt Brecht's poem "A Worker's Speech to a Doctor":

> When we come to you
> Our rags are torn off us
> And you listen all over our naked body.
> As to the cause of our illness
> One glance at our rags would
> Tell you more.
> It is the same cause that wears out
> Our bodies and our clothes.
>
> The pain in our shoulder comes
> You say from the damp:
> and this is also the reason
> For the stain on the wall of our flat.
> So tell us:
> Where does the damp come from? (1987: 292)

These bodily conditions were the direct result of living conditions, and those
living conditions were the direct and indirect consequences of human decisions to shape geography, in the form of administrative urban renewal efforts
and civic initiatives to address the need for housing.

The residents protesting such conditions were elaborating what some scholars have called a "body politic" (Scheper-Hughes and Lock 1987: 23–28). They
sought to overcome the biomedical tendency to view illness as individual pa-
thology by demonstrating connections between their bodily health and the
physical environment in which they lived, an environment shaped by governmental decisions and actions. In addition to revealing the historical depth
and geographical linkages underlying present conditions (Farmer 2003: 42),
analyses of poverty ought also to account for how the bodies of the impoverished materialize social, geographical, and historical distress.

Medical anthropologists have elaborated the social body as an integration
of self and social relations. In this model, susceptibility to illness is related
to both bodily vulnerability and external dependence (Scheper-Hughes and
Lock 1987: 16–23; see also Henry 2006; McCallum 1996); bodily symptoms

are avenues through which individuals and communities express trauma and thereby assert a measure of control over disempowered lives (Henry 2006: 380; Scheper-Hughes and Lock 1987: 23–28). Elaborating connections between broader politics and the body, Ellen Foley's work in Senegal demonstrates how the intersections of neoliberalism and ecological decline fostered a socioeconomic crisis that became "written on the bodies of young men" (2008: 258).[12] Mum Alice's neoliberal crisis was the connection between the damp permeating her home, which she attempted to absorb with newspapers, and the damp that seeped into her lungs, which manifested in her constant colds and general lack of well-being, and which required frequent trips to the doctor, explaining her tardiness for part-time organizers' meetings. These concerns were pervasive; in other communities, activists cited environmental pollution as exacerbating asthma and tuberculosis.

The ARP produced an outcome similar to the one Maurya Wickstrom described for Irish Travellers, who were confirmed as being supernumerary to Ireland's neoliberal project through their visual association with waste: Alexandra residents displaced by the ARP were in effect spatially discarded and neglected—to the extent that the municipality allowed a supplier's contract for portable toilets to expire. The fact that Silver Town residents were displaced from entire homes (some, like Mum Alice's, had been multistory houses) and relocated to one-room shipping containers to create space for privately owned shopping centers makes clear the ARP's neoliberal foundations. Alexandra residents were sacrificed for the benefit of private corporations working in concert with state agencies. In a reversal of the dynamics Wickstrom mapped, the state's spatial maneuvers in Alexandra altered the residents' status from one of fixed settlement to an interminable suspension with no resolution in sight.

SELECTIVE INVISIBILITY

The people's inspection was a concerted effort, supported by the APF, to overcome the inadequacies of ANC housing policies, but the APF itself was often blind to the ways in which its own patterns of organizing and using space segregated its membership, distancing those operating at the city center, many of whom were the administrative drivers of the coalition, from the broader constituency the movement sought to serve.

Much of the APF's social base was composed of unemployed workers (particularly women and youth), casualized workers, those in the informal sector, and the elderly. Many relied on government subsidies in the form of pensions or child grants, lived in overcrowded households in dire conditions, and were being pressured by South Africa's socioeconomic crisis into "narrower survivalist modes" (McKinley 2012: 17). The APF had implemented a number of procedures that recognized the impoverished economic status of its primary constituents. For instance, the forum reimbursed travel costs to the office (with reimbursement rates varying by region), and meals, or money for their purchase, were often provided for daylong meetings.

Yet, there were limits to the APF's recognition of the economic inequalities faced by many of its members. When impoverished residents transport themselves from the urban peripheries they inhabit to participate in activist coalitions, the conditions of their day-to-day lives remain selectively invisible, just as they themselves might be unseen or discounted in a civic distribution. This invisibility held for the APF and its members as it would for any centralized organization. A former APF facilitator, visiting Mum Alice's home for the first time, commented that she had had no idea of the inadequacies Mum Alice had been living with because Mum Alice was always well-presented, good-natured, and cheerful in the APF office. The facilitator offered her comment as a testament to Mum Alice's dignified strength of spirit, but it also revealed the erasures occurring even in the pursuit of collective action against the very conditions Mum Alice was living with.

The people's inspection, then, provided experiential evidence intended to create mutual recognition of shared humanity and dignity. In this pursuit, it was premised on a logic of intersubjective connection: if external observers could only experience the residents' challenges, these observers would understand on an existential level that the residents' circumstances fell short of their worth and violated their dignity, and that recognition would secure commitments to act. Among performance ethnographers, this intersubjective connection through shared location entails copresence, or what Dwight Conquergood refers to as co-performative witnessing (2004: 315), an embodied participation with others in their own environment. D. Soyini Madison remarks that a shared vulnerability of aliveness with others "in the spaces they help make and that in turn help make them" amplifies empathy by deepening shared feeling through the experience of the affect a space generates, the emotions it harbors (2010: 126). A demand for reciprocal presence, then, like that created by the people's inspection, seeks refuge from alterity. It seeks a geographic experience that recasts judgment, not on its inhabitants but on the systemic origins that rendered the space inadequate. A demand for shared presence calls for mutual recognition, an affirmation of another's dignity generated through embodied commitment.

Dignity, here, operates as a counterclaim to the state's neoliberal inversion of ubuntu, a worldview that, with its emphasis on interrelationship and collectivity as the core of being human, would presumably root activists' desire for intersubjective connection in a South African context. However, official ideologies of ubuntu compromised the term to serve neoliberal disciplining aims, using it to support a case for individual fiscal responsibility in the provision of municipal services. Activists have not, by any means, ceded ubuntu to the state's maneuvers, but the concept's state-driven prominence as a national brand is of little salience to those with whom I worked. I noted the use of the concept only once in all the APF meetings I attended, as part of a broader discussion of socialism during which an elderly male speaker, in a manner that suggested he was stating the obvious, offered that "socialism is a simple word—ubuntu. Stokvels [savings collectives], burial societies, cooperatives, and self-sustenance projects are being done by women in our communities; we can copy from them. There's nothing that prevents us from doing socialism now." Alongside his gendered ascription of mutual aid efforts, the speaker's appeal to simplicity through the quotidian grounding of socialism in ubuntu's preexistence confirms the group took the term for granted.

But activists do not ground their claims in ubuntu, despite the term's ready availability to them. Rather, they make claims on the state by adopting a language of rights (von Schnitzler 2014: 337) and mobilize through logics of rightness and justness. Recurring reminders of this focus come through songs that remind participants and listeners alike "Thina silwela amalungelo wethu" (We are fighting for our rights), and admonish opponents "L'ento'yenzayo, alunganga" (What you're doing is not right). One is due what is right, what is just, merely by virtue of being, regardless of individual financial capabilities. Rights are to be claimed and fought for, not prepaid, as extractive state ideologies of ubuntu would have it. Dignity, then, as it inheres in mutual recognition of shared humanity, is a right that existence accords.

"NEVER DEFINED BY THEM": CLAIMING DIGNITY THROUGH SELF-SOVEREIGNTY

A key factor in the APF's activist campaign was the indignation residents of Alexandra expressed to attendees at the people's inspection. Their assertions— "I'm not supposed to stay like this"—indicate a refusal of their circumstances and an enduring claim to their dignity. Activists' favorite struggle songs echo that insistence on dignity in relation to their life circumstances. The role of song in the APF's work is not unique. Scholars have shown how song, along with other technologies, historically constituted "shared, public political sensibility and practice" in ongoing struggles for self-liberation "through which

Africans had challenged their subordination to colonialism" (Chikowero 2015: 239; Mavhunga 2014). The South African activists I worked with drew on "elastic cultural traditions" (Mavhunga 2014: 8) as they sought possibilities for transcendence over experiences of overwhelming, long-standing privation. Theirs was an experience of self as preeminent over external challenges, even when—especially when—the body is subjected to violence. That is the crux of human dignity.

> Do you see the mystery of our pain?
> That we bear the poverty
> And are able to sing and dream sweet things.
>
> —BEN OKRI, "AN AFRICAN ELEGY"

Some protest songs express a refusal to yield to the conditions or external authorities that activists confront. For instance, I asked one activist about the significance of the song "Angeke sizwe ngabo." My interviewee, a thirty-eight-year-old male activist from the Thembelihle Crisis Committee, translated the lyric as "We cannot hear anything from them." He explained what that meant for him: "There is nothing they can tell us as long as we have ourselves. We will tell us what we want, you see. I'd rather be directed by someone from the same crew [as] I . . . not you, you are my enemy, so how can you come and tell me something? There is nothing you can tell me."[13] This refusal to be directed by the expectations of others enabled the activist to claim himself and assert the legitimacy of his and his community's experience against an imposed authority. In this way, this song and its interpretation reveal a view of self that is not subject to the routine authority of someone else's dominion.

Similarly, the favorite song of Khabane, a twenty-year-old male activist from Khutsong, exemplifies internal resolve and resistance to external forces. Its lyrics include the line "abasazi basizwa ngendaba" (they don't know us; they hear about us through newspapers). That is, they are unable to penetrate the surface of who we are. This song is a particularly apt revelation of the limits of newspaper clippings as an index of struggle. Much lies beyond the surface of newspaper stories like those posted on the APF's walls. Khabane told me the song shapes his sense of himself, revealing that there is more to him than meets the eye of newspaper readers or the imagination of journalists: "They don't know what's inside us, the strength of our spirit. They only know us through the news, but they don't know where our true spirit lies." Through this interiority of engagement, the song yielded for Khabane an expanded sense of self and personal capability that transcended the immediacy of his circumstances. The lyrics of these songs were not perfunctory chants but expressions of profound sentiment.

In refusing to yield to abject conditions or the impositions on their selves by brutal authority, these activists claimed their human dignity. Manifesting a tragicomic hope (West 2004), they did not disavow feeling; rather, it was feeling and affective "response-ability" that spurred them to agitate for change.

These individual assertions of human will in claims for justice call for communion with like-minded people, requiring sociality to affirm one person's sense of what ought to be. Dignity remains critical to fulfilling the potential of shared struggle. Furthering claims to dignity, activism is also a call for ethical collectivity. As differently positioned individuals and communities come together in collective action, each must be supported within their own conceptions of what is at stake. Otherwise, solidarity becomes misguided. Without recognition of the dignity of the fellow activists to whom each individual pledges solidarity—that is, a recognition of the immeasurable human freedom that considers each person's struggle on its own terms—solidarity efforts are easily misplaced or ruptured.

CONCLUSION

The people's inspection at Alexandra elaborated the housing crisis around which many APF-affiliated community organizations mobilized. While Alexandra presented a particular set of cases, other APF community affiliates experienced the housing crisis through brutal eviction from their homes. Many struggled for access to water and electricity, both of which were increasingly regulated with prepaid meters. With steep retrenchments and high rates of unemployment, many families subsisted on a grandparent's pension or a child's social grant.

In encounters with researchers, as well as the occasional journalist or foreign camera crew, impoverished individuals were often driven to dramatic lengths to communicate their plight. In Itereleng, for example, I watched as a woman lay down in front of a small construction of wooden poles holding up a blue plastic sheet, looking up to check that the Australian media crew in attendance was filming. As I observed the enactment, perhaps with apparent skepticism at the obvious staging, a male activist and close friend commented, "I know it seems that they are making a drama for the camera, but the conditions that they are living under are real." This kind of staging of poverty for external audiences was not uncommon—indeed, the people's inspection involved dramatizations of the everyday—and it can evoke cynicism. But such staging reflected a sincere effort to communicate the reality of impoverishment as "a chronic state of emergency" (Taussig 1989: 4).

Simply detailing the extent of the abjection risks reducing the experience of structural violence, constituting suffering as the defining condition of impoverished communities. Yet not interrogating the inhumaneness of these living spaces perpetuates the invisibility that shields the consciousness of the more affluent from them. This dilemma is a large part of the difficult task movement participants face: establishing regular practices that bridge divides and work toward a balance that upholds dignity while raising critical awareness for themselves and for bystanders. Enactments—like the people's inspection, which insist on shared presence in protesters' environments—are one such practice that works toward that balance.

While the need for embodied commitment was felt on the ground and recognized by APF's target constituents, the arenas activists used for demonstrations were not spaces entirely of their own making, and, aided by song, their selves were sometimes the only dominion they could lay claim to. The basic goal of establishing dignity remained fundamental to residents even as they sought to expose state deficiencies manifested in their immediate environments. Whether in encounters in activists' homes, through protests on city streets, or even in meetings at the APF office, space was a precondition for the assertion of dignity and indeed of everyday enactments of both governance and dissent. Frustratingly for many activists, various behaviors interacted to form a pattern in which demands for recognition and change encountered spatial divides the state induced deliberately, or in which the APF's internal organizational practices, including the focus on a central administrative core that sometimes made the organization blind to its members' needs, induced inadvertently. In Remmoho, the APF women's forum I describe more fully in chapter 5, a member remarked that she felt she had to come to the APF's office dressed as a comrade in a uniform—that is, in jeans and a struggle T-shirt. The APF's red T-shirt was an index of its public visibility and notoriety, but as a uniform, it also symbolized a disconnect many members expressed. It stripped away individual practical concerns—the children's gnawing hunger, domestic abuse, and other problems at home—and promoted a uniform(ed) mass, making individual need invisible.

These erasures were difficult to capture because APF's leaders readily acknowledged that the bulk of the collective's constituents lived in impoverished communities. But the APF's political interventions were not pitched to ameliorate day-to-day survival concerns, and so the organization had limited avenues to address these everyday needs. One member described the dynamic thus: "We have to struggle. We don't have housing, we don't have water, sanitation, whatever. The APF is doing something to help us to go and do those struggles, but what about this poverty?"[14] The APF left poverty alleviation efforts to interested affiliates, but only a few affiliates made such efforts. In the Vaal, for example, the Orange Farm Water Crisis Committee extended its scope beyond agitating for the delivery of basic services to include member-driven relief initiatives, such as a community garden, a daycare center that served children two daily meals, and a recycling center that offered payment for containers. The allowances the APF did make for the financial limitations of its members—reimbursing travel to the office and offering lunch during all-day meetings—ultimately prevented the collective engagement needed to share political stakes and eventually disrupted rather than facilitated internal solidarity, a dynamic I will examine in detail in chapter 4.

Recognizing that it lacked sustained visibility into local affiliates' conditions, the APF organized visits to individual affiliates by its part-time organizers, but these visits were sporadic and were only partially completed before the movement's disintegration. Because day-to-day life concerns were precisely what drew activists to the movement, the invisibility of APF members' daily conditions remained a crucial irony and a critical shortcoming. These divides were reinforced through movement routines that encouraged a unidirectional orientation toward the APF's administrative center with little or no reciprocal engagement with marginalized conditions in the peripheries.

The APF's performative constitution in the years following its emergence was proliferated through spatial practices and normalization that produced blind spots in the APF's program of action. Those blind spots, to some extent, reproduced the durable spatial disadvantages of impoverished South Africans, first entrenched in apartheid and then reified by the new, neoliberal regime. Thus, impoverished South Africans—many of them among the APF's constituency—remained spatially disadvantaged, whether through the regulation of public protest gatherings or by being relegated to inadequate physical environments. These kinds of maneuvers are easily overlooked in coalitional movements that operate in centralized locales far removed from activists' residents. Attention to the routinized spatial practices that produce and limit collective dissent sets the foundation required to appreciate moments and experiences that transcend those routines; for instance, protest performances. Even though state agents can curtail collective assembly (and have done so), the presence and possibility of performance (particularly through song) allows for a channeling of movement and emotions that cannot be preplanned and can therefore more deftly escape state regulatory efforts. Chapter 3 takes up these affordances of performance.

NOTES

1. For more on states' spatial regulation, see Fanon (1968), Foucault (1977), Cell (1982), Scott (1990), Gordillo and Hirsch (2003), and Bozzoli (2004).

2. This phenomenon has been manifested compellingly in the temporal and spatial diffusion of collective protests ranging from Occupy movements to the Arab Spring revolts, #BlackLivesMatter demonstrations across the globe, and #FeesMustFall protests in South Africa (Juris 2012; Razsa and Kurnik 2012; Hamdy 2012; Smith 2016; Gillespie and Naidoo 2019). In these demonstrations, the spatial constitution of people as masses, a *demos*, is evident in places from Cairo's Tahrir Square to the Wisconsin State Capitol, from Greece's anti-austerity protests to Nigeria's fuel strikes, from Ferguson, Baltimore, and Charlotte to university campuses and city streets across South Africa (see Collins 2012; Gordillo 2011). Protesters saturate space with presence, laying their claim to the public space.

3. The Rosa Luxemburg Foundation is a German foundation named for the Marxist theorist and economist. The foundation, which has offices across the world, supports political education and considers itself part of the movement for democratic socialism. It is funded by the German government.

4. Tshwane is the name of the metropolitan municipality to which Pretoria belongs; a proposal to change the city's name to Tshwane, as well, is the subject of an ongoing saga.

5. This event is discussed in detail in chapter 4.

6. The act arose from recommendations made by the Goldstone Commission of Enquiry, which then president F. W. De Klerk had appointed to inquire into public violence and intimidation in anticipation of the transition from apartheid. Prior to 1991, the state imposed a blanket ban on public demonstrations and gatherings. Nonetheless, protests were widespread and prominently featured in South African communities. Police responses to these events were often brutal, with state violence resulting in further commemorative protests—for example, of the Sharpeville massacre (March 21) and the Soweto uprisings (June 16). In the period of transition, from 1990 to 1994, an escalation of public violence led to the formation of the Goldstone Commission, which was charged with making recommendations on the prevention of such acts of violence. The commission convened a multinational panel to assess approaches in the United States, Canada, the United Kingdom, Belgium, the Netherlands, and other countries, seeking a potential model for South Africa. Its recommendations, based on the premise that

activists and the government share responsibility for the enactment of peaceful protest, constituted a break from the government's previous repressive practices. The commission argued for the recognition of gatherings as a protected right of citizenship rather than as political threat (see Heymann 1992; Duncan 2016).

7. The Goldstone Commission report refers to the triumvirate of protest organizers, local civil authorities, and police as the "safety triangle" (Heymann 1992: ix).

8. Interview with the author, June 16, 2010, Johannesburg.

9. Recent interventions on the significance of home in South Africa include Mark Hunter's *Love in the Time of AIDS* (2010), a case study in Mandeni, KwaZulu-Natal, that traces shifting intimate relationships involving love, sex, and marriage and demonstrates how the various social and emotional configurations that go into "building a home" are materially conditioned, historically and in contemporary South Africa. Anne-Maria Makhulu (2015) similarly examines the shifting political economy of intimacy through the lives of shack dwellers in Cape Town and their contested claims to a city that has denied their very existence. Fiona Ross's *Raw Life, New Hope* (2010) explores the pursuit of decency and the shifts in social relations that hinged on one Capetonian Coloured community's hard-won move from informal settlement to formal housing.

10. Internal document, shared with the author by an ACR organizer.

11. Anthropologist Thayer Scudder coined the term "developmental refugees" to capture the displacement of communities by development projects such as World Bank–funded megadams in India (see Nixon 2011: 152).

12. In spite of the usefulness of Foley's interventions, I find this phrasing to be inadequate, because it suggests an objectification of the body (rendering the body a text on which power is inscribed) that scholars of embodiment have critiqued (see, for example, Csordas 1999: 182; Howes 2003: 29–30; Stoller 1997: xiv–xv).

13. Interview with the author, October 16, 2010, Johannesburg.

14. Interview with Ellen Chauke, conducted by Dale McKinley, August 20, 2010, Johannesburg.

ACTIVIST PORTRAIT

Kanelo

.

I WAS ATTENDING A POLITICAL education workshop at Khanya College in August 2010 when I received word that people were being evicted in Quagga; I immediately made my way there, along with three APF activists involved with mobilization in the area. As we approached the complex, we saw police vans parked outside. Furniture, clothes, and household items were piled along the outside of the wall enclosing the complex. Allen, the APF's regional organizer for Tshwane (Pretoria), met us at the gate, where he informed us that the eviction was done. Kanelo, an APF activist who lived in Quagga, came out as well, to tell us she had been evicted. They ushered us through the gates to see for ourselves. As we entered the complex, we saw the infamous Red Ants—employees of Wozani Security, a private security firm often employed to evict people from inner-city buildings and informal settlements, recognizable by their uniform of red coveralls.

The red ants the name refers to evoke terror across the world in the marginalized spaces occupied by African descendants. Across the Gulf Coast of the United States, red ants congregate into floats when it storms, drifting through water until they reach dry land. These floats, and the red ants that constituted them, were among the many dangers people in New Orleans confronted as they fled their homes after Hurricane Katrina, as did those in Texas following Hurricane Harvey. Linda Bui, an entomologist at Louisiana State University, recalled the bodily conditions of Katrina evacuees who had encountered the ants as they waded in floodwaters; they emerged with bands of rashes around their legs and waists. "They were like something none of the medical professionals had ever seen," she said. "I was like, 'Those are literally fire ant stings on top of fire ant stings'" (quoted in Zhang 2017). The relentless sting of the fire ant compounded the susceptibility to bodily damage that evacuees confronted in fleeing for their lives.

In South Africa, human beings willfully become red ants, converging in clusters, often acting in concert with the police to devastate communities already in distress, making recovery almost impossible. They descend on a location with crowbars and other implements, emptying homes, bulldozing shacks, and forcibly removing people. "When red ants come," a male activist once explained to me, "they take everything so that people will not be able to rebuild, even your small nail polish." When they appear, they create bodily injury in addition to utter dispossession. In Quagga, these clusters of men in red were sitting and lying down in the shade of cars, some wearing red caps with "redant" written in black across the front. As they were lounging about, their capacity to create havoc was not readily apparent; these were ordinary men, the only thing remarkable about them being their red uniform(ity).

Kanelo informed us that some of the residents had received a notice of eviction, and a few who knew they were targeted had managed to get their things outside. For those who were too slow, Red Ants would gather all the items in a flat, dropping everything in their trucks without bothering to separate items. The trucks would then be driven away. Owners could only retrieve their items after they paid their arrears; otherwise, the items would be sold to recover the amounts owed. In the newly emptied flats, management and Red Ants were installing burglar doors to prevent those evicted from accessing these flats again.

Two local filmmakers from Media for Justice arrived. As they set up their equipment, residents gathered singing, and constituted themselves into an impromptu march. Singing "awuyaz'oyifunayo" (you don't know what you want), they marched right up to the Red Ants, deriding their inability to secure what they were after. Kanelo elaborated in a later interview that Red Ants wanted to occupy the evicted flats that night, but "that's the message we sent to them, that they won't get what they think they were going to get, and really we didn't allow them to do that." In this instance, the song enabled a talking back, opening up possibilities of refusal.

Once residents who had space to share had taken in those evicted, we prepared to leave to contact lawyers to intercede on behalf of the evictees. In the lull of activity before we left, I sat down beside Kanelo on the sidewalk with the contents of her home. It was not until she started to cry that I began to register the emotional impact of the day. Activists confront security and state agents motivated to fight; a mobilization of energy propels them through the encounter. But the vulnerability, fear, and indignity of exposure lingers beyond the intensity of pitched battles.

I sat next to Kanelo with her children, their humble possessions laid out on the sidewalk, as she wept.

"WE CAN'T GO AND BARRICADE WHILE WE'RE THIRTEEN"

Kanelo's life had been marked by uprootings and relocations. She lived with her family in one place from her birth in 1978 until 1992, when the petrol-bombing of her home led to her mother's death. "After burying my mother, we never went back to that house," she explained. With her father still in the hospital, she and her siblings stayed with her paternal grandmother, who mistreated them. After she became pregnant at eighteen, Kanelo moved temporarily to Limpopo to stay with her maternal grandmother, although she later returned to live with her siblings at the home of her paternal grandmother. After some time, the grandmother chased them all away, and Kanelo and her siblings resorted to squatting in other people's homes.

When Kanelo's sister started working and wanted to reclaim their parents' house, she found out their uncles had sold it. "So we started being homeless, and we started hiring a place just to stay." Kanelo and her siblings rented a Reconstruction and Development Programme (RDP) house but had to move when the owner wanted it back. Her younger brother found the flat in Quagga Estates in 2007 and signed a lease agreement, but he had to give up the flat after a series of large rent increases. Kanelo felt stranded by her children's schooling—her two siblings' accommodations were both too far to allow Kanelo to transport her children to school inexpensively.

Quagga Estates had been housing for employees of Iscor, an iron mining and steel production corporation now known as ArcelorMittal, the largest steel producer on the African continent. After Iscor sold the housing complex, former Iscor employees living there claimed the buildings they inhabited—they believed they had paid down the bonds on their blocks and alleged Iscor sold the complex without consulting them or paying them back. The new owners in turn rented out unoccupied flats, creating two streams of inhabitants—former Iscor employees and those residing there under a lease from the new owners. The new owners, seeking to standardize all residents under lease agreements, tried to enforce the leases through evictions, but the former Iscor employees would not relinquish their claims to their homes. Instead, the employees formed committees and sought litigation.

These two streams of residents converged in shared struggle when abnormally large rent increases led some renters to seek the perspectives of former Iscor employees living there. Kanelo, who had leased her apartment from the new owners, approached the committee of Iscor workers for assistance when she was stranded. The committee connected her with another tenant, and she and her children stayed with that family. Because she was not working, one of the committee members paid her rent and even helped provide clothing for her family. She was elected to the committee's leadership, and when the committee decided, as a point of combative strategy, that residents should occupy empty flats in the apartment complex, Kanelo and her children were assigned their own flat.

The situation at Quagga created intersecting issues, which Kanelo laid out for me. The community's protests were not only about the rent increases; they also concerned land insecurity due to the dispossession of Iscor workers and environmental pollution from the industries surrounding the complex. "Every morning when we wake up, we'll have black dust," Kanelo noted. "Most of the people are old and they never had asthma but most of them now, we are using pumps." Kanelo herself had been born with asthma. Her left lung was no longer functioning, and her susceptibility to attacks was compounded by stress: "To be honest, the issue is that I'm not working, I can't provide for my kids, it's very tough. That one I can't lie to anyone, I'm stressing from it a lot so sometimes maybe I'm thinking something, and it triggers the asthma because I don't have to be overexcited, I don't have to be upset. I just have to be normal; otherwise, I'll get attacks." Iscor had maintained a hospital to test its workers in the area, which for Kanelo demonstrated the corporation's awareness of its pollution and the impact of that pollution on workers and the environment.

On the basis of these three factors—abnormal rent increases, dispossession of former Iscor workers, and environmental pollution—Kanelo and others sought to negotiate a more reasonable rental agreement with the management company. The management company refused, arguing that it was not Iscor and was not responsible for Iscor's acts. When negotiation yielded no progress, the committee found an advocate to take its case to court and sought to hold Iscor accountable for sick residents. Kanelo wanted the government to buy back the fraudulently sold estate and reestablish a political contract for the provision of adequate housing. In the meantime, Quagga residents battled evictions and attempts to evict.

Kanelo joined the APF through her work with the Quagga committee, which was an APF affiliate. Often under siege in her home, Kanelo was among those who relied on the political acumen and solidarity available through the APF. But she encountered a challenging disconnect between what happens in the APF office and the reality of her home: "In the office it's not struggle, there are only like personal politics that are not taking us anywhere." The APF's lack of visibility in moments such as her eviction worried Kanelo. "What did the office bearers think about the evictions?" she asked. "Two hundred people get evicted? Doing nothing about it. I mean that's where APF was supposed to jump in and go crazy. They should have sent taxis from the affiliates or from the regions, maybe two taxis per region so that they can come and support. APF was so invisible here. That's why the people are running back to the [political] parties. And then automatically DA [a distrusted political party] is going to take advantage."

More than verbalized commitment, Kanelo needed the physical presence of her comrades, whom she expected to rally to her aid. She felt a gap between the struggles on the ground she was experiencing, with their urgent and fervent need, and the roles APF office bearers inhabited. "But what about the struggles that are here that are happening? Where is the housing coordinator?" she queried. "We need something that can help us now, help the people who are still on the streets now. It's raining daily, some old men are sleeping on the streets, some women took their kids home to Limpopo, to KZN, to Cape Town, they are no longer going to school."

Kanelo also identified a disconnect between the APF's championed tactics and the reality of her immediate environment. The APF suggested barricading as a response to evictions, but this tactic requires numbers and assumes the willingness of individuals to put their bodies on the line. Those elements are not always available, as Kanelo pointed out: "They must understand that we are dealing mostly with old people. We can't go and barricade while we're thirteen [in number]. You see and most of the people here are so scared, I don't know for what but they are so scared that's why when you say, 'Let's go for barricading,' only twelve or fifteen people will come. The rest won't come."

"OKAY, I'M AN ACTIVIST NOW"

The fear and timidity that dampen motivation to protest was something Kanelo herself learned to overcome. Describing her first protest event, Kanelo remembered feeling shy and inhibited: "I started like at the back, standing at the back and watching others." Although she felt shy, Kanelo longed to join protesters at the front of the march. She watched one older woman who was particularly demonstrative:

> She started singing the song, and she started lying down, and I said to myself, if an old woman can do this, why can't I do it? . . . The minute that I came to the front from the back, [she] said, "You and you lie down." . . . We lay down,

and after that she started singing the song. And then I didn't even know what they were doing, so I couldn't close my eyes, so I was watching them, what they were doing, so that I can do what they were doing, see. . . . The minute I stood up, I felt like I wanted to sit down, like we were doing our legs like up and down, the minute I stood up, the cameras shot me. . . . And that's why I love the song, because that was the first time I was on the newspapers, being part of the protesters singing on energy. And actually I felt like, "Okay, I'm an activist now."

For Kanelo, that song, "Sizolala" (We will sleep here [until you address our concerns]), became encoded with her identity as an activist because it, along with the newspaper image, captured the moment she learned to bypass her inhibitions and express dissent through spontaneous bodily engagement, achieved by apprenticing herself to those around her, following their lead until she could find her own embodiment of protest. Song enabled her to send a message during protest events, to disrupt a particular distribution of the sensible— "because we know that they [the police] can't hear . . . they do hear us, but they are ignoring us." Being seen and heard offered relief: "So when I'm performing like in the protests, it's like I'm sending the message and I'm relieving a bit of stress, because it's like when I come back home, then I say, 'Yes, they saw us, what we wanted, we actually sent the message.' So at least I relieve something."

At the Quagga evictions that August, song enabled the residents to talk back, enacting a reclamation of the humanity that had been denied, a reassertion of choice by those who had been forcibly removed from their homes. The lyrics of one of the songs driving the residents' confrontation with Red Ants, "awuyaz'oyifunayo," can be translated as "You don't know what you want. We offer you our hands, we offer you our elbows, we offer you our breasts. That which you are really after, you'll never get." The song asserted its singers' fundamental bodily sovereignty, encapsulating their power in their right to offer or deny access to themselves. In taunting the Red Ants with this song, Quagga residents answered back to a force that sought to overpower them. They returned the insult on their dignity and humanity not from powerlessness but from a position of authority. Song fostered the reclamation of space as the community denied the men further access to the flats they had emptied. Protesters used song to confront their vulnerability to pain, suffering, and humiliation without being defeated or immobilized by it.

The Kanelo I saw in protests did not display the timidity of her early activist years. Not only was she uninhibited, often charging ahead to lead the procession; she had become quite adept at reclaiming her power through song. When, for instance, she was among those caught in a standoff with police officers who had formed a human wall to prevent protesters accessing a main artery and larger audience, Kanelo addressed the standoff in song:

Maphoyisa sukan'endleleni	*Policemen move out of our way*
Aniboni siyazabalaza?	*Can't you see that we are uprising?*

THREE

—ɯ—

EFFLORESCENCE

IN OCTOBER 2010, THE FREEDOM of Expression Institute (FXI), a Johannesburg organization some Anti-Privatisation Forum (APF) members also belonged to, tried to hold a silent protest against a bill that would curtail public access to government information. The silence, though, was inevitably upended by song. Silence felt counterintuitive to collective procession; that fact became evident the moment the marchers took their first steps—and tried, unsuccessfully, to quell their impulses to clap, stomp, and raise their voices in song. Protesters, who had symbolically gagged themselves with duct tape, began to sing as soon as the march started. I later asked one of the organizers, an FXI staff member and APF activist, if he thought it was possible to hold a silent march in South Africa. "I don't think so," he chuckled. When I asked why, he responded that the songs "add something to that activity [protest], and the character has been that, you know, you sing [during marches]. If there [were] academics, journalists, you know maybe [the October march] was going to achieve its purpose of being a silent march, but getting us from the township . . . but I know also that some academics also can't . . . they've been involved in those struggles, so I'm just saying it's not easy."[1] In his estimation, what could distinguish academics and journalists from township activists was their level of experience with song as a mode of protest. Academics and journalists might be unfamiliar with township distributions of the sensible, to use Rancière's phrase. The sensible, as was expressed by my FXI interlocutor, can be described as "how you get used to doing things when you're in that community." Because distributions of the sensible entail bodily sense-making that becomes taken for granted, silence as protest would not seem as strange or unsettling to those who do not have embedded bodily associations of protest with song and patterned movement. For many activists present that day, however, song was not only a powerful vehicle for expressing discontent but also an essential mode of establishing geographic and temporal continuity within far-reaching, ongoing struggles.

Apartheid-era freedom songs remain an important resource for contemporary activists resisting neoliberal reforms and making claims on the state through public demonstrations, litigation, and infrastructural opposition (von Schnitzler 2014).[2] One constant across these strategies of political engagement has been the prominence of collective singing, whether activists are marching through city streets, demonstrating outside courthouses, blockading highways, reconnecting households to vital water and electricity, or opposing their own or their neighbors' evictions. For many South Africans, including the activists I worked with, protests are moments of utter immersion in the embodied experience of singing, clapping, and dancing together. In these moments, sound, bodily sensation, movement, and emotion converge.

The APF's early years typified these manifestations of the musical underpinnings of collective protest. Direct action—and the performances intrinsic to it—generated a collective bond even when the diversity of members' ideological commitments threatened to create rifts in the nascent organization. Song was an element at the APF's birth. When the activists who would later form the APF stormed the Urban Futures conference at Wits University, they accompanied their action with song. As the organization emerged and took hold, these expressions remained prominent in APF activities—in meetings and internal practices as well as in protests and public confrontations. In the collective's later years, the use of participatory performance to facilitate collective bonds only accentuated a dynamic already established during the APF's emergence.

APF activists employed a range of performance practices, including the use of freedom songs to punctuate meetings and coordinate protests, the enactment of collective rituals in activist education, and the presentation of poetic and theatrical pieces by youth groups. Among APF members, freedom songs constituted a particularly rich domain of embodied and emotive transmission. In deploying these practices, the activists drew on a long history of strategic expression. Singing together fostered an alternative experience of leadership and affiliation that contrasted markedly with the APF's formal organizational structure and its observable shortcomings. The presence of song in the movement's activities is all the more significant for the experience of community that such collective performances afforded, even in the context of the organization's stratified spatial and social dynamics.

PROTEST SINGING IN SOUTH AFRICA: SONG AS
MANIFESTATION OF EXPRESSIVE CULTURE

In their use of song, protesters draw on a deep history of singing in South African activism. Freedom songs are so deeply connected to struggles for the nation that the acclaimed trumpeter Hugh Masekela once attributed the loss in the decisive Zulu war of 1879 to Zulu warriors' singing on the battlefield.[3] Freedom songs emerged as tactics of liberation struggles against the ravages of war, against colonialism, and, most notably, against apartheid. Their origins can be traced to historical forms, such as Zulu *amahubo empi* (or war songs [prominent in precolonial and colonial warfare]), and to oral art that is embedded in daily life (Mthembu 1999: 1; Xulu 1994; Gilbert 2007; Jolaosho 2014). The theater practitioner Duma Ndlovu describes how song permeated daily practices under apartheid to the extent that "our parents would break into song at the slightest provocation. When your mother couldn't figure out what to feed you for that night because she didn't have any money, she came back from looking for a job, she would break into a dirge that would be expressing how she felt" (in Hirsch 2002). Occasions when people gather—including weddings and funerals—provide opportunities for song as well, and many freedom songs emerged from and contributed to these practices.

Freedom songs also have ties to religious singing; many protest songs are adaptations of church hymns. As playwright Fatimah Dike put it, "People had faith in God so much that they even took hymns and used them as songs of protest in testing the waters of apartheid."[4] Many of these songs adapt the moral grounding of Christian hymnody to query the apartheid system and seek divine intervention. The political element complicating the link between song and religion appears in Dike's statement of an all-consuming concern in her activism: "If we are the children of God, why does God allow what just happened in South Africa to happen?" The strategic transformations of religious texts for political ends come through clearly in the way many song adapters replaced Jesus in ascriptions of salvation with struggle heroes and leaders. One song, which originally asserted "somlandela, somlandel' uJesu" (we will follow Jesus), was changed to "somlandel' Lutuli" (we will follow Lutuli) in an effort to popularize the leadership of Albert Lutuli, the then president of the African National Congress. This kind of appropriation illustrates the plasticity of the protest song as a medium that allows it to leverage religious tradition for political aims.

As "songs of the people," freedom songs were not only adopted and sung by the masses but also composed and adapted by them. While certain individuals, such as Vuyisile Mini[5] and Reuban Tholakele Caluza,[6] are recognized as composers of particular songs, the identities of many composers and the origins of most songs are difficult to trace. Regarding this phenomenon, pop culture journalist Peter Makarube notes, "African people always made music. Nobody ever said, 'I wrote this song in three minutes,' or 'I wrote it in three months. This is my song.' Because you start a song and someone backs you, and people just build up a song" (in Hirsch 2002). Many liberation songs have call-and-response structures that allow for incessant repetition, constant ad-libbing, and nonstop improvisation. These songs were built together by protesters, evolving with every performance. Their composition, like their performance, is inherently participatory and collective. Further, protest events provided opportunities for songs to develop and circulate across communities. One manifestation of this circulation is linguistic: freedom songs tend to mix the different languages performers speak—including isiZulu, seSotho, isiXhosa, sesTwana, English, and Afrikaans—reflecting the accessibility and wide adoption (and adaptation) of the form.

Ndumiso, an activist leader, describes the felt experience of protest singing as a phenomenon of expressive culture: "[Even if] you can't speak out the verses of the song, but then you feel it, that means it's in your heart, it's there, so there's some other energy which we feel going into our marches, going to our meetings, wherever, that's the culture we should never lose of song and dance." [7] I met Ndumiso at the first collective protest I attended as part of my fieldwork in 2009. It was billed as a nonpartisan protest. The intention was not to advance the aims of any political organization but to present the claims of the community at large to municipal officials. Ndumiso was clearly a leader—he held a bullhorn, spoke at the podium, and led the collective in some freedom songs—but he had taken care to conceal his features. A cap shaded his face, and he wore large sunglasses that shielded his eyes from view. He concealed his facial features so well that when I met him for an interview in another setting, at a fellow activist's home, I did not immediately recognize him. What I could access in my initial encounter was the gritty texture of his voice and the manner with which he sang, select elements that clearly distinguished him. During our conversation later, Ndumiso demonstrated an awareness of the historical underpinnings of singing practices among South African protesters. Echoing Masekela's reflections, he asserted that protest singing "is like fighting a battle. You can't go to war without song because that's the only thing that will keep you going."

When I arrived in South Africa for fieldwork in 2009, an established and flourishing repertoire of freedom songs articulating post-1994 grievances had developed, many adapted from apartheid-era songs. These songs were felt as intrinsically political and embodied expressions among South African protesters, as Khanyisa, a male activist in his fifties, attested: "If I go to a march and the

songs are not good, I will tell you there is something not good with the movement, because it means they are not together. It means they don't march a lot.
Yes, they might all know the song, but it doesn't move them, it's not spirited."[8]
Khanyisa further explained that the creativity needed to create or perform a
protest song required a "febrile mind." Indeed, febrile creativity was crucial to
activists' attempts to adapt apartheid-era freedom songs to ongoing struggles,
in an effort to access the powerful legacy of these songs as culturally sanctioned
practices that interrogate the existing state of affairs, articulate common grievances, and mobilize toward shared visions.

The contemporary repertoire of protest songs thus rested on the sanctioned
authority of anti-apartheid singing practices, but it offered distinct shifts in
sentiment that reflected the new challenges faced by postapartheid activists
opposing the neoliberal policies of the democratically elected African National Congress (ANC) government. During the immediate posttransition
period (1994 to the early 2000s), songs lingered, often unchanged, from the
anti-apartheid struggle. But activists in new postapartheid social movements,
such as the APF, needed to distinguish the emerging class struggle from the
forgoing racial one. They used song—and especially adaptations of apartheid
protest songs—to highlight the ANC's changing stance as it shifted from a
liberation movement to a governing body.

Vuyiswa, a female APF member who was actively involved in the organization's early days, described the challenge the emergent movement faced:

> Moving people from that position of seeing the ANC as the saviour was a
> long process. So while you're conscientizing them theoretically, the songs also
> played [their] role.[9] For instance, you'll be in a protest or in a workshop and
> then you talk about, let's say, GEAR, and you have many people and some are
> still members of the ANC. And let's say you start a song, and people will be like,
> "We can't sing this song, we are full members of the ANC!" But then gradually
> people understood and were like, "Ok, we are members of the ANC but we
> don't have electricity, we don't have water, while these guys live in Sandton [an
> affluent suburb of Johannesburg] and other areas, and what is there to gain if
> we don't sing this song?" So it was a process that ran parallel with theory and
> song. And eventually you have now a solid group that now knows that the ANC
> is actually failing the poor and that can be seen in all aspects of life.[10]

Thus, the transition to postapartheid freedom singing came about gradually,
as people were convinced to be more vocal about the ANC's shortcomings.
It proceeded through both spontaneous and organized formations. In organized practice sessions, struggle-aligned performance groups—including
Sounds of Edutainment, Bophelong Youth Choir, and Sedibeng Concerned

Artists—adapted songs and created new expressive forms (including new songs, poems, and plays). The plasticity of the freedom song form, with its antiphonic, repetitive, and embodied rhythmic structure, enabled more spontaneous adaptations during protest events. As Vuyiswa recalled,

> I would come to a protest and then just in my mind work the lyrics [to preexisting tunes] and then try them out, and then people join in, you know. . . . Sometimes you are protesting and then something happens, and then you're just carried away and quickly you look for a tune to fit the words, and then it fits and then people get to join you. And then the next protest, they say, "Let's sing that one." Sometimes you forget the lyrics, they'll be the ones reminding you. You'll be the one who will be forgetting, and then they remind you. That's how the songs grow.

Many freedom songs were made relevant through lyrical transformations, but such transformation is not absolutely necessary. A translation of sentiment—in which preexisting lyrics encode current grievances—can also help activists and their audiences relate to an apartheid-era song. For example, the song "Siyaya (ePitoli)" (we are going, no matter what [to Pretoria]) was popularized during the 1956 Women's March to the seat of the apartheid government in Pretoria; it can still be heard in contemporary South African protests. The song expresses activists' resolve to keep going despite the risks of psychological and physical harm (including death and sexual violence) they confront by airing their grievances against the state and other opponents.

By the time the APF released its album of freedom songs, *Songs of the Working Class Volume 1*, in 2007, South Africa's collective oppositional singing culture had not only survived the apartheid transition but thrived, providing a fertile resource for protesters, who creatively deployed their legacy of freedom songs. These songs supported educational aims, serving as vehicles to inform communities of the shifts and continuities within emerging struggles against a democratically elected government that had dashed the hopes of many for national transformation. Rooted in a long history of an expressive culture that was functional in its aesthetics, freedom songs survive and thrive due to the plasticity of their musical forms. Even more than the textual dexterity they employ, the musical structure of these songs enables their adaptability and ongoing relevance in changing political circumstances.

THE MUSICAL STRUCTURE OF COLLECTIVE PROTEST

Scholarship on the subversive functions of songs often locates their political significance in their lyrical content. For example, one definition of protest songs describes them as musical expressions "whose lyrics speak out against a specific social, political or economic injustice" (Lockard 1998: 33). In this text-based analysis, lyrics are understood to convey sociopolitical sentiments and reinforce ideological commitments (see Denisoff 1983; Corte and Edwards 2008; Turino 2008: 189–224). Singers employ verbal artistry, using repetition, adaptations, and extensions to amplify ideas, to create avenues of persuasion and recruitment for social movements (cf. Lieberman 1995; Roy 2010: 5–6). These practices underpin a temporal and spatial emergence, expressed in lyrical juxtapositions through which the relevance of the past is made explicit and geographical circulations are made audible (James 1999: 84; Gunner 2009: 38–39).

While this text-based analytical emphasis has been extremely productive, the political significance of musical expression is not conclusively revealed by relying only on its lyrical content (Ahearn 1998; Roy 2010).[11] For instance, the lyrics of protest songs might belie any political connection, as was the case with many songs of the US civil rights movement. Understanding the political efficacy of such songs requires more inclusive consideration of the interplay of elements constituting a musical encounter. Attention to the musicality of collective protest singing reveals how song functions, not just as a discursive site for articulating protesters' sentiments but as an aesthetically constituted politics.

As a form of participatory performance, the musical framework of freedom songs involves three distinctive elements: antiphony (call and response), repetition, and embodied rhythm. These formative elements establish a somatically grounded mode of relationship among protesters, structuring patterns of exchange, evaluation, and conduct.[12] These aesthetic dimensions form the basis of protest, supporting key functions like organizing and sustaining demonstrations and fostering solidarity among those gathered. Beyond these functions, the musical structure of freedom songs affects emotions and shapes identities, thereby rendering politics a deeply intimate phenomenon. If, as Margaret Dorsey suggests, we "situate our glance earlier and allow it to linger longer" than the time frame of events explicitly marked as political (2004: 61–62), new insights into music's role in mediating individual and collective activism through protesters' emotions and embodiment can emerge.

Antiphony

At the 2009 Orlando East march, where I first met Ndumiso, activists constituted themselves in song and dance, a phenomenon similar to countless other protest events across South Africa. Protesters were gathered on a circular traffic island around a blue pole that held up billboards on three sides. A backless concrete bench had been built underneath the billboards, creating a convenient raised platform around which protesters had gathered. A young woman who appeared to be in her twenties stood on this makeshift platform and read the memorandum of grievances drafted by that march organizers. It was an especially hot day, and many of the *gogos* and *'mkhulus* (grandmothers and grandfathers) who turned up for the march held an assortment of colorful umbrellas over their heads to ward off the scorching sun. Others wore wide-brimmed hats, leaving their hands free to display cardboard protest signs. The signs carried such messages as "Step Down To All Councillors: Ruby, Vusi, Queen," "All the Consilors are useless and corrupt," "Away with Eskom, we want city power," "You cut electricity, we shoot to kill, be warned," "Ruby and Ruth [municipal councilors] have title deeds, Orlando residents have toilet papers," and "Stop stealing houses from grandmothers." The memorandum of grievances echoed these commentaries, accusing municipal councilors of corruption and financial mismanagement, particularly in the handling of housing allocations, and demanding that they step down.

Because organizers did not want the agendas of political organizations to overtake residents' grievances, they framed the march as a nonpartisan gathering. Despite this intention, attendees declared their varied political affiliations with T-shirts. Some bore symbols of the governing alliance and read, "Do it For Chris Hani/Vote," recalling the ANC struggle hero who was killed in the run-up to South Africa's first democratic elections. The back of the shirt listed "Six Reasons to Vote ANC." Another T-shirt supporting the ANC read "Born in the Struggle and Baptised in Revolutionary Fires." Oppositional movements were also represented. APF supporters wore red T-shirts bearing the logo of the APF in front and proclaiming on the back "APF says: Stop Electricity Cut-Offs/No to Privatisation." Another T-shirt bore the logo of the APF-affiliated Soweto Electricity Crisis Committee. Some displays manifested no explicit organizational ties. Protest marshals wore vests emblazoned with the acronym FIFA, calling attention to the 2010 World Cup, which was then months away. The woman reading the memorandum wore a T-shirt that fixed a locational rather than an organizational identity: "Orlando East state of mind." These sartorial choices were forms of embodied performance, communicating activists' positionings in relation to one another and to bystanders.

Cultural performances were also more explicitly deployed, in song. Ndumiso was the first to raise a song. After the crowd's cheers on the conclusion of the memorandum died down, he exchanged the vuvuzela he was blowing for a bullhorn and began, his gravelly voice lifting, "sithi lelizwe elabogogo bethu" (this nation belongs to our grandmothers). He moved rhythmically as he sang, lifting one bent leg after another, marching in place in time with the song. "Asoze," the crowd responded, joining his easy sway and clapping along. "Asoze saphela 'mandla" (Never shall it lose power), Ndumiso completed the phrase. The crowd responded, bringing the exchange to its melodic conclusion: "Asoze saphela 'mandla." In the next stanza, others joined Ndumiso in the leading line: "Elizwe elabogogo bethu." "Asoze," came the collective response. "Asoze saphela 'mandla," the song leaders continued, finishing the melody. A woman now assumed the lead: "Sithi Orlando elabogogo bethu," she sang. (Orlando belongs to our grandmothers.) "Asoze," the crowd assented, Ndumiso now joining its ranks, dipping his torso in dance. One of the marshals, who was holding a bullhorn, offered it to another marshal, who sang the next leading line, "sithi Orlando, elabomkhulu bethu" (Orlando belongs to our grandfathers). When the stanza ended, marshals held up their hands in a signal to stop singing.

This exchange exemplifies a fundamental feature of South African freedom songs: their use of antiphony, or call-and-response patterns. Call and response is a critical organizational element of collective protest singing. The antiphonic pattern structures a musical exchange among those gathered—a leading line can raise a question, offer a comment, or provide an incomplete starting phrase that the responding line finishes. The interaction organizes the proceeding: the raising of a song provides everyone gathered an opportunity to come into synchrony, by recognizing the song and taking their place in its musical framework. It thus eliminates the need for a conductor to coordinate the group.[13] Furthermore, it highlights the interdependency among individuals in the creation of community. The leading line can be sung by one individual, but often song leadership is not exclusive to one person; other individuals can join the leading line or take it over (as they did in Orlando East). Protesters will often reinforce or harmonize with the original song leader's voice, especially if the song resonates with them. This practice highlights the particularly democratic nature of song leadership. As Khanyisa noted, "Anyone can sing and songs are democratic in the sense that no one is elected to start the tune. We don't have our songster who always starts the song."

Aside from its organizing functions, an antiphonic pattern is also evaluative. Raising a song—putting out a call to draw a response—is a proposal of sentiment that can be vocally affirmed or suppressed. The strength of the collective's response demonstrates the group's assessment of the call. As Ysaye Maria Barnwell notes, "If you don't like [the message], you say so . . . and we give each other permission to act in that way because that is the cycle of communication."[14] A lukewarm or absent response communicates a lack of support.

In this way, antiphony becomes significant as a musical play that crafts power. In the terms of ethnomusicologist Kyra Gaunt, protesters "learn to improvise with what it means to be dominant and subordinate in musical and nonmusical relationships" (2006: 14). The play of leadership and response is revelatory of power-laden internal dynamics that can manifest as uneven participation. In the sonic interplay, silence is as perceptibly meaningful as sound. As S'bu Nxumalo noted, anyone can raise a call: "It is only the master orator however that can ignite an unarmed gathering into a response that strikes fear in the hearts of military men. The cry must read the signs of the time. Capture the mood of those gathered and resonate with a response that sets the intended tone of any protest gathering" (2003). While song leadership can be claimed by anyone, that leadership is made powerful only by skillful assessment of and response to the needs of the collective.

Repetition

Repetition underlies the antiphonic pattern of freedom songs (cf. Snead 1981: 150). In Orlando East, as the march proceeded from its point of origin, Sizwe, one of the organizers, ran ahead of the crowd, bullhorn in hand, to lead the march. A police van drove ahead, clearing traffic for the marchers. A few individual police officers lined the road, carrying video cameras and cellphones to record and photograph the marchers. The APF activist who had invited me to the march explained that it was standard police procedure to record the faces of marchers. Ndumiso's concern to strategically conceal his face seemed all the more sensible in light of this revelation. Marshals in orange and neon-green vests held one another's hands to create the front line of the march. The rest of the marchers fell in behind them and began to move. But even with all this action, it was not until Sizwe raised the call—"sithi kudala"—that the march began in earnest. "Kudala sisebenzel' amabhunu," the crowd responded, stepping forward and clapping in time with the song.

Call: Abasebenzi—
Response: 'Basebenzi mas'hlangane.

"For too long have we worked for the whites. Workers, let's unite," the song urged. Just those two repeated melodic phrases—"kudala sisebenzel' amabhunu" and "abasebenzi mas'hlangane"—formed the entirety of the song, a song marchers sustained for almost six minutes.

This kind of repetition, as Chernoff notes, is a shared aesthetic feature in much African-derived music: "In almost all African music there is a dominant point of repetition developed from a dominant conversation with a clearly defined alternation, a swinging back and forth from solo to chorus" (1979: 55).[15] The alternation between lines or "swinging back and forth" between leader call and group response is only one manifestation of repetition. Songs often repeat lines; some songs consist entirely of one repeated refrain. "Senzenina" is one example. "Senzenina?" the leading call queries (What have we done?). The collective response repeats the question, "Senzenina? Senzenina?" The song consists of that one question, repeated over and over again in musical exchange between the leader and a chorus. South Africans ascribe a wealth of meaning to the unceasing repetition. Sibongile Khumalo, for example, interprets its relentlessness as an unsettling incitement to action: "It's like hammering somebody" (in Hirsch 2002). With such unease, she says, "you have no other option but to stand up and go and fight." Repetition, in other words, can serve to amplify feeling.

Repetition is also the bedrock of improvisation. In leading the song at the Orlando East protest, Sizwe varied his leading line while adhering to the established melody. "Amandla," he sang in one instance in place of "kudala." "Amandla wasebenzi" (power of workers), the crowd responded. "Orlando," Sizwe continued. "Orlando, mas'hlangane" (Orlando, let's unite), the crowd urged, concluding the melodic phrase. Many songs, particularly those relying on chants, do not have fixed lyrics; rather, leaders improvise lyrics in the moment with the group providing a responsive refrain. With the assurance of an underlying refrain, a song leader can lyrically, melodically, and rhythmically expand on any theme, as long as it does not disrupt the shared framework. In this way, "a call-and-response sequence may go on for several hours, with apparently monotonous repetition of the same short phrase sung by a leader and answered by the chorus, but in fact subtle variations are going on all the time" (Small 1977: 54–55). This kind of repetition with variation is generative of new commentaries, interpretations, and sentiments.

Repetition with variation enhances the plasticity of song, allowing it to adapt to changing sociopolitical circumstances. As an example of both the generative and evaluative power of song, one protester I interviewed, Khabane from Khutsong, commented on his attempt to introduce a new "slogan" he felt was needed: "It was off of 'dibaka mona, dibaka mona, rebulay'inja' (stop this side, stop that side, we are killing these dogs). It's not good to say you're killing dogs. Basically, I was coming up with a slogan that was 'dibaka mona, dibaka mona, rebulay'icapitalism' (stop this side, stop that side, we are overthrowing capitalism). I was coming up with a slogan like that, but people didn't consider it, I know, because of the sensation—I could hardly hear [the slogan taken up]. Some of the people considered it, but I cannot say that a majority of the people considered it."[16] The song reflects the practice of many apartheid-era protesters, who referred to white opponents as dogs. Khabane thought capitalism a more appropriate target of present ire. In the repeating refrain, he exchanged "inja" ("dog" in isiZulu) for "icapitalism," while maintaining the melodic frame. He had hoped that with repetition, the new slogan would be more widely adopted. But based on what he heard, he concluded there was a dearth of support for his proposition. Nonetheless, his attempt to change the response line exemplifies the ongoing adaptation enabled by patterned antiphony and repetition with variation.

One final aspect of musical repetition relevant to protest relates to its temporal implications. As Christopher Small noted, "A call-and-response sequence may go on for several hours" (1977: 54). Repeating structures mean that a song can be sustained as long as protesters have energy for it. Besides prolonging the singing and heightening emotion, repetition can also be experienced as a liminal suspension of time (1977: 54–55). As it builds emotion and elongates time, repetition lays the foundation for an emotional or rhythmic episode, building to a height of tautness before dissipating, only to be recovered again. As an aesthetic phenomenon of freedom songs, repetition contrasts with a teleological approach to music production (in which a song is expected to progress toward a defined end or final cadence), shifting focus from the teleological push to the ending to the prolongation of shared experience (see Rose 1994). In this way, call-and-response singing feeds a sustained craving for experience that escapes the passage of time.

The suspension of time is also evaluative. The base of support for a song can be aurally assessed through the strength of the responding sound and how long the song is sustained. As Khanyisa noted, "If you start a song badly, people sing one stanza and then someone comes in with another one." Songs rarely end. Rather, they gracefully morph into other songs, dissipate into momentary silence, or are cut short by a shouted "bopha" or "sixteen," which means, as Masekela phrased it, "Stop this fucking song" (in Hirsch 2002).

The suspension of time repetition occasions is also significant for understanding the interplay of history and memory. Certain songs can become associated with past feeling, taking on a meaning that can be particularly individual or can cement a collective bond. Khanyisa's words capture this process: "Sometimes there is one song which, like, everyone just goes mad about, because it was started in a certain way, *it was the right register, you know. It's got the lyrics which hit the thing and it brings back memories, you know*" (italics mine). Khanyisa is describing a phenomenon of resonance, the way a song can ignite a profound response by striking at a point (both vibrationally embodied and cognitive) of maximum amplitude. In such moments, song touches people, evoking memories and associations in a shared immediate encounter that circulates affectively. Repeating songs across events can then become an act of reconstituting previous emotional achievements and aesthetic sensations (Yang 2000; Juris 2008b; Samudra 2008). Jeffrey Juris describes the empowering dimensions of protest as opportunities to live "moments of freedom, liberation, and joy" (2008b: 66). The height of these feelings, encountered in protests, is ordinarily absent from routine interactions and can thus be experienced as personally transformative (Juris 2008b: 66; Routledge and Simons 1995). Song, especially through repetition, provides a way to reach those heights, in the moment and in the memory of past singing.

The transformative significance of these emotionally embodied dynamics helps explain activists' attachments to these songs. Repetition across events becomes a mechanism for revisiting affirming experiences. However, such intensity is not always buoyant. Some protesters have told me that, for them, freedom songs could never be anything but sad, given their painful associations with South Africa's liberation struggle and its postapartheid evolution into community struggles. Despite these painful associations, however, freedom songs did not elicit activists' aversion. Such considerations raise the possibility that repetition works toward a different kind of catharsis by agitating unresolved frictions. Repeated songs, recycled from previous protests and past grievances, pick at scabs. The persistence of old songs that repeat or reenact past experience could represent a refusal of memory where "instead of a dialogue about a history already past, one has a re-staging of the past" (Snead 1981: 150). This confrontation with the past through song is particularly significant when the past remains unresolved, as it is for many in South Africa.[17] Refusing to move on from the past, by restaging memory, could be a response to the changing politics of the present, but it could also stand in the way of mobilization to address more immediate challenges. APF activists' transformation of the song repertoire to address present struggles works to overcome the immobility of memory and redeploy the songs in service of a new generation of protest.

Rhythmic Embodiment

The third structural element of participatory music-making in protests is the rhythmic embodiment of singing. Francis Bebey's aphorism defining African music as "a music that speaks in rhythms that dance" (Bebey 1975 [1969]: 92) epitomizes rhythm as music's connection with the body. More recently, Kofi Agawu described conceptions of rhythm among Northern Ewe in Ghana as indicative of rhythm's entanglement with other embodied processes, including those of "stress, duration, and periodicity.... Rhythm, in other words, is always already connected" (2003: 63; see also Agawu 1995: 5–7).[18]

Singing, like much human action (Farnell 1994, 1999), is an embodied production. It engages the mouth, tongue, vocal cords, sinus and nasal passages, lungs, and indeed the entirety of an individual's physical structure. The sound produced depends very much on the shape and placement of various elements within this bodily structure (Feld et al. 2004: 333–36). Song is further embodied through rhythm—that is, the organization of sound duration and emphasis. Writing on the prominence of rhythm in African vocal music and its intrinsic connectedness with movement, Agawu noted, "There is no song proper without a sense of associated movement" (2003: 94). For many of the activists I worked with, rhythm is how music *moves* them, the way in which music is danced. As Khanyisa put it, "You sing with your mouth and your chest and your lungs, but that is only one part of you, so when you start moving, then the whole of you is involved. . . . Now the song has got you, the song moves you like literally. So even an old man, a granny with a stick, you'll see them swaying."

Movement cannot be separated from song, as one interviewee made clear: "When you listen to music, there's got to be rhythm. When you are dancing, it's got to go with the rhythm. When the rhythm goes this direction, you can't just go that direction."[19] The integration of movement and song serves to unify protesters. Gatsha, a male protester I interviewed, described the phenomenon: "Dancing when we sing creates a rhythm within the space, and people get along with the rhythm, it brings another incitement within the people. The space just becomes more positive with connective energy, having the same aim or objective. So you cannot separate dance from music."[20] Freedom songs, like many African music forms, involve polyrhythmic layering—"the simultaneous use of two or more contrasting rhythms in a musical texture" (Agawu 2003: 79–80; see also Rose 1994: 66); in the same way, an individual's rhythmic perception and enactment can be idiosyncratic even when inflected by communal expectations. Movement serves as a uniting force in song production, as the individual use of the body in stomps, clapping, and guttural punctuation emphasizes established rhythms and creates new ones. The results of individual rhythmic perception and interpretation can be chaos. But the mutual embodiment of a shared rhythm through movement—by clapping, stomping, or swaying together or through shared vocal punctuations or gestures—becomes a resource for entrainment (Black 2011: 10, 2014: 385–87; Clayton et al. 2005).

The Aesthetic Affordances of Musical Structure

The musical elements of antiphony, repetition, and rhythm together constitute a framework through which collective participatory singing unfolds during protests. The sensory exchange of antiphony affords an experience of sequential interrelationship. Repetition with variation sustains collective singing, facilitating a liminal suspension of time (cf. Small 1977: 54–55) during which emotional ripples continually undulate within individuals and across the collective. Finally, rhythm orients the collective and the individuals in it to the music through movement, generating connective energy. As these effects manifest during protest performances, they contribute to an emotional encounter with freedom songs that some describe as an experience of being "stirred up"— "basivusele usinga" in isiZulu.[21]

SINGING DYNAMICS AT PROTEST EVENTS

In our 2010 interview in Orlando East, Ndumiso, who carefully concealed his features during public demonstrations, recounted feeling anxiety before attending protest marches, severe enough that it would paralyze his will to attend. "You'll be scared at the last minute," he told me. "I'll be like here we are, going to this march, but now there are many elements. Are the police going to shoot rubber bullets? What if we get shot? You don't know what they have planned, you're wondering what is going to happen." These concerns were, however, superseded by "this envy [where] you have this feeling that no, I have to be there."

Ndumiso's description exemplifies the affective mediation that many activists confront around protest events. He experienced his body as vulnerable to unforeseeable state violence, creating dread, a fearful aversion to the event. Yet this distancing was countered by an awareness of the potential sensory reward of protest, the knowledge that "once you're there, a whole new world opens to you, somebody is just on you shining a bright light." Songs open the door to this bright new world. As Ndumiso attested, "There's some other energy which we feel going into our marches, going to our meetings, wherever, that's the culture we should never lose of song and dance." Singing drives protesters' energies, producing desirable sensations that Ndumiso did not want to forgo. The desire to experience for himself the intensities of the protest encounter, particularly as facilitated by song, explains Ndumiso's use of *envy* to describe the feeling that "no, I have to be there." Even ahead of the scheduled protest, song already played a critical role, generating an affective pull toward the event.

The sensations of activists during protests, while amplified, were not necessarily pleasant. Ndumiso, concerned for his security, experienced a hyperawareness of the environment: "Your blood boils, you sweat a lot . . . even your heart doesn't beat at the same normal rate, because you don't know what's coming, you can't foresee what's coming. If only you could foresee [what the police have planned]." He interpreted his bodily reactions as indicating the presence of anomalous spiritual elements: "When you invade such spaces, you should be alert at all costs, that here there are other elements playing their role." Perhaps because of the pressing discomfort, song acted as a crucial mitigator—"That's the only thing that will keep you going," Ndumiso noted.

Ndumiso's sensitivity and hyperawareness lend power to his analysis of protest as a battle waged in and ameliorated by song—you can't go to war without song, he had said. His perspective on song as spiritual warfare could be explained by his experiences growing up in the Zion Christian Mission: "When you sing truthfully from the bottom of your heart, there are spirits within you which nobody else can relate to in a way, but then you can feel yourself that no, something is inside me, you know. That's why you find when you go to churches like the one I used to attend when I grew up, the church I grew up in, you find people when the song, the rhythm is going, and the song is going on for long, people faint . . . and stuff like that, because they've just fought a battle." Ndumiso's and others' comparisons of protest singing to religious experiences, including church services, illustrates how freedom songs exist in continuum with other spheres of participatory singing. For Ndumiso and other protesters, protest singing presented a parallel phenomenon to the religious experience, one in which song shored up individual and communal strength, reinforced the motivation to continue, and thereby provided crucial armament for protest. Key to such processes is a sublimation of pain through song.

Interior and Exterior Mediations

A number of APF members describe mobilizing artistic expression to address past hurts. Many activists expressed similar sentiments to those of Ma Patrycja, who described how collective protest singing spoke to her pain, allowing her to expel it: "Let's say you are thinking something, and that thing hurts you. Then if you can start singing, you take all that sorrow out of you. If you are a comrade who have been suffering, struggling under apartheid regime, if we sing sometimes you remember where are you from and where are you now, so you say, 'Yes, I've suffered.'" Ma Patrycja recalled being arrested under apartheid for her activism, being interrogated by state police when her only son went underground to join umKhonto We Sizwe (the military wing of the ANC), not hearing from him or knowing of his condition for five years, traveling alone by foot to Zambia when she finally located him, and enduring the loss of his eventual passing. Freedom songs stirred up these painful memories in affective encounter, but they also strengthened her resolve to stand strong in defiance of the violation wrought by the current ANC regime and its agents. These songs, she noted, "make us happy and they make us strong, even if you can say, 'Here the police are coming!' We don't mind. Instead, we'll be singing more and more, dancing, or if we want to sit down on the road, we sit down."

Presenting another example of the channeling of aesthetic encounter toward activism, a different APF member remarked that singing freedom songs helped sustain her fervor. When her comrades would remark that she was so strong and could sing until the end of an hours-long event, she would respond, "You don't know people, what is inside me." She told me, "By singing these songs, . . . I am healing myself . . . because after I did sing and gather with the comrades, I feel that yes, something have calmed down in my heart, and I can say that now, that is something that have happened within me, so that is why I'm saying the songs are healing me." Like Ma Patrycja, this woman was burdened by loss: She never fully recovered from injuries to her ribs sustained when police officers kicked her during anti-apartheid protests in 1978, and her physical pain was compounded by the loss of her brother, who was beaten to death by soldiers during the protests. Under South Africa's ANC regime, she had lost her son, a twin who was mistaken for his APF-activist brother. He was hanged in 2007, she suspects by the same ANC-aligned agents who had been trying to intimidate her and sabotage the APF. In dealing with these experiences, song, as she phrased it, "calms her heart." She elaborated, "Because you see if something, maybe let me say, you lost someone that you love, then comes people they are singing, then you are singing with them, talking with them, doing things, because after the songs, we sing and sing and laugh. After that, then I feel that something have calmed down for me." This process of sublimation—channeling unresolvable personal pain into shared performances and occasional levity—spurred her on. Caught up in the spirit of what she was doing, she often spent whole days away from home attending to community struggles.

Such profound affective mediation is interior, taking place within the self. Song also offers a conduit to transcend the constraints of individual subjectivities. An elderly female protester I met during a December 2009 march to express solidarity with Abahlali baseMjondolo, a Durban-based shack-dwellers' movement whose members had been targeted and attacked in their homes, described these possibilities. The elder, commenting on her sadness that "now we're fighting against the Black government that we voted for," described how singing became embodied emotional expression. Tapping her chest, she detailed how singing freedom songs enabled her to "feel pain from inside" and "take out the pain," so that even a passerby could "feel the same pain through the songs" and come to know that she was hurt.

This response, and others like it, signals "bodytalk" (Weiss 2002) or "body-based image schemas" (Csordas 1994: 20, n. 2)—the descriptions, metaphors, and metonyms of the body that mediate between physicality and sociality. The elder identified pain as residing within a particular part of her body, but she was not helpless before this occupation; singing enabled her to expose the pain and transmit its exact qualities to those who heard her.[22] Through song, she traversed the isolation of the body in pain (Scarry 1985). Song, in its affective circulation, becomes a vehicle of transcendence that generates intersubjective connections.

The affective circulation of song also establishes the boundaries of collectivity through exclusion, especially of the opposition and observers. Singing, as integrated bodily performance, has historically constituted an embodied, aural, and emotive shield marking a distinction between the collective and its other. In a 2003 reflection, Gillian Slovo, an anti-apartheid activist, highlighted the disparity between the experience of protest from within as a vibrant, joyous collectivity and its external presentation as an intimidating force. She was referring in particular to the toyi-toyi, a shared dance that combines movement from foot to foot, fist pumping, and improvised commentary from a leader that the crowd endorses through repeated assents. Unarmed protesters using this form often intimidated the armed soldiers and riot police charged by the apartheid government with containing the protest.[23] Slovo reflected on her experience of toyi-toyi: "From its centre, [toyi-toyi] is a joyous, collective demonstration of togetherness. What had not occurred to me, however, was what it must have felt like from the outside. The white nation's nightmare—a huge Black crowd, armed only with imitation AKs, voices, and thumping feet, and yet surging forward as if it were they who held the power" (2003). Such anecdotes of anti-apartheid protest highlight the contrasting emotional significances embedded in one social action—the impenetrable joy of togetherness among protesters in contrast to the terror those outside the boundaries of the group experience. The circulation of sound accumulated affective intensity for both participants and bystanders, although the intensity took on different registers, delimiting boundaries around participants.[24]

Similar dynamics persist in contemporary South Africa. One activist articulated this correspondence, noting that singing together as a group "creates its own environment."[25] Like Ndumiso, this interviewee equated protest singing with church services: "Once you get to church, there is a certain atmosphere now, [the churchgoer] is in a different place and he's in a different planet. [Worshippers] are changing. It's because of that consciousness, it's because of that spirit that says now I'm in a different space now. Also with these songs, it's the same thing."[26] Collective singing during protest events "creates its own space" and sets activists, who are within the collective experience, apart from outsiders.[27]

Sonic Armament and Community Stylings

In encounters with authorities, song can serve as an offensive weapon, as the toyi-toyi did. South African writer D. P. Kunene sees the singing of liberation songs as "an act of self-emancipation to be able to confront your oppressor face to face and tell him in uncensored language what you think of him . . . the accusatory 'you' is hurled like a barbed spear at the white oppressor" (Kunene 1986: 46 quoted in Gray 1996: 11). Through the "hurling" of accusation in liberation songs, these songs serve a function similar to that of the stones protesters would sometimes throw at riot police during protests. In this sense, the sonic solidarity of protesters serves to mitigate the harshness of contentious encounters with the police and other opponents: protesters hurl insults at their antagonizers in place of stones.

One body of protest songs addresses the police as primary antagonizers. Lebo, an activist from Protea South in Soweto, discussed his love for one such song, "Asinandaba namaphoyisa, thina sisebusotsheni" (we don't care about the police, we are in the regiment [fighting for our rights]).[28] Lebo was active in the Landless People's Movement (LPM); with his partner and three children, he squatted in a consenting householder's backyard, but he was often subjected to harassment. Recognizing the vulnerability to police violence inherent in his historically entrenched status as a "landless person," Lebo maintained, "What we are experiencing now, it's the real apartheid." His attachment to the song expressed his acute awareness that the police "are the ones who give us problems—most of the problems—when we are taking out our grievances or aims . . . because they are there to protect the very same system that we are fighting." Through the song, he expressed his disgruntlement "when those people are around."

Songs insulting the police and other specific opponents often employed such uncensored vulgarity that many protesters attributed an "age restriction" to them, considering such songs to be culturally inappropriate. Perhaps because they are so steeped in taboo, these songs are a relished and potent part of the protest repertoire. Their blatant vulgarity expresses a freedom from norms of etiquette that is often tempered musically—the sweetest sounds convey the harshest sentiments.

An example of this phenomenon is the song "rona reakena," sung to a sweet melody, which I heard during a standoff with police at the opening match of the 2010 World Cup. The police had created a human wall to keep the APF's modest protest away from a major roadway leading to the stadium, where the protest would gain a greater audience. After the protesters had lambasted the police with songs that admonished them to "voetsek" (fuck off) and decried the police action in speeches, someone in the crowd began the scatological song: "rona reakena / rekena kamasepa / dumelang mmesono yalona." Because I was unfamiliar with seSotho, the sweetness of the melody was the only element of the song available to me. I naively embraced that sense of the song until a friend's translation corrected me. The literal translation, which few interviewees were willing to offer, could be rendered, "We are entering, we are entering through shit, greetings you assholes." In fact, the meaning is apparently even more vulgar. Unable to find the English equivalent for "mmesono yalona," a friend suggested I substitute "asshole." "Asshole is a vulgar word," he said, "but it's much nicer [than the intended concept]."[29]

This incongruence between message and melody featured in many protest songs, particularly during apartheid, when the opponents were mostly white officers unfamiliar with Black vernacular, allowing protesters to get away with very direct subversive statements in song. In this context, song allowed for a certain freedom of expression, for what Vail and White call "licensed criticism" (1991: 41)—"frank and free" expression unhindered by social norms. By framing their insults in song, often with coded lyrics, protesters were able to say much more—and much more directly—than is conventionally sanctioned (cf. Scott 1990).

Shifting beyond the referential functions of language toward the poetic (Jakobson 1960; Bauman 1975), the innovation and suspension of interpretive conventions in protest singing create even more subversive possibilities. The malleability of protest songs is evident in contemporary shifts. Mass demonstrators drew all the more on coded language after South Africa's formal transition from apartheid, when the police officers regulating large gatherings were likely to be Black inhabitants of the same townships the protesters inhabited. Once language was no longer a barrier, subversion had to rely on other linguistic and musical affordances, including coding meaning through melodies and using words whose surface meanings conceal singers' guileful intent. These modes of linguistic play—language taken primarily with itself, with its own forms rather than external contexts—are what theorist Roman Jakobson refers to as the poetic functions of language.

A common quip among the APF protesters illustrates these subversive possibilities in song. In a number of feedback interviews, activists pointed out chanted provocations aimed at the police. One male interviewee who had been an APF organizer expressed his admiration that APF comrades resist police control: "Even if you can send your top policemen, these ones that they say if the state deploys these ones, then there's going to be trouble, [APF comrades] don't give a shit. We do whatever we want and at our own time."[30] Referring to more "humble comrades" from other activist organizations, he noted that APF protesters "are not used to being controlled, we are not used to being told how to fight our struggles, we set the trends for our battles . . . we know that we will not achieve anything trying to be humble comrades, we need to show that fighting spirit." Besides joining with Ndumiso and others in describing protest in martial terms, the interviewee illustrates how some daring provocations of the police are not direct. Pausing the video footage of a recent march he attended, one that was heavily policed, he highlighted one line in the song the protesters were singing, translated as "Look at that monkey, he's carrying a gun." He further explained:

> It's referring to the policemen, and they can hear what we sing but they can't come to us because they are monkeys. That's what we are saying: look at these monkeys, they are carrying guns. If you check, they are the only people with guns, monkeys . . . there's nothing [the police] can do [to retaliate]. . . . Even if [a police officer] wants to fight, he would have to explain why he's fighting. . . . So if they are monkeys, they will have to show us they are monkeys because we are only singing about monkeys, we did not say look at the policemen carrying guns, these policemen are monkeys. We just said look at the monkeys carrying guns.

The lyric uses metaphor as a form of critique, and in doing so it creates a verbal trap for the police. Responding to the insult would indicate that the officers had interpreted the metaphor literally, taking the insult as a direct reference to themselves—a reference protesters deliberately did not make.

Beyond the subversive potential of the language, the incongruence between message and form in many protest songs was perhaps also an intended musical articulation. In introducing one of his songs at a concert in 2010, the late Zimbabwean musician Oliver Mtukudzi discussed how its melodic sweetness defused lyrical tension. Such an impulse may be present in the disjuncture between the melodic features of songs like "rona reakana" and the rawness of the songs' lyrics: euphony can mitigate the friction of undisguised vulgarity or highly charged lyrics that express contempt, anger, frustration, and pain.

Song, then, provides an emotive armament in the form of its affective mediation within individual interiorities and in intersubjective exchange; its sonic delineation of impenetrable collectivity; its creation of a space for direct, charged insults; and its ability to provide musical refuge where raw sentiment is conveyed in sweetened sounds. These emotive mediations offer but one dimension of the creativity with which songs are unleashed during protest events. Gillian Slovo's reflections on the intimidating impenetrability of protest singing suggest that what the uninformed may find inscrutable are in fact elaborations of patterned behavior. Singing together over time, activists create a shared framework that grounds collective action, improvisation, and emotional mediations within the group and in confrontations with opponents. This shared framework provides orientation, so that each protest performance can be created anew based on cultivated expectations. The constitution of community through singing practices is particularly evident when protesters from different areas come together. In these gatherings, familiarity cannot be taken for granted, and each group's unique performance approaches must be negotiated to form a larger collective. Through such encounters, activists learn from one another and adapt the singing practices they experience into their own collective sonic identities.

I witnessed a particularly remarkable instance of such adaptation in Protea South, where I met Lebo. As I was marching with activists clad in red T-shirts exhibiting the symbols and slogans of the LPM, I heard songs layered one over the other in unexpected yet ingenious ways. The connection between songs was thematic, as when "Mama we ma" was brought together with "Nantsi Mellow Yellow." In "Mama we ma," the song leader enumerates sufferings in a lament to a mother figure; for example "we Mama, kuyabanda emjondolo" (Mama, the shacks are freezing). The response to the leader's improvised lines, "Mama we Ma," is similar to a response for "Nantsi mellow yellow," which is simply "we Ma," also addressing the mother. "Nantsi mellow yellow" was a phrase used during apartheid to alert township dwellers to the presence of South African police vehicles, which were called "mellow yellows." LPM members took full advantage of the similarity between the refrains of the songs, alternating the two until they came to sound as one.

Commenting on such practices, Lebo explained that he and his fellow LPM activists "grab" new songs they encounter from other activist collectives and make them their own. They practice in private, trying different approaches to hear what works as a manifestation of their own "style" and "rhythm." With these two words, Lebo articulates his awareness of an audible group character—a collective sonic identity—constructed through the manipulation of musical elements. After successful rehearsal, the transformed songs are presented at marches, meetings, and other public events. By elaborating their own style, LPM members in Protea South evince the febrile creativity that Khanyisa noted is important for collective mobilization; they establish, through sound, their distinct place in the struggle.

Not Letting Her Song Die: Singing and Self-Construction

In accounting for music's political efficacy, it is worth considering that the most significant impact of freedom songs might be on individuals. Just as collective identity is sonically performed, individual identity is constructed through singing as a form of self-expression in which each individual voice is patterned by a unique frequency. This uniqueness is further styled through tonal and embodied rhythmic articulations. In collective protest singing, individuals experience and construct a keenly felt sense of self. Activists express their concerns in an amplified manner; the person becomes more than the contours of their individuality. Describing this heightened embodied experience, some activists I interviewed said they feel *un*like themselves in protest, in that they act in ways they would not otherwise. Others, like Khanyisa, described feeling *more* like themselves. Despite these different interpretations, the experience often becomes one that is immediately identifiable and sought after. Multiple individuals who had been inactive protesters for months, maybe years, spoke in interviews about "getting that feeling again, that feeling of being me" from their first reimmersion into collective protest singing, however brief. A friend who was no longer able to attend protests due to his work at a social movement nongovernmental organization (NGO) once commented on missing this experience as a result of taking on a more administrative role. In casual communication with me on my return from a demonstration that he missed, he lamented, "What are they [his employers] doing to us, keeping us at this desk?" The rhetorical question contrasted his work routine with his desired experience of self in collective protest.

> I'm emotional, but you know when I talk about music, about struggle, I get
> really emotional. It's when I can really be what I am.
>
> —KHANYISA

Individuals often come to claim a particular song as a favorite or become associated with a song because they repeat it across protest events and show concern for how well it is sung. Such identifications endure in life and in death, sometimes becoming compelling commemoration. For instance, Ayize, an activist with the Black lesbian women's organization Forum for the

Empowerment of Women (FEW), raised the favorite song of a murdered friend and fellow activist at every protest she attended. "Nantsi Mellow Yellow" was a song that Ayize could not let die.[31] Were her friend still alive, she would still be singing the song, Ayize reasoned, so her continuation of it furthered her friend's spirit and work. Ayize's efforts recall an insight shared with Frederick Klaits during his fieldwork with an Apostolic congregation in Botswana: "A person's song . . . remains with us as the word dwells in the flesh; when a person is absent or has passed away, his or her song is a memorial (*segopotso*, literally, something that causes 'remembering')" (2010: 69; italics in original).

"IT WILL GO DOWN AS FAR AS YOUR OWN STRENGTH": SINGING APF'S DECLINING YEARS

In all life-forms, dying is a complex journey that can sometimes entail height-ened vitality. A terminally ill individual sometimes experiences a period of energetic flourishing before death. Hospice caregivers call this "rallying." Re-latedly, some plants are monocarpic—their flowering triggers changes within the plants that cause its death. These organic models suggest a trajectory for the APF, itself an organic form, between its moments of heightened connec-tion and the underlying ruptures that signaled its imminent end. Even amid organizational decline, whenever APF members gathered in sung protest, they experienced moments of efflorescence. That APF members experienced such depth of feeling, which momentarily made them effervescent despite organ-izational rupture and downturn, is a testament to the power and relevance of freedom songs in all stages of shared struggle, including in moments of decline.

Because songs offer vocal and aural recollections of life, they are critical barometers of the ebb and flow of collective struggle. The APF's decline could be heard in its performances; as the collective aged, its songs more and more recalled earlier years of vigor. These recollections did not come without pain. During my November 2010 interview with Khanyisa, we discussed the song "That's Why I'm a Socialist." The song had the following lyrics:

> My mother was a kitchen girl
> My father was a garden boy
> That's why I'm a socialist
> I'm a socialist
> I'm a socialist.

Khanyisa asserted that the song was popular because it was identity affirming. "Now that song, I think the reason it's popular," he said, "it's got a nice theme with it, a nice call and response but it's an identity-forming song or an identity-affirming song. It says, 'We are the Socialists.' Yes, that's what we are but we are not the poor, you know, 'We are . . .'" For Khanyisa, the significance of the song was its affirmation of an identity beyond classifications of poverty in the context of specific historical circumstances to which many could relate. Many activists, including Khanyisa, had either themselves been or had parents who had been "garden boys" and "kitchen girls."

That connection was strong for Khanyisa. As he was offering his interpretation, he had visible and audible physical responses. His eyes watered, his voice thickened with such emotion he could no longer continue speaking. Following a protective impulse, I offered to stop the interview, but Khanyisa preferred to continue rather than break the moment to regain his composure. I asked why Khanyisa was emotional. His answer spoke not only to the history portrayed by the song but also to the APF's history: "It's because we're missing that," he responded. "It's gone you know, or it's going. But it will come back," he offered, as if to reassure himself.

Tears are useful sites of analysis in arguing for an embodied epistemology. Khanyisa's tearful response can be understood in light of his insistence that song served as a measure of activist engagement. His evaluation of the connection between a song and its singers—that the singers must be moved enough to produce spirited sounds—indicates the broader context of his concern about the apathy in the APF. The potency of identification Khanyisa had perceived in past renditions of "That's Why I'm a Socialist" was particularly significant because song served as a barometer of the struggle. That potency and resonance was missing, he sensed, in more recent times. As a long-term activist who had been involved in community movements since the apartheid era, someone who developed his sense of self in the struggle, the absence of resonance was deeply upsetting because it signaled the decline of collective mobilization with direct personal effects. "The struggle is not a straightforward thing you know," he continued: "So it's got its ups and downs, so sometimes when it goes down, it will go down as far as your own strength. So when you're weak it goes really down . . . and also now it's even more obvious that the social movements are declining because everyone else is fighting, you know like protests, strikes, but we, we're just quiet, so that means we're out of it." The decline in the APF's external visibility, as the organization's energies were absorbed in internal struggles, affected its members profoundly. The strength of the struggle was identified with the strength of its constituents, a further elaboration of the identification between self and struggle that occurs in activism. As Khanyisa revealed, such processes of identification are critically elaborated through song. An absence of feeling in renditions of much-loved and much-shared songs can cause profound sadness and disquiet.

Despite the APF's decline, the movement lingers on through its songs, particularly as the struggles it galvanized during its years of activity have been taken up in subsequent mobilizations. Indeed, one of the APF's many adapted songs warns, "APF ayilalanga / ayilala iguqe ngamadolo" (APF is not sleeping, it is merely genuflecting [in prayer and solemn reflection]). In the latter months of 2015, South Africa was engulfed by protests. Demonstrations among university students, including at Wits, against the outsourcing of labor and the increase of tuition fees declared that #FeesMustFall. Communities rallying in solidarity with the students insisted that #ThePriceOfBreadMustFall. This convergence of worker, student, and community struggles recalled the constellation of the APF's emergence more than a decade earlier, suggesting that the genuflecting figure had perhaps risen again in a different guise.

Apartheid-era protest singers recognized freedom songs as a legacy to be passed on for use in an actively unfolding future. In 1990, at the Smithsonian Folklife Festival in Washington, DC, Nenze, an anti-apartheid activist, explained how South African freedom songs evolved from past practices and were bequeathed to the future as blueprints for a robust cultural sphere: "People tend to think that when they look at South Africa, for instance, where we sing songs of struggle, songs of apartheid, that that is the only way song will always be. [But] we are not going to be static and live today the way of oppression and exploitation. I think in the process of struggle we are also creating a new South Africa and in that new South Africa, we are also creating an aesthetic of the future."[32] Nenze recognized in 1990, as apartheid was beginning to unravel, that the songs that gave voice to South Africans' oppression and exploitation would remain relevant, not as relics of the past but as aesthetic offerings that would be sustained even after the advent of the freedom activists had sought for so long. She spoke with the assurance that freedom songs would maintain their aesthetic form, offering distinctly South African sounds even as their substance changed "to indicate the context in which people are living at a particular time and moment."

Contemporary activists have heartily received and built on this legacy, particularly as, contrary to Nenze's expectations, South Africans' struggles did not end. The words of Ayize, who would not let her friend's favorite song die with her, provides a pertinent example of the perceived legacy of protest songs among contemporary activists. She sees in her forebears' songs a platform that can be adapted to the current moment: "It's our great-grandmothers who made that song and made that platform to use it in the future. Because can you imagine we are using it now." These are the songs Ayize learned at her grand-mother's feet, and these are the songs she and others are adapting to shifting postapartheid challenges. Their plasticity, enabled by musical characteristics of antiphony, repetition, and rhythmic embodiment, provides the bedrock for melodic, rhythmic, and lyrical improvisation that generates new commentaries, interpretations, and sentiments. As a result of the familiar framework they provide, protest performances can be continually created anew based on cultivated expectations; this is freedom sung.

NOTES

1. Interview with the author, November 9, 2010, Johannesburg.

2. The case I present provides an alternative perspective to Shana Redmond's portrayal of protest anthems as "reformed and tamed in the postdemocracy moment in South Africa" (2014: 20). Marginality and political exclusion remain a critical analytic for the salience and efficacy of liberation music, as freedom songs continue to foreground counter- and transnational pathways of belonging and collective formation that, as Redmond herself notes, remix "the modalities of the state in order to foster alternative exercises and experiences of freedom and justice" (2014: 4).

3. In an interview featured in the documentary film *Amandla!* (Hirsch 2002), Masekela noted, "I think part of the reason why we lost the country to a certain extent is that before we attacked the enemy, we'd sing and then they'd know where we are. You know, I don't know if you ever saw the movie *Zulu*, and there are the Zulus all over these mountains you know, and like at dawn they sang so beautifully. There were a few British guys but they said, 'Before we hit them, let's let them finish this song; it's a nice song.' You know what I mean?"

4. Interview with the author, June 7, 2007, Cape Town. All quotes from Fatimah Dike in this chapter are from this interview.

5. Vuyisile Mini (1920–1964) was a South African trade-unionist often tagged as the father of freedom songs. He was arrested and hanged by the apartheid regime. Purportedly, he went to the gallows singing the song he is now well known for, "nants' indod' emnyama, Verwoerd" (here comes the Black man, Verwoerd).

6. Reuban Tholakele Caluza (1895–1966) was a South African composer who trained and taught at the Ohlange Institute, a private college outside Durban.

7. Interview with the author, January 22, 2010, Johannesburg. All quotes from Ndumiso in this chapter are from this interview.

8. Interview with the author, November 14, 2010, Johannesburg. All quotes attributed to Khanyisa in this chapter are from this interview.

9. *Conscientize* is a frequently used term in Latin American and South African activist circles. It refers to the act of making someone more aware of social and political conditions and, in that way, preparing that person to challenge observable injustices and inequities.

10. Interview with the author, November 15, 2010, Johannesburg. All quotes attributed to Vuyiswa in the chapter are from this interview.

11. The persuasiveness and effectiveness of lyrics in conveying contentious messages are increasingly the subject of debate (Roy 2010: 13). Lyrics, however, are more accessible to scriptocentric modes of analysis and knowledge production.

12. Regarding the intrinsic correspondence between musical structure and social dynamics, M. Xulu noted, "Sound directions serve not only an abstract aesthetic musical purpose, but they also serve a concrete social purpose. The rise and fall of a melody is not only an aesthetic occurrence to be admired on its own, but it is more a social realisation of specific ideals" (Xulu 1994: 97). I similarly argue that song serves a sociopolitical purpose that is not just expressed through lyrics but cultivated in the structure of the music itself.

13. I am grateful to Ysaye Maria Barnwell for this insight.

14. Interview with the author, May 11, 2009.

15. African musical practices do not constitute a monolithic phenomenon, although early scholarship tended to uncritically generalize features as representative across the continent, a phenomenon Kofi Agawu terms *unanimism* (Agawu 2003: 58–62). Uninterrogated unanimism and a concern with African difference underpins racially essentializing concepts of, for instance, "African rhythm" (Agawu 2003: 55–96; see also Burdick 2013: 23–24). The designation of "African music" is not to be completely discarded, however. Critical analysis of music originating in African communities is needed all the more in confronting the politics of knowledge production, the ethics of representation, and the incongruities of postcolonial lived experiences (Waterman 1991; Falola and Fleming 2012; Erlmann 1996).

16. Interview with the author, May 26, 2010.

17. In her analysis of South Africa's Truth and Reconciliation Commission (TRC), a forum with a legal mandate to effect South Africans' reconciliation with and transition from the atrocities of apartheid, Catherine Cole discusses the continuing unwieldiness of the past, noting that years after the culmination of the TRC's work, "the past in South Africa still requires 'dealing' in the present continuous sense"; history, she asserts, remains "a site of unresolved trauma," despite the aspirations of reparative resolution embedded in the TRC's mandate (2010: 121).

18. Aiming to capture the synesthetically integrated nature of vocal musical expression suggested here, Coplan proposed the term *auriture* "to represent

vocal art in which verbal text, sonic qualities, and rhythm are interdependent expressive resources" (1991: 190, n. 1).

19. Interview with the author, January 22, 2010, Johannesburg.

20. Ibid.

21. Innocentia Mhlambi, personal communication, May 2015.

22. South African narratives are pervaded by an emotional ideology regarding the necessity of expelling pain from the individual body. This idea was evident particularly among the female activists I worked with, who saw the harboring of sorrow, anxiety, and pain as particularly destructive to physical health. This phenomenon is further exemplified in Cole's interview with Nomonde Calata, the wife of a murdered anti-apartheid activist, whose wailing cry during her testimony before the TRC has become iconic as the defining sound of the commission. When asked about her response to this association, Calata explained that she screamed in that moment of her testimony "because I wanted the pain to come out. I was tired of keeping it inside me" (2010: 79–80). In her scream, she sought a similar transmission as the female elder, for people to "feel as I felt that day" (2010: 79).

23. In the documentary *Amandla!*, a group of white apartheid-era riot police officers discussed how terrifying the toyi-toyi was, particularly for young recruits, who had to be exhorted to stand their ground when confronted with the surging crowds.

24. Sara Ahmed discusses how affective value accumulates and intensifies; passion is therefore "that which is accumulated over time" (2004: 120). She notes that affect is not a positive feature of objects or persons but rather something that moves through them and accumulates value in that movement. In this economy of affect, "feelings appear in objects, or indeed as objects with a life of their own, only by the concealment of how they are shaped by histories, including histories of production (labor and labor time), as well as circulation or exchange" (2004: 120–21).

25. Interview with the author, November 18, 2010, Johannesburg.

26. Ibid.

27. Reflecting on this phenomenon in the context of the US civil rights movement, Bernice Johnson Reagon noted that as long as activists were singing together, "they [police officers] cannot change the air in that space, the song will maintain the air as your territory." This clip is available at http://vimeo.com /43608959 [03:17].

28. Interview with the author, April 30, 2010.

29. Interview with the author, June 2, 2010. Subsequent quotations in the paragraph are from this interview.

30. Interview with the author, November 18, 2010. Subsequent quotations in the paragraph are from this interview.

31. Interview with the author, May 27, 2010, Johannesburg. All quotes attributed to Ayize in this chapter are from this interview.

32. Archived festival recording of the "Struggle Narrative Stage: Music as an Educational Tool," July 4, 1990, Washington, DC; housed at Smithsonian Folklife Archives, reference: FP-1990-CT-0133. The subsequent quote from Nenze in this paragraph is also from this recording.

ACTIVIST PORTRAIT
Lebo

LEBO WAS ACTIVE IN THE Zabalaza Anarchist Communist Front, an affiliate of the Anti-Privatisation Forum (APF), although he did not consider himself an APF member, a self-attribution indicative of the complexities of individual alignment within the APF's structure. Zabalaza was among the political groupings that maintained APF affiliation even after the organization shifted to emphasizing community affiliates. The APF did not have an active community affiliate where Lebo lived, in an informal settlement in Protea South, Soweto. The Landless People's Movement, which was active in his location, attracted his political involvement because it sought to address the daily hardships he faced as a shack dweller. The unemployed thirty-one-year-old and his wife earned money to support themselves and their three young children (three, five, and eight years old) by doing hair—he was a loctician and she was a braider. They also kept a vegetable garden to ease the family's food insecurity.

A SMALL MORTUARY

Lebo had not always lived in a shack. He and his mother moved to the Free State in South Africa from Lesotho after his parents had a falling out. From the Free State, they moved to Pretoria, then Lebo and his mother eventually came to Moletsane in Johannesburg in 2000 to live with his aunt, his mother's elder sister. His father passed away in 1996.

Lebo dropped out of school in the eleventh grade because he was having problems at home. His aunt expected him to contribute more financially. "Life was starting to be difficult," he explained, "and I had to now see [how] to make myself get through it so I had to drop out and try to see how to make money in order to survive." He attended a catering school in 2002 and started working as a bartender, waiter, and chef's assistant in the hotel industry, primarily in the affluent suburbs of Sandton. In 2003, his aunt kicked him out of the house, so he rented a garage nearby, paying R300 a month. After he lost his job, he moved in with a friend in Berea, but even there, things were tough. From Berea, he moved to Dobsonville; in the intervening years, he married and became a father. From Dobsonville, he moved his family to their current residence in Protea South.

After Lebo lost his job in the hotel industry, he sometimes struggled to get food for the kids. The comparison between his current conditions and his time with his aunt was stark. In Protea South, "we don't have taps, we don't have electricity, we don't have roads like proper roads, even toilets as well." His life with his aunt differed strikingly:

> I wasn't living in a shack, I wasn't using fire to cook. . . . Electricity is there, you are able to buy things that you are short of. . . . You can't buy a fridge in a shack because you don't have electricity, but if you are in a house with electricity, you are able to buy your own things, so that when you pass away then your kids are able to take over those things, and also maybe you are able to get some new items for their kids and growing. In a shack, it's tough. During winter, it's like you are [living] in a fridge. Actually, it's like you are in a mortuary, I take it as a mortuary. [A shack] is a small mortuary.

Lebo's comment captures how the impact of displacement accumulates over generations, with parents unable to establish a cycle of inheritance for their children. Even in the present, the shacks offered inadequate shelter, leaving their inhabitants exposed to the weather. In winter, ice accumulated on the roof, "and when the sun comes it's like you are outside, it's raining inside the house when it defrosts."

Following service delivery protests in his community in 2007, Lebo attended a meeting of the Landless People's Movement (LPM). In the organization, he found a leader who valued his insights, a movement that was receptive to his ideas, and a community that focused on issues that affected him, including education and employment. Lebo noted that African National Congress (ANC) councilors often favored members of the party over others when it came to housing allocation and job offerings on paid projects. When he attended community meetings with the councilor, Protea South was never represented among the councilor's concerns. The LPM, by contrast, focused its mobilization on Protea South. The organization received support from the APF in making pamphlets and posters for marches and was part of a broader network of activist organizations in Johannesburg and across South Africa.

Although Lebo was an active participant in the LPM, his political ideology differed fundamentally from many other participants; specifically, he profoundly distrusted government structures. That difference alienated him; he would skip LPM meetings when local government elections were on the agenda because when he discussed his views, "it's like I cause chaos." In the Zabalaza Anarchist Communist Front, Lebo connected with like-minded individuals who shared his anarchist ideology. Zabalaza met every fortnight as a reading group, and its members rotated roles. One person might be the secretary at one meeting, and someone else would take that role at the next meeting. This system worked for Lebo because it enabled him to receive broad-based leadership training: "Because, for instance, maybe I don't go to school for being a secretary or what, I don't know how to file things, I don't know how to do these things, but with Zabalaza I do get that education for free. . . . We believe that for people to have a certain knowledge, they don't have to pay. Everything should go equally." Zabalaza supported the LPM and other organizations and would often work in solidarity with them. For Lebo, affiliation with both the LPM and Zabalaza meant he had two activist communities he could appeal to in moments of need. Given the precarity of his life and his visibility as an activist, that support was much needed. His activism led to his being targeted by owners of bond houses in the area who were displeased about informal electricity connections and worried that the presence of the informal settlement depreciated the value of their homes. Such tensions would not come to a head for Lebo until May 2010, but they simmered under the surface.

"SOME SONGS NEED YOU TO DEMONSTRATE"

In July 2009, the LPM won a court order preventing the city of Johannesburg from evicting activists and others residing in the Protea South informal settlement of Doornkop. The averted relocation would have further cut the residents off from transportation, education, and employment options. The court directed the city to provide housing, electricity, and other basic services in Protea South, where the activists were living, instead of removing them. I was invited to a celebration of the interdiction in November 2009. The celebration began at LPM headquarters, a hall constructed of corrugated iron painted red; a red flag waved on its roof, bearing the acronym of the movement. In the lull as we waited for comrades to gather on a Sunday morning—activists were expected from as far as Benoni, about forty-five miles away—one of the male comrades got too familiar with me. When confronted with my stiffness, he explained that he was already intoxicated: "All right, I'm drunk," he said, adding as justification, "It's a celebration."

On the arrival of the activists from Benoni, one of the comrades, Kungawo, invited me to walk over to the bus stop to meet them. Kungawo probably felt responsible for me because I was not participating in the mirthful imbibing that had already begun. He checked on me throughout the day, making sure I was all right, and introduced me to movement leaders, including the LPM's lawyer. As we walked to Protea Gardens mall to pick up the Benoni activists, Kungawo and I had a stretch of time to talk without interruption. He told me he was the second of five boys.

"You all must have been quite a handful for your poor mother," I teasingly remarked.

His response was surprisingly solemn. "Boys are not as much trouble for mothers as girls," he said. "There's a problem in Protea South with school-age pregnancy, and people know our high school has the highest rate of school pregnancy in Soweto. The girls in Protea are not serious." He then went on to explain that there were also issues with rape. He gave the example of hearing a young woman screaming and not knowing what to do. "If you're a mother, you consider that it could be your own child, yet if you go to that person's rescue, you're in trouble with the rapist." In his quiet reserve and the seriousness with which he carried himself, I sensed that this was a sadness that weighed on him.

On our return to the LPM hall, the contrast between the festivity of the day and the gravity of my conversation with Kungawo lingered. But the day proceeded nonetheless. As more people gathered, comrades retrieved the LPM's banner from the hall as well as two additional flags and arranged themselves in marching formation. Those holding the banner made up the front line, and the others fell in behind them. After posing so I could take a few snapshots, the group of about fifty comrades proceeded, singing.

"Dubula, dubula," began a male comrade in khaki pants and a denim hat who was positioned toward the back of the march.

"Dubula, dubula, dubula," the others responded, clapping along and marching forward at a slow pace. One man raised his fist and offered some vocal accents, laying a quicker tempo over the foundation set by the song. His contribution momentarily heightened the sonic and kinetic experience before the energy dissipated. But something had shifted. It was as if he had roused the song from slumber. The song's foundational tempo did not change, but the man had highlighted the potential to fill in its gaps and draw out different rhythms. Suddenly, the slowness was not tedious but the basis for further exploration. Others began to offer different accents, both kinetic and sonic. Those marching in line with the song leader momentarily changed the manner and rhythm of their stomp, landing kicks on the offbeat, as one of them punctuated the song with staccato "oh"s. Intermittently, that line of people employed kicks to accent the song, which switched leaders as this exploration unfolded. The new leader called out "Ja! Ja! Ja! Ja!" in staccato, and that call prompted kinetic response down the rest of the line, with kicks that became fuller and more defined with each iteration, while the rest of the group maintained the song and the steady pace.

As the march proceeded, others joined along the way. Norman, a tall, thin man with his full hair covered by a cap, joined the front line. Standing between two members who were holding the banner, he also carried a knobkerrie. The knobbed stick became an extension of his body; he held it up in full pronounce- ment at the head of the march. When a chant died, leaving a quiet interval in its wake, Norman started a song, "thina senza nje." A young woman behind him began a different song, "Sinyova sinyova." Norman, however, was unrelenting in this sonic conflict. He maintained his song choice while holding out the knobkerrie to lightly reprimand the young woman behind him and assert his authority. She laughed off the bullishness but did not continue her choice of song. His assertiveness won out, and the crowd picked up his song with the response, "thina senja nje, masizabalaza, thina senza nje" (we do things in this way, let us struggle, we do things in this way).

Lebo would later elaborate that songs like "thina senza nje" call for demon- stration. Since its lyrics specify a particular way of action, whoever proposes the song should also have an accompanying gesture that demonstrates what exactly "we do."

> Thina senzanje
> Thina senzanje
> Masizabalaza,
> Thina senzanje.
> Asideleli siyashaya,
> Thina senzanje
> Masizabalaza
> Thina senzanje

As others joined the group, another knobkerrie appeared among them, al- though the person wielding this second knobkerrie did not do so as insistently as Norman had. Behind the second knobkerrie, one of the marchers carried a stick; another carried a broom. "Some songs need you to demonstrate," Lebo explained. Knobkerries, sticks, and brooms satisfied an impulse to extend the body's gestures and recruit the material environment into the articulation of a song.

These objects were also meant to perform power. The demonstration peaked when a car met the marchers on the red dirt road. With Norman at the head, wielding his knobkerrie, and the group as energized as it was, the march refused to give way to the car. A standoff developed, until Norman stepped onto the hood of the car and ran across its top, jumping off at the other side. "Suka, man!" A male voice shouted, urging the driver to move. The driver acceded to the group and reversed away, clearing the road for the marchers, who continued through the red dirt roads of the informal settlement to the school hall for the planned program of celebration.

Lebo was among the marchers that Sunday in November, and we would meet at other activist events as the months passed.

"OUR LIVES CANNOT DEPEND ON FOOD PARCELS"

Around 8:00 one Sunday evening in May 2010, as Lebo and his partner were preparing to sleep, they heard loud banging against their door. "Vula! Sifuna indoda!" (Open! We want the man!), one of the knockers shouted. Unsure who was at his door or why they wanted him, Lebo hid, and his partner opened the door to find that five men—three armed with guns, one with a machete, and one with a hoe—had jumped the fence to their yard. They pushed past her to search the shack with a torch. When they found only the couple's small children, sleeping on the bed, they roughed up Lebo's wife and declared they would be back.

While the men were knocking on Lebo's door, one of the neighbors came out to investigate the noise. After the men left, the neighbor harbored the family in his home in case the men returned, and he lent them his phone. Lebo and his wife reached out to their comrades in Zabalaza for support and solidarity.

The armed men continued around the settlement, intimidating and attacking others. One resident was shot and killed, and some were wounded. The police did not arrive until around midnight.

Lebo and other members of the Landless People's Movement believed they were targeted for attack by some inhabitants of bond houses in Protea South, in an attempt to run them out of the informal settlement. A number of bond-house inhabitants were displeased about the devaluation of their homes due to the informal settlement and by shack dwellers' informal electricity connections, which raised electricity costs for the bond-house inhabitants. These connections had increased in the lead-up to the World Cup, and tension remained heightened in the subsequent weeks. During a community radio program on Kaya FM focused on the situation in Protea South in June, a bond owner phoned in to vent her complaints: "When Protea South was established, there were no shacks here. . . . And [the shack dwellers] have been offered to be moved but they won't move. We are trying to get the government to buy our houses because we can't sell them otherwise. It's not fair that our bills are increased [due to unofficial electricity connections]. You pay and you pay and what do you get for that?" Protea South was also the subject of much discussion at a community workshop I attended earlier in the month. The workshop, which was held on a Saturday at the University of Johannesburg, began with a report on struggles across communities. The chair of the workshop shared that two people had died in Protea South and a funeral for one of them had been held the preceding Thursday.

"We have said that people must help themselves, in fact, help the government in its task to provide free electricity and basic services. Now the bond payers have a problem with this," the chair said.

"As social movements, we have to talk about how we can fight state repression," a comrade from Soweto Electricity Crisis Committee (SECC) offered in response. "There is a deployment of the government who send officials to infiltrate and disrupt movements. These officials can then point out the leaders of social movements, they call it 'operation crackdown,' because if they arrest our leaders now, others will scatter."

When one of the APF's part-time organizers proposed a march to highlight these concerns, another comrade, a woman from the SECC, responded that even more than a march, "we need to educate people about councilors and the strategies they use, for example providing food parcels and blankets [during election season]. They target the poorer of the poorest and gogos [grandmothers] who will then say councilors are working" rather than seeing through the diversion.

The chair fully agreed: "Our lives cannot depend on food parcels," he said, "or on blankets, but on our power. When we educate people, people will be the one to defend you. That is why you find out that LPM is dead. It's because people were bought for money." He felt that divisions between bond owners and shack dwellers had been stoked by state agents through diversionary tactics, which placed individual financial self-interest ahead of any recognition of shared exposure and vulnerability to an exploitative political economic system that stripped many of their dignity. By drawing people's awareness to the common issues they faced through education, these divisions would be eradicated. At least that was the vision.

A week after the community workshop, a contingent of people living in bond houses marched to Eskom, the electricity parastatal, to demand that power be restored to their homes. LPM comrades and other shack dwellers had not been invited—for Lebo, a glaring exclusion. He was aware that shack dwellers and those in bond houses shared a vulnerability to the ravages of South Africa's neoliberal turn. "Those living in the bond houses are also the victims of the capitalist system" he noted. "All of us are facing issues of poor service delivery, exploitation, oppression, and poverty. Fighting each other will not solve these problems. All we are doing is squabbling for the breadcrumbs that fall off the table where the bosses and rulers are having a feast."

Similar conflicts and ruptures were evident in the APF's internal meetings. As I discuss in the next chapter, APF activists were not unified in confronting a common external enemy. Some could not see past their self-interest; their participation in the social movement was an avenue for personal gain that they pursued without consideration for their fellow comrades. Due to this and other dynamics, a combative atmosphere of suspicion and one-upmanship eroded the ethical activist community that the APF had sought to foster.

FOUR

—ᴍ—

RUPTURES

ON JUNE 11, 2010, THE opening day of the nineteenth FIFA World Cup in Johannesburg, South Africa, members of the Anti-Privatisation Forum (APF) planned a mass rally to protest the opulence of the event. The APF activists claimed that the World Cup benefited political and corporate elites at the expense of impoverished South Africans, including themselves. The rally they planned would, in their vision, disrupt the opening match, leverage international media presence, and draw attention to their struggles. In early planning, the APF intended for ten thousand protesters to march up to the First National Bank Stadium in Soweto, where the opening game was to take place. This number was later reduced to five thousand protesters during a series of meetings to negotiate march logistics with the South African Police Service, in accord with the procedures laid out in the Regulation of Gatherings Act.

On the day of the march, however, fewer than fifty people had gathered by 11:30 a.m., when the march was to have concluded. Roadblocks and traffic prevented many protesters from arriving at the designated gathering point, including those on nine of twelve hired buses. In spite of the diminished numbers, however, the group included a diverse set of individuals: APF activists from Soweto, Central Johannesburg, and Tshwane (Pretoria); students from Wits University; and members of allied organizations such as the Zabalaza Anarchist Communist Front (an APF affiliate), the Landless People's Movement, and the One Voice of All Hawkers Association.[1] A researcher from the Netherlands, a documentary film crew from the United States, and this anthropologist were all there to document the event.

The organizers were unsure how to proceed in the face of such low numbers. One organizer wanted to issue a statement that because the buses were stuck in traffic, the number of people gathered "would not make an impact" and the march could not go on. Another organizer wanted to have the march, deliver the memorandum of grievances anyway, and still make the statement that the march did not have many people because the buses were stuck in traffic.

In the lull while the organizers were absorbed in decision-making, the activists constituted themselves through song and dance. Some toyi-toyied to the APF's CD compilation of freedom songs, *Songs of the Working Class, Vol. 1*, which blasted from a pair of large speakers propped up on the bed of a truck. One of the songs was "isibhamu into yami" (the gun is my thing). Matt and Wesley, two members of the Immortal Art Group, a youth performance troupe from Quagga Estates in Tshwane, danced next to each other, jumping from foot to foot with synchronized flair. Moving in proximity, they urged each other to bolder expression. Those gathered around them swayed and offered their own grooves in response to the song. Suddenly, the music was cut off, interrupting the shared moment. Belying the timidity of her earlier activist years, Kanelo grabbed the microphone and started singing the song's leading line, perhaps to prolong the moment beyond its rupture. Before she could complete the line, the speakers offered a different song from the CD, "We Nyamazane (Yiyo Ehlal' Ehlathini)," which refers to "an animal residing in the forest." The group quickly found its bearings with the new song and resumed its toyi-toyi–inspired grooves.

To begin the day's proceedings, Boipelo, the organizer who had initially wanted to cancel the march, asked those present to gather. He requested that someone lead a song.[2] A young man who appeared to be in his late twenties, wearing a baseball cap and sweatshirt, began the song "Eli Lizwe logogo bethu, sizabalaza eli lizwe" (this country belongs to our grandmothers, we are fighting for the country of our grandparents). After a few songs, Kanelo asked speakers from organizations other than the APF to offer comments and support for the protest. As these speakers were coming to the stage, the police—who had been driving by the meeting point all morning—stopped. One officer asked Joseph, an APF office bearer, for a private conversation. Other organizers joined them. After that consultation, Boipelo came to the microphone and announced that the police wanted the march to begin, and so the group would stage a "symbolic march" up to the intersection of the main road, which was around the corner. As was typical for such marches, the group proceeded, singing, and danced forward, with Kanelo leading the frontline. At the main road, however, the police stood in a line, blocking the marchers from going farther. Activists' speeches and songs followed, addressing the standoff. But the march eventually dispersed, leaving the protest's organizers with the bitter taste of disappointment and unfulfilled visions.

Even allowing for the numbers lost when the buses could not make it to the venue, five thousand protesters had clearly been an ambitious goal. Yet, there were moments in the APF's history when such turnouts were exceeded without difficulty, including in 2002, when the APF mobilized more than twenty thousand protesters to target the World Summit on Sustainable Development convened by the United Nations in Johannesburg. This march, among the organization's first mass rallies, demonstrated the extent of public support the still-young organization could summon. By 2010, however, such numbers were not assured; the World Cup march with its low participation highlighted the diminished reach of the APF in Johannesburg.

From a theatrical perspective, public-facing endeavors like the World Cup march constitute the APF's front stage, with the backstage consisting of internal activities among APF organizers and general members.[3] With intensifying disappointment at the APF's front-stage showings, the organization's backstage was rife with discontent. In meetings, members often expressed frustration with the APF's decline; the feeling that the organization had passed its glory days was pervasive. Some activists hoped that the collective spirit could be recaptured, while others were more cynical. This chapter addresses the APF's backstage dynamics in consideration of members' frustration, disappointment, and perceptions of failure prompted by the organization's front-stage decline. My concern with the APF's backstage is an elaboration of performance as it manifests through everyday interactions, and how these quotidian exchanges contribute to and—even more so, as described in this chapter—undermine collective goals. Although the APF's falling short of its goals, for instance with the World Cup march, can readily be interpreted as failure or a lack of performance (in the evaluative sense), this chapter furthers an alternative argument: performance happens in the breaks—in the ruptures that conflict occasions, and in the gaps between idealized intentions and disappointing outcomes.

The disappointing World Cup march was not the only sign that the APF was losing its visibility and front-stage effectiveness. One activist's comments during a meeting I attended in October 2009 exemplified the unease many members expressed about the APF's loss of relevance: "We could spend the next seven months talking amongst ourselves while struggle happens elsewhere. We need to get back to struggle. This country is on fire right now and where is the APF? Nowhere."

The activist was referring to a recent wave of what the South African media had problematically dubbed "service delivery protests"[4] that marked a shift from large, centralized disruptions to local insurrection. Service delivery protests tended to be community-based—taking place in low-income

settlements—and to occur outside the purview of social movement organizations. The emergence of these community protests across the nation is trace-
able to an incident in 2004 in Intabazwe Township in the Free State province,
during which a seventeen-year-old student, Teboho Mkhonza, was injured and
subsequently died due to police efforts to quell protesters' attempted blockade
of a national highway. The protest was an expression of community dissatis-
faction with local government—including the flight of industry from the area,
which fueled unemployment, inadequate provision of water and electricity,
and bitterness over the development of an adjacent town, Qwa Qwa, that was
perceived to be at Intabazwe's expense. As later investigation revealed, police
fired into the crowd of youth protesters and continued to fire at their backs
even as they fled for cover. At least twenty young demonstrators were shot and
hospitalized; only Teboho did not survive. Protesters were arrested and battled
charges of public violence that took years to resolve, but no one was charged in
Teboho's death. The tragedy at Intabazwe "marked the start of a rise in direct
and antagonistic action to convey messages of discontent with matters local"
(Booysen 2007: 24; see also Booysen 2009; Alexander 2010). Similar protests
against untenable local conditions arose in other Free State towns and snow-
balled across the nation.

As impoverished communities learned through media coverage of protests
in Intabazwe and other locations, they plotted their own revolts, hoping for similar results—including visits from municipal officials and national ministers
that would elicit government commitments to improve their locations. These
protests often emerged following trigger events, were responsive to disruptions
in adjacent areas, and were typically viewed as spontaneous (due to nearsighted
and short-term media coverage that overlooked the local organizing underpinning the revolts). Over time, media coverage of the protests dwindled. The
early waves of protest in 2004 and 2005 were covered extensively, but later
coverage focused on major disruptive actions (for example, the blockading of
main transport routes). Declining coverage encouraged the amplification of
disruptive repertoires designed to secure and maintain—through the media—
the attention of the nation and government officials. Although APF members
organized some of these community-based protests, the scope of activist and
media attention generally shifted away from coordinated actions under the
aegis of broad-based social movement coalitions like the APF and toward local
community-level insurgence.

For many activists, the limited attendance at the June 2010 World Cup march
was further evidence of the APF's decline in public relevance and visibility.[5]
Backstage, the APF spent much time analyzing the outcomes of the march,

seeking to understand how the organization's reach could have been so diminished. Many viewed the march as a dismal failure and as evidence of the APF's disorganization. Despite the disappointing turnout, protesters at the World Cup march exemplified contemporary activists' associations of protest with performance. As organizers decided what to do, and again as negotiations with police were taking place, those gathered sang and danced to freedom songs that blasted from speakers. Indeed, the day's proceedings began with song.

Because performance is attuned to *doing*, the carrying out of action and its role in failure, loss, or disappointment can easily be neglected. Correspondingly, failure is often not a result of inaction or the absence of performance; rather, failure frequently arises out of the incongruence of human endeavor with broader historical, material, and sociopolitical environments. Locating performance in the gaps such incongruence creates, this chapter examines these gaps as they manifest in conflict—conflict-ridden interactions and conflicting enactments of supposedly shared priorities, including of upholding dignity among members. Chapters 1 and 2 revealed one performative aspect of the APF's formation—how various decisions and practices over time achieved a particular kind of collective mobilization. This chapter presents the flip side of that achievement, focusing on the role of performance in the dissipation of collectivity. This discussion is a necessary follow-up to chapter 3's focus on the protest aesthetics through which song energizes activist participation in the immediacy of shared experience. In the APF's later years, however, those moments of heightened collectivity generated by song were weighted by a disconnect rooted in the loss of love, interpersonal integrity, and affirming bonds among the activists.

Chapter 3's reminder of how fortifying collective activism can be, throws into relief the significance of such losses. Coming together in pursuit of justice is not merely a matter of publicly interrogating the failings of the present normative order. It is a means of constituting shared beliefs, ideals, desires, and imaginings of what ought to be and how people ought to be together. Although freedom songs foster collective togetherness, these experiences of connection are immediate and therefore momentary. To maintain the collective bonds needed to sustain a purposeful and unified movement, backstage practices of collective alignment are necessary. These backstage practices nourish and expand members' commitments over time and underpin front-stage outcomes. Such practices support the building of ethical collectivity on which activism thrives.

APF members had specific needs in this regard. The organization's target constituents—those living with dire poverty—confronted routine indignities that fueled their participation in collective oppositional action. These routine indignities highlighted a need to reinforce humanizing practices in activists' interactions with one another. Aside from the momentary togetherness of collective song, terms of address such as "comrade" index the alignment activists sought to create with one another through the sharing of political and ideological orientation. However, the APF was a stratified coalition that fell short of these alignment goals during its declining years, in part due to conflicting engagements regarding dignity.

APF members were anxiously aware of the organization's shortcomings. Buyisiwe's description of the APF's decline as a failure of performance offers but one example of the ongoing assessments APF members voiced. Reflecting his passion for all things automobile, Buyisiwe had described performance in vehicular terms, as what happens when a car's engine—the community—connects with its gearbox: movement leaders. According to him, performance is the car's movement that this connection enables—without the gearbox receiving power from the engine and transmitting that power into the forward or backward rotation of the wheels, a car cannot move. Analogically, without leaders fully embedded in the community and transmitting the community's directives and raw power into coordinated front-stage action, there can be no social movement.

For Buyisiwe, intensity, pacing, and consistency are of particular importance for performance; he was intolerant of slowness or inconsistency. His assessment of the APF was that "there is not enough performance."[6] He decried the World Cup march as "a poor performance, the poorest performance," and he attributed that poor performance to meek leadership. "The leaders and the organizers were supposed to challenge everything that can come across their face," he said, continuing: "but due to a lack of understanding each other, I mean they were like mumbling you know. There were buses that were stuck on the traffic, they have rights . . . to go and tell the Metro police officers that, 'Okay, our buses are stuck on the traffic so can you please go there, and make means and ways for the comrades to come down here?'" In this view, by not standing up to police curtailment and not recruiting the police to serve the needs of the protest, the day's organizers had dropped their charge and let down their community. The result was not only diminished numbers but also demobilization. Disappointed that what had been envisioned would not occur, Buyisiwe went home early—"That's why I can say I've seen the performance but it's now low!" Such evaluations lead to the insights of this chapter, in which performance is understood in relation to the gap between activists' ideals and the inadequacy of their lived experience.

While the APF's front-stage appearances disappointed and frustrated members, conflict pervaded the organization's backstage. In its latter years, the APF's meetings were often dominated by bickering, personal attacks, confrontational exchanges, and other alienating practices, including gossip. These practices reflected, and themselves produced, deeper domains of activity beneath perceptible verbal and visual surfaces.[7] Further, the practices were symptomatic of power struggles that manifested in the cultivation of tacit and oblique political acts that eroded collectivity. Over time, and with neglect of these concealed domains of meaning and activity, intragroup conflict becomes rupture, an outright separation or breakdown in social relations that creates openings for counter-intentional outcomes and limits avenues for redress. Under such conditions, a performance analysis embraces the primacy of human action. Whether or not it yields intended interpretations or consequences, the occurrence of an act cannot be denied. Thus, I am not interested in pronouncing the failure of the APF's engagements. Rather, in this chapter, I continue to trace the variety of ways differently situated individuals came to constitute the organization, however unevenly, through interactions with external opponents and with one another during which they each strived to uphold their dignity.

"I FELT THAT THIS WAS A WAR": RUPTURES IN ACTIVIST SPACE

Many of the APF's target constituents had met with extraordinary violence in their encounters with the police. But they grappled even more with wearying, routinized structural violence based on race and class. They confronted routine denials of their worth in their living conditions, in their bureaucratic interactions with government and other officials, in media depictions and scholarly representations of themselves, and even in their intimacies. Both kinds of challenges—extraordinary and routinized—can occasion the assertion of human will, an insistence on dignity, against dominion and degradation. The courageous refusal to be defeated by circumstance prompts further reflection on dignity's role in collective efforts at social transformation.[8] Within the APF, attributions of dignity were not only inherent in indomitable responses to abject conditions; they also arose from ethical stances regarding principled activist behavior.

These varied ascriptions to dignity became performatively significant as conflicting enactments that deterred collectivity, rupturing it in ways that eventually proved insurmountable. To grasp the ruptures within the APF that disconnected its members from one another and thwarted fulfillment of the group's participation aims, the circumstances that fostered the activism of a particular grouping of APF comrades—those constituting its mass base—must first be clarified.

The quotidian spaces and experiences on which these constituents' ascriptions to dignity rest are evident in the descriptions of activists' bodily experiences and living conditions that frame this discussion. Recall Ma Lindi's refusal to be pitied for her bodily limitations; Ma Patrycja's strivings to maintain her home; Mum Alice's battle with the damp seeping into her dwelling and her very body; Kanelo's vulnerability, fear, and exposure following her eviction from Quagga Estates; and Lebo and his family's experience of harassment as "landless people," not only by the police but also by homeowning residents who sought to expel the shack dwellers from Protea South. Attuning to the lives of these activists highlights the politics of the APF's constellation and illuminates the uneven relationships among its constituent elements. As differently positioned individuals and communities converged for collective action under the umbrella of the APF, each came with their own conceptions of what was at stake, creating gaps in the organization's practice. These varied priorities often arose from economic disparities in the immediate circumstances of activists' lives, disparities that articulate race with class and environment in complex ways. Consequently, the pivotal challenges that drove a key segment of APF activists to collective action diverged from other motivations and ascriptions to dignity that were active within the movement.

Coalitions like the APF, which brought together communities and individuals from various class positions, can constitute spaces of collective ethical engagement in which dignity is upheld. Yet the APF often did not meet this potential. The perception of many activists that their immediate circumstances could not be addressed within the APF's collective struggle signals an overlooking of their priorities, a falling short of the potential for shared struggle.

Other problematic internal dynamics also manifested the decline in the organization's backstage cohesion and front-stage visibility. During the very first APF office bearers' meeting I attended in 2009, the number of confrontational exchanges caught my attention. One such exchange took place between the deputy secretary, a woman in her forties, and Prudence, the APF's media coordinator, who was then completing high school. During a finance review in which affiliate requests for monetary support were considered, Prudence suggested that one of the requests be forwarded to the APF-allied Coalition Against Water Privatisation, since it had to do with water. The deputy secretary vehemently disagreed with Prudence's punting on the request, arguing that it regarded housing and electricity as well as water. I did not clearly hear Prudence's response, but it was sharp enough to elicit a word of caution from others in the room. The chair, an activist in her early fifties, told Prudence that she should consider that the deputy secretary was sitting across from her and could jump across the table to get her. Prudence brashly responded that she could also jump. The deputy secretary complained that she was being disrespected, and the chair asked Prudence to apologize. The young woman insisted on receiving an apology herself. This antagonistic interaction was not an isolated one—the chair herself was pulled into a similar confrontation with the project and campaigns coordinator. In my reflections on the day, I wondered what was boiling under the surface of APF meetings.

The next day I was at the office, the chair and I were first to arrive, providing an opportunity to debrief the previous meeting. As we walked from the elevator to the office entrance, the chair explained that these confrontations had not always been prevalent in meetings, that the APF used to be more focused, but hostile exchanges arose from people taking things personally and holding grudges. In my interpretation, members carried sedimented histories from prior engagements with one another that exerted influence on present interactions. An "underneath of things" (Ferme 2001) exerted force over the surface of APF meetings; the past could not let go of the present. Holding grudges hindered the organization, the APF's frustrated chair concluded. She equated such conduct with childish behavior, saying she had already raised her children, they now had children of their own, and she was here for the struggle, not to parent.

Against such tendencies to dismiss heated internal exchanges as childish distractions from the organization's success—and they certainly demonstrated ruptures in the organization's internal solidarity—I ask what it means to consider these grudges and interpersonal conflicts as competing claims to dignity. Such consideration renders dignity performatively significant for the illumination it offers on a political field that had become obscure—conflicts within the APF were not merely petty squabbles but also enactments at the core of what it means to claim one's humanity. Compellingly, such enactments by some came to be seen as conflicting with the efforts of others to uphold a principled activism. These conflicts generated ruptures within the APF that disengaged its members from one another and from their collective activist aims, hindering the movement's performance.

Such ruptures arose from at least two sources. The first is the stratification of APF membership according to a number of factors that connect to privilege, including class, race, geographical location, and political competency. The second related to a prevalent mode of mistrust generated by practices I call "playing politics." The two elements are interconnected in the jostle for power, although the first is more reflective of hierarchy, and the second represents a more horizontally charged wrangling.

Stratification: "Briefcase Comrades" and "Street Comrades"

A celebrated feature of the APF—the heterogeneity of its participants and its concern with democratic participation, enacted through different categories of membership—nonetheless reflected and fostered power imbalances. Different categories of members had entirely uneven stakes and consequently fractured into different forms of participation and different activist identities. In a comment on these divisions, one activist I worked with described APF comrades as falling into two categories: "briefcase comrades" and "street comrades." Briefcase comrades, who could also be glossed as the organization's middle-class activist-intellectuals, represented the APF at conferences, international forums, and other such spaces; they served as the APF's "idea workers" (Garner 1996: 24). Street comrades, on the other hand, constituted much of the movement's social base; they engaged the work of protest in the streets, a relatively more marginal occupation.

Class privilege often intersected with racial privilege, geographical location, ease of access to higher education, and the cultivation of certain forms of political competency (ranging from facility with political ideologies to practicalities involving accounting, communication, and document processing) to shape an activist's identity and role in the organization. In addition to their typically middle-class positioning, briefcase comrades were less likely to be township-based; that is, they did not reside in the communities where the majority of APF members lived. Such privilege indicated an experiential remove best captured by one activist's reflection on his political inspirations during apartheid: "I never imagined myself . . . as a subject to be liberated as such. I mean I grew up in the middle-class household, as such, so the kind of political inspiration for the stuff that I got involved in, you know, stemmed not from a sense of wanting to free myself from oppression but from creating some sort of idea of a just society, which never was personalized to, I think, the degree where I saw myself as a victim of apartheid."[9] This kind of motivation toward collective activism, rooted not in a survival crisis but in a broad political vision, echoed the distinctions that separated community-affiliated APF activists from individual activists and those from political groups: "So, you know, the only thing that makes our credentials different is that people come in there from communities who are generally there because they are directly affected by something. And not always, by the way, but very often that would be the thing. I have been cut off, so your day-to-day living is on the line in your struggle, whereas for someone like me and other members of Keep Left, we were there because we have a vision of change in society more broadly."[10] The APF thereby connected those driven by ideological commitment with a mass-based constituency driven by need—both economic need and a need for recognition of their innate humanity, of their dignity.[11] The bifurcation between the two types of comrades reflected a fundamental shift in the APF's composition, from its initial formation as a loosely structured activist forum premised on facilitating and coordinating struggles among students, union workers, community activists, individuals expelled from ANC-allied structures, and others directly affected by neoliberal initiatives. With the evolution of the forum toward a focus on community struggles, the basis of relationships shifted from commonalities in subjective commitments to solidarity and linkages between two prevalent layers of membership—that is, between members of affiliated community organizations seeking to improve local conditions and individual activists and members of political groups.

In these shifts, the imbalances among APF members became more prominent, particularly in the perceived dominance of individuals who were in several ways better resourced: "The uncomfortable thing about that is obviously that thing of people who are coming with much more experience, much more resources in terms of like your background, that you're more confident to speak and so on. And so, yes, there was always the danger of these few individual voices dominating at the same time."[12] To the APF's credit, the organization attempted to buffer individual dominance through structural changes that privileged community affiliates in representative numbers and decision-making. These changes, discussed in chapter 1, bear further elaboration here. Dale McKinley discusses the rationale behind the APF's structural choices: "There was a core group of individuals, which brought with them serious organizational, political, theoretical, as well as literary and media skills, and those activists and others had to contribute. But the way in which they needed to contribute was not to dominate the organization politically, necessarily, but that the community organizations which had the numbers, which had the political legitimacy, which were the ones who were actually engaged in the battles, which were the ones who were feeling the effects of the policies needed to have their own voice. I think the organizational form tried to reflect that."[13] These efforts to structure the relationship between the APF's two membership layers—the briefcase comrades and the street comrades—were rendered inadequate by the legitimation of some forms of participation over others.

One case exemplifies the pattern of concerns. Much resentment cohered around one prominent figure, a founding member who had long served as the organization's treasurer. Although he was scrupulous in his handling of APF matters, his manner was perceived as brusque, leading a number of people to feel belittled. Some felt that he represented a pattern of engagement by middle-class members who neither shared the stakes in the struggle of the APF's social base nor reciprocated the solidarity efforts of members from that base.

A written complaint against the treasurer, discussed at an APF meeting in October 2009, surfaced some of these issues. The treasurer, who was white, had insulted a Black office bearer out of frustration over the office bearer's tardiness and abiding disregard for organizational procedure, calling him a "mother fucker." The insulted office bearer's written grievance described his "long standing hostility with the APF treasurer who seems to have issues with every Black person who can stand on his own without asking guidance from a white man." At the meeting where the grievance was discussed, the treasurer responded that he was glad the complaint had been put in writing because it could be easily picked apart. This, he said, was the response he had received from other APF members when he exposed their negligence. Accusing him of racism, he argued, was an attempt to deflect the discussion away from the complainer's own unreliability. As treasurer, he added, he did the number crunching no one else wanted to do. He cited his struggle record in anti-apartheid movements and as a founding member of the APF. He had taken nothing from the organization, he pointed out; he had donated all his time, even his money, and his push had been for greater transparency. He said that he was not perfect, he probably should not have uttered the word he did, and he was willing to apologize for it.

However, the meeting also offered others an occasion to air deep-seated grievances. A female member, speaking in isiZulu and English, asked people to raise their issues with the treasurer present. A former staff member spoke about "things that have been eating us inside regarding [the treasurer]," her description of resentment drawing on vivid bodily imagery. She alleged that he had been abusive in his demeanor, swearing at meetings without being reprimanded. "Personally, I have received abuse from [the treasurer] for the eight to nine years I've been an activist, I've felt humiliated, and I felt that this was a war." Addressing the treasurer's record of service and contribution of resources, she argued that the stakes of her participation were more significant. He "may have contributed in terms of time and money," she said, "and some of us may not have the money to give, but we've given our lives. I grew up in this organization, I came to APF at nineteen, a naive teenager. At nineteen, I was arrested, [the treasurer] may have contributed to it, but it's our struggle." With those words, she claimed the struggle as distinct from his contributions, contrasting her courage in encounters from which he was spared by his resources—the

resources on which he based his claim to status in the APF. Core to the staff
member's complaint was what she perceived as an assault on her dignity: when
she was an APF staff member, she said, the treasurer had treated her with constant suspicion. "These are the things that break a person," she said.

The claims to dignity in activist spaces are complex given South Africa's
apartheid history of racial domination and the worsening impoverishment of
the APF's core constituency after apartheid. Often, conflicting claims to dignity reflected activists' different experiences and socioeconomic situations. The
treasurer's legitimate concerns about financial mismanagement, unprincipled
behavior, and lack of transparency were based in an appeal to dignity that
insisted on the maintenance of ethical standards of accountability, honesty,
integrity, and other aspects of principled commitment. Similarly positioned
individuals placed comparable emphases on such standards in the enactment
of personal integrity and disciplined commitment. As a former treasurer commented, "By the time I left the APF, I don't think it mattered whether I was
white or who I was, you know but I think it was the fact that my actions spoke
for who I was and then people recognized that and that they were appreciative
of that."[14] Such perspectives drove expectations around personal transparency
and accountability.

Most APF members shared these concerns, regardless of their social position, but members diverged in their emphasis on such elements. In that October meeting, many attendees contended that the treasurer had missed a greater
point regarding the importance of recognizing their humanity at a level that
affected their sense of self-worth. For those individuals, who had faced routine
indignities in their daily circumstances that made the struggle against privatization of primal significance to them, to encounter disrespect and humiliation
in the movement representing their aims was too much to bear.

Furthermore, no institutionalized instruments existed to capture the extent of these abuses or to document them in organizational records; the only
outlet for them was informal grumblings outside organization meetings. As
the staff member who spoke noted, "Comrade [the treasurer] is talking about
opportunism. It's just that some of us, we don't keep minutes, we speak in corridors." "Speaking in corridors" is a symptomatic response to powerlessness,
demonstrating how inexpressibility seeks alternative outlets, echoing similar tropes of marginalized discontent, particularly with regard to the silencing of women's voices. A 2004 article by a female activist, urging the APF to
consider its problematic gender dynamics, alluded to a similar dynamic: "We
should look at gender, not have women in a corner talking about women" (in
Paley 2004). Activists submerged their complaints because they did not feel

empowered to address their issues openly in the central forum. In decrying among themselves behavior they deemed unjustifiable, marginalized individuals formed bonds that provided alternative channels to the main organization and, through their talk, sought to affirm values and norms that the organization was not recognizing.

Some groups managed to formalize those alternate channels. Female activists who came together on the basis of their discontent with the APF's internal dynamics founded Remmoho, the APF women's forum, as a mechanism to further their critique of gender dynamics in activist spaces. But the APF's efforts to address its class- and race-based contentions institutionally proved more amorphous and inadequate. The October meeting about the treasurer devolved into a discussion of one person's affect, with a male activist wondering whether there was a way to deal with the treasurer's temper organizationally, perhaps through mandated anger management classes.

While "speaking in corridors" was one way that disempowered groups asserted their voices, the phrase also encompassed gossip—verbal denunciations of a person, often including unverified details, in that person's absence. Gossip is itself a tool of the disenfranchised. Gossipmongers are often dissatisfied or frustrated with the subject's behavior and may feel, for any number of reasons, unable to openly confront the person. However, gossip is not an unalloyed negative. Anthropologists and historians have noted the role of gossip in group constitution and maintenance, particularly among those set apart from wider society. Gossip helps group members maintain their unity, morals, and values (Gluckman 1963: 308; see also Handelman 1973; Paine 1967). By creating in-groups and out-groups, the circulation of gossip and rumors helps regulate and affirm social norms and ideals, especially among groups hegemonically distanced from power (Ross 2010: 160–64; White 2000). And, as Fiona Ross points out, "in communities in which well-being rests on intimate knowledge, gossip serves as an alert to matters that might need redress" (2010: 162). People gossip about the things that bother them, things that might require organizational attention.

The corridor exchanges in the APF underscore the difficulty of coordinating diverse contributions to a broader struggle in the context of historically entrenched inequalities. The challenges the APF faced as a heterogeneous organization raises questions that are important for considering activism in its plurality, regarding how differently positioned individuals can share a struggle and which organizational forms can accommodate divergent contributions without devaluing or marginalizing diverse constituents. The idea that middle-class intellectuals coopted the movement, as Buhlungu suggested (2006: 82), is rather too simplistic a framing of APF dynamics.[15] Some of these intellectuals also felt alienated; their participation in the APF was questioned through claims to experience that could not be countered. Furthermore, these racialized contentions, examples of which surfaced in the October meeting, rang to some as opportunistic attempts to manipulate tensions inherent to the APF's heterogeneous engagement through caricatures of racial domination. This assessment is not to deny that racism was active within the organization—race, gender, and class were significant delineators of power in the APF. Members' critiques of racism were urgently valid, but these critiques also played into maneuvers by some individuals to better position themselves for direct access to the organization's resources for their own gain. Such manipulations can be better understood in the context of the second source of rupture in the APF's internal dynamics, playing politics.

Playing Politics and Pushing Pocket Struggles

The voicing of perspectives became complicated in the context of the APF's representative structure, in which most members participated as representatives of their organizations or political groups rather than on their own behalf. Only a few individuals participated without any kind of separate affiliation. This structure made some activists hesitant to speak out, as Claire Ceruti of Keep Left observed. Ceruti, whose perspective I discussed in more detail in chapter 1, suspected that activists' diffidence may have submerged individual opinions and concealed major concerns. This hesitancy was certainly an aspect of the dynamic, as the focus on "speaking in corridors" revealed. Elaborating on Ceruti's observation, an activist described how she tried to encourage women's participation in the broader forum: "The women in APF, they are afraid to come forward because they said always the men in the APF, even in the meeting or CC [Coordinating Committee] if you are a woman talking, it seems like you don't know what you are saying. So I used to tell them just stand up and say what you want to say. Those who are listening, they will listen to what you are saying, and don't tell yourself that people are undermining me."[16] A lack of self-confidence about contributions to meetings was not unique to women. Another activist explained it thus: "You find that our comrades do not have the trust in themselves to say they can do that [stand up in a meeting and speak their issues], so it takes one to do it. Maybe I had been exposed to a lot of events where I'm able to stand up in front and speak, so I think we are trying to capacitate them."[17]

Some of the hesitance to speak was related to an element of obliqueness that pervaded APF proceedings, resulting from individual maneuverings to secure political ends. Rather than expressing a straightforward disagreement that could be engaged openly, some activists advanced their aims by delegitimizing those with opposing views. Ceruti elaborated on this dynamic, pointing out that "some of the political arguments amongst us [were] being fought out by organizational means rather than directly politically. There was a lot of stuff that went on that wasn't entirely open somehow and kind of backbiting, like questioning people's credentials."[18] As a result, individuals' contributions to meetings could not always be taken at face value. Subtexts, sedimented histories, or shrouded intents shadowed what was directly verbalized. For instance, underlying Prudence's verbal tussle with the APF's deputy secretary over the secretary's request for funding for a local protest was suspicion about money. I later learned that concerns had been circulating that the deputy secretary's affiliate was a "ghost" affiliate, existing in name only without evidence of active membership or local activities. While these concerns were ultimately never verified or openly discussed because the part-timers did not complete their affiliate visits across the APF's regions, a number of people operated from the assumption that financial grants to the affiliate went directly into the pocket of the deputy secretary's family. Prudence may have sought to punt the deputy secretary's request based on these circulating concerns, or the two women may have had a personal history that shaped their interaction. Whatever the case, the deputy secretary defended her request as vehemently as she did because she understood that, were the decision delayed until a later affiliates' meeting, it might never get funded. In the APF's operations, to delay was often to deny.

This kind of dynamic was one reason, Ceruti suspected, that individual activists were afraid to speak as themselves. Due to these forces, despite the importance of unhindered participation to the APF's democratic aims, a stratum of the organization sat in silence. In the noise of the confrontational exchanges that dominated APF meetings, what was not being said—the concerns of reticent members—did not simply evaporate. They were submerged: driven elsewhere (into inaccessible private forums in "corridors" and "corners") or left to fester beneath the surface, unspoken but animated. For adroit participants, the APF's structure provided a coded system within which they could maneuver and that they could utilize to their benefit. For those with less confidence or decoding ability, the system was less navigable or manipulable.

For some members, advocating debate was an oblique strategy to cause delay for their own ends. Usually the intent was to run out the clock and thereby defeat an otherwise certain outcome that would have been to their disadvantage. The APF valued debate in meetings as a way to guarantee that divergent views were not suppressed. However, as a result, meetings often degenerated into unfocused squabbles that, again, focused on the vocal few to the detriment of silent (silenced) onlookers. During a coordinating committee meeting I attended in September 2010, I was approached to act as a neutral party to chair a breakout session involving members from the Tshwane region, who could not reach agreement among themselves. During the breakout session, a participant charged that I was suppressing him because as chair, I would not allow him to debate what I judged to be an insignificant point. Against such an accusation, I had to allow him to make his point, and the session continued in the unfocused vein I had tried to avoid. At the end, the participant approached me with a hug, saying I had made a good presentation. "Even though in the meeting you said that I was repressing you?" I asked, frustrated. His response offers a sharp perspective on the maneuverings I describe: "This is politics," he said. "And politics is like a game. There will be fighting, sometimes someone will die, but they will be quickly replaced."

This viewpoint, approaching participation as a game to be won at all costs with little regard for fellow participants, is what I mean by "playing politics." Playing politics in this sense is rooted in a destructive individualism that privileges the player's needs and desires over the collective. A forty-six-year-old female activist critiqued this motivation to win at all costs: "It was all about making your point and not giving up as long as you can. . . . I think that it was also sometimes quite destructive, the nature of those discussions, and I think quite unhelpful often."[19] Her words provide insight into the obliqueness and combativeness of APF space, particularly as it manifested in the confrontational exchanges I observed.

When describing these dynamics, APF members called them out as "dirty politics" or "personal politics," and many complained of the challenges such practices created. One member spoke about the tendency of some activists to sabotage the contributions of others in jostling for position: "Some comrades are actually becoming, they start to put their personal issues on the struggle, whereby if a particular person is having a particular position, instead of supporting that particular person, they will try to crash that particular person even if that person is doing good things for the organization."[20] Another member described these activities as "power mongering," in which "it's not about the struggles anymore, it's about who is holding which position, which has got a negative impact on the struggles of the APF."[21]

In addition to jostling for position, the APF's internal dynamics were also distorted by disputes over resources. The organization's access to funding was often experienced in contradiction.[22] In the organization's first two years, external funding helped address a problematic dynamic in which a few better-resourced individuals bore the burden of providing for the group's financial needs and allowed the organization to enable broader participation and more accessibility to communities that did not have financial or geographical advantages. However, even as the funding resolved the APF's dependence on its financially advantaged members, the subsidies enabled by the funding fostered a different kind of dependence, by providing access to money for members made desperate by poverty. It was an open secret, one activist explained: "Now people are seeing the APF as an ATM; if they do not have money, then they go to the APF, they will be given money and they will be left with R10 to buy bread, those kinds of things."[23] In other words, the APF's transportation subsidy could be stretched to cover other expenses if members used cheaper forms of transport.

Many members saw these tactics as problematic, both for the organization and for the activists who employed them. The activist quoted above joined others in calling for "a program that could assist the unemployed comrades in order to make a living for themselves so that they shouldn't be depending on APF."[24] Such appeals sought to help members preserve their self-reliance and uphold their dignity. But they also complicated the APF's identification as a social movement organization, rather than a relief organization for poor folks. The APF's focus was on addressing systemic inequity by radically transforming South Africa's system, not on helping individuals cope with poverty.

Individual affiliate organizations were free to take up their own relief efforts, which a few did. The Orange Farm Water Crisis Committee ran a recycling center that employed its affiliate members and a crèche that offered young children daily meals. The broader APF, however, offered no systematic initiatives in that regard. This disconnect between the organization's stated aims and constituent needs made poverty alleviation an individual rather than a collective challenge and, within the broader forum, drove personal relief efforts underground. Against this ideological stance, people used APF resources to cope with poverty, including by claiming more transport money than they needed to provide funds for other needs. These efforts were widespread and relatively petty, but some members were blatantly opportunistic about drawing on APF support. Access to financial resources, through leadership positions and assumption of increased responsibility for various tasks, was valuable in such maneuverings. During a meeting I attended in September 2010, an APF activist from the Vaal aptly characterized these abuses as "pushing the pocket struggle."

These patterns of behavior led to frequent accusations of corruption or misuse of funds. Leveling such charges against other members, whether or not the charges were founded, was useful in discrediting those members, making room for the accuser to maneuver. This behavior provided context for much scrambling among activists and cultivated an atmosphere of suspicion and mistrust. Thulani—the activist from Kanana who had slept on a bench in Park Station following a meeting in the APF's earliest days—found himself caught by such an accusation. He had attained leadership positions with the APF, at one time serving as the regional coordinator for the Vaal region. Responding to comments at meetings that, for example, raised "concern about [Thulani's] conduct on finances as he usually [claims] money for things which are not there," Thulani often invoked his good name. He was cleared of wrongdoing in one meeting, but similar charges were repeated at later junctures. He confessed to me that he was thinking about quitting the APF because the persistent accusations were sullying his name, which was important to him as a preacher and as someone devoted to serving the community. He complained that even when charges proved unfounded, the accusations were still entered into the organization's minutes and thus were irreparably associated with him. For Thulani, the politics of participation ultimately became too much to bear.

In light of such considerations, the APF's racial contentions can be interpreted as political maneuvering. While accusations of racism raised significant concern about problematic dominance among a segment of the membership, the organization's internal politics rendered plausible the impression that these accusations were also opportunistic manipulations of tensions inherent to the APF's stratification. The alienation of individual activists created avenues for a few people to attain power and maintain it in undemocratic ways. After the APF treasurer stepped down, refusing to run for office at the next annual general meeting (AGM), his elected replacement began making decisions without following a democratic process. Other office bearers complained that he called meetings without informing them and that he wanted to control everything without transparent communication. He sometimes justified his behavior by invoking South Africa's violent racial history. He claimed the material resources of his role (including a new laptop for himself purchased without collective approval) as a welcome reversal of Black South African impoverishment and disenfranchisement. Although he touted his material claims as communal gain and collective restitution, his hoarding of resources and use of funds were only to his personal and nepotistic benefit. This treasurer was eventually suspended from his post, but not before his actions severely destabilized the organization.

A CODA: RECONSIDERING PERFORMANCE
AMID ORGANIZATIONAL DECLINE

As a result of the APF's stratification, the organization fell short of the promised rewards of togetherness during its declining years, in large part due to divergent claims to dignity. Its members privileged different aspects of the import of dignity in activist space, and those differences were manifested as racial tensions. Other tensions, including disputes over resources and leadership positions, created an atmosphere of distrust. These ruptures in the APF's collective bond revealed just how far the organization fell from ethical collectivity.

These ruptures also caused anxiety over the decline of the organization's public visibility, a decline that Buyisiwe noted as a failure in performance, particularly in light of the disappointments around the World Cup march. In contrast to Buyisiwe's pronouncement, I would urge a more integrated understanding of performance in everyday life as practice itself, repetitive and uneven, with accretive outcomes that exceed or fall short of intentions individually and as an aggregated whole. The APF did not stop performing in its declining years; rather, through members' routine engagements with one another, the connections that structured the organization began to degenerate, and the sense of interlinked struggles that was foundational to the APF's emergence was lost. Alienation affected APF activists in ways I will continue to trace, in the efforts of Remmoho members to restore their social bonds through different methods of mobilization and in the demobilization among youth activists arising from the APF's internal conflict.

While the APF's ruptures did not represent the absence or breakdown of performance, the APF clearly fell short of its intentions for ethical collectivity in a number of ways. The distance between intention and practice—which some might term failure—designates a space that offers opportunity for the reflection needed to generate action that is responsive to circumstance. Such reflection thus enables more performance. An exemplification of this possibility entails a return to the World Cup march and an examination of how lessons learned from that march guided the execution of another demonstration two weeks later.

The World Cup march provided external evidence of the APF's internal fissures, which became evident to observers as profound disorganization. Tseliso, a friend who was not an APF member but was involved in other movements in Johannesburg, called the World Cup march a failure, an evaluation he maintained even when I challenged him. The reasons he offered, from his vantage point outside the organization, suggest key lessons from the march for APF members. According to Tseliso, significantly fewer people assembled for the march than anticipated because many got lost. He himself was at Soccer City, the designated end point for the march, because he did not know where the march was supposed to start. He had called every APF member he knew to get directions, but he could not reach anyone—two organizers' phones were off, or they were perhaps busy. Prudence, the APF's media coordinator, whom he reached, was at home sleeping. For Tseliso, this experience provided evidence that the march failed because of poor organization.

Tseliso's complaints highlight communication gaps within the organization and the external constraints faced by march organizers. Prudence had not been among the APF office bearers coordinating the march, and organizers did not hold or communicate expectations regarding her involvement. She may have informed fellow office bearers that she had alternative plans on that day, but she may not have. The two organizers whose phones were off were at the starting point for the march, where I was, dealing with disappointing numbers and negotiating with the police to create a proceeding that would allow the organization to save face. It is unsurprising that they were not reachable in such circumstances. These communication problems were compounded by external issues. Unsuccessful negotiations with the police regarding the details of the gathering, undertaken in compliance with the Regulation of Gatherings Act, had not gone well for the APF, creating further challenges: The march had been relegated to an obscure starting point to minimize its visibility and thereby avoid presenting South Africa in a negative light at the debut of the World Cup. APF representatives tried to push back on the assignment, but they were given little choice. Rather than cancel the march altogether, they went ahead, hoping that fervent discontent from a significant assembly would overwhelm the police's attempts to keep the march hidden and unheard. In that hope, the APF's leaders miscalculated.

Tseliso was unaware of and did not account for the external constraints that stifled the demonstration. APF members, however, took notice and were determined not to repeat the perceived disaster of the World Cup march. For another demonstration held on June 25, two weeks later, APF organizers responded with more agility when faced with similar constraints. They scaled back expectations while keeping in mind the broader goals of raising international awareness. In this case, the Johannesburg Metropolitan Police Department downgraded the intended march to a gathering, because, they said, Library Gardens, the intended starting point for the march, was covered by city bylaws that required permission to gather there, and organizers had not acquired this permission. As a result, the police said, protesters could not assemble there to begin the march. Instead, protesters could gather at the end point rather than march to it. An APF organizer researched the city bylaws and found no such law. When he challenged the police department with this knowledge, the police called another meeting, which the organizer was unable to attend. That meeting was not successful for the APF; the gathering remained a gathering, not a march. The organizer felt the APF's leaders had capitulated too easily, echoing frustration from the World Cup march negotiations and the externally imposed limitations the APF had to contend with in organizing both events.

The June 25 event coordinators nonetheless worked to make the gathering successful. On our way to the Department of Housing, where the gathering was being held, the APF's administrator asked Boipelo and me to stop by Library Gardens to pick up some people who had gone there, thinking the march would start there. Reflecting on the World Cup march prompted me to suggest that someone should have been at Library Gardens as a matter of procedure, to make sure people who came to Library Gardens for the march could be redirected. Gese, another researcher in our group, mentioned that Boipelo had had a brilliant idea the previous day, to have a checklist and timeline of what needed to be done in preparation for a march or demonstration.

"Are you going to create this checklist?" I asked Gese.

"No," he responded, "but I'll push Boipelo to do it, and I'll help him. Documents like these are more important than spending time writing endless meeting minutes and reports." The "failure" of the World Cup march prompted many such discussions on how the organization could refine its procedures.

We arrived at the Department of Housing to find at least two hundred demonstrators. Many organizations were represented among those gathered, including the One-In-Nine Campaign and the Lesbian and Gay Equality Project. Among the protesters gathered was Mum Alice from Alexandra Concerned Residents. She had spearheaded this demonstration as an initiative of the Johannesburg Region of the APF. She almost caused a stampede passing out posters decrying the economic neglect of impoverished communities because South Africa had diverted funds to host the World Cup—people rushed to her wanting to get one.

Those gathered were particularly activated, especially in comparison with the deflated energy of those at the World Cup march. When Department of Housing representatives requested that the memorandum be delivered early so the protest could end and the entrance to the building be cleared, Siya, an APF leader for the Johannesburg region, addressed the crowd, telling those gathered that they needed to be vocal about what they wanted. "Sizolala la" (We will sleep here) was the response. The demonstration continued past the time negotiated for its end; those gathered had to be asked to leave. "We will come back," one of several older women asserted.

Thus, within the span of two weeks, the APF held two events that yielded very different but related outcomes. The disappointment over the World Cup march drew the organization's attention to its processes and set the stage for the comparative success of the June 25 housing demonstration. Failure or frustration, then, is not antithetical to performance. Rather, it is a constitutive element of performance, implicating the tenacity and agility that make political expression possible even in the face of attempts to foreclose it. Sustained engagement with disappointing outcomes or an overall condition of inadequacy engenders the reflectiveness required to sustain a collective's striving toward its goals. This turn inward, toward collective self-evaluation and reflection, can refine action, and often it is the bitter sting of disappointment that draws attention and sharpens critiques. Failure and frustration destabilize facile narratives of progress or togetherness, revealing the breakdowns or ruptures that compel interrogation of the assumed framework for being and working together.

Such destabilization need not be terminal. Disappointment reminds those affected that practice can be scrutinized and reworked. Ruptures do not so much weaken collective efforts as establish openings to pursue fortifying action. I explore this pursuit of preferable political collectivity in the chapters that follow. Chapter 5 examines Remmoho, the women's collective that sought to constitute collective politics on a different, more humanizing basis than the precedent set by the APF. Willeen's experience (see the Activist Portrait following this chapter) reveals one Remmoho member's journey toward that alternate feminist collective, through discovery, loss, and reclamation of spirit.

PABALLO'S PASSING: MOURNING AND MARKING DISTRESS

In the APF's declining years, the ruptures in its internal dynamics meant that the organization did not meet its ideal of collective action as ethical collectivity premised on mutual recognition. Regardless of their positioning—as individual members or community affiliates—members experienced estrangement from the APF as a result of the combativeness of the movement's political practice. Having witnessed the personal attacks and the atmosphere of suspicion that pervaded the APF's internal practices, I was not surprised to see, in February 2012, an article on the South African Civil Society Information Service pronouncing the APF's demise, "Lessons of Struggle: The Rise and Fall of the Anti-Privatisation Forum." Although the article was not surprising, it was sobering. I had assumed that the APF's survival through various evolutions over the years meant that it would persist well into the future. I was in no way prepared for the news that the APF as a movement was no more. It immediately pulled me into a space of mourning.

"We cannot mourn those whom we do not respect," political theorist Drucilla Cornell has said (2002: xx). Mourning entails recognition of the persons or entities we mourn beyond the constraints of their lives, beyond evaluations and judgments of their shortcomings, beyond disappointments in our unfulfilled visions for them. Excavating, or at least attempting to imagine "who or what they might have been in their struggle" attributes dignity to those fallen, those whom we mourn (2002: xx). Such an excavation is a particular ethic of memory. Mourning charges us "to do justice *through* remembrance" (2002: 195, n. 7).

In the space of mourning, I recall other passings during my time in South Africa and since I have been away. The precarious lives of many APF activists demand a familiarity with illness and dying, events that have proven too frequent for comfort. In particular, I recall my friend Paballo, an APF-affiliated activist whom I keep close to me since her death at the age of thirty-five. I have a postcard of her name by my front door so that I remember her in my coming and going. In seeing her name at my door, I recall this woman so full of love who lamented during an interview at her home, as her eyes darted restlessly between my camera and me, "Life in Joburg is not like [back home] in Lesotho. If you can see Tayo, there is love because love is from God, but here, there are no people for loving. Now it's about money."[25] This woman felt so unvalued and that her worth was so unrecognized in the city she had adopted as her home that she declared an absence of love, finding herself among people who focused on monetary assessments rather than on love. In the grip of this estrangement, she gave up romantic relationships. Months later, she tested positive for HIV, the condition that eventually led to her passing. With a sense of bitter irony, I wondered how she might have contracted the virus, from which partner. My rage and sorrow at her inability to access the resources for spiritual and personal development that she desperately yearned for spur the choices I make. I keep her close to me as an incitement to do justice to her memory through the ways I live my life.

This chapter is a further response to that charge to do justice through remembrance. Justice in this sense entails a recognition of dignity, maintaining a vision of the worth in the being we have lost so that we can uncover, as Drucilla Cornell said, "who or what they might have been in their struggle." As such, justice is not an attempt to temper the past with exoneration but rather to consider the entity or person lost on its or their own terms, with recognition of will and intention, recognition of a humanity that transcends circumstance. In the APF, I mourn a social movement organization, an organic constellation of individual and group affiliates. The decline of the movement, and the significance members attached to this decline, colored members' frustrations in the movement's later years. The beginning of mourning can be heard in members' lamenting the loss of love, interpersonal integrity, and affirming bonds among one another in the movement's quotidian routines.

It was against the combativeness pervading the APF's meetings that activists, including Paballo, lamented the loss of love and the rise of rampant jealousy and bickering over money. Paballo herself was affected by the pervasive suspicions that accompanied the disintegration of the APF's bonds. While I was still in South Africa, as she took ill and before she was diagnosed, she became convinced that she had been poisoned by a friend, another APF member, who wanted her leadership position. This suspicion drove Paballo into a deeper isolation, not only because of her own mistrust but also because other members, seeking to distance themselves from the gossip and rumors, withdrew from her. An external facilitator who worked with the APF suspected that Paballo's support base within the organization declined because fellow activists did not want to be entangled in the "gossip" around her suspicions.

I have previously addressed gossip as a particular challenge for the APF; in this case, it was a marker of distress indexing Paballo's perception of a threat to her well-being. While gossip can work to affirm collective bonds among marginalized individuals who espouse alternative values when they "speak in corridors," it can also undermine individual and collective well-being. In interdependent communities, to be denounced as the subject of gossip is to be without peace, a state of unease that can yield bodily consequences, as I learned through activist commentary. In a particular instance, when I asked after one of the administrators of a Soweto-based APF affiliate who had seemed quite unwell at a community meeting—she had red, runny eyes, and her chest was heaving—her comrade responded with suspicion that the administrator was physically unwell because of all the "gossip" surrounding her. The specific details of said gossip were never disclosed. Being the subject of gossip can engender a loss of well-being, and labeling someone's talk as gossip can ostracize the person labeled, minimizing her concerns and marking her as dangerous and unsociable.

Spiritual and material insecurity have converged since the advent of South Africa's democracy, as Adam Ashforth has shown (2005). In this convergence, as climates of suspicion erode collective trust, being associated with gossip puts at further risk individuals whose lives are already precarious. When Paballo voiced her spiritual insecurity by expressing suspicion of another APF member, others dismissed her claim as gossip. While gossip can function as power among marginalized individuals and collectives, its truth does not depend on the veracity of details shared but rather on the extent to which an indirect accusation indexes social ills. Paballo's suspicion that she was poisoned highlighted her intuition that her friend and fellow comrade bore her ill will due to jealousy over the leadership position she held. By refusing to listen and engage openly with Paballo on this account, her fellow APF activists discounted Paballo in the context of her own life and understanding. Engaging with Paballo's concerns need not have entailed abandoning either the accused or the accuser. Rather, collective mediation to surface the tensions and clear the air between the two parties through sustained, committed dialogue could have revived strained interpersonal bonds.

As her physical condition visibly worsened, Paballo made various appeals to me to help her secure a place where she could have peace of mind, but my attempts to do so were woefully inadequate. Her case was not unique—in the APF's atmosphere of distrust, members often interpreted their illnesses as evidence that others in the organization bore them ill will. Some fortified themselves through consultations with diviners and herbalists, whereas Paballo clung ever more fervently to her Christian religion, at one point informing me that she and her pastor fasted and prayed for four consecutive days. Her eventual passing was a profound loss that grated against the decline of the APF as a movement. It grated because, in hindsight, it is impossible not to lament how the APF's internal dysfunctions, which heralded the organization's decline, distanced Paballo from an important avenue of support in her illness—community. In the combative atmosphere that pervaded the APF's internal efforts, members sacrificed community to the detriment of individual and collective well-being, a loss that exacerbated the precarity of members' lives.

Paballo's passing, as I experienced it, ran parallel to the APF's decline. Paballo was ostracized and misunderstood, a reflection of the loss of care APF members experienced. The APF lost external relevance, visibility, and reputation due to carelessness about its pulsing underneath of things—submerged tensions, oblique political maneuvers, unspoken intents, and hidden domains of discontent that weighed down the organization and obscured its declared goals. Both the individual and the organizational entity were worthy of dignity and respect; both deserved to be mourned. In engaging with the APF's internal dynamics, I have revealed some less-than-ideal tactics among its members, and I have kept other unsavory internal conflicts outside of this treatment. I intend not to condemn but to decode and excavate the uneven grounds of the APF's efforts, because, like Paballo, the APF deserves to be mourned in its decline, and such mourning is only possible through clarified understanding. The aim of mourning to do justice through remembrance entails not idealization but rather acknowledgment of what made the individual respectable, of what made the movement respectable, tempering disappointment with consideration of the broader, deeper contexts of each entity's struggle.

NOTES

1. In organizing the protest, the APF reached out to stadium hawkers who were banned from selling at the stadiums during the World Cup by two Special Measures Acts of 2006 that created exclusion zones surrounding stadiums and fan parks.

2. In isiZulu, he said, "Asishay' ingoma, Comrades" (Let's hit [or strike up] a song, Comrades).

3. I am drawing here on the dramaturgical approach exemplified in Erving Goffman's *The Presentation of Self in Everyday Life* (1959).

4. In "The Service Delivery Myth," Richard Pithouse (2011) critiques media and scholarly commenters' designations of these protests as "service delivery protests." He points out how doing so depoliticizes these local struggles by offering technical solutions (more efficient service delivery) that do not recognize protestors' lived reality—in many cases protests arise from state delivery of services, especially when "delivery" means the installation of prepaid meters that make essential services inaccessible. Pithouse echoes James Ferguson's argument in *The Anti-Politics Machine* (1990) regarding the depoliticization of development. Focusing on the contradictions that local municipalities are caught up in, Gillian Hart also demonstrates the inadequacy of the label "service delivery" in relation to these protests (2014: 95–154).

5. For an extensive consideration of how visibility matters to social movements, including the effects of unintentional invisibility in moments of political opportunity, see Ashley Currier's *Out in Africa: LGBT Organizing in Namibia and South Africa* (2012).

6. Interview with the author, June 16, 2010, Johannesburg. Subsequent quotes are from this interview.

7. Regarding interactions between surface appearances and hidden depths in African life, see Mariane Ferme (1999, 2001), Achille Mbembe (2001), and Constance Smith (2020).

8. To maintain dignity in the face of abject conditions is to assert a fullness and vitality of human life that deprivation does not constrain. It is to envision a world beyond the immediacy of circumstance and to uphold a self-image that transcends the disdain of a society that is not "faithful to our freedom" (Cornell 2002: 2). This vision of the self and of the world turns abjection into a source of creative energy (Gikandi 2001: 319; see also Njoya 2010) and captures an understanding of the sublime put forward by a number of theorists, including Immanuel Kant.

9. Interview conducted by Dale McKinley, February 19, 2010, Johannesburg, housed in the Anti-Privatisation Forum collection of the South African History Archive.

10. Interview conducted by Dale McKinley, February 23, 2010, Johannesburg, housed in the Anti-Privatisation Forum collection of the South African History Archive.

11. Lucien van der Walt, a former APF activist described this connection: "It linked up a whole layer, rather let me say the independent Left with a constituency. That was great, I mean I don't think that sort of access had been there since the early '80s, and with the rise of the ANC in the '80s, a lot of that

space was just gone." Interview with Lucien van der Walt, conducted by Dale McKinley, March 23, 2010, Johannesburg, housed in the Anti-Privatisation Forum collection of the South African History Archive.

12. Interview conducted by McKinley, February 23, 2010.

13. Interview of Dale McKinley, conducted by Ahmed Veriava, March 1, 2010, Johannesburg. All of the quotes attributed to McKinley in this chapter are from this interview.

14. Interview conducted by Dale McKinley, February 17, 2010, Johannesburg, housed in the Anti-Privatisation Forum collection of the South African History Archive.

15. For a review of Buhlungu's portrayal of the APF offered by a founding APF activist, see Ahmed Veriava (2008).

16. Interview with Mammy Tladi, conducted by Dale McKinley, March 30, 2010, Johannesburg, housed in the Anti-Privatisation Forum collection of the South African History Archive.

17. Interview with Meshack Tladi, conducted by Dale McKinley, April 6, 2010, Johannesburg, housed in the Anti-Privatisation Forum collection of the South African History Archive.

18. Oral history interview with Claire Ceruti, conducted by Dale McKinley, February 23, 2010, Johannesburg. All of the quotes attributed to Ceruti in this chapter are from this interview. Interview housed in the Anti-Privatisation Forum collection of the South African History.

19. Interview conducted by Dale McKinley, March 9, 2010, Johannesburg, housed in the Anti-Privatisation Forum collection of the South African History Archive.

20. Interview conducted by Dale McKinley, April 6, 2010, Johannesburg, housed in the Anti-Privatisation Forum collection of the South African History Archive.

21. Interview conducted by Dale McKinley, August 19, 2010, Johannesburg, housed in the Anti-Privatisation Forum collection of the South African History Archive.

22. While Arundhati Roy's stance against the "NGO-ization" of politics—that "real resistance has real consequences. And no salary" (Roy 2004)—is a relevant critique of APF dynamics, I find it a bit too stark given the benefits of external financial support in APF's earlier years.

23. Interview conducted by McKinley, August 19, 2010, Johannesburg, housed in the Anti-Privatisation Forum collection of the South African History Archive.

24. Ibid.

25. Interview with the author, 2010, Johannesburg. Subsequent quotes are from this interview.

ACTIVIST PORTRAIT

Willeen

WILLEEN IDENTIFIED HERSELF AS SOMEONE who was passionate about art: "I always tell myself that I am an artist, I am because there is nothing else that I do with love besides art, you see." Her passion for art manifested primarily in song and theater, and she especially loved theater games and exercises that connected her with her breath and body.

Willeen's love of art disappeared, however, when her family moved to Drieziek in Orange Farm. After the move, her personality completely changed. She became unrecognizable even to herself: "I started to hang out with lots of guys. I was the only girl maybe in a group of eight boys. I would be the only one, smoking ganja, and even the neighbors didn't like me because I was living a not so good life." These developments reached a peak with the onset of mental illness. At the time, Willeen felt like she was being bewitched, but in hindsight, she recognized that she was stressed, and her stress led to severe depression. "That's why I ended up looking like a crazy person." She identified her stress as being rooted in bottled-up issues, "really personal issues," that she had to deal with on her own, not knowing that she could talk to someone. As a result, she turned to marijuana for comfort: "Smoking ganja was my only friend, my only comfort and consolation." Her anguish eventually worsened to the extent that she could no longer continue: "I saw that if I don't talk now, I die because I was feeling that I'm dying, I'm suffocating, I'm dying because this thing is killing me so I just burst with tears." In tears, she confided her issue to her sister, who subsequently told their mother what had been happening.

Rather than recount Willeen's story, I share it in her own words, recognizing how hard-won her voice, her power to express her concerns has been. As she told her story, Willeen stood by her kitchen sink, facing me. I was seated nearby, at her plastic-covered dining table. Her sister was in the one bedroom, allowing us space to talk. Her seven-year-old daughter had been with us moments earlier but was off playing as Willeen spoke. She was already self-conscious because her face had broken out into lesions of some kind two weeks earlier, although the lesions were now healing. She began delicately:

> It was a very personal thing, but as I grew up I learnt that the truth sets you free, and as long you have things that you are hiding, you will never be healed and you will never get help and you will never help others, you see. So what was happening there, it was the fact that . . . let me just tell you. My father died [in] 2007, so the fact that we grew up with a very abusive father, he was abusive verbally and physically. So at my side he used to beat me a lot more than the others because he told me that "you are older than them, you should be doing the right thing, they should look up to you. You are doing wrong things, what will they learn from you?" And then every mistake I had to account for it, you see, so when I was little, I was like eight, he sexually molested me, so that came out when I was twenty-one, that thing came out, and it was like a nightmare to me. I didn't understand, it's like it was the first time understanding what really happened that day and it was a—

She paused, and her eyes focused on the camera I had set on the table. Her daughter and I had been playing with it earlier that day. The little girl was only inches taller than the table; standing at her full height, drawing with her crayon set, her eyes barely peeked above its edge. Willeen might have been that size when she was that age, when the story she recounted now took place. Referring to the camera, Willeen continued:

> You see, when you record here, it was like someone was playing a video camera and I could see each and every move, each and every word I could hear, each and every move, each and every reaction.
>   I chose to block it because of the person he was that time. I was very afraid of him because I knew that he would beat me. Like there were other friends of mine who I will just talk to and tell them that "you see, in such a year something like this did happen." And I would cry and they would say, "Does your mother know?" "No, she doesn't." She only found out when I was twenty-one.
>   It was only once.
>   And then along the years there was this . . . you see, the constitution says now even in the workplace, when someone bounces you, that's sexual assault, they are assaulting you. So there were occasions like that in between from my father, and that made me really scared, because one time I was washing myself and my friends were sitting in the kitchen and he got into

the bedroom, and I was naked there washing and he would just tap my bums. And that thing just . . . you see, I just remembered, "Oh my God, he did it!" So I didn't entertain it that much, but only after the divorce, and it was as if something was separating, something had to happen, I don't know, improvement or growth, and other things had to come out you see.

So my mother asked me, "Why did you keep quiet all along?"

And I would say, "No I didn't just keep quiet, it blocked itself in my memory, it just came out now."

What really, really struck me is the fact that, how can he? How can he? Is he really my father? And I used to hate the word "rape," and I used to hate rapists but when I had to come to terms with it, to come to terms with the fact that my father is one, eish, it was really—When I think about it I would like just—

In that moment, Willeen gestured with her hands to indicate a forceful attempt at separation, demonstrating her mental break. "Please, please, and it would be like, yes, yes, and I would be like, no, no, and it was like yes, yes. So it says, 'Look at me, I'm the truth you see.' But I wanted to run away from it, so it really got my head to spin. And I smoked more. The more it comes, the more I'll smoke, and it would be like, 'Oh, you are smoking like that? Okay, fine I'll wait for you until you—' And then I would come back." When Willeen's anguish finally forced her to disclose, she began with her sister, who did not share Willeen's hesitation about telling their mother. When her mother was informed, her response was not what Willeen would have wanted. "Let me just liberate myself," she said to me. "Let me just tell the truth because what I expected from my mother I didn't get and that is the truth. I love the truth, I love God, and God is the truth! What can you expect, Tayo? Your kid is telling you that this happened, what will your reaction be?" Without waiting for my response to this question, Willeen continued, in full voice:

Embrace me! Comfort me, be more understanding, more there you see.

Yes, and share my pain with me, because I was crying and I wasn't playing, I wasn't acting, I am an actor, yes, but I wasn't acting. I was crying, I was feeling the pain, and that pain was very deep, it was very deep. It's just that sometimes we tend to undermine the pain. The pain that other people feel, we are not there when we are being needed. So to tell the truth, to tell the honest truth, after that, I regretted telling her because I didn't get the reaction that I thought I would get, because the only thing she said was, "Oh, your father is so cruel, I suspected that he did."

Her mother's response deflated Willeen. Rage layered over her disappointment. In that moment of disclosure, her sister had summoned their mother, who had been outside. Willeen had tearfully confirmed the story her sister had shared, only to receive a terse response, after which her mother went back outside, leaving Willeen with her tears. "That thing got me very angry, I didn't even want to question, 'What did you do? What did you do when you suspected? Why didn't you talk? Why didn't you say something, you see, why didn't you ask me?' Another thing, I was so good, oh my God, I was so good at blocking things that really hurt me, because I was so afraid of pain, so I would just block everything and pretend as if everything is fine." What jump-started Willeen's healing was forgiveness:

The only thing that healed me was forgiveness, because you get tired of this heavy load, this burden on your shoulders, to hate people and to hold these grudges against them, "Oh, she wasn't there for me, oh she said that, she hurt me like this, she called me this name, you see she was supposed to do this but she didn't." All those things, and I think God created us for a purpose, and those purposes, they differ, so are their pains, so are their struggles, so are their, even their rewards, you see. So I told myself that whatever happened happened for a reason and whatever I didn't get that I was supposed to get, God knew. As of now, I'm still living, so that means he gave me the strength to go through that. You see what happens, people tend to take you the way you react to life even to situations. They know that that one is strong, she will make it. Or that one is like this, this one is weak, he needs to be handled with care, that one is strong, she can manage. You see, we're different characters, and that is shown by the struggles that we find ourselves in, and the way that we deal with them.

Yes, so I was really angry at first. I was really angry and I got really upset, and I have this really bad heart you see and [I] said, "It's one and the same thing, why did I tell? What difference does it make, because even right now, I'm still feeling the pain, even right now it's even double, because I don't feel any comfort, I don't feel any ease." Nothing eased my pain, instead it doubled, and then I told myself that no it's fine, it's fine, it's life. But as I go on, as I move on with life, I understood that my mother was in an abusive relationship for a very long time, you see. She was not in a state where she could give comfort because she also wanted to be comforted. After twenty-one years of loving, caring, understanding and supporting a person, and then after twenty-one years that just disappears as if it was nothing. So she was sick, if I can say that, she was sick, so she didn't have the energy and the heart to help me deal with my situation, and I thank God that as time went on, I did understand and I forgave.

Overwhelmed as she had been by her circumstances, Willeen ended up in Ma Patrycja's orbit. The elder, recognizing a young woman needing help, brought her to a meeting of Remmoho, the women's group affiliated with the Anti-Privatisation Forum (APF), thus inaugurating Willeen's activism.

Willeen came to Remmoho harboring burdens from her father's sexual abuse and an ensuing disconnection from her mother. Regarding such burdens, Willeen was not alone. Her experience resonated with those of other Remmoho members, who had also lived the intimate connections between structural violence and sexual vulnerability. Neither was Willeen's experience unique to her Johannesburg or South African origins: I heard many parts of my life history as a survivor of childhood sexual abuse in the United States when Willeen shared her experience with me, proving sexual violence to be of worldwide prevalence and concern. Willeen's pain, her desire for justice, and her need to be restored through another's *compassion* ("feeling with," from the Latin *compati*, "suffer with") also extended beyond her generation. Ma Patrycja recognized Willeen's emotional life because she was a survivor of domestic abuse and had resolved to channel her rage from that experience into helping women. The elder woman had found in Remmoho a community that acknowledged the significance of her relational and domestic life, and extended the support of that community to Willeen. Chapter 5 focuses on Remmoho, Ma Patrycja's offering to Willeen, detailing its origins within the broader APF and the practices its members cultivated to foster much-needed community.

FIVE

—ᴙᴥ—

COUNTERMOBILIZATION

AT THE BEGINNING OF 2007, recognizing problematic gender dynamics in the Anti-Privatisation Forum (APF), some women activists formed a women's organization independent of the main forum. By creating an independent group, these activists sought to counter the marginalization of women in the APF, a trend that continued despite women being the majority. The women's group founders were adamant that their group, which they called the Remmoho Women's Forum,[1] not be seen as a women's subcommittee of the APF. Such an arrangement, they felt, would ghettoize women's issues. They rejected the idea of a group composed of both men and women because such a structure would threaten to replicate "the way issues are discussed in the movements where it is impossible to construct a women's agenda."[2] Mixed-gender groups addressing gender issues, they felt, often "focus[ed] on women's gender roles not to critically analyse these roles but to entrench them e.g. we end up thinking about issues like childcare, projects for women and not the power dynamics in the organization." Addressing such power dynamics, the founders felt, required an alternative space for women to reflect on their experiences as activists, a space that challenged the parallel binaries between public and private, social and embodied.

As the ruptures described in chapter 4 made evident, the plurality of activist practice often produces irreconcilable tensions between the movement's philosophical intents and the persistence of social stratification along vectors of race, class, and gender. Within the APF's context, Remmoho members employed novel methodologies to foster community and empower themselves as individuals and activists. These methodologies involved adapting embodied performance techniques, particularly ritual, to support wellness and contest male domination in collective endeavors. Remmoho's attention to well-being and care is particularly significant in the context of the structural and symbolic violence that pervaded members' everyday lives.

Remmoho's founding and its innovations in collective activism serve as a testament to the regenerative potential of "failure," manifested in the search for alternatives that a state of crisis necessitated. But the narrative does not end there. The APF's receptivity to Remmoho (or lack thereof) shows how stratification within movements can contribute to perceptions of feminist interventions as being unstable and incompatible with the organization, in spite of ideological commitments that should support such interventions.[3] Coalitional movements are sometimes constituted by conceptual frameworks and assumptions that hinder receptiveness to feminist approaches, particularly those emphasizing embodied, affective sociality. In the case of the APF, despite the organization's verbalized commitments to parity, gender interventions within the movement became conflict-ridden, ambivalent, and ghettoized, and some criticized them as being foundationally at odds with the aims of broad-based activism. Against this background, Remmoho's founders sought to create an independent, fully supported space for women activists to explore their commitments and needs.

These dynamics were not unique to the APF. In South Africa, the dissonance of feminist interventions within broad-based activism is highlighted by a number of long-standing factors. Historically, due to a "hierarchy in the struggle" to end apartheid (Eriksson 2007: 38; see also Geisler 2004: 71; Hassim 2006: 32; Meer 2007: 99), gender parity was a deferred cause, often seen as peripheral or unimportant in coalitional anti-apartheid movements: "Only for a few did the search for freedom include eradicating women's subordinate position resulting from patriarchy. For many, the task was to organize women, workers and youth, so as to ensure there were greater numbers in resistance organizations" (Meer 2007: 99; see also Hassim 2006: 38–39).

After apartheid, the assertion that social inequities were rooted primarily in economic factors limited the scope of gender interventions that could be deemed legitimate. In its early years, as the APF worked to galvanize communities that the African National Congress (ANC) government's neoliberal policies adversely affected, impoverished Black women constituted a significant portion of the organization's base, as they did for other such movements. In movement analysis, women were readily recognized for their vulnerability to the ANC government's neoliberal shifts. The privatization of basic services increased domestic burdens on women as homemakers, who (due to the sexual division of labor) had to compensate for the government withdrawing utilities it had provided in the past, such as water and sanitation (Naidoo and Veriava 2005; Xali et al. 2005: 25; see also Eriksson 2007: 71).

As a result, women activists constituted a majority in the movements that arose in response to post-1994 contestations, contributing numbers and vibrancy to protest demonstrations. But even though women were a target constituency, the new movements were not avenues of female empowerment. Women were not well represented in the male-dominated leadership structures of these movements (Eriksson 2007: 49; Pointer 2004; Xali et al. 2005). The APF's membership patterns also reflected this reality. In reports, Remmoho members pointed out that women constituted up to 90 percent of most mass meetings and marches, demonstrating women's presence as the bulk of the APF's target constituency, yet they were nearly invisible among the organization's leadership. Apart from the issue of female leadership, APF activists noted the absence of women's voices in meetings and workshops. In one activist's account of a meeting in 2004, men dominated the floor, while the few women participating were "women with lighter skin, for whom English is their primary language" (in Paley 2004). Thus, the dynamics of the organization marginalized Black women even within a movement that claimed to represent their aims. According to one activist, in a comment I noted earlier, they were relegated to "a corner talking about women" (in Paley 2004). Another activist alleged that women were caught up in men's ambition and were "being used by men who are looking for power within the social movements" (in Paley 2004).

Postapartheid movements also subordinated gender equality to a universalized class struggle, echoing the priorities of anti-apartheid coalitional politics.[4] Class was a readily recognized vector for collective mobilization, but a commitment to promoting gender equity, by challenging patriarchal cultural systems or sexist ideologies, was harder to find in postapartheid movements (Meer 2007). Addressing gender issues would entail focusing on them internally rather than just opposing the state and challenging the values and power dynamics within movements, something activists had been hesitant to do.[5] As a result, rather than being venues for addressing gender inequality, these organizations became sites at which "daily forms of oppression are being normalized in the name of the struggle" (in Paley 2004).

This chapter advances inquiry into the aesthetics of collective action by retracing Remmoho's interventions within this political landscape. The emergence of feminist critiques within the APF further reveals the significance of activist embodiment for mobilization, particularly for hypermarginalized populations. The women of Remmoho experienced repression not only from the neoliberal political-economic struggles that originated their activism but also as women in a male-dominated social movement organization. In their gendered interventions, the different modes of activist practice they inaugurated emphasized an internalized pursuit of healing and communal support over contestation with external opponents. These activists' bodily encounters and sensory perceptions influenced their shifting motivations toward collective action. Their motivational shifts reconceive mobilization as intimately embodied through attention to the physical and psychological processes that occur within individuals and foster collectivity during activist events. In contrast with activists' dynamic embodiment in protests through singing, which afforded heightened but episodic and momentary experiences of collectivity, Remmoho deliberately attempted to construct community through ongoing bodily and affective practices of reclamation.

In this chapter, I profile Remmoho and the Gender Reference Group that preceded it, detailing the origins of both, the distinct practices they employed to mobilize women, and the rationales behind these practices. Following these profiles, I examine the implications of their efforts for scholarly understanding of activist embodiment—how Remmoho's particularly embodied approach addressed activists' need for critical outlets, and how voicing (the transmission of experience through speech) provided a pathway for activist transformation. I subsequently detail the tension that arose when other APF members did not receive Remmoho's novel methodologies well, viewing them as incompatible with the the APF's views on collective politics.

The Gender Reference Group that preceded Remmoho brought together about twenty women across community organizations in Gauteng and nearby provinces from 2005 to 2007. The facilitator of that group, Nancy Castro, advocated the transformation of androcentric/male-dominant approaches to collective mobilization and the creation of new approaches to gender activism. The ways in which Remmoho's founders and members drew on Castro's work in their own interventions, examining the mobilization strategies within both the Gender Reference Group and Remmoho—and how these strategies differed from conventional mobilization approaches—reveals the scope and effects of gendered countermobilization within the activist coalition that was the APF.

THE GENDER REFERENCE GROUP

In 2005, Khanya College, the Johannesburg-based nongovernmental organization (NGO) dedicated to supporting social movements (including the APF) through education and strategic planning, hired a gender coordinator to identify and implement strategies to support women's empowerment and gender equity in its programs. This was just one measure Khanya took to assess the gender implications of its support of community activism. That year, Khanya also made "Gender and Neoliberalism and the Social Movements" the theme of its annual winter school, a weeklong workshop that typically brought together activists from NGOs, social movements, and trade unions from across Southern Africa.

Given the workshop's theme, Khanya recognized a need for women activists to lead its planning, design, and evaluation. The organization therefore recruited women activists from the organizations it supported; those women became the Winter School 2005 Reference Group. The group began with a three-day women's empowerment workshop in June, followed by media training workshops. One of the group's responsibilities was the production of a daily newsletter circulated to winter school participants. Its members helped shape Khanya's winter school program that year and continued to meet after the workshop, when the group was renamed the Gender Reference Group. In a report after the winter school, Khanya staff members noted that the school was "different" from past workshops, not only in its emphasis on women's leadership but also in its teaching methods.

Khanya's newly hired gender coordinator, Nancy Castro, facilitated both the Winter School 2005 Reference Group in the run-up to the winter school and its ongoing meetings as the Gender Reference Group after the workshop ended. In explaining the group's work, Castro discussed the need for alternative approaches that would not perpetuate the male-normative organizational forms and patriarchal rules that occluded women's democratic participation (see Lorde 1984: 110–14). In the everyday operation of activist groups, male dominance was normalized and thus rendered invisible. The activist space was disembodied and depersonalized, with personal lives and bodied experiences separated from the political endeavor. One woman described the effect of this disconnect: "*You go to a march, you go to a campaign and you fight for the rights of everyone. And then come back to your problems, the fact that you are not working, and you have kids. And you have family that is looking after you. And then those things are still there, looking at you when you were out there, fighting. So there is that world and your world*" (in Eriksson 2007: 114; italics in original).[6] Castro, noting this disconnect in the women she worked with, asked, "When my reality is that my husband is kicking me, and I am unemployed, and I need to put bread and butter on my table for four children, and here they say capitalism . . . how do I link that with my reality?"[7] She sought to connect the overarching themes of political protest directly with women's everyday concerns.

Castro's assessment of the disconnection between coalitional activism and women's everyday lives was still relevant when I came to work with the APF

in 2009. APF conventions in the period I was there further illuminate the
environment the Gender Reference Group sought to change. In my fieldwork,
I observed three features of APF meetings that were alienating for women.
The first was that meetings often ran late in the day, privileging participants
who could travel freely. Because traveling late entailed particular security
risks for women, many left early, and important discussions continued in
their absence. Second, the APF did not provide childcare, which put many
women who were responsible for children in their families at a disadvantage.
Finally, discussions and procedures were sometimes difficult to follow due to
the oblique practices detailed in the previous chapter. In APF meetings, the
words spoken were often shrouded with subtexts and sedimented history. In-
explicit codes underlying public words privileged those comrades (often male)
who could draw on authority, prior experience, and their embeddedness in a
racialized and patriarchal society to assertively voice opinions. In meetings,
participants jostled with each other in their attempts to maneuver discussions
and outcomes to their benefit. These features were evidence of underlying assumptions regarding APF members' mobility, availability, and facility with
public speaking and confrontation that, left unquestioned, mostly benefited
male participants and further normalized the combative engagement within
the APF that women had to master if they wished to participate.

Indeed, many women perceived APF meetings as not welcoming. In my
interviews, a few women reported feeling physically intimidated in meetings.
Some were afraid to speak because they thought male members would hit
them. One woman recalled an incident in which a male member threatened
to throw a pregnant woman out of the window "because she was a woman and
she was vocal and assertive."[8] Another woman was adamant in her refusal to
attend APF meetings, so unpleasant was her experience in one of the meetings
she attended with another Remmoho member: "We were just sitting like this
[arms crossed], we were sick and we were stressed because we've got something
to say but we can't, so for me APF, no. Those men, they are bullies and they do
whatever they think is right for them, and as a woman, you don't have a say in
those meetings."[9] Others who did feel comfortable speaking reported not being taken seriously.[10] The words of one male APF member in 2004—the year
before the formation of the Gender Reference Group—still rang true in 2009:
"It's all about who has the biggest cock. And if [a woman activist] is going to
succeed, it's because she's got a big cock also" (in Paley 2004). Women activists
voiced similar interpretations in meetings I attended.

Within such a combative environment, Castro argued for the transformation of male-dominant practices so that mere female *inclusion* was not equated

with female *empowerment*. In her work with the women of the Gender Reference Group, who met actively between 2005 and 2007, Castro aimed to engage "holistically [with] the full female human being and not only [her] activism, [drawing together] all the different identities of the woman."[11] This holistic engagement entailed excavating multiple possibilities of being that were buried under conformity with dominant societal expectations. Castro sought to validate her collaborators' experiences so that they could come to know and trust themselves beyond the definitions imposed on them by the world and by the movement. To draw on Marilyn Strathern's formulation of the import of experience in feminist knowledge production, Castro's techniques aimed "to restore to subjectivity a self dominated by the other" (1987: 288). In the US women's movement, feminist attempts "to turn those who had been constituted as others into selves" precipitated a crisis of difference (Abu-Lughod 2006 [1991]: 155) regarding exactly *whose* selves were being surfaced. The differently marked experiences of racial and ethnic marginality, as well as those based on gender identity and sexual orientation, problematized any inference of shared identity under the banner of "women." Such social distinctions belied the assumption of gender-based commonality in the holistic ideas the APF's women members sought to surface through Castro's practices.

Nonetheless, Castro's techniques acknowledged the futility of the conceptual engagements that dominated the APF's mobilizations for transforming social dynamics; she privileged women's direct experience over abstractions. Runciman (2011: 612) characterized APF's political praxis as rooted in a translation (quite literally), through political education workshops, of capitalist and neoliberal social relations to people's ordinary circumstances that are designed to allow participants to locate themselves within those political structures. Castro argued that engaging gender parity through this conceptual lens would achieve only limited gains "because conceptually it is very easy to agree with the gender position. [It is] different [however] when you start to touch the individual" (in Eriksson 2007: 98). For Castro, transformation had to first engage the embodied individual through breathed, felt, and lived experiences.[12] Addressing gender disparities required methodologies that personalized interactions and drew on spiritual, emotional, and embodied knowledge. Whereas other facilitators were predominantly concerned with whether or not workshop participants understood the "translated" concepts, Castro inquired into how the women were feeling.

Castro's interventions link to a feminist politics of translation (Alvarez et al. 2014) that highlights how the dissemination of ideas across geopolitical borders and sociocultural barriers "is always already caught up in relations of power and asymmetries between languages, regions, and peoples" (de Lima Costa

2006: 63). Yet, discursive flows are not inherently one-sided, limited to mere complicity with or uncontested submission to externally imposed ideologies; possibilities for refusal, resignification, and strategic appropriation also exist (Thayer 2010). While translation may reinforce local and transnational power dynamics, it is also a terrain for struggle, facilitating interventions against "discursive aggressors" (Thayer 2010: 202) and collaborations across difference to create composite formations and new modes of political enactment. As a transnational subject (Castro had migrated to South Africa from her native Colombia), Castro could herself be understood to be a translator—a broker facilitating the circulation of ideas across geopolitical borders and cultural, racial, and other barriers. Attenuating such an interpretation is Castro's disavowal of conceptual engagements as foundational to gendered activism. In place of the imposition or adaptation of concepts (even if contestable) to suit women's lived experiences, Castro espoused methodologies that privileged women's embodied ways of knowing.

Thus, in the Gender Reference Group and later Remmoho, the women's collective work was essentially a refusal of translation, a talking back on their own terms, terms that were at odds with the social-movement milieu in which they were embedded. Castro sought to disrupt the patterned alienation imposed by the translation approach and lead the women to discover new forms of connection to self and others. She wanted to create an environment in which participants could freely discuss immediate concerns involving their "real" lives (encompassing but extending beyond their activism), including their familial relationships, sexuality, and living conditions.

Sexuality was an important theme in discussion because, Castro argued, it directly impacted women's mobility in the world. "If I am in charge of my body, I can see freedom . . . that doesn't mean that patriarchy won't hit me, obviously, but I have tools to deal with it. In the opposite way, [if I am not in charge of my body,] I can have all the theory here but I won't have the mobility to use it." Nomvula, Ma Lindi's soft-spoken soprano daughter who was one of the participants of the Gender Reference Group and a founding member of Remmoho, noted the transformation that came with discussing sexuality:

> The biggest concept that gave us [Remmoho members] a breakthrough was being the owners of our own bodies, because we realized that as women, we don't own our bodies. We're owned by the communities, we're owned by children, we're owned by mothers, and sometimes by our in-laws, because even when a woman is not ready to have children, the in-laws can tell you that we want a child now. They dictate how you should have sex and how

many times you actually have it and so . . . I think sexuality is key when you're doing gender work, because until someone knows how all these gender roles are actually constructed and what it means to me as an individual and as a woman in society, you can't really get a breakthrough.[13]

Addressing sexuality allowed those who worked with Castro to make direct connections between absences of bodily autonomy in their individual lives and societal gender dynamics.

Furthermore, to transcend patriarchal devaluation of women, and the silencing of their voices, the women had to cultivate a new sensibility, to discover what they had to say.[14] This process, which Castro ritualized as "putting on female glasses," privileged the women's own experiences over any others: "[It is] not what the male or what the movement, or what the social movement, think and say, it is how we see and read with our own eyes, and how that is connected with our real lives, our private, our public, our involvement with the community but from our eyes. The process was beautiful beautiful beautiful." The women had to let go of ideologies of female submission to patriarchal authority and incompetence in political spaces to cultivate their own independent perspectives, to trust their own perceptions in decoding their external environments. It is significant that Castro and both women's groups based their interventions on sensory grounds. Demonstrating the "crucial correlation between aesthetics [as modes of sensory experience] and politics" (Wolfe 2006; see also Mookherjee and Pinney 2011; Jolaosho 2015), the women strove toward a new sensibility that privileged their experiences and disrupted a dominant sensory order, the effect of which had been numbness, silence, and repression. For the Gender Reference Group, Castro drew on techniques from her work with women in her native Colombia. These techniques used ritual, food sculpture, dance, and other embodied practices to move the women out of the realm of the "traditionally normal." Considering popular associations of the aesthetic with beauty, it is very informative that Castro and other women I interviewed described the work they did as *beautiful*. In doing so, they reconfigured sensory categories to include their own experiences. Other instances in which beauty came up included the reclamation of self-image, a process in which women address themselves and each other as beautiful to encourage participation in activist spaces.

Rituals were a key element of Castro's practice. Rituals created material manifestations of the women's cognitive and emotional processes and encouraged testimony on women's experiences of poverty, sexual violence, physical abuse, and other daily struggles. These rituals revalorized the things women encountered in their everyday lives. For instance, through one such ritual, during a three-day workshop, water—the privatization of which had caused deprivation and driven some women to activism—became a reclaimed agent, representing the energetic contributions of female participants to the workshop. At the beginning of the workshop, the women introduced themselves and described how they were feeling. As they did so, they drank water from their containers, contributing their energy to it; they then poured some of that water into a bowl. "To have that bowl, that is all our energy, it's not water from the municipality, it's ours," Castro elaborated. During the course of the workshop, whenever the women had new ideas or experienced a change in their understanding, they contributed water to the bowl. Every morning, they began by checking in, drinking water, and pouring it into the bowl, and they repeated the ritual over the course of the day. At the end of the workshop, the women carried the bowl outside, singing, and poured the water over soil to nourish new growth: "All our energy and all our new understanding . . . maybe it's touching another woman, and maybe it's permitting flowers to grow. It's the individual, and at the same time it's the collective," Castro explained.

Another ritual involved fire. Åsa Eriksson, a researcher with the group at the time, described an intervention in which participants wrote down their most painful memories:

> Tears are starting to roll down the cheeks of some of us. When everyone is done, we go out on the yard, lighting candles. Sitting there together, arms crossed over our chests or comforting each other, freezing in the cold June weather, we use the candles to burn the pieces we have written, in silence and with sincerity. . . . Slowly, some of the women started to speak. Memories of poverty, sexual violence, lack of respect from parents and other struggles are shared. When no one else wishes to speak, we end with a song to clear the pain. The atmosphere for the day is low, but carries a sense of respect and vulnerability. (Eriksson 2007: 117–18; italics in original)

Such methodologies represented a radical departure from conventional modes of organizing in South Africa, and a few male activists criticized them as being more psychologically than politically driven.[15] In the face of this criticism, Castro asserted that such work was intrinsically political because it challenged the devaluation of women and humanized the activist experience.

REMMOHO: "WE ARE TOGETHER"

Four Gender Reference Group participants who were also APF members sought to implement some of Castro's interventions within the APF. By November 2006, as the group was completing its process, they had begun discussing with other female APF members the creation of Remmoho as an independent group for women activists. The goal was to apply the techniques the Gender Reference Group had used to humanize the activist experience. When it was established in 2007, Remmoho was not a typical project for South African social movement organizations. That difference was deliberate and deliberately cultivated. In fact, members' listed aims included the objective to "change the nature of the space of the movements and create a women friendly environment." Furthermore, the founders sought "to take up the issues that movements are not taking up from women's point[s] of view."[16]

Although, through Remmoho's efforts, the APF became more sensitive to women's involvement and strove to achieve gender balance in leadership, women still had to battle patriarchal attitudes and a sense of alienation. Remmoho reports noted that women lost their investment in leadership and interest in sustained involvement due to "male behaviors for power." One woman complained, "Why should I waste my time watching men fight with each other when I have more important work to do in the community?" Further, women encountered male attitudes that dismissed their concerns as inconsequential to "real politics."[17] One woman reported, "After I shared some of the problems facing women, the response from one of the male comrades was that I should take these problems to Oprah, because in the meeting only real politics was being discussed."[18]

Part of Remmoho's aim and ongoing challenge, then, was to identify and depart from ingrained power dynamics and male-dominated movement culture. In their attempts to create and articulate a new "space for women," Remmoho's leaders invited members to attend activities as women, not as representatives of community organizations, a significant departure from the APF's primary membership structure. As a result, the group's membership featured a diverse group, including women activists from the APF, women activists from community groups and organizations not affiliated with the APF, and women who were not involved in any form of collective activism. Many Remmoho members were recruited by individual women, although some were sent to the group by their community organizations.

Remmoho drew these members from four primary areas—the Vaal Triangle, Khutsong, Soweto, and East Rand. About forty to sixty women attended each Remmoho general meeting I participated in from 2009 to 2010. In 2008, its members ranged in age from fourteen to sixty-five, with mothers often bringing their daughters to participate in activities. Those who were not students were primarily unemployed. A few had formal employment with community-based organizations, some were pensioners or received social grants, others engaged in informal trading (running tuck shops or selling Tupperware, for instance), and others participated in income-generating communal projects. Those with no sources of income relied on household members and piece jobs to sustain themselves and their families.

Recognizing the resource disparities among its members, Remmoho subsidized the costs of attending meetings in Johannesburg. Before the group received organizational funding from Oxfam Canada, its members covered one another's expenses. Once it received the Oxfam funding, Remmoho reimbursed a portion (if not all) of meeting transportation costs and provided lunch and childcare options; childcare was particularly important to women's ability to participate. In late 2010, Remmoho sought to rework its subsidies to foster member responsibility. Leaders encouraged members to bring lunches from home, and childcare was available only to women who could not attend meetings without that support. To address spotty attendance, Remmoho worked to create a core group of twenty-five consistent members who would receive gender training, coordinate campaigns, and pass their experience on to other women in their communities. Through this model, Remmoho aimed to reach an additional five hundred women.

Initially, Remmoho met about three times a month. At the beginning, members rotated leadership and administrative roles from meeting to meeting, to build a nonhierarchical structure based on shared organizational responsibility. However, driven by the need for consistent accountability as a prerequisite to external funding, the group eventually developed a formalized leadership structure. At that point, Remmoho was led by a coordinating committee consisting of a chairperson, deputy chairperson, treasurer, secretary, deputy secretary, and two additional members who observed and assisted as needed.

Remmoho members gave a variety of reasons for their initial interest and subsequent participation in the group, including a desire to learn about the abuse of women and take steps to address their own situations. For example, one interviewee commented, "In my first meeting, they were talking about the abuse of women, those women who are having problems with their husbands and even the children, the abused children. So I found that place being the right place for me because that's where I found other women who are having problems as I was having problems."[19] Other women expressed as motivation curiosity about women's lives and a desire for an organization that would further their growth (a few women glossed this as an organization that would "build me up"). One woman explained, "You see, talking to women, interacting with people, getting their ideas, getting to know where they are, you see that really builds me, that really does something to me, you see because . . . it unlocks another door in my life."[20] Finally, members sought an organization that would protect their voices and support their lives. One woman stated, "I think that's why Remmoho is there—to give each other support, to have a family outside the house."[21] These reasons are critical to understanding the nature of the organization that the women were building in terms of the political interests they sought to address.

Remmoho's early meetings and workshops used Castro's methodologies to cultivate the space for women its founders and members envisioned.[22] It was a period of intense excitement and energy, feelings that would subside in later years. When I mentioned the absence of rituals and other techniques attributed to Castro in the Remmoho meetings I attended, one founding member characterized this absence as a gradual erosion symptomatic of organizational growth rather than a conscious shift away from those practices. As Remmoho cultivated partnerships with other entities aligned with its aims, its mobilization repertoires expanded to incorporate other embodied approaches. In late 2008, Castro and other practitioners connected Remmoho members with Gender at Work, an NGO that supports institutions and community-based organizations in promoting gender equality. Gender at Work facilitators bring together peer organizations in a series of workshops to learn from each other through a gender action–learning process. Four Remmoho members participated in an eighteen-month Gender at Work learning process that culminated in February 2010. The process included overnight peer-learning workshops and individual visits from an assigned Gender at Work facilitator. This partnership introduced to the group new methodological approaches that complemented Castro's techniques.

Relaxation, self-care, and the cultivation of positive, supportive sociality underpinned Remmoho's activities as its members were influenced by Gender at Work facilitators. Amina, one facilitator, explained, "When people are more relaxed, they can look deeper inside themselves" to honestly identify the sources of the challenges they face and generate sustainable solutions. Remmoho's activities included overnight healing workshops and Capacitar exercises, which included elements of tai chi, acupressure, visualization, breathing techniques, hand and head massage, and other modalities.[23] Remmoho members valued these practices. In fact, my interest in the group was initially piqued by exploratory interviews in which APF-affiliated activists observed that women in Remmoho were most interested in tai chi and other physical exercises as the focus of their meetings because they recognized such practices as fulfilling the most significant need in their lives. Remmoho's emphasis on wellness introduced positively regarded techniques that were absent from the women's daily lives, heightening recognition of the collective's potential for transforma-tivity (see Juris 2008b: 66). Remmoho members anticipated workshops; during introductory check-ins, they said they came to be healed or to be energized. Discussing "personal problems" was a critical outlet, necessary for physical health, and Remmoho provided the space to do this.

In their attempt to create a cohesive women's group, Remmoho members made three key interventions into movement practice. First, they asserted the personal as the most pertinent foundation for political engagement. Second, they demonstrated the intrinsically embodied nature of social ties. Finally, they highlighted group cohesion as an ongoing process involving love, respect, and care, sentiments that are critical to sustaining social relationships in the face of economic inequities and health crises, as Deborah Durham, Frederick Klaits, and Julie Livingston have shown in Botswana (Durham and Klaits 2002; Klaits 2010; Livingston 2012). Three ethnographic moments that exemplify Rem-moho's activities during my research tenure provide explication of the group's many complementary approaches. The first two events were weekend work-shops with members, and the third event was a group visit to a sick member.

Called by Possibility: The Political As Personal

I experienced Remmoho's emphasis on the personal as the foundation for col-lective politics at my very first meeting. From the spatial setting to the ses-sion's activities, the meeting contrasted remarkably with my experiences of the APF thus far through its attention to the bodily sensorial experiences of its participants. The meeting, which took place in the APF's conference room on January 30, 2010, was planned as a workshop to identify the challenges women faced regarding public transportation and to plan a campaign to address these issues. The Remmoho executive committee had organized this workshop in an attempt to regain the momentum of previous years. By 2010, Remmoho's front-stage campaign activities had dwindled: its last public event had been a march in 2008 to protest violence against women who used public transporta-tion. The workshop was intended to allow members to reconnect with another, experience their collective purpose, and articulate a campaign strategy. As I entered the APF conference room, I noticed that the room—usually arranged so that tables formed a huge rectangular block in the middle—now had open space, with chairs arranged in an oval along the walls. The intended effect was immediately evident: I could fully see all women across the room. Complete bodies, usually hidden from the waist down by tables, were now visible. This arrangement set a different tone, one that was further emphasized when the workshop leader, Gender at Work facilitator Amina, began the meeting by writing "Welcome" on the board and drawing a smiley face. ☺

About twenty women gathered for the workshop, which, at its start, purposively drew on the bodily visibility that its spatial setup enabled. We stood, and Amina led us through a series of physical exercises based on Capacitar's adaptation of tai chi. Some women in the room were already familiar with the exercises from earlier workshops. Then, each attendee introduced herself and described how she was feeling. Thami mentioned feeling a bit depressed. Emily discussed how disturbed she felt at the passing away of her sister's daughter; she had come to the workshop to be healed, she said. When Ma Patrycja mentioned feeling "101 percent," we all laughed because it was such an enthusiastically anomalous response. After everyone had spoken, Amina expressed concern for the number of people who said they were feeling depressed. She joked that she should have come stocked with Prozac. She hoped that the workshop would help to alleviate some of the women's concerns "so that we can all get to Ma Patrycja's 101 percent."

As the workshop proceeded through Amina's wry commentary and, more importantly, through physical and theatrical exercises, I felt a level of commitment and investment I had not noted in other activist gatherings. Everyone in the room was invited and committed to participate fully, without distinction between researcher and member. I felt completely invited into the space but also nervous about the possibilities made available by the openness and vulnerability the women shared. I was not the only one who felt called by these possibilities. In a later interview, Willeen—also experiencing her first Remmoho meeting that day—described the joy of that meeting. "Let me tell you the truth," she confided: "I went to the toilet at lunch, if you remember we did break for five minutes, I went to the toilet and I closed my eyes and I said, 'Thank you Lord, thank you, you know exactly what I need. And this is it.' And there were just small tears in my eyes and I said, 'Thank you, Jesus, this is what I need in my life.' And when I got back I was so . . . I felt very important, after a very long time, I felt alive and I said, 'Oh my God, this is it.'"[24] What seemed distinct and valuable about this collective to Willeen and others was its emphasis on sensory experiences and energizing sociality. Emily, who came to be healed, and others who knew what to expect nurtured a sense of anticipation about the space created by the workshop exercises. Those new to the encounter were immediately attuned to its significance.

From this first meeting, it was clear that what would ordinarily be conceived as personal, particularly within the APF—body states, emotions, and familial challenges—not only could be voiced in Remmoho but was in fact the starting point for mobilizing the forum's members. Willeen's experience is instructive in that regard: she was bodily moved through tears to recognition, gratitude, and desire to partake further in the collective. For Willeen and others in the room, the workshop invited the whole person to collective participation. Members engaged through their full embodied selves, sharing physical exercises in addition to both voicing and hearing emotional states, including despondency, grief, uncertainty, and even passionate enthusiasm. They came with needs and desires for healing; the women's work together, as exemplified and reactivated by that workshop, would draw activists' pursuits of healing and collective recovery to the fore.

"You're Not a Comrade if You Cry": The Social As Embodied

A discussion during another workshop with the same group of people raised concerns about how interpersonal connections within Remmoho affected the health of its members, as participants processed the intrinsically embodied nature of their social ties. This second workshop, which Amina also facilitated, took place two weeks later, on the weekend of February 13 and 14. When I arrived, people were checking in, sharing their current physical, familial, and emotional states. Mum Alice mentioned her lingering illness and expressed hope that the workshop would give her some good energy. The woman next to Mum Alice also did not feel well.

Ma Patrycja, as at the last workshop, felt 101 percent, but she mentioned a hospital visit she and three others had made to see Rose, a Remmoho member who had had a stroke. After the hospital visit, she said, the four women had gone to Rose's house. The neighbors told the women that before her hospitalization, Rose had locked herself in her house. She had been unable to move, and no one knew what was happening to her. The self-imposed isolation ended when Rose was hospitalized. Allowed in at last, Rose's neighbors sought to help; they looked after her children (one of whom had epilepsy) and maintained her household.

Writing on Soweto at the advent of South Africa's democracy, Adam Ashforth (2005) charts a convergence of spiritual and material insecurity (stemming from increased socioeconomic inequality, the AIDS pandemic, rise in violent crime, and fear of witchcraft) that eroded collective solidarity and trust among neighbors. Rose's self-isolation was most likely a manifestation of this erosion of security in postapartheid Black community life. With neighborhoods being such an environment of insecurity, presumptions of malice from one's fellow residents proliferate, lending to social isolation and severance from avenues of needed support. Because Rose could not trust her neighbors, she could not seek their support in moments of need.[25]

Rose's condition shaped the ensuing discussion among the women. Nomvula, in her check-in, pointed to the need to develop a support system for group
members. She mentioned that Rose was the second member to have suffered
a stroke and that an increasing number of Remmoho members were seriously
ill. Amina agreed with Nomvula's suggestion to develop a support system that
could keep the group aware of what was happening with its members. "I wonder
how many illnesses are our contribution really as an organization?" she asked.
With this question, she was suggesting interconnections between members' social environments—in which Remmoho played a part—and their well-being.
"Are these illnesses coming from stress, from HIV/AIDS? . . . What support
systems are in place in members' lives?" she wondered.

"I'm always thinking about Comrade Rose," Talent said when it was her turn
to check in. "That picture is stuck in my head." She bent her head, her body
shaking; we heard her crying. Nomvula got up, but she did not approach Talent
to comfort her, as I thought she had intended. Rather, she started moving chairs
away from the middle of the room, markedly making space as Talent cried.

Amina next addressed Rose's isolation. "When you start working together,
you become more than friends, you become like family," she offered. "Why
couldn't Rose tell somebody that she was really ill? . . . Why is it that Rose
couldn't trust anyone?" she asked.

Talent tearfully responded, "She told me, but I didn't take it serious."

"Did she tell you that she was ill?" Amina asked.

"She told me that she had problems at home," Talent said.

Nomvula interjected, "Is this a safe space where people feel safe and that
they can share? . . . [because] more than once the space has been broken."
Reflecting on how the insecurity of everyday life was absorbed into social relations, as had been the case with Rose, Nomvula gave an example of a woman
who no longer attended meetings because another member had reported to her
husband that she had discussed their marital problems in meetings. The loss of
trust from that incident indicated that the insecurity that pervaded members'
neighborhoods was also seeping into Remmoho's internal dynamics.

"If we can't bring our personal issues to this space, then what is this space
for?" Amina asked, again questioning Remmoho's role in supporting its members. "Is it for campaigns?" With this question, Amina identified a key characteristic of Remmoho's organization. Coordinating campaigns, she suggested,
was not the primary purpose of the women's communion. Rather, its members
relied on the group for restoration, a reality evidenced by the emotionally open
check-ins, by the willingness of the women to talk about being depressed or
feeling down, as well as by the examples of women like Mum Alice, who came

to meetings hoping to receive restorative energy. This need for restoration was also evidenced by the profound gratitude Willeen felt for her discovery of the group. The break in trust within the group endangered that restorative function because it closed off the possibility of expression and release needed to restore well-being. Amina expressed a view of illness echoed by many of the women I interviewed: "When you stifle something that is bothering you it manifests in terrible issues. That is why when I hear that a woman is sick, I ask what is going on in her life." The group could provide a space to release, rather than stifle, feelings, but only if its members cultivated it as a safe space, one where they could be free to release the things they were stifling, the things that contributed to physical dis-ease.

The women continued to discuss Amina's question about the purpose of their collectivity, identifying a number of elements. Members offered intentions to use the space to build up one another as women, cultivate trust with one another, love one another, and praise one another's attributes. On this last point, Nomvula elaborated how, on a daily basis, women hid their real conditions, giving a standard response that they were okay. "Why are we continuing to play the game to appear as if we are okay if we are not?" Amina asked. "What is wrong if people see that we are going through a rough patch? . . . We want our kids to be truthful but all our lives, we have been told to lie, to cover up. . . . We only react when things fall apart."

"For me, this space is for us to affirm that we are beautiful," Nomvula responded, saying that she would tell pregnant women they were beautiful, which was not often done. "Sometimes I let people cry," Nomvula later explained, an explanation that encompassed her earlier behavior when Talent cried, "Because that's the only way that will heal you. It's not a space for you to wear makeup [to cover up imperfections]." Picking up on this point, another participant, Celiwe, raised the importance of "redefin[ing] this space away from the APF, because you're not a comrade if you cry." Nomvula's philosophy to embrace unconcealed bodily conditions and responses as restoratively beautiful, to let people cry, thus stands against the constrictions on activists' vulnerability and emotional repertoire embedded in the APF's organizational ethos.

Remmoho's discussion of illness and social support at that February meeting invoked the intrinsically embodied nature of social ties. Social ties, even when virtual, are built through the sharing of bodily presence with others. In a recursive dynamic, the strength or weakness of these ties feeds back into individual bodily well-being. Fractured ties contribute to isolation, which exacerbates physical dis-ease. However, such ties can be repaired through purposive to-getherness, as Remmoho members would strive for by supporting Rose.

Rose's Song: Group Cohesion as Cultivated through Care

The presumption of malice that manifested in the APF's community life was apparent in the erosion of trust Remmoho members experienced. The women's choice to consciously cultivate support and take responsibility for one another is all the more significant in light of this erosion. One manifestation of that conscious community is a decision members made during their February meeting to visit Rose at the hospital together. While visits to ailing people are customary in Southern African communities, hospital visits were not an established collective practice within Remmoho. Members would, of course, visit one another of their own accord, but Remmoho's visit to Rose was compelling as being the organization's first collective visit to an ailing member. This decision stemmed from the group's avowal at the February meeting to cultivate care and support one another. Following up on those intentions, the members hired a van to transport them to the hospital on the Tuesday after the meeting. I invited myself along for the hospital visit because Rose had been among the first activists I connected with at the start of my fieldwork.

When we arrived at Rose's room, which she shared with three other patients, we found Rose connected to an IV. She seemed swallowed by her hospital bed. Both her hands were bandaged into fists—to prevent her from hurting herself, a nurse explained. She had lost a lot of weight, which showed in the deep set around her high cheekbones. Nomvula immediately went to Rose's bedside and started addressing her and caressing her face. Paballo, who had not yet taken discernably ill (described in chapter 4), asked us to join hands for a few moments. Charmaine raised a church hymn, in Sesotho: "ha le mpotsa tshepo yaka ke tlare ke jesu. Ke lapetse. Ho Jesu, anthe Jesu o ne a mpona ha ke lela jwalo a mpitsa are tlo honna." At the conclusion of the hymn, the women started praying aloud. Nomvula stood at Rose's side throughout. Rose did not have the strength to sit up; the nurse had to be called in to give her water through a plastic syringe. Nomsa, standing next to me, said that Rose looked so much like her own mother and began to cry. I put my hand on her back to comfort her. Charmaine mentioned a poem Rose had written based on the song "'Mshini wam" and tried to recall the words. She and others fondly brought up memories of the songs Rose used to sing with such spirit, including "We'ndoda awuyaz' oyifunayo." Someone sang another song, and Nomvula prayed.

In the van, I asked Mum Alice about the church hymn in Sesotho, as it was unfamiliar to me. She translated it for me as "When you ask me who is my savior, I will tell you it's Jesus Christ. He is the one who saw me when I was crying, when I was suffering, he told me come to me. Even if I walk through the darkness, he was with me and what I found there, I felt happiness and peace." Mum Alice insisted that Rose was singing that song with us. "It started out humming and you could see that her mouth was moving," she said. Because of its spiritual nature, Mum Alice offered, the song was "like a shock going through your body. . . . If you understand the songs, you feel it in your body. I think that was the main thing that Rose was feeling, that's why she had to sing."

Personal circumstances often frame our experiences in the field. My grandmother passed away about six weeks after I visited Rose in the hospital. Bereaved, I was away from Johannesburg for about ten days. When I returned, Charmaine informed me that Comrade Rose had passed away, and that the women had held a memorial service for her. I felt sad not to have been there. Her passing set loss in a deeper groove.

Remmoho members' deliberate cultivation of care through specified actions, including visiting one of their own who had taken ill and mourning her loss together by holding a memorial, highlights a revived attentiveness to collectivity and group cohesion. This ongoing cultivation drew on love, respect as the accordance of dignity, and collective nurturance to sustain the supportive relationships that members needed amid economic insecurity and pervasive health crises. The women's togetherness seemed to unfold effortlessly as they drew on personal, social, and religious repertoires of sharing caring presence, as in the visit with Rose.

And yet, these seemingly effortless acts remain instructive. In claiming Rose's bedside, Nomvula exuded such love toward Rose, transmitting to all present a willingness not only to draw nearer but also to embrace the infirm in her moment of vulnerability and with a bodily condition that might otherwise repel. In doing so, Nomvula assured Rose of her inherent dignity, unchanged by her physical environment or body state. No matter how Rose's shrunken and enervated body might register to her visitors, Nomvula understood the critical need to provide a reassuring presence through facial and bodily comportment and thereby communicate to Rose that her social bonds remained secure, that she remained safe. The assurance that she would be harbored in community was all the more important given the uncertainty and anxiety Rose had exuded by not revealing her health decline to neighbors and friends sooner.

Nomvula set the tone, putting us all at ease. Members drew nearer, not only to Rose but also to one another, constituting themselves in an approximation of that eternal group formation, a circle, with Rose's bed serving as the head. Paballo's request to join hands was perhaps inspired to physically embody the sense of connection already present in the room, generated by the intimacy of our bodily proximity. The sonic emerged from the haptic. Having established touch, the women's connection was further actualized in sound when those present joined their voices together, with Rose making her own contribution. Sonically and spiritually ensconcing the women, singing circulated physical sensations and evoked bodily responses evident not only in Rose's pull to sing—like a shock going through her body, as Mum Alice had said—but also in Nomsa's sensitivity and ensuing tears. Laughter came even with tears as Charmaine and others teased Rose with memories of more humorously spirited times. With the assurance of laughter and fond recollection, Remmoho members again reminded Rose of her inherent dignity and belonging within this community, a belonging she would not lose. Rose's illness and eventual passing would continue to reverberate among the women as they reflected on the interconnections between their own activism, physical health, interpersonal bonds, and the responsibility they bore each other.

Remmoho's claim to such responsibility for self and others must be carefully delineated, given the neoliberal economic inequities of its members' lives. French sociologist Pierre Bourdieu (2000 [1997]) uses the concept of symbolic violence to explain how systems of inequality can remain unchallenged even among those who are structurally disadvantaged. For Bourdieu, perceptions and interpretations of the world are filtered through the social contexts in which individuals live. It therefore becomes easy to believe that one's social world and the inequalities embedded in it are inherent and natural. When groups and individuals come to assume the rightfulness and deservedness of their social positions—for instance, when the impoverished blame themselves for their conditions, or when women activists assume they are not smart enough to lead collectives or their knowledge and experiences are not the stuff of politics—this symbolic violence benefits those with power because it undercuts opposition to inequities.

It is tempting to interpret the women's assumption of responsibility—individually for their illnesses and collectively for promoting one another's well-being—as an internalization of symbolic violence (see, e.g., Holmes 2013: 172–74) or as a manifestation of false consciousness that serves to naturalize and thereby obscure the sources of structural inequities.[26] However, I want to advance a different set of considerations. Reconciling critical analysis with the women's perspectives reveals Remmoho members' efforts as a *resocialization* away from the systemic silencing of women within patriarchal formations. Remmoho's work also incorporates attempts to combat the individual alienation attendant with the postapartheid neoliberal dispensation by cultivating interpersonal and collective bonds grounded in care for the body. This care included work to relieve the body of its burdens through movement exercises and vocal catharsis.

"YOU CANNOT DO TAI CHI WITH YOUR BAGGAGE": THE BURDENED BODY AND CRITICAL OUTLETS

Remmoho's understanding of ill health as the embodiment of structural distress, and its focus in practice on physical exercises and voicing of one's issues, echoes philosophical and anthropological understandings of the connections between bodily health and sociopolitical inequities. Judith Butler's descriptions of the body as "the legacy of sedimented acts" (1988: 523) is suggestive of how everyday stresses and tensions manifest in bodily conditions, whether fatigue, depression, or other illness. Medical anthropologists, including Nancy Scheper-Hughes (1992, 1994) and Seth Holmes (2013), have shown how illness, as physical and mental anguish, can be a direct embodiment of structural, symbolic, and environmental violence. Conducting fieldwork at a farm in Washington State, Holmes found that the health concerns of Triqui migrant laborers he worked with corresponded with and were determined by their marginalized positioning at the bottom rung of the farm's social hierarchy (2013: 88–110). Triqui workers were subjected to structural violence (discriminatory international policies, inadequate living conditions, severely strenuous physical labor) and symbolic violence (racist insults and xenophobic stereotypes), and they coped with the legacies of direct political violence (including the bodily damage and persisting trauma torture had caused). Each formation along this "violence continuum" (Holmes 2013: 89–90; Bourgois 2001; Scheper-Hughes and Bourgois 2003) yielded different but intersecting bodily effects, cumulatively revealing the suffering endured by the migrant laborers.

Remmoho members similarly experienced illness as an obtrusive recurrence in the group—Nomvula noted that Rose was the second member to have a stroke and the third to be seriously ill. Understanding the recurrence of ill health in Remmoho requires considering, as Holmes did, how the women were physically affected by their structural positioning with regard to class, race, and gender and their social roles as daughters, sisters, wives, mothers, and activists. Like Triqui migrant laborers, who were caught between the United States and

Mexico, Remmoho members, many of whom bore the physical and emotional scars of apartheid, lived through postapartheid structural violence, manifested in inadequate housing conditions and financial instability that rendered uncertain their prospects to meet their basic needs. They endured the social stigma of being among "the poorest of the poor." These are the very manifestations of structural violence that social movements mobilized against; they also affected women most adversely because women most often bore primary responsibility for their families' livelihood.

In addition to their exposure at multiple points of the violence continuum, Remmoho members' experiences were also determined by their socialization as women within patriarchal formations, which produced further bodily dispossession. As wives, they were subjected to the authority of their husbands and his family. Social and physical violence—including restrictions on women's mobility and bodily autonomy as well as physical and sexual abuse within households—shaped women's structural conditions. Recall, in particular, Nomvula's realization that "as women, we don't own our bodies. We're owned by the communities, we're owned by children, we're owned by mothers, and sometimes by our in-laws, because even when a woman is not ready to have children, the in-laws can tell you that we want a child now." This bodily dispossession cemented their social identities at the expense of a sustaining sense of self.

In addition to these structural stresses, the multiple responsibilities of Remmoho members exerted unrelenting physical and emotional pressure. Reflecting on the considerable number of women who expressed feelings of depression or fatigue at Remmoho meetings, Amina hypothesized that the daily stresses Remmoho members experienced, left unresolved, built up in the body. Their tired bodies were the material "legacies of sedimented acts": "Imagine if you're not allowed to put down your suitcase if you're at an airport. You have a five-hour wait and you have to carry this all the time; you are going to be tired. And that's exactly what happens to them. They carry this huge amount, they haven't had the chance to offload those, and you go to bed with it, you get up with it, and you clutch it everywhere you go."[27] Biomedical science understands this legacy of stress as "allostatic load"—the accumulation of bodily damage from chronic stress. Subjected to an unrelenting allostatic load, the body becomes overburdened in ways that hinder receptivity and effective participation in collective activism. As Amina explained:

> In many ways, what you're clutching becomes your defense, so you are not open to anything—you are not open to understanding who you are, you are not open to finding who you are as a woman, because you just have your

baggage that you are clutching all the time. You go to meetings [at the APF], and you can't really get your voice heard because you have your baggage with you. And that baggage impacts on your self-esteem, it impacts on your relationships, it impacts on how you are functioning at work, it impacts on how you operate in the family, in the community, in all given situations. So when you come in a given environment, you're still a bit tired, and your body starts only seeing that tiredness.[28]

That bodies become overburdened due to accumulating structural disparities is rarely a point of activist critique. Feminist praxis, however, accounts for Amina's and Remmoho's intervention.

Establishing the domestic, private, and personal as a realm of critical analysis with sociopolitical implications has been crucial to feminist praxis. Remmoho members' challenges within the APF echo the experiences of American women's liberation activists from the 1960s who asserted the personal as political (Hanisch 2006 [1969]). Extending from this insight, Remmoho women also attest that the social is embodied. Accepting that the personal is political and the social is embodied contextualizes intractable individual challenges within wider dynamics, allowing each woman's experiences to resonate with those of other women and fostering collective action toward social change. Attending to the structural implications underpinning the prevalence of ill health among Remmoho members offers an avenue for suturing together individual experiences to build toward collective understanding. Such a move would render structural inequities visible and mobilize powerful critiques of the conditions the women are living through. Yet, in their willingness to assume individual and organizational responsibility for ill health, Remmoho members would at first seem to bypass this political move.

From one point of view, this apparent sidestepping of the political through assumption of responsibility for each other could be seen as playing into neoliberal logic. Harvey (2005), Rose (1996), and others (see McElhinny 2010: 315–19) discuss how proponents of neoliberalism idealize self-sufficiency, individual autonomy, and an entrepreneurial spirit in a way that shifts social responsibility from the state to individuals and civil society organizations. Methodologies that emphasize self-care and affective social ties, like those the Gender Reference Group and Remmoho relied on, could be interpreted as furthering these aims of neoliberalism rather than subverting them. Such an interpretation, however, would overlook Remmoho members' conscious intentions and the gendered countermobilizations of their bodily practices toward wellness.

Attunements to the political significance of illness as a structural critique from disenfranchised bodies offer a model of subversion that is powerful but also passive and oblique. Through illness, the body reflects individuals' exposures along a violence continuum; it is passively inscribed on and overdetermined by historical and political-economic configurations. Remmoho's practices rendered bodily orientations around health and wellness more intentional and active by offering means of shifting and ameliorating their physical, emotional, and social states. Rather than allowing members' bodies to merely reflect the structural strains of their lives, Remmoho worked through their bodies to restore well-being, by incorporating movement practices that required members to momentarily lay down their baggage, as it were, and root their bodily assemblies in the accordance of care, respect, and dignity to one another. By claiming organizational responsibility for checking on and supporting one another, they created avenues for action that defied structural constraints.

"How Words Do Things with Persons":
Speech, Healing, and Political Transformation

Remmoho members' cultivation of positive sociality among themselves alleviated their physical burdens. Discussing personal problems became a critical outlet, one that was necessary to their bodily health. Ma Patrycja saw talking out issues as self-healing: "Because if you keep something, Tayo, inside, you don't want to take it out, it hurts. And that thing it kills you because it's ... it's a secret killer, because it takes a bit, a bit inside of you. Then at the end of the day when you go to the doctor they say you've got depression or you are stressed. Most of those people who are secretive, who don't want to cough things out they usually get those sickness and they don't last [survive]."[29] Thus, Remmoho offered the potential to enhance well-being by providing a supportive environment for airing out issues and challenges. Feminist philosopher Denise Riley describes this impact of language as a shared rather than individual phenomenon. Seeking to address "How Words Do Things with Us" (an inversion of J. L. Austin's famous title), Riley conveys "language's affect as that outward unconscious that hovers between people, rather than swimming upward from the privacy of each heart" (2005: 3–4).[30] In recognizing the intersubjective force of language, it is possible to appreciate "how words do things with persons" (Klaits 2010: 165), not only in constituting interpersonal relationships but also, as Remmoho members attest, in reconstituting the body's health.[31] In Ma Patrycja's elaboration, Remmoho members did things with their bodies by transmitting through words—"coughing out" in an expulsive voicing—what their burdened bodies had been holding on to.

Amina shared and encouraged such voicing, reflecting a belief that collective activism is not only inadequate but also potentially harmful if it stifles individuals' voices and yields poisonous interpersonal relationships. In her facilitation with Remmoho, Amina was inspired by the importance Paulo Freire placed on dialogue in promoting inclusivity within political communities (1972). Amina encouraged talking as a process of collaboration through which Remmoho members recognized the issues that were important in their lives and created the space for their voices to be heard. As voices emerged and gained strength, the members could then identify possibilities for transformation together. In order to meet members' needs for restoration and collaborative transformation, some practices had to be encouraged (like the freedom to cry), deliberately cultivated (visiting Rose as a group), or openly disavowed (gossiping, backbiting, and the aggressive organizational culture of the APF).

"My Spirit Remembered My Soul": Bodily Reclamation and Wellness

Individual members registered and expressed positive effects from Remmoho's methodologies, particularly as facilitated by Amina, not only on their physical bodies but also within their spirits. Through physical exercises involving visualizations of the body's energy, of the wholeness and beauty of co-participants, of lives and communities, Amina encouraged a different kind of presence (distinct from that fostered by the APF's practices) in the workshops she facilitated. By doing exercises that encouraged relaxation, women experienced the freedom of laying their burdens down, even if only temporarily. As Amina stated, "You cannot do tai chi with your baggage." The relief was so profound that, at one workshop I attended, some women started crying after the exercises. Ma Patrycja described her experience of the exercises as one of losing weight: "When I'm doing these exercises I feel something [taken] out of my weight."[32] Willeen described it as an energetic release of an obstruction: "Those exercises, it's like in a way they liberated something, they opened something in me, they released some certain energies and when I saw it, my spirit remembered, you see, my soul."[33] In the unburdening of accumulated energies, Willeen experienced reconnection with herself. These two distinct elements—the effect of language in reinforcing positive sociality and the palpable experience of relaxation cultivated through physical exercises—charged Remmoho's space.

In light of these assessments, it must be noted that while many women sought to heal themselves through collective ties, the impulses to offer care and support were not innate to the women. Remmoho members had to renew commitments to creating a safe space because the group itself became conflict-ridden. When Amina "wonder[ed] how many illnesses are our contribution really as an organization," she was referring to the problematic dynamics within the group, involving gossiping and backbiting that disrupted the safety of the space. By questioning the group's contribution—positive or negative—to the health of its members, she had hoped to prompt the women to dig beneath the surface and identify the reasons they perpetuated the very dynamics they had formed the group to transform. Remmoho members struggled together to articulate the meanings of the space, to identify those moments that changed their outlook (like Nomvula telling pregnant women that they are beautiful), the transformations they sought, and the possible ways of getting there.

ACCOUNTING FOR BACKLASH

Like the efforts of the Gender Reference Group that preceded it, Remmoho's undertaking met with opposition. The nurturing, intuitive approaches the group used jarred with political praxis within the broader APF collective. A few male activists criticized these efforts toward gender mobilization as being psychologically rather than politically driven. One male activist critiqued the Gender Reference Group as engaging people "as if you are counseling them" (Eriksson 2007: 85). Counseling, it seemed, had no place in coalition politics. Further, efforts to highlight gender inequality and contest patriarchal orders within the movement were interpreted as diverting attention from the "real" politics of anti-neoliberal struggle (see Eriksson 2007: 80–87). Besides being viewed as distraction, these practices, and the women's critiques of the APF's practice, were also accused of promoting individualism and thereby neglecting or undermining the collective. As one male activist asked at a 2006 meeting, "What is the point of these person's [sic] individual experiences if we cannot hear how these people collectively experience water privatisation?" (Eriksson 2007: 83). Many shared the perspective this activist expressed, that the Gender Reference Group did not do enough to draw attention to the wider neoliberal context.

These critiques were not solely male-driven, a fact that marked the depth of the disjuncture between these feminist interventions and the broader collective. The groups' methodologies did not appeal to all female APF members, and some of the differences between the women Remmoho mobilized and those who disagreed emerged from racialized and class sensibilities. Many of Remmoho's members were impoverished Black women who felt viscerally alienated in APF meetings—one woman described getting sick at APF meetings due to the silencing of her voice. A number of them lived with traumatic experiences (of rape or physical violence, for example), which could be unitary or prolonged violations. Reclaiming their selves involved cultivating empowerment over these facets of their lives and relationships. Remmoho's methods facilitated this endeavor, providing space for women to process together and garner collective insight.

For some, such work held no appeal. Clara, a forty-year-old woman who self-identified as white, described feeling disconnected in the one Remmoho session she attended, during which attendees recounted experiences of sexual abuse. Finding little to connect with in these narratives and seeing no indication that Remmoho's scope extended beyond such recountings, Clara doubted whether she had a role in Remmoho's collective project. Although she was concerned with combating sexism, she did not experience voicelessness in the same ways Remmoho's members experienced it, and she sought a more expansive engagement with gender-based activism than Remmoho offered. For Clara, Remmoho's lack of focus on the wider systemic issues, the lack of a wider structural perspective on the women's intimate narratives limited its effectiveness. While her reflections suggest that Remmoho could have been more inclusive of a wider range of experiences by drawing more focus to wider cultural and political-economic systems, Remmoho's work was undeniably political.

The disjuncture between Remmoho's interventions and these APF perspectives can be better understood by considering how feminist practices tend to fit only "awkwardly" within broader assemblies. In her engagement with awkwardness, Strathern posited essential differences between feminist commitments and disciplinary practice, particularly in anthropology. Strathern's observations suggest two possible avenues for analyzing the backlash against the methodologies of gender mobilization that Remmoho and its predecessor used.

First, she describes feminist analysis as perspective transforming (1987: 280), a quality echoed in Remmoho's and Castro's insistence on creating new activist practices rather than duplicating existing organizational forms. A perspective-transforming approach to activist mobilization challenges the privileging of external opposition by emphasizing internal dynamics and excavating previously unvoiced experiences. The second avenue Strathern suggested, closely related to perspective transformation, is a focus on the inadequacy of compensatory restructuring—gender equity in social movements could not be achieved simply by accretion, by placing women in leadership positions. Rather, such goals require radical reconstruction; at least, that was what the gender activists I interviewed insisted (see Strathern 1987: 282). Such reconstruction, which is inward-looking, challenges established practices and contracts the domains of activist engagement, shifting the scope of political impact into intangible registers. This disjuncture—between the external focus of the wider collective and the need for internal focus to transform the collective and allow women's voices to be heard—is the source of the tension between the "real," presumably material, politics of anti-neoliberal antagonism, which were the focus of the wider APF, and the emotional, testimonial, restorative work the women conducted in Remmoho.

The APF was not without such emotional registers; a politics of confrontational antagonism, like that practiced by the APF, generates its own emotional practices (Gould 2009). But APF members were practiced in particular ways that Remmoho's gendered interventions challenged. Rather than anger and obdurate resistance, Castro and Remmoho emphasized beauty and sensory receptivity, emphases that allowed some women to pointedly feminize their activism. This contrast is especially evident in the constraints women experienced around the ascription of "comrade," a male-normative uniformity exemplified in dress (ragged jeans and a struggle T-shirt) and as particular emotional characterizations, as Remmoho members noted in statements such as "You are not a comrade if you cry." The experience of Rethabile provides insight in this regard. In Remmoho's February meeting, when Nomvula had said, "For me, this space [Remmoho] is for us to affirm that we are beautiful," Rethabile elaborated the significance of that intervention in her experience. She described how, when she first came to the APF, she would dress down "to be like a man." She wore jeans and a comrade T-shirt, "so that men would accommodate me." She had come to the group pregnant, and when Nomvula told her she was beautiful, she dismissed it at first. But when Nomvula repeated her affirmation at the next meeting, she was considerably affected. "Through that [Nomvula saying you are beautiful], then I was revived to start taking care of myself. [Things like that,] it revived us, and made us who we are."

The contrast in emotional praxis extended to attitudes toward the care routines that were at the heart of Remmoho. Many male activists derided sensitivity to bodily care as the antithesis of struggle and comradely effort, as a luxury that activists could ill afford. Such activities as overnight workshops emphasizing relaxation and wellness modalities were unrecognizable as consequential in the context of the APF's broader aims. Yet these seemingly small actions proved impactful, not just in personal transformations but also in collective participation. A founding Remmoho member recalled how, in the group's early attempts to get women into APF leadership positions, members would meet right before APF meetings to encourage each other and, through such encouragement, generate a sense of capability that encouraged women to volunteer for leadership roles.

Broader critiques of these gendered interventions highlight the challenge of expanding the conceptualization of the political to encompass more intimate sites of encounter, including how "comrades" should relate with one another, as well as the embodied and emotional resonances of activist practice. Another challenge is recognizing the authority of Black women's experiences without depending on interpretation or translation into a broader systemic framework; in other words, to make these expressions recognizable as political interventions in themselves (Lewis 1996: 100). These interventions involve not only the voicing of what may otherwise be silenced or undervalued (Craven and Davis 2013: 8–9) but also, through such voicing, the disruption of patterned alienations and cultivation of new sensibilities.

NOTES

1. *Remmoho* means "we are together" in seSotho. While I have chosen to identify the group, I use pseudonyms for its members to protect their privacy, except for people already identified in published accounts and Nancy Castro, one of the facilitators of Remmoho's earlier processes.

2. This quotation and the next are from Remmoho's files, including organizational minutes.

3. A related conceptualization of incompatible relationships is Anna Tsing's discussion of friction as "the awkward, unequal, unstable, and creative qualities of interconnections across difference" (2005: 4). "Friction" is viewed here as a productive and enabling feature of collaboration across agents' disparate agendas. Yet awkward alliances, like the one between feminism and coalitional activism, for example, can reinforce inequality in spite of their productivity (Carrier-Moisan 2013).

4. For parallels within anti-apartheid movements, see Kompe (1985) and Reynolds and Richards (2003). For a nuanced discussion of the subordination of women's specific interests to universalized goals, see Molyneaux (1985).

5. For example, Rebecca Pointer discussed a reluctance to engage with internal dynamics in the Mandela Park Anti-Eviction Campaign: "Mandela Park activists claim to be 'revolutionary' in their thinking, and to want to overturn the systems that create oppression. But this is predominantly viewed as attacking the State, capitalism, privatization, and so on; not as an attack on their own oppressive 'cultural' systems or their own oppressive thoughts and actions" (2004: 277). It

must be noted that APF activists interviewed in 2010 considered insensitivity to gender dynamics a shortcoming of their mobilization, in retrospect.

6. This quotation has been slightly edited for clarity.

7. Interview with the author, December 15, 2010, Johannesburg. Unless indicated otherwise, all quotes attributed to Nancy Castro in this chapter are from this interview.

8. Interview with the author, November 19, 2010, Johannesburg.

9. Interview with the author, December 7, 2010, Johannesburg.

10. One woman said, "You can speak in APF and say whatever you wanted to say, but they will never take you seriously. It's like you are playing" (interview with the author, March 18, 2010, Johannesburg).

11. Interview with the author, December 15, 2010; also see Eriksson (2007: 83–84).

12. Castro argued, "*To change culture is impossible under the normal tool of the patriarchy. [It] needs to be something like you breathe and you feel and you live. If we start with conceptual [discussions] I am sure nobody [is] going to discuss to disagree because conceptually it is very easy to agree with the gender position. [It is] different when you start to touch the individual*" (in Eriksson 2007: 98; italics in original).

13. Interview with the author, November 19, 2010, Johannesburg.

14. In the course of my more recent fieldwork, one meeting participant discussed how she experienced a "double or triple mindedness" arising out of fear, doubt, confusion, and lack of confidence that interrupted her routine endeavors and decision making: "There was something that made you not believe in yourself and when you grow, it stays with you," she said.

15. One male activist's critique of the group was that it engaged people "as if you are counseling them" (Eriksson 2007: 85).

16. These objectives were listed in a 2008 proposal for organizational funding.

17. See Kaplan (1997) and Hodgson (2017: 133–55) on the political authority of women's community activism.

18. The quotes in this paragraph are from Remmoho's internal organizational reports.

19. Interview with the author, December 7, 2010, Johannesburg.

20. Interview with the author, September 8, 2010, Johannesburg.

21. Interview with the author, March 18, 2010, Johannesburg.

22. In fact, Remmoho invited Castro to facilitate some sessions; one member credited Castro as being "very instrumental in making Remmoho and us what we are today" (interview with the author, November 19, 2010).

23. Capacitar is an international network with a mission of empowerment, healing, and solidarity, particularly with communities that have experienced violence, impoverishment, and trauma. Dr. Pat Cane developed early Capacitar

programs through popular education workshops in Nicaragua in the 1980s; the programs have since grown to a global presence. Capacitar adapts and blends a number of wellness modalities to create exercises for its participants. Remmoho adopted Capacitar exercises through Gender at Work facilitators.

24. Interview with the author, September 8, 2010, Johannesburg.

25. Paballo, who was a member of both the APF and Remmoho, noted the effects of this fundamental instability. As I prepared to leave her house after our interview, Paballo said, "This is life in the location." When I commented, based on the quiet of that still September afternoon, that it was peaceful, she corrected me: "No, it's stressful." The tranquility I sensed belied the stress Paballo experienced in her life. Her response articulated the tension and disquiet residents inhabit daily due to the fundamental insecurity and distrust among neighbors. Paballo and her fellow residents were continually managing their social impressions so as not to expose themselves to judgment or bad intentions. Especially when it was quiet, residents never knew what unseen and unheard development could be brewing—hence Paballo's stress. Interview with the author, 2010, Johannesburg.

26. *False consciousness* is a term from Marxist discourse that suggests that individuals and groups can hold views of the world or adopt goals that are contrary to their best interests given their class positions.

27. Interview with the author, October 26, 2010. Both Julie Livingston (2012) and Didier Fassin (2007) consider how the body absorbs the injustices of history and political economic disparities in accounting for epidemics of cancer and HIV/AIDS, respectively, in Southern Africa. In doing so, they mobilize historically attuned analyses highlighting the pathological legacies of colonial migration, apartheid, and postcolonial inequities as they are embodied in an ongoing present by those who have been marginalized and rendered invisible. Similarly, the burdens Remmoho members carried in their individual lives have been infiltrated by history and are embedded in political-economic insecurity.

28. Interview with the author, October 26, 2010.

29. Interview with the author, May 25, 2010.

30. Denise Riley signals here the affective turn in the humanities and social sciences in the early 2000s that drew attention toward unspoken, ineffable, and nonconscious dimensions of experience. If feelings arise from personal sensations, and emotions are shared collective categories to register the expression of feelings (anger, sadness, happiness, and so on), then affect is a movement of intensities that is preconscious, subconscious, or nonconscious (for more on this delineation, see Shouse (2005); also see Brennan (2004), Massumi (2002), Thrift (2004), Ahmed (2004)). These shifting intensities circulate among people, objects, and environments and are registered bodily, although they may bypass conscious awareness.

31. Kathryn Geurts presents a similar cultural model of affliction arising from acrimonious speech among Ewe in Ghana (Geurts 2002: 204–9). Remmoho members' emphases on speech as an unburdening of the body in the pursuit of well-being resonates with these insights.

32. Interview with the author, May 25, 2010, Johannesburg.

33. Interview with the author, September 8, 2010, Johannesburg.

SIX

—⚏—

REDEMPTION

THE SOWETO ELECTRICITY CRISIS COMMITTEE (SECC), an Anti-Privatisation Forum (APF) affiliate, holds its meetings at Funda Center in Diepkloof, Soweto, tucked away but readily accessible once a visitor knows to proceed through a BP gas station to the gates leading into the center's grounds. Funda is one of a number of community arts initiatives founded under apartheid, in its case as a response to the 1976 youth uprising in Soweto. In the aftermath of the uprising, Funda's founders sought to offer arts-based education as a means of engaging young people for whom the state education system had fallen short. Following the 1976 protests against Bantu education and the use of Afrikaans as a language of instruction, many South African Black youths were not in school but "languishing in jail"; others journeyed across the border to join liberation movements in exile (Charles Nkosi, quoted in Jason 2015). To bridge this gap, Funda highlighted the role of the arts in collective recovery amid the turmoil of life under apartheid. Given Funda's struggle history, it is fitting that the SECC holds its meetings and events on Funda's campus.

In November 2009, I arrived at Funda for the SECC's Soweto Heroes Day. This annual commemorative event had been initiated only the year before as a way to honor the memory of SECC members who had died since the movement began. On the first Heroes Day, SECC members went to the cemetery to clean the graves of their departed comrades. In the year I visited, the organization planned a program and reception to draw in more people. Still an inexperienced driver, I scraped my car against a pole as I pulled in to park. Before I could lament the damage, two teenage boys approached me to express sympathy and volunteered to wash the car to minimize the appearance of the scratches from the accident. I would later find out they were part of a youth choir performing at the event. As I moved from the parking area into the event hall, I noticed several photographs on display along the entranceway. These were portraits of the deceased heroes; the person's name and SECC branch were listed beneath each photo. Inside the hall, I was greeted by activists who had swapped the red SECC T-shirts usually worn at movement events for yellow ones that read "In Loving Memory of Bongani Lubisi and Sihle Mahlangu."

The day's program included speeches and recollections by families and friends of those being remembered and a performance by the youth choir. Following the choral performance, one of the young people approached the stage to give a solo dance performance. She was Bongani Lubisi's daughter. Lubisi had been the SECC's organizer and leader until he died at the age of thirty-four from an unknown illness. He had opposed electricity cutoffs by reconnecting those affected, despite the risks to himself. "I'm not afraid of the prison anymore," he had said. "I always prepare my family that one time they might get a call that says: I'm dead" (in Opitz 2006). The community's esteem for Lubisi was evident, and the young dancer bore the mantle of her descent well. She stood timidly at first, covering her face out of shyness, but the moment she started dancing, the crowd was moved to rapturous cheers and ululation. In the face of shared grief over her father's passing, and concerns for her welfare on his loss, her dance affirmed life in a generational continuum. Her present vibrancy recalled his past determination.

Performance served as a site of intergenerational transmission throughout the day. As was typical of activist gatherings, the program of speeches was punctuated not only by scheduled performances but also by spontaneous singing sessions during which some participants, mostly elder women, would cluster in front to dance. During one of these sessions, a community leader urged the young people in attendance to join in the singing and dancing. Asserting that the youth "must know these songs," she highlighted the political stakes of young people's participation in activism. At an event that explicitly acknowledged the pervasiveness of death—commemorating activists who had passed away not from police bullets but from the structural violence that pervades life under impoverished conditions—the leader revealed what was at stake: the transfer of struggle to the next generation. If young people forgot, if they did not take up these songs, the aural manifestations of collective dissent, the activists' efforts of past generations would be lost. The struggle could not continue if young people did not participate in its cultural performances and thus claim it as their legacy. Such sentiments echoed the words of then African National Congress (ANC) secretary-general Kgalema Motlanthe, albeit from an entirely different political configuration: "If we lose the active support of young people, then our struggle would have been in vain. We have to engage the youth on issues that interest them. They are going to inherit this country. A revolution that does not produce future cadres and leaders from among the young is doomed" (quoted in Jubasi 2000). For both ruling party politicians and community activists, youth participation was key to sustaining their efforts over time.

In South Africa's history of political mobilization, broad-based movements had often relied on their young members to further activist aims. Indeed, youth were frequently the radicalizing faction in such movements. The APF shared in this history; youth were integral to its formation right from its founding. Young people, particularly university students, energized the APF's earliest efforts. They struggled alongside workers, many of whom were trade union members, and community residents in multifaceted campaigns to stop privatization as it was introduced on campus, in municipalities, and in township neighborhoods. This constellation of young activists was foundational to the APF's organization, as it enabled the collective to leverage the differential capabilities of diverse groups. While workers found themselves constrained from direct action by union agreements, students could occupy the offices of Wits University leaders and, at great risk to themselves, disrupt routines to compel leaders to address their concerns. These first attempts to stop outsourcing did not succeed, and subsequent protests calling for an end to outsourcing did not yield results, but outsourcing at Wits did end in November 2015, after a new groundswell of student protests under the banners of the #FeesMustFall and #EndOutsourcing campaigns. Thus, the abandonment of outsourcing at Wits was the result of years of effort by youth working in coordination with broader activist communities.

The organizational context in which these youth efforts played out is relevant. Although APF leadership recognized youth as a vital component in its work, the marginalization of their concerns caused youth members to became alienated in ways that were similar to the marginalization of women's concerns within the APF. Before the 2015 protests—and leaders' response to them—affirmed activist faith in young people's political impact, many young South Africans had been establishing continuities with their anti-apartheid predecessors' mobilization efforts by cultivating explicitly political subjectivities. However, activists and scholars had largely discounted their activities as apolitical or frivolous, so their work had been done without mainstream recognition and in the face of structural economic pressures. Given the liberationist aspirations, political innovations, and possibilities for self-making that have become evident in South Africa's recent youth movements, the historical contexts, investments, and merits of young people's activism necessitate reconsideration.

Thus I recontextualize the experiences and motivations of young people who became active in social movements like the APF, especially prior to 2015, when such activist involvements were not in favor among their peers. This chapter demonstrates how the political engagement of youth is rooted in an aesthetic of relationship—what draws young people to collective action, sustains their participation, and can cause their disillusionment are encounters, often intergenerational, that are charged with the import of sensory perception. By drawing this relational dimension further into focus, I aim to show how that aesthetic of relationship encompasses the intimacy of interpersonal interactions sustained over time, the immediacy of individual embodiments, and the power of public or collective encounters with other activists and with art. Ultimately, for APF youth, this aesthetic of relationship entailed a connection to others that had important implications for the evolution of political subjectivity, with performance as a key mode of expression.

THE SHIFTING FIGURE OF YOUTH IN SOUTH AFRICA'S TRANSITION

The radicalizing contributions of youth in South Africa's history of liberation struggle are highlighted in the life of the country's first democratically elected president. Nelson Mandela, in his autobiography *Long Walk to Freedom* (1994), described his involvement in the formation of the African National Congress Youth League (ANCYL), which was created to serve as an agitating force within an organization many young members perceived as slumbering. The ANCYL immediately embarked on a mass program of action, including boycotts, strikes, stay-at-homes, and demonstrations, which represented a radical departure from the ANC's previous law-abiding stance. In community actions, young activists often adopted strategies that were perceived as extreme by older counterparts, such as school and consumer boycotts. For example, in Diepkloof, Soweto (home to Funda Center), during a consumer boycott of white-owned shops in 1985, youth enforced the campaign by seizing grocery packages and strewing food items on the ground, much to the ire of onlookers. As much as older adults condemned these tactics, however, they did not cast away the young. They still entrusted youth organizers with the task of addressing community dilemmas, especially those involving crime (Marks 2001: 54–55).

Youth leaders, including Mandela, also spearheaded the militarization of the ANC through the formation of its military wing, Umkhonto we Sizwe. Young recruits were sent to military training camps in other countries. The lyrics of the song "sobashiy' abazal' ekhaya" speaks to that experience: "We will leave our parents at home, entering other countries in the quest for freedom." Some youth would covertly travel between these training camps and South Africa's townships, carrying out underground missions meant to destabilize apartheid's infrastructure. Many died in what became an outright war between apartheid military forces and militarized liberation movements, including the ANC. Umkhonto we Sizwe members were not the only youth who sacrificed their lives in anti-apartheid struggles. Others who stayed in the country, including some who were only bystanders, also died in protests. In one moment deeply etched in South Africa's history, government forces brutally killed protesting school-children in Soweto, including Hector Pieterson. In contemporary South Africa, National Youth Day commemorates the event, which occurred on June 16, 1976. Partly as a result of the actions of the militarized young people, the apartheid government came to see *youth* as encapsulating the notion that freedom fighters were troublemakers (predominantly Black and male) who opposed the state.

Despite the rich history of youth contributions to activism, many young people today are ambivalent toward the legacy of anti-apartheid struggle. As the "juvenile black counternation" (Comaroff and Comaroff 2006: 270) exemplified by Mandela and his compatriots has grown from state opposition into state governance, contemporary South African youth are impoverished and have limited employment prospects, caught in an economic predicament that neoliberal capitalism's global advance on the country's postapartheid trajectory have exacerbated. The urgency of their economic need led some to disengage from political resistance. As Catherine Besteman describes, the young men whom she worked with in Cape Town "respectfully acknowledge that people gave their lives in the struggle against apartheid but argue that defining their contemporary situation through the lens of the struggle would hinder their opportunities" (2008: 238). One young man explained to Besteman, "If I'm trying to understand what happened then, and not being attentive to what is going on right now, how am I going to survive? How am I going to look for work?" (2008: 238). Another clarified his perspective, suggesting that the victory of the anti-apartheid struggle was limited: "For me, the struggle would be a great memory if we had fought and won the freedom. And then everyone would be free. But nobody's free.... It's like, we won the freedom, but certain people are enjoying the freedom, and it makes me so mad about the struggle. People fought and did their absolute best, and I'm so proud of them. But now, the freedom that was captured doesn't even serve the people who fought for freedom. That's why I'm saying the struggle was good, but it doesn't inspire me" (in Besteman 2008: 238). Excluded from the economic promises of their young nation, in spite of their predecessors' sacrifices, contemporary young South Africans at first seem to have responded with political disavowal.

Scholarship on protest and on youth has, in turn, been ambivalent toward postapartheid youth. Grappling with the apparent apathy of this generation of "born-frees," popular-culture theorists writing in the mid-2000s asserted that the political intentions of cultural practices among youth have shifted from mass mobilization to the pursuit of justified enjoyment (Coplan 2005; Allen 2004; Nuttall 2004). During apartheid, the commercial prospects for youth cultural workers were severely limited; those who devoted their creative energies to political struggle usually did so without financial reward, and the international boycott against South African products meant few outlets were available even for those who sought compensation. With the end of apartheid, youth devoted their energies to practices that seemed to break with the past. Young artists expressed their cultural self-confidence through demands for enjoyment: "In those first heady [post-struggle] days the first freedom the youth demanded was to freely enjoy themselves" (Coplan 2005: 15–16). Apartheid-era leisure opportunities served a restorative purpose.[1] In contrast, youth demand for enjoyment postapartheid was tinged with materialism. These tendencies were most highlighted in a new musical genre, *kwaito*, which provided a platform for a celebration of township innovations in style. Exponents of kwaito reflected a global trend in which young people were empowered as consumers. The genre combined a middle-class consumerist ethos with the "unapologetic bravado of the youth of the township streets" (Coplan 2005: 18). In embracing a new materialism, South Africa's youth cast aside the burdensome mentality of their elders' preliberation morality and actively composed street culture through musical, bodily, and sartorial departures.

These activities, innovative as they were, contributed to portrayals of postapartheid youth culture as decidedly apolitical. Coplan, for example, writes that while some kwaito does lament the failure of the democratic government to address social problems, "direct involvement in South Africa's current political processes is not a favoured activity of either black youth or their popular musical heroes" (2005: 21). Similarly, Gavin Steingo, associate professor of music at Princeton University, writes of kwaito as embracing material and social aspirations while overlooking actual political-economic conditions, depoliticizing the music (2005, 2007).

Yet, this rejection of traditional politics ushers in a new political and aesthetic configuration, a repartitioning of the sensible. Thus, kwaito becomes "the embodiment of a radically new politics, even if it is not political in the traditional sense. By rejecting politics, kwaito becomes political. By being apolitical, kwaito becomes extremely political" (Steingo 2005: 343; see also Steingo 2007).[2] Despite Steingo's sharp analytics of power (especially in Steingo 2007), his attempt to politicize kwaito's anti-politics of enjoyment furthers a narrative of disinterest among youth. These portrayals of youth as apolitical risk neglecting other participatory domains in which young people explicitly engage the state, including youth involvement in community work (see Besteman 2008), the rise of generational factions within the ANC's ruling alliance (Gunner 2015), and the ongoing activism among university students that gained national prominence in late 2015 (Gillespie and Naidoo 2019; see also Becker 2016; Nyamnjoh 2016). In particular, the emergence and endurance of #RhodesMustFall, #FeesMustFall, and #EndOutsourcing campaigns across South Africa's university campuses in 2015 demonstrated the power of youth mobilization and generated renewed scholarly attention to the transformational capacities of youth in South Africa's political landscape. These are welcome developments that encourage a reconsideration of earlier characterizations of the generation's political involvement.

The lack of opportunities many young people face also affects their political involvement. Youth participation has typically been recognized as key to sustaining collective struggles over time, but the precarity of many young people's socioeconomic positions has made recruiting youth to social movements challenging. High rates of unemployment mean that any opportunity to work often takes precedence over movement activities, and the ready acknowledgment that community activism is not a path to financial security means that youth seeking security will direct their energy elsewhere.

These circumstances might lead to an assumption that young APF activists engaged with the organization due to a lack of alternatives and passively participated only until something better came along. Such an assumption is insufficient. At least two factors undermine it: First, many young people were involved in the APF at great risk to themselves, including some who would disavow a life of material accumulation as antithetical to their politics. Second, when asked to describe their motivations for participation, young APF members used terms that were rooted not in consumerist concerns but in logics of connection—language that evoked the importance of alliances and affiliation with other human beings. It is through their experiences that I elaborate an aesthetic of relationship—how connection to others can generate and sustain political subjectivity. To advance understanding of these political motivations as embedded in the social, I first clarify how the already flexible category of *youth* figures within the activist practices of the APF.

Youth Participation in the APF

While Remmoho provided a structure of association based on shared (although not uniform) gender identifications, the APF offered no similar coalition-wide structure for youth. Within the APF, people *became* youth more by contrastive association than due to numerical age. The elusiveness of the category extends beyond the APF; no consistent, universal characteristics, not even age, demarcate youth among the wider public. Youth or adolescence is not a highly significant life stage in all societies, and where it is demarcated, the designation can span a wide age range. South Africa's National Youth Act of 1996 categorized as youth those between the ages of fourteen and thirty-five. Although this legal categorization reflects some social realities, the experience of youth is shaped more by life circumstances and social status than by chronological age.

This flexibility in the identification of the category lends support to scholarly insights that challenge overly fixed conceptualizations of youth. As a category, youth mediates social interpretations of biological chronology, foregrounding age "not as a trajectory but as identity . . . [where identity is] agentive, flexible, and ever-changing" (Bucholtz 2002: 532). Attention to youth as a social category and a subjective identification supports an understanding of young people as cultural agents in their own right, emphasizing "the here-and-now of young people's experience, the social and cultural practices through which they shape their worlds" (Bucholtz 2002: 532).

Youth, therefore, can be considered a "social shifter" (Durham 2000; Jakobson [1957] 1971; Silverstein 1976) that draws much of its meaning from situated use and alerts us to social structures at play: "As people bring the concept of youth into bear on situations, they situate themselves in a social landscape of power, rights, expectations, and relationships. . . . They do so not necessarily . . . in a static manner, but in a dynamic, contestive, and imaginative way" (Durham 2000: 117). Thus, the category of youth is relational; an individual's existence within it is fundamentally tied to shifting familial, economic, state, and broader social structures that shape life trajectories (Cole and Durham 2007: 14).

Youth are often able to act in public spheres and take on public roles, and have established certain levels of autonomy but are still dependents. They are not in the position to fully claim authority over others' or their own life choices (Durham 2000: 116). These circumstances render youth a liminal and ambiguous experience, particularly in the context of political involvement. If we are to foreground age as a basis for identification in and of itself, and not as one element in a trajectory toward adulthood, youth is nonetheless a social positioning with a keen orientation toward others and toward the future.

Demarcations of youth in a generational context often involve the interplay of power. For example, differing claims to knowledge by elders can lead to the subordination of the young by the old (Durham 2000: 115; Meillassoux 1981). Within the APF, these generational considerations focused primarily on the economic. Concerns of household maintenance, including housing, electricity, and water, dominated APF community struggles. These were responsibilities that many young people had not yet assumed; consequently, APF youth found themselves outnumbered by activists of older generations, particularly grandparents, whose pensions often sustained their families. APF affiliates often cited their membership as consisting of young people and the elderly, reflecting a generational gap prevalent both in the movement and in many South African households.[3] Younger APF members also had economic concerns—particularly around employment and education—but many were motivated by a desire, aesthetically rooted in intergenerational bonds, to relieve suffering, seek political understanding, and claim collective belonging.

AN AESTHETIC OF RELATIONSHIPS
IN POLITICAL LIFE

The internal and intersubjective characteristics that motivated youth toward collective activism point to an aesthetic of relationship at work in shaping their political trajectories. This relational dimension of political becoming reflects not only the interplay of power in generational dynamics but also an embodied interdependency among people. Relationships are emotional and sensorial, unfolding through felt exchanges in which bodily experience maintains primacy. Social movement scholarship, relying on false Cartesian oppositions between mind and body, reason and feeling has historically bypassed these embodied dimensions of activists' interpersonal dynamics. Such scholarship was limited by an inability to reconcile theoretical abstractions with activists' lived experience and their inner life of movement participation.

To counter the legacies of Cartesian duality in scholarly accounts of political collectivity, conceptualizations of activist being must not only reunite mind with body but also situate embodiment firmly within a relational world. Lest attempts to reembody the aesthetic limit the scale of attention to individuals' immediate sensory mediations, no less than a complete reexamination of the relational and dialogic basis of being in the world is necessary to fully grasp the embeddedness of the aesthetic within social and political domains. The self must be placed within the social, and the individual actively emplaced within their environment (Cavell 2006: 64; Wittgenstein 1953).

Models for the sensorial embeddedness of the individual in community already exist among embodiment scholars. These scholars generally agree that sensory perception and the capacity for thinking are socially produced through the individual's connections within a community (Downey 2002: 488; Chau 2008: 488; Meyer 2010: 754–55; Cavell 2006). Furthermore, relationship, the basis for community, is already built into conceptualizations of the aesthetic;

Kant, for example, characterizes aesthetic judgment as claims perceived to merit the agreement of others (Kant 1931; Cornell 2002; Budd 2007). However, although these conceptualizations acknowledge relationships in the abstract, they do not map the relational unfolding of the aesthetic through everyday interactions with others. Neither do they fully explain how the social worlds we inhabit, and the sensations we perceive from being with others, transform our political trajectories.

An aesthetic of relationship provides these missing elements by attending to how nascent political subjectivities emerge through inherently embodied relationships. It considers the impact of empathetic resonance and affective attunement with another on activists' trajectories, beginning with the proposition that interpersonal relations initiate individuals into political subjectivity and sustain political engagement. Interdependency can hamper or facilitate activism, and interpersonal relations are fraught with all of interdependency's risks and rewards: the joys of connection, the affirmation of social belonging, and the strength of discovering personal potential for impact, along with the pain of loss and disappointment and the frustration of being rejected. Because of the transitional nature of their positioning, young people are particularly sensitive to their social environments. The quality of their connectedness with others feeds back into their sense of belonging. This sensitivity of youth (by which I mean their susceptivity to *feeling*) is often the basis of political commitment. While some young activists may not yet shoulder the political and economic responsibilities that often spur the activism of older adults, many are driven to act based on affective ties and desires to understand and alleviate the suffering of parental and ancestral generations.

Relational Aesthetics of Youth Mobilization

When she joined the APF-affiliated Working Class Crisis Committee (WCCC) in 2004, Charmaine found the affiliate to be composed mostly of "grandfathers." At her first meeting, "there were so many, many grandfathers and I didn't even understand what I am going to say or do so I just stood there and listened."[4] When I asked how she felt participating in the organization as a younger person and as a woman, she responded that her experience was good: "You feel so special; they always tell you, 'My child, you are doing great work! Keep it up and you will see how well you will develop.' They make you feel so special, they make you feel like what I'm doing is right, I'm doing a right thing." The grandfathers' encouragement positioned Charmaine in a moral landscape that affirmed her choices to participate.

Buyisiwe, the energy-craving activist in his midthirties who had assessed the APF's performance through his passion for cars, also noted a generational gap in activism. He had left the SECC, his affiliate organization, in 2002. On his return in 2008, he was "seeing a lot of pensioners only, one [other] youth member . . . striving hard to build the organization."[5] Unlike Charmaine, he decried the situation and lamented the absence of youth involvement, which was a change from his earlier participation. He attributed the decline to the death of a key organizer: "People do believe in other people. . . . Let's say you go to church, you believe in your pastor, he's the good preacher, then you can get healed by his voice, you know. People are believing in people. Then after [the organizer passed away], I heard that community branches are starting to drag slow, like branches are dying, you know, so the stem can't do nothing without the branches, or the roots can't grow up without anyone who is watering the plant." Buyisiwe's reflection highlights the impact of single individuals on collective efforts, which are steeped in an emotive investment that manifests aesthetically; that is, through sensorial evaluation. In his example, the good preacher's voice produces healing—by extension, he is a comrade worthy of one's investment. In his ethnography of a church community in Botswana, Frederick Klaits writes about the power of the voice to affect others, an effect that is particularly embodied. Buyisiwe's comments can be understood through the lens of Klaits's observation that "apostolic Christians in Botswana cultivate methods of apprehending and reshaping their sense of who they are in relation to other people, since they are keenly aware of the power of their own and others' voices to affect each other's sentiments and bodily conditions" (2010: 168). Buyisiwe's comments describe such an intersubjective bond, established through "the reciprocity between the addresser and addressee" (Jakobson 1990: 96), a phatic connection that builds community. In other words, APF members established who they were in relation to other people and sustained intersubjectivity through emotive investment—"people are believing in people."

The significance of this phatic connection for enabling young people's political action is perhaps best revealed through the story of Comrade Rose, the late activist around whom Remmoho members rallied. Still reeling from Rose's death, I was surprised to learn that one of the young activists I sought to interview had been mentored by her. I was drawn to Khabane and inspired to request an interview with him, due to his vibrance as he sang. He had tried to change the lyrics of "dibaka mona" so that the song specified capitalism rather than dogs as the target of protesters' ire, a marker of his attunement to the sensory import of song. In seeking out Khabane, I did not know of his connection to Rose, whom I grieved despite our brief acquaintance, continuing to register the silences that pervaded her passing. When Khabane told me he was from Khutsong, and that Comrade Rose founded the study group that initiated his activism, it tugged at my heart to hear her name from an unanticipated source. The APF was not active in Khutsong, but Rose connected Khabane with the organization, and he attended events sporadically.

More than simply facilitating Khabane's connection to political collectives, including the study group she had founded and the APF, Rose helped transform his sense of capability. She told her cadres that "we have the power to show who we are," referring to how young people in Khutsong changed the concept of politics in South Africa and internationally when, through prolonged dissidence, they prevented an unwelcome change to Khutsong's provincial demarcation. The power expressed by youth in those demonstrations overwhelmed opposition from the state in ways that reverberated through the nation, the continent, and the world. When Rose made her assertion to the group, urging members to bear in mind their often unacknowledged potential, Khabane at first questioned it. Perhaps it was the incongruence of Rose's portrayal of his power with the neglect that pervaded his community that caused Khabane's initial disbelief and spurred his further inquiry into the significance of the Khutsong struggle. Through this investigation, however, he became more aware of Khutsong's reputation—"I heard information from different people, from different sources that Khutsong is famous in America, Khutsong is famous in Europe, Khutsong is famous in Africa, Khutsong is famous in South Africa."[6] The confirmation of Khutsong's prominence led Khabane to a deeper sense of recognition not only of his community's capacity but also of his own power. He saw that youth were fundamental to Khutsong's political achievement. "We are the people who made these present conditions that we have in South Africa," he said, "and I started growing there . . . from that perception."

Rose's urging that "it's up to us to show ourselves" was at the root of Khabane's self-identified freedom song, which includes the lyrics "abasazi, basizwa ngendaba" (they don't know us, they only know of us through the news). The song drives him to nurture a strength of spirit that is concealed from the fleeting interest of outsiders who hear of protesters' exploits secondhand (through the news) and form their own judgments but are unable to access the core of the protesters' powerful being. Khabane's identification with this song is a refusal to yield to life challenges that threaten to break him, a recognition that he is more than the overwhelming conditions that consume him. In our interviews, he talked about his daily pain as indescribable, asserting that there are things I cannot know from seeing him, from hearing his voice. "Right now, I can say to you I'm fine," he told me, "but you don't know actually what has happened [to me] . . . yes, I've been truthful throughout the interview but *eish*, you know there are some aspects that I cannot just articulate on my life." Despite a struggle so unrelenting as to be ineffable, he refuses to yield. "But I will make it, I think so," he told me, later adding, "I must be a strong African."

Khabane's expression of a profound interiority of activism, conceived as the act of cultivating hidden depths that can be harnessed through "the power to show who we are" was engendered through Comrade Rose, a testament to the significance of intersubjective transmission in the mobilization of youth. A process of triangulation (Cavell 2006) was foundational to Khabane's activist emergence, a triangulation that involved Rose and Khabane and Khabane's attempts to fix the meaning of Khutsong's provincial struggles. Rose made a proposition—that young people have changed the nature of politics not only in South Africa but also in the world. Uncertain but curious, Khabane investigated and in the process was assured of the impact young people like himself had had—and by extension could have in the future.

Rose's original proposition, and Khabane's orientation toward it, is heavy with implication. Rose's proposition sought evidence. As Cavell notes of propositional thought, it "commits the thinker to certain conclusions, invites challenge or trust on the part of another, makes promises and reneges on promises, is open to doubt, challenge, question, reflection" (2006: 70). Through the interpersonal and intrapersonal dialogue that such thinking enables, Khabane's transformed understanding of Khutsong committed him to Rose's proposal that the personal power of Khutsong's youth was unhindered by the destitution within their immediate environment. Rose's proposition invited him into an activist continuum and to an expanded sense of his self as a potentially inexhaustible font of strength that resists capture by an oppositional gaze. Khabane and Rose lived out in their shared encounter one response to the question of survival in a world counter to our being: harness concealed power.[7]

Individuals like Comrade Rose and the organizer whose passing Buyisiwe noted leave significant voids in their wake. But those absences do not necessarily lead youth to abandon activism. Although with the passing of Comrade Rose, Khabane lost an adult whose care for him he could readily perceive, he remained driven in his activism, particularly within the study group Rose founded. However, it is more often the case that the transformative investments that capacitate young activists erode with the departure of key individuals, particularly if interpersonal bonds within the broader collective are tenuous. When he left the organization for a time in 2002, Buyisiwe heard that "lots of youth decided to quit. . . . What that probably means is [it was] the community who decided that, 'no, as long as there is no so-and-so, and so-and-so we are not going to work.'" The passing of the organizer Buyisiwe identified as pivotal further eroded connections and commitments that had already weakened.

Thus, the movement of young activists toward, or away from, the core mobilizations of the APF were never far from a key relational vector: the intergenerational affinity between youth and older mentors. These intergenerational connections provided a site for the transmission of political capability, with individual engagement drawing young people to collective commitment and shared struggle. This intergenerational engagement is only a beginning, however; if the investment of key individuals is the sole avenue for political belonging, the collective participation that is fostered through this belonging cannot persist after the departure of these individuals. Young people, indeed activists of any age, must cultivate their own sense of purpose and political drive. They can be encouraged in this, just as Comrade Rose's proposition catalyzed Khabane's investigation and eventual commitment. Considered in contrast with the departure of young people from Buyisiwe's affiliate on the organizer's death, Khabane's persistence on Rose's passing demonstrates that intersubjective connections—as embodied and profoundly affective as they are—can support enduring political commitment if they are integrated into a budding activist's sense of self. Apart from the integration of intergenerational connection with personal commitment, economic factors weigh on youth collective participation and are also significant to the embeddedness of relational aesthetics in collective politics.

Challenges of Youth Engagement

In accounting for an aesthetic of relationship and its impact on young people's political trajectories, a key consideration is what happens when connection in one sphere competes with obligations in another. When Buyisiwe returned to the SECC in 2008, he was elected youth leader because he was deemed the only young person who could "manage that position." The other active youth in the SECC, Thokozani, was already serving as a media officer. Part of Buyisiwe's role as a leader was to recruit youth to the organization, a task he found particularly challenging, even though he was successful: "You know it's difficult again to recruit the youth but at that time I was trying hard, so I managed to get at least from different communities eighteen members of the youth who wanted to work with the SECC." These numbers were not sustained, however, because youth dropped out when opportunities to work arose: "We worked hard, then others got jobs, they don't pitch in because . . . they only pitched in when they are off at their jobs . . . so now we are like, only left with two."

Buyisiwe's experience speaks to a wider trend of organizations losing young activists to professional opportunities. Concerns about employment, which are particularly acute among youth, have endured even after South Africa's transition to democratic governance. In 2011, the unemployment rate among fifteen-to-twenty-four-year-olds was 51 percent, more than twice the national unemployment rate of 25 percent.[8] As Buyisiwe discovered, the opportunity to work can often conflict with involvement in social movements. Buyisiwe himself had returned to active participation with the SECC only after exhausting his employment possibilities—he had left a previous job due to harsh treatment and had been unsuccessful in his subsequent job applications. "So I said, 'Okay, for now let me give myself two or three years here without a job, see if there'll be ways to survive you know.' 2008, I decided, 'Let me go back to SECC and help the comrades with the struggle [because] the struggle is for everyone so no one owns the struggle.'" In other words, his decision to accept his unemployment prompted his return.

Buyisiwe's decision to return to his social movement only after an exhaustive job search reflects broader dissociations between community activism and economic stability. Many youth members had people in their lives who questioned their choices to participate in activist organizations. For Charmaine, the reservations came from her younger brother. Inside her family's shack, as he was sitting over a paraffin stove cooking pap (a porridge made from maize meal), I teased him, asking why he did not join the struggle. Unsmiling, he told me to ask Charmaine how long she had been in the struggle, to which she responded, "Five years." He then said to ask what had resulted from her engagement, what she had gotten from it. After some thought, Charmaine responded, "Nothing." A moment later, as if to ease the bleakness of her response, she added, "It takes time." Such doubts did affect Charmaine, who, as we got to know each other, expressed frustration about her appearance, which she considered was made homely by her lack of funds. She wondered where those of her age and material circumstances found money to get their hair done and buy nice clothes while she wore tattered jeans and struggle T-shirts.

While visiting young activists, I often encountered friends and family members who disavowed activist life as inimical to their aspirations. Engagement in community struggles was often perceived to be a path of unnecessary sacrifice. Khabane's mother was disappointed in his focus on activism. In his words, "Yes, she's a very proud mother but because of this political thing, she became now, you know, very, very disappointed in me. You know, 'I wasn't expecting such from you, I was expecting you to accumulate education and money.'" A friend of Khabane's told me that he did not consider himself an activist; rather, he intends to become a politician, because he could not pinpoint a difference between activists and politicians. Aside from the obvious opposition to state policies among the activists I worked with, the unspoken subtext was the opportunity for affluence that comes with being a politician.

Education was another stress point in youth activism. Many younger people had completed their high school final exams—known as matric exams—but were forced by financial constraints to delay or give up the pursuit of further education. Tshepang, for example, who was twenty-four when I interviewed him in 2010, had matriculated in 2005 but did not continue his education "because my mom had like these huge debts so I said, 'No, what's the point of being into school when my mom is suffering you know? Let me just, leave school a bit, I will help her with her debts.'"[9] He found intermittent work and enhanced his skills through sponsored training opportunities in museum management, research, and tour guiding. He was enthusiastically volunteering with a community center in Bophelong, where he lived, and he sought to distance himself from the workforce by not seeking remunerative employment. He was also preparing to enroll in college.

Tshepang was not alone. His colleague and fellow activist, Disebo, twenty-two, who participated along with him in sponsored training opportunities, had matriculated in 2006 and began college in 2009. She had to interrupt her studies, however, because she was unable to pay enrollment fees. Thokozani, who was twenty-eight, had also abandoned a university degree because he could not afford it. He mitigated the severity of unemployment by pursuing training similar to what Tshepang and Disebo had done—he was completing a project management course he hoped would enhance his employment and financial prospects.

While training such as that pursued by Tshepang, Disebo, and Thokozani might offer future benefits, these short-term courses also served as a way youth with limited finances could keep busy. The young activists with whom I worked largely depended on household members and sporadic income-generating activities for daily survival. For example, Buyisiwe earned money as a private long-distance taxi driver. Many youth lived with a female parent or grandparent, whose wages or pension often provided the entire household's upkeep. Tshepang, for example, lived with his grandmother and uncle in Bophelong, while his mother lived in Kensington to be close to the East Gate Mall, where she worked as a cleaner. An only child, Disebo lived with her mother in Bophelong as well, and they both depended on her mother's pension, which Disebo was sometimes able to supplement by working as a tour guide.

Although financial and familial obligations would generally seem to conflict with the activism of young people, the opposition was not absolute. For instance, Thokozani was inspired to become politically active by an economically driven intergenerational connection. When his mother passed away in 1999, his grandmother became the only person supporting the whole family. As he witnessed her struggle, he was motivated by his love for her to identify the root of their stressful conditions. "I could see that it was strenuous for her. . . . She was supposed to pay for services and also give us money, pocket money to go to school also, and buy groceries and all those things were very strenuous for her."[10] He started attending activist meetings in 2000. Through those meetings, which gave rise to the SECC, he came to understand that his grandmother's struggle was part of a wider trend related to the privatization of basic services: "We talk about those things and start questioning you know, what can be done? Why people are so quiet about those issues?" Through such questioning, "I started to open my eyes in terms of politics."

Thokozani's experience shows how intersubjective connections that are economically driven can be the basis for a young person's activism if that activism is connected to the desire to make a better life, for himself or for family members. For Thokozani, becoming an activist was a process of aligning subjective emotional states with the political-economic analysis that participation in the movement offered. Even though he was not financially supporting a household, his *feeling for* his grandmother, who was overwhelmed with responsibility for hers, located him within South Africa's trend toward neoliberal strategies. The SECC's analytical sessions shed light on his lived experience, making the path toward positive transformation clearer—through activism, he could envision and agitate for a better life. Thus, in the context of competing economic obligations, relational aesthetics account for youth activism not merely as a matter of cross-generational ties but also as a mechanism of aligning these personal ties with a movement's broader aims of economic transformation.

MOBILIZING YOUTH THROUGH PERFORMANCE

While intergenerational economic solidarity was the pathway to activism for some, for others, political engagement came through performance. In the APF's earlier days, the performing arts had been particularly prominent. "Almost any meeting would have cultural activity," recalled one activist.[11] At meetings and protest demonstrations, troupes such as Sounds of Edutainment (an arts collective that particularly featured poets) would dance, sing, and perform poetry and plays. As the same activist recounted: "These groups, they just exist. In all townships here, there are these groups of dancers, singers, and people using some forms of theatre and every activity. People would come . . . I think the reason why small groups were so important is that they had a more clear political role that they saw themselves, so there was also a community group, but they were trying to shape their work in a way that it had a message, and basically they were very young people."[12] Four APF affiliate organizations had been formed solely on the initiative of young people and boasted a membership that was exclusively youth. Of these, two affiliates further distinguished themselves by structuring their groups as performance troupes. Although these two affiliates also experienced eventual declines due to the erosion of intersubjective investments, their members' accounts of their activist origins highlight the considerable significance of performance in fostering the positive relationality that is essential to engaging youth politically.

For one youth member, Disebo, the attraction of performance preceded, and served as the gateway to, political participation. In 2003, when she was fifteen, Disebo and her friends sought out a group that developed dramas in their Bophelong community. Disebo's curiosity about the group was particularly piqued because of her performance background in primary school. When she and her friends arrived at the rehearsal, Disebo realized that the site was also the source of the drumming she heard on the afternoons she visited her mother's friend. She had always wondered what was happening, and she was quite taken with her discovery. "It took me by surprise because there were young people who were my peers and they were fun. Even though they did not know me, I was like, I was family. Even though I was new, but they welcomed me, they showed me the warmth."[13] Disebo felt so connected to the group that she returned every day over the next week "up until I said, 'Okay people, I want to be part of you.' And they said, 'You are welcome, you know.'" Only when she attended a march with her newfound friends, who were then dressed "in red T-shirts written APF on them," did she realize that "these people are also involved in community struggles." Her mother had mentioned the APF in passing, and when she saw the T-shirts, Disebo began making the connections. Members of the Bophelong Community Service Forum (BOCOSFO), an APF affiliate founded in 2001, had conducted the rehearsals Disebo attended, though she was also unaware of that connection until that march: "I didn't know we were also BOCOSFO; I just went to the rehearsals. And then it took me by surprise, everything took me by surprise, it opened my eyes, my mind, you know, it challenged me!" Once she made the connection between the BOCOSFO's performance initiatives and the community struggles with which the group was involved, Disebo wanted to learn more.

Performance also led to political involvement for Charmaine. In 2000, while she was still in school, Charmaine joined the Sedibeng Committed Artists (SCA), which, along with the BOCOSFO, performed regularly at APF events. In her early days of involvement, she particularly enjoyed opportunities to compete with the BOCOSFO. "And that's what makes me like APF," she exclaimed.

When she moved from Small Farm to Sebokeng Zone 20, to a shack that she and her family built, Charmaine gained the personal context to understand the APF's efforts. She met an activist in the Working Class Crisis Committee (WCCC) who invited her to their meetings. Although she was no longer actively performing when we spoke, she credited her political involvement to those days with the SCA: "Because of SCA, I have joined the struggle, I've become an activist. If I didn't join SCA I wasn't going to be informed, you see. Because of SCA I knew APF."

Collaborative Competition: Early Artistic Flourishing among APF Youth

Charmaine and Disebo were part of the two APF affiliates that used performance ("cultural programmes" in APF parlance) to mobilize youth for community struggles. Their efforts expanded the role of performance in the APF's mobilization.

The BOCOSFO was a key driver of cultural activities among APF youth. The affiliate was founded in 2001 to agitate for service delivery and education in Bophelong. One of the group's earliest successes was in abolishing school fees and securing free uniforms for students in Bophelong. The group formed a Concerned Learners Committee that fought for learners' rights within the education system, as well as Tsibo, a group focused on adult basic education and early instruction through crèches (day care centers). The BOCOSFO also had a group that dealt more pointedly with community struggles for basic services. The youth cultural programs served to link all three sections—the Concerned Learners Committee, Tsibo, and the basic services group. In the cultural programs, members introduced their organizations to the public through drama, music, dance, and poetry. These cultural activities also linked the young people to older generations. Two members discussed the importance of "organizing through culture" and maintaining a tradition of performance established in Black political movements and trade unions. Furthermore, performance allowed youth activists to connect with parents and grandparents who were illiterate: "We saw that most of our grandparents and parents had not been to school, so we educate them via culture because they cannot read or write. We make them understand the present compared to the past. We use culture not only for entertaining people but to mobilise and educate them as well" (Mosinki and Moiloa 2005: 30).

In its affiliation with the APF, the BOCOSFO would perform along with the SCA at APF events, often on themes APF organizers commissioned. Initially, the group focused on drama, but in 2004 it incorporated gospel music into its repertoire and formed a choir.[14] The group decided doing so would expand the reach of its efforts and raise its profile. "We saw that we were doing only drama and poetry and other groups were not doing that, they were singing gospel," Disebo recalled. "You only find only a few selected groups that are doing cultural performances, so that is how we changed our approach." The choir enabled the group to build connections with youth beyond Bophelong; some members traveled to Khutsong to help with the formation of a community organization there. The gospel choir also enabled the BOCOSFO to connect with other young choirs through competitions. Charmaine, then with the SCA, referred to these kinds of experiences when she recalled the excitement of going to compete with the BOCOSFO.

Tapping in to a competitive spirit while remaining committed to community-based struggles generated innovations in cultural forms and was key to a period of artistic flourishing among APF youth. For instance, the BOCOSFO's choir adapted the gospel genre to deliver its political message, developing innovations the choir members were proud to present. Disebo recalled hosting a choir from Khutsong in Bophelong. She said that when it was the BOCOSFO's turn to sing: "We wanted to show them so we went on stage, we sang the gospel song, but later we changed, we went through the cultural songs that we have created, and they were like, 'Okay, that's the new thing for us you know.' The songs had a message, the songs were direct, they had everything that we wanted people to hear." The event demonstrated the creative charge and dynamism of the moment, as the group blended gospel music with "cultural songs" that delivered their message and framed this presentation as a competition with their peers. Through playful rivalries that furthered activists' imaginative growth, the BOCOSFO and the SCA were incentivized to realize their best artistic contributions. Their competition was collaborative, functioning as a relational orientation that drove broader creative effects than either could have achieved on its own.

Regarding this period of artistic flourishing among APF youth, a former Khanya staff member who had worked with the BOCOSFO raised questions about how the organization valued these performance activities. Although commissioning such performances was an established practice for the APF, she suggested that the group saw them as mere entertainment. "It worked to keep people energized but [was] not the real struggle . . . I don't think we ever explored it as a real kind of tool."[15] This devaluation was partly a result of intergenerational dynamics, which the predominantly youth performances were key sites for registering. According to the former Khanya staff member, older activists did not take the youths' efforts seriously: "I think because the older people were too busy with the serious, and because it wasn't viewed as a real tool that you could use for proper mobilization."[16] Among the youth, however, the dynamic energy of performance fostered creativity. The BOCOSFO in particular used its performances to build up its organizations—to recruit youth and coordinate with other organizations regarding pertinent issues affecting employment and educational rights. The performances also provided vehicles for working in schools and coordinating organizational meetings. Unlike APF meetings, which tended to run long, BOCOSFO meetings were often rehearsals. In this way, performance deployed as an organizing tool served to keep focus, maintain energy, and generate further involvement. But the APF more broadly never fully realized the political potential of these performances.

Differential Aesthetics of Youth

Assessments that the APF collective did not take young people's efforts seriously call generational conflict to the fore. The tendency to compartmentalize youth, relegating their energy to a contained role, frayed the aesthetic fabric of relations within which the movement operated. Generational divides encompassed a differing appreciation for the role of artistic performance in the movement and threw into relief a unique aesthetic of relationship, binding youth to each other and to the antiprivatization mission.

An aesthetic of relationship not only enables political continuity through being with others; it also must account for rupture and distinction by considering moments when being with others highlights difference rather than enabling connection. One example of such a moment regards the concern for energy levels as distinct sensorial standards younger people held for collective performances and for meetings. This aesthetic distinction between generations was especially prominent in song. Buyisiwe and others expressed a preference for faster tempos when singing freedom songs at marches and meetings. Buyisiwe recognized the emotionally embodied impact of song, particularly that sad songs could spur his anger, an experience he did not relish, "so I don't sing those songs hard, you know." Buyisiwe preferred faster-paced chants "so that people will have the hype and run. Like the soldiers, you know, taking that giant step which was taken during [the] apartheid regime." He preferred martial songs and chants that placed him and the crowd in directed motion. Such songs generated energy, producing the vibe that was appropriate to his sensibilities around what was needed in the current political dispensation. He did not have much tolerance for slower-paced sad songs: "If they sing them, I rather go and stand somewhere on the side."

Many youth shared Buyisiwe's preference for faster-tempoed songs, and young people would often intercede in collective singing to direct it toward their preferred energy level. Buyisiwe drew my attention to a march in Orlando

East, Soweto, in which protesters were dragging and getting tired: "They will sing one song walking slow, I mean it never gives that oomph you know, and where we were at, [we] started to chant, then the people started to have that vibe and hype of chanting, running slowly because they want to listen to the vocalist. They are like the drums because the chanting songs like give an instruction, 'Shay'izandla' (clap your hands), then you will see the whole crew, you will hear the whole crew clapping hands." Matt, a college student from Pretoria who was a member of the Immortal Art Group, described a similar impulse. At his first APF meeting, he and his friends (all members of the art group) started clapping at a faster beat than APF members. As he explained: "It was to lead the rhythm of the song. . . . I wanted the song to go a bit faster so that people will be able to dance to it, that's why I was clapping a bit faster, so that they will go with the rhythm of my hand. . . . When it's slow, it's like boring, it doesn't give you time to like just be yourself. . . . When it's fast, if you want to dance, you dance."[17] For Matt, a fast rhythm established a base from which he could more fully express himself. Slow singing evidenced a lack of energy that was unappealing and stifling—"it doesn't give you time to . . . just be yourself."

Younger people did not always shun slow or sad songs, however. I was particularly taken by university students, members of the Pan-Africanist Congress (PAC), singing plaintive apartheid-era songs during a protest against the ANC ruling party. Singing the same laments as their predecessors, without any change in lyrics, they built a connection to the suffering their ancestors had experienced. Khabane, who was also a PAC member, attempted to describe in our interviews how singing freedom songs engenders in him physical sensations and emotions connected to his attempt to grasp the pain of "our forefathers and mothers" whom history had betrayed. Attuning to the pathos of ancestral suffering—including under conditions of slavery and apartheid—produced feelings that propelled his unforeseeable but fervent song delivery and protest participation. As he noted, "It's like an instigation to my soul, like an instigation to my soul, to just go forward and trust my instincts."

This variation of aesthetic preference even among youth reveals the futility of generalization; the case for distinction here is not to affix taste along generational lines. Rather, aesthetic distinction entails personal peculiarities that may or may not intersect across social categories, including of class, race, ethnicity, gender, or generation—for both Buyisiwe and Matt, the external tempo called up responses within themselves that they felt as either enabling or constrictive *for different reasons*. For Buyisiwe, slow, sad songs threatened to overwhelm his emotions and paralyze him. Thus, he preferred songs that facilitated active movement. For Matt, sad songs weighed heavy, dampening rather than supporting his creative expressions and preferred experience of self. By contrast, the songs that Khabane and many other young PAC members I interviewed took to were soul-instigating laments that connected them to ancestral generations, a performance of collaboration between the living and the dead.

FINDING REDEMPTION: RECONSTITUTING
THE PERFORMING ARTS IN THE APF

Recognizing performance as a critical concern, I was encouraged during fieldwork to seek out the young people who had been responsible for the APF's past artistic flourishing. I succeeded in establishing contact with members of the BOCOSFO, who in 2009 were still actively meeting. The SCA was inactive, although some of its members had joined the Small Farm Crisis Committee. One of the SCA's past leaders, Redemption, was a particularly interesting, and elusive, figure. No one could give me a number to reach him (he no longer had a phone), yet interviewees repeatedly referred to him. One afternoon, as I was dropping Thulani in Kanana after a research excursion, he mentioned that Redemption lived nearby. After futile attempts to reach him by phone, I quickly agreed to stop by his house. As we were about to turn the corner onto Redemption's street, Thulani exclaimed that he was right across the road at a produce stall. He hailed him over, with much joyful excitement bouncing between us. Redemption was surprised to hear I had been searching for him for months. He wedged his lanky figure into the backseat of my car, his long legs pressing against the front seat as we talked.

His conversations with me led him to reconnect with Thulani and the APF and to revitalize his political engagement. Thulani explained weeks later that he had been trying unsuccessfully to reengage Redemption in community struggles. He had been sad to see Redemption step away, because he had seen the extent of his talents. Redemption could fill a stadium with youth because he "spoke their language." He could invite Redemption to perform at a meeting tomorrow and "he would write the play today, gather youth to rehearse, and have it ready for tomorrow."[18] Because he had stepped away from the struggle, Redemption had been engaged in some "politically messed-up activities," according to Thulani. He had volunteered to be a street patroller, a service the ANC organized, which greatly saddened Thulani, given the APF's oppositional stance toward the ruling party. When I teased Thulani that he had used me to draw Redemption back into the APF, he responded rather soberly without disavowal, "Yes, I used you to get Redemption." For Thulani, Redemption's talent was needed in the struggle. Just as Rose helped to inspire Khabane's activism, Thulani sought to anchor Redemption to use his talent in service of community struggles.

I witnessed the extent of this talent within a week, when Redemption and others at Small Farm devised a performance for May Day observances at Khanya College. Redemption had been disappointed when Small Farm delegates did not show up for a performance at a March APF conference for which they had been paid a stipend. He did not want comrades from the Vaal Triangle to develop a reputation for being unreliable, so he did his best to make sure the May Day performance went well. He wrote the script the Monday before, and the group rehearsed every day leading up to the Saturday performance. The play, in Sesotho, dealt with AIDS, a topic of life-and-death import to youth. It was organized around a meeting. Redemption was a speaker at the meeting, and the audience members presented a range of responses. A choir formed at the conclusion of the "meeting" accompanied by an impromptu performance by Prince Shapiro, one of the poets from Sounds of Edutainment, whose verses further highlighted the play's themes:

"I attack"
If you are cantankerous
And feel dangerous
Perhaps adventurous
Know that . . .
Out there exists something malicious
A beast voracious and poisonous
Every time getting enormous
Becoming even more ferocious
So be cautious

Color don't matter
Whether you black, brown or white
I assault
I am AIDS
I attack

Under the guise of love alive
In I dived
Then landed in your blood
And now I mug
I am AIDS
I attack

Through experiments
Experience

Sex obsession
    Ignorance
Fat pockets of prosperous man
Even in caring and sharing
    I enmesh
AIDS attack
I molest

Injection of so-called legal drugs
Drew me closer like home searching bugs
To terminate but I can't discriminate
    Infect
Affect
    Divide
Destroy
    Sweep
And swap
    I assault
I am AIDS
I attack

I know now that you hate me though
But tough luck I shall not go
Not from your blood
I am a flood
I assault
I am AIDS
I attack
I molest . . .

On the conclusion of Prince Shapiro's performance, one of the Small Farm group, not to be outdone, segued seamlessly into his own poem. The Small Farm poet continued with the theme of communities being under seige, but he highlighted a different target of enmity:

On top of the mountains
I see the enemies
Who is the enemies?
The police
Whoa Africa
What the hell Africa

How are our mothers
How are our fathers
How are our brothers
How are our sisters
The police arresting in the middle of the night
Harassing
Shooting by rubber bullets
And real bullets
Whoa Africa
What the hell Africa

His final lines were drowned out by audience ululation as he used his voice to imitate a machine gun. The wave of emotional response among the audience at this expressive display harkened back to the flourishing of such activities in the APF's earlier years. The transition from speaker to speaker was so smooth that an audience member could not have known the poetry was unplanned. Building on a "shared repertory of theatrical (including poetic, literary, musical, gestural, and spatial) as well as everyday social conventions" (Seizer 1997: 66), the diverse singers and poets integrated their performances without prior arrangement.

Reflecting on that May Day performance, which he had brought to fruition, and on his reengagement with the APF more broadly, Redemption talked about rediscovering a part of himself he had not felt in a long time. Singing the songs, performing, and being in protest connected with something emotional in him that made him feel restored and that affirmed for him that "Yes, I am back."[19] Thulani's attempts at redeeming his friend from politically misguided activities by reconnecting him with the APF activist community seemed to have succeeded, at least momentarily.

After the performance that day, members of the Immortal Art Group from Pretoria, among them Matt and Wesley, became keenly interested in the APF. They connected with the activists from Small Farm and started discussing the formation of a performance squad with branches in the Vaal and Pretoria. Unfortunately, with the APF's broader decline, those plans were not to be realized. But for a moment, that May Day performance made the revival of such activities seem not only within reach but necessary.

THE AFTERMATH OF STRUGGLE: PERFORMING YOUTH DISENCHANTMENT AND DISILLUSIONMENT

Along with joy, relational aesthetics also bring the possibility of rupture—disappointment, loss of trust, the frustration of not being listened to, received, or harbored in one's vulnerability. All of these feelings erode belonging and can generate feelings of futility. Movement participants, in their relationships with one another, treaded this delicate line. Due to such rupture, young people's artistic revitalization of the APF did not last. The structural conditions imparted by the state with regard to AIDS health policy, neoliberal economic policy, and police militarization, among other issues, set the stage for losses in leadership and internal strife within affiliates and the broader APF that cut out the heart of the relationships that bound youth to the movement. Suspicions of misguided behavior by leaders complicated matters further. Through it all, performance again was available as the means by which the fissure was articulated.

The BOCOSFO succeeded for a time in using performance to keep up the energy level among its members, a success that can be more fully appreciated in light of the varied import of pacing in facilititating desired aesthetic encounters. In their performances, the BOCOSFO members expected to draw energy and be engaged actively with one another. The group's early efforts were disrupted, however, when Tsibo split from the BOCOSFO around 2003, due to internal disagreement and conflict over accusations of theft by a founding member. When the alleged thief and the BOCOSFO decided to part ways, he continued working with Tsibo's education initiatives, and the BOCOSFO lost a key mentor. Disebo described the BOCOSFO's driving force during this split: "I think most of us, we did not know what challenge . . . or battle that we are taking on, because it was very huge, and our driving force that time was, we wanted to show [the departing mentor] that we can do it even though he turned a blind eye, that we are not doing it for [him], we should be doing it for our community." As a cultivated practice that can be claimed apart from disagreement with or disappointment in others, performance facilitated individual and collective drive among BOCOSFO members, providing a source of refuge in the face of loss. The BOCOSFO achieved much following its split from Tsibo. Its members traveled to festivals and considered cultivating careers in the arts. But the group's drive was again halted when the estranged mentor died of HIV-related illness. "Everything started to deteriorate up until now, now it's like silence. There is no more action, like nothing you know. We've lost the vision, that [reason] we wanted to fight, we've lost everything," Disebo mourned.

The BOCOSFO lost another two members to HIV-related illnesses within the span of a year (2007); the losses deeply shook the organization. Tshepang commented on the sorrow of that moment, the grief still evident in his comportment: "We were very young, and we did so many things for this community, and one by one, the members fell." The losses raised members' awareness;

the remaining members got tested for HIV and expressed their determination to stay "[HIV] negative and keeping positive," in Tshepang's words. The members' somber new awareness could be heard in the BOCOSFO's performances. Consider, for instance, the lines from a poem, "Ingculaza (HIV/AIDS)," which was included on *Revolutionary Songs and Poems*, a CD the group recorded in 2008. In the recorded performance, each stanza was recited by a different BOCOSFO poet over a humming chorus:

Condoms are there at the clinics
And are free to use
To use it
Having sex with virgins
It is no cure for AIDS
Youth
You must take this alphabet
From ABC
Abstain
Be faithful
Condomize

I don't think the reality of AIDS
I take it as a joke
I thought it was a way for parents to keep their children from sexual activities
HIV/AIDS is not someone else's
It's my problem
It's your problem too

Open communication should be a way of life
Not an event
I would like to advise my fellow South Africans
We can't hide
Just because our parents in the olden days did not talk about sex and
    relationships
Now is the time to be open and realistic and talk about it
In churches and in schools
Children are being taught about HIV and AIDS
So now is the time to be open and realistic
Safa
Saphel' isizwe sakithi
Ingculaza Mama
Iyo

The sung chorus, "*Safa saphel' isizwe sakithi,*" lyrically referenced Mbongeni Ngema's "Safa Saphel' Isizwe," a song that appeared in his 1992 musical *Sarafina!*, which honored the youth activists of 1976. Ngema's song lamented the dying of a Black nation and called for a leader the people could look to in the escalating struggle to end apartheid. The BOCOSFO's chorus used a different, slower melody that hung heavy, grounding the poets' words to an inescapable reality. The lament of "our dying nation" was now articulated with regard to HIV/AIDS, "ingculaza." Calling back through that reference to the youth anti-apartheid struggles *Sarafina!* memorialized, the BOCOSFO placed the ravages of HIV/AIDS on the nation's continuum of political struggle, with young people particularly implicated.

The BOCOSFO was further diminished by the time I met its members in 2009. I attended a few meetings, but activities no longer occurred consistently. Disebo and Tshepang sought to extend the BOCOSFO's efforts by starting a group for girls between seven and thirteen, a change from the teenagers who had previously constituted the group's core membership. They taught the girls poetry and dance, including stanzas Tshepang wrote for them:

> Living the days of fear is not a good life
> Living with AIDS is not a punishment
> But it is a challenge to us to take care of one another
> Beware that AIDS is there
> Brothers and sisters take care of yourself
> Staying away from sex to stop AIDS from killing us

These efforts to engage preteens were not sustained. Disebo felt that, with the BOCOSFO no longer active, "it's kind of like we let them down, because they were young at this and they wanted to learn from us."

Khabane was also dealing with disappointment in the aftermath of struggle when I met him. The Khutsong community had achieved its demarcation goals, allowing it to remain within the better-resourced Gauteng province, but the town was left in ruins. State symbols (the library, councilors' houses) had been destroyed in the demonstrations against government interference. Khabane lamented this destruction of already-meager facilities, particularly libraries, "because without those things, we are lacking resources." Destruction may have alerted the state to Khutsong's crisis, but residents had to live with its aftermath. The community's successful show of strength, wiping out symbols of state occupation ripe for destruction, left Khabane and his peers with even fewer resources. When destruction is the only language that provokes state response, protest fires may win the moment, but they leave disturbing disquiet in their wake, a disquiet that colored Khabane's ambivalence toward community struggles, which he saw as shows of strength but also as self-harming.

Through such ambivalence, Khabane was confronted with his own limitation, and that of his community, in bringing justice into the world. Haunted by the impossibilities of resistance and self-actualization in the shadow of incessant material deprivation, he bore the brunt of history. The burning of the library particularly pained him for the loss of access to knowledge. Yes, Khutsong protesters obstructed the provincial demarcation, but at what costs and with what consequences? For Khabane, the consequences were material destruction, physical insecurity, and cognitive neglect. The aftermath of the struggle was not just, and yet neither can acquiescence be just. The unresolvability of that dilemma also haunted me; on my return from fieldwork, I sat in a Princeton restaurant and, invited to discuss my research on protest, I was pulled back to that conversation with Khabane and could not help but cry. The tears that escaped my attempt at public composure became an occasion to reflect on bodily responses as sites of knowledge.

Other factors contributed to youth's growing disillusionment with activist organizations. The two most-cited causes for concern were money and internal strife, elements of the APF's problematic internal dynamics that I discussed in chapter 4. Young activists were understandably suspicious of financial support, as they had witnessed acrimony within the APF and affiliate organizations due to funding.[20] As Thokozani explained: "We end up having in-fights in our organizations because of the particular funding, and for me it's kind of like demoralizing our struggle. You can look into it in two ways, but most of the time, people will say, you can't survive without funding. But I think if issues affect you in that way, you can survive without it, and after all if you want to make change, you won't rely on someone to make the change, but you have to say that I'm going to be responsible to make that change." Tshepang was particularly embittered by his experience working within an organization that was part of Johannesburg's broader activist network. As he explained, "Your day has been spoiled because you know that you are going to meet the people who depress you more." His disenchantment was why he chose to volunteer at a community center "instead of going somewhere to work for money, but in return you are not happy. So I said, 'No, let me just quit [the job], quit APF, and just come and help the community.'" He saw volunteering as a more direct way to serve his community than through organizations like the one he quit or alliances like the APF. Disebo also decided to withdraw from her activities with the APF because of gossip: "I cut myself from this because it's too much. It's way too much."

Redemption also fell prey to disillusionment. Within three months, Thulani's triumph with him had waned. When I visited him in August 2010, Redemption was working at a panel-beater workshop (auto body shop) in front of his house. Although he still came to APF meetings when he could, attending them was no longer a priority. He explained, "It's hard for youth to engage with those veterans because they politicize personal issues and then you end up in the middle." His words draw the particular challenges of youth activism into relief. In the APF, youth were caught in the middle between opportunity and constraints, between creative flourishing and the interpersonal politics that weighed down the movement.

If performance registers as the language of youth, drawing on Thulani's designation in his assessment of Redemption's capability, it is its affective qualities—generating positive sensory associations and sociality—that were especially motivating for the young people I worked with. Such motivation occurred in a manner similar to Remmoho members' experiences, but it drew on different techniques. Recasting a contemporary politics of enjoyment in light of these preferences is critical. Youth activists were demoralized by strife and motivated by intergenerational solidarity; interpersonal relationships with individuals like Rose and Thulani who looked out for them; and by performance, which seemed frivolous to elder activists. Their political engagement was not an escapist enjoyment; its potential exists not only in the recognition of performance as the ground on which to generate activism among youth but also in recognition of the intergenerational relationships through which young people act on the world.

NOTES

1. As Johnny Clegg said at the height of the struggle in the 1980s, "The weekends are for reconstitution.... 'Good time' music is reconstitutive because it says, climb inside and I'll make you whole, get up off your chair, don't feel so bad, let's move together, a bit more strongly with each repeated cycle of the song.... It is defiant. It expresses the determination that every one of us will be free one day. It cannot be explicitly political ... it expresses in its tone, in the sound of the voice and the sound of the instruments, the soul of the black South African" (quoted in Taylor 1997: 80, 82).

2. A further interpretation of kwaito's political operation could be that, despite its seemingly apolitical emphasis on enjoyment, its stylistic ingenuities subvert the status quo by pushing beyond the boundaries of the parental generation's moral universe. See Ortner (1995) for arguments against

the dichotomy between resistance and accommodation that pervades the conventional contours of political intervention. Xavier Livermon's *Kwaito Bodies: Remastering Space and Subjectivity in Post-Apartheid South Africa* (2020) shows how kwaito transcends such a resistance/co-optation binary through his portrayal of the genre as a performance of freedom for young Black South Africans navigating the limits of national recognition.

3. These skipped-generation households reflect both a regional history of labor migration that tended to separate parents from their children and the devastating effects of the HIV/AIDS pandemic, which decimated South African communities. As individuals of childbearing age succumbed to the pandemic, grandparents were often left to raise their orphaned grandchildren.

4. Interview with the author, March 18, 2010, Johannesburg. All of the quotes and comments from Charmaine in this chapter are from this interview.

5. Interview with the author, June 16, 2010, Johannesburg. All of the quotes and comments from Buyisiwe in this chapter are from this interview.

6. Interview with the author, 2010, Johannesburg. All of the quotes and comments from Khabane in this chapter are from this interview.

7. Such concealment in the face of domination has sustained Black life both on the African continent and in the diaspora. As Gikandi notes of artistic practice under enslavement, it was "sustained by an underground symbolic order that spoke a cabalistic language, unintelligible or inaccessible to the dominant culture" (2001: 346–47).

8. According to Statistics South Africa's quarterly Labour Force Survey, as reported in *The Times* (2011).

9. Interview with the author, August 23, 2010, Johannesburg. All of the quotes and comments from Tshepang in this chapter are from this interview.

10. Interview with the author, October 18, 2010, Johannesburg. All of the quotes and comments from Thokozani in this chapter are from this interview.

11. Interview with the author, October 16, 2009, Johannesburg.

12. Ibid.

13. Interview with the author, August 30, 2010, Johannesburg. All of the quotes and comments from Disebo in this chapter are from this interview.

14. For more on the centrality of choirs and other musically driven associational forms to young people's social transformation in South Africa, see McNeill and James's (2011) examination of young women's strategic combination of multiple genres to transmit biomedical discourse on HIV/AIDS to the general public in the Venda region. In addition, see Steven Black's (2014, 2019) work with a Zulu gospel choir in Durban that also served as an HIV support and activist group. Austin Okigbo (2016) draws out music's connection to the politics of health through ethnographic engagement with a choir formed to combat HIV/AIDS in Umlazi (near Durban). As these works show, music groups remain

realms of social intervention for young people even beyond kwaito modes of consumption, particularly as the HIV/AIDS epidemic is recognized among some as South Africa's next terrain of struggle. For more on these dynamics on the African continent more broadly, see Bourgault (2003).

15. Interview with the author, October 16, 2009, Johannesburg.

16. Ibid.

17. Interview with the author, June 2, 2010, Pretoria.

18. Personal conversation with the author, 2010. The subsequent quotes and comments from Thulani are from this conversation.

19. Personal conversation with the author, 2010.

20. As Disebo put it when she recalled her involvement with Remmoho, "When the money came, it was fighting and fighting."

—⁓—

CONCLUSION

IN AN INTERVIEW IN 2010, Ahmed Veriava described the advantage of pursuing a project on the Anti-Privatisation Forum's (APF) history at that particular point in time. He noted that with "so many narratives of the APF told before the story was over—you never knew how it might conclude. I think you can finally tell the story of how the APF finally concludes. But hopefully that end is also a new beginning."[1] Awareness of the APF as a movement that is no more has colored my analysis in this book. That knowledge encouraged sober reflection on the APF's strengths and the impact of its members' struggles even as it required an ethical commitment to understand the ruptures in the organization's internal solidarity and the disenchantment among its members and constituents.

The APF undeniably changed South Africa's contemporary political landscape. The African National Congress (ANC) government has shifted its policies in response to the agitation of the movement and other mobilizations it spurred. Lucien van der Walt described this achievement:

> We stopped the state commodifying basic things—in a limited way, true—
> but a decommodification from below, basically through those struggles,
> helped. Not solely the APF, but the APF was an important part of the
> struggle. Helped *de facto* to prevent the commodification of those resources,
> and the state had to accommodate to that. I mean what it did when they
> wrote off those debts? They were essentially recognizing a fact on the ground
> that we had already helped create. When the state started giving free water, it
> was recognizing the fact that they couldn't actually enforce their policies, all
> right, then and there. So it had big victories in that sense.[2]

The APF was one of the first organizations to consolidate budding discontent with the postapartheid political landscape in dispersed communities.

Its visibility and notoriety changed that landscape, paving the way for later struggles over service delivery. The movement also produced personal transformations among its members, many of whom credited the political education they received through the APF with helping them project authority in their community organization work. For some, this political education contributed to the cultivation of careers in unions, academic research, community-based organizations, and activist philanthropy.

This book is concerned with how the APF's legacies are captured through the organization's multiple performances. In activists' performance of everyday life, routine negotiations of political sensibilities shaped the APF's emergence and organizational form. The APF constituted itself through its members' acts of reproduction, acts that came to be taken for granted over time. These reproductive acts involved the structure of membership, the conduct of meetings, and the tactics for political confrontation the organization adopted. While early APF activists sought to inaugurate new approaches to collective mobilization that would overcome the shortcomings of apartheid-era organizations, their attempts generated new dilemmas. For example, in seeking to be as inclusive of different perspectives as possible, APF activists encouraged debate in its meetings. Over time, that debate took on a combative tone, which alienated many members and made them less willing to participate in meetings. APF founders sought to prioritize community struggles by recognizing three categories of membership and curtailing the privileges of some members to serve that overarching goal. That structure contributed to a complex imbalance of power that belied the ethical intentions underlying it. As a result, the organization fell short of its ethical ideals through ruptures in its internal solidarity.

Alongside the APF's performative emergence and decline, another dimension of performance was rooted in creative expression. Singing freedom songs, creating rituals for collective wellness, and staging dramas enhanced the public face of the organization and generated alternatives to the combativeness of the APF's internal workings.

PERFORMANCE AND COLLECTIVE POLITICS

Performance holds the potential to both uphold and transgress, to both reinforce and trouble boundaries. Fraught with political implications, performance appears in the analysis presented here both as the conduct of politics, including members' appraisals of one another and of their organization, and as creative expression that materializes the emergent. It troubles current states of affairs, offers recourse, and serves as a mechanism by which marginalized groups can re-center their world.

An examination of the interconnections between performance and politics benefits from an expansive consideration of the many meanings of *performance* (Hamera and Conquergood 2006: 419–20). Such expansive consideration is aided by the ubiquity of performance in sociopolitical considerations. Performance is a core consideration in phenomena as varied as job evaluations, organizational reviews, software algorithms, machinery, human prowess, ceremonial observances, and creative expression.[3] As an "essentially contested concept" (Strine et al. 1990: 183; cf. Carlson 2004: 1–5), performance is useful in studying the spectacular and the mundane (Palmer and Jankowiak 1996), particularly in political contexts.

Defined as "restored behavior" (Schechner 1985), performance acknowledges the cyclic and minute acts underpinning the present while presenting possibilities for transcending what has come before and stretching into previously unknown modes of being in the world. This transformative potential and the experience of alternative paths, for practitioners and their sociopolitical contexts, registers as "anathema to those who would police social borders and identities" (Diamond 1996: 2). These multiple considerations contribute to an expansive view of the performance of politics and the politics of performance in two ways: the facilitation of political expansion through creative expression and the fostering of alternate forms of participation through members' appraisals of the organization's "performance."

Creative Expression and Political Expansion

In her discussion of the strengths of tactical diversity in social movements, Angelique Haugerud posits a direct connection between play (an activity cognate with performance) and collective politics. "It is play that keeps political life healthy," she proposes (2013: 196).[4] Play and, by extension, performance do not just contribute tactical diversity; they also facilitate political action. Such a connection between members' creative displays and their political life is evident in the APF's enactment. Singing together enabled cohesion and provided respite from the divisiveness that pervaded activists' interactions, as I demonstrated in chapter 3. This cohesion was transient, however, lasting only as long as the performance continued. Furthermore, variation existed within that cohesion. Attention to gendered and generational distinctions, through, for instance, the Remmoho women's forum (chapter 5) and youth efforts to create a space for themselves within the APF via theatrical performances (chapter 6), engaged with such variation. The wellness modalities that were the focus of many of Remmoho's meetings offer one example of performance as a source of countermobilization. Remmoho's emphasis on healing and collective care sought to establish an alternative mode of political engagement that was not fully appreciated within the broader APF forum. In a parallel manner, the APF encouraged but also undervalued the performances its young members enjoyed and used to build their organizations, and they considered the performances mere entertainment rather than substantive political engagement. Prior analyses either overlooked these sites of meaningful practice or took them for granted; attention to them contributes to a greater appreciation of their political implications.

Performance and politics both proceed as aesthetic, sensorial experiences. Examining performance through the lens of political aesthetics—showing how politics erupts through the reconfiguration of sensory experience—illuminates the ways that APF activists are dynamically embodied, constituting the organization in ways that can be visibly manifested, but are not always. Internal processes—emotions, sensations, and sensibilities—however delicate, are no less powerful than externally discernible performances.

These sensorial experiences shape aesthetic preferences and influence the mobilization experiences activists pursue. This book presents many illustrations of this dynamic: the pull to attend protests that Ndumiso described as envy (chapter 3); the glimpse of personal connection that drew Willeen to Remmoho, a moment she described as her spirit remembering her soul; the warmth and positive sociality that secured the commitment of Disebo and many APF youth members. Sensorial experience also yielded aversions: the distress of not having a say in APF meetings resulted in refusal to attend future meetings; pervasive combativeness in meetings eroded solidarity and alienated many members. Such examples constitute the inner life of participation and its manifestation in ways that mattered, profoundly, for the organization as a whole.

If, indeed, it is play that keeps political life healthy, APF members' experiences suggest that performance and its cognate activities, including play and ritual, keep political life not only healthy but also desirable. For youth members, for instance, performance was the pathway to their involvement in community struggles. And returning activists found a sense of reconnection and recommitment in their immersion in collective protest singing.

That reconnection was perhaps fueled by remembered rapture, an idea made apparent to me during an interview with Charmaine, an APF member who had been active with Sedibeng Committed Artists. I had asked her about where activists used performance, and she mentioned road barricades. I confessed my inexperience, saying that I had never been present at barricades. "You've never participated in barricading a road . . . oh!" she exclaimed. "That's funny, you have to try it."[5] When I asked why, she responded, "Because you put tire, put petrol, and police will come after you, but if they catch you, you are going to stop smiling. I remember that time when we were barricading there." She pointed down the dirt road. "I really enjoyed that day, I enjoyed it, it was like a good experience to me."

"Why is it so good?" I asked. Her response focused on how road barricades involved coordination and were stimulating. Activists would agree to meet at a certain place and time, usually at a major roadway in the middle of the night, with the needed materials in hand so that, by the morning, if the activists had not been caught by the police, the whole location would be set ablaze, halting traffic. These procedures are not inherently fun, yet Charmaine highlighted the playful dimensions of the activity: "So first, we are going to the grounds and discuss what we were going to do, how we were going to do it, then we go there, and we start singing." These songs, she told me, involved vulgar lyrics, and her younger sister, for example, would be prohibited from singing them due to her age. The playful atmosphere these performances generated provided a sense of freedom from social norms and contributed great enjoyment. "I don't know . . . it was so good," Charmaine recalled. "Even if I was arrested, I would have enjoyed every minute when I was arrested and in the cells." Pressing further, I asked, "But what made it feel good?" She responded, "Because I know I did that." For Charmaine, road barricades yielded a sense of delightful capability and accomplishment, despite or perhaps because of the risks involved. Capturing the attention of the police, and the subsequent chase, become a game; part of the enjoyment is in not getting caught. The efficacy of protest in immediate experience is the delight of provoking the authority represented by the police, and the reward of achievement that is a performance of power. As Charmaine noted, the element of enjoyment was wrapped up in her experience of her capability—knowing that she did that. This enjoyment took place in a context of coordination with others, and the activists' collective bond was enabled through song and strengthened through shared risks.

Charmaine's associations were not unique. Redemption offered similar sentiments. He told me he had missed street actions during the time he was not involved in the APF. Returning to participation in marches and barricades, he said, reminded him of a part of himself that had been missing. The significance of night vigils and song to participation in demonstrations was a part of the APF's tactical toolbox, as one activist recalls learning from APF members before his community became affiliated with the organization:

I remember at one stage we had a march, and previously we did not have night vigils. But the APF comrades came to us and said, "No, you see, in order to have a successful march, you start the night before, hold a night vigil, sing all night long, and you'll see no person will go to work. They would want to join this march." And it happened that way, and we had a massive march. A very huge march, which made a very huge impact, and that march went to the office of the President. That was one of the biggest marches that our affiliate had at the time and it was because of the relationship that we had with the APF.[6]

Group singing secured participation; a march was invigorated by a singing vigil the night before.

Appraisals and the Seeking of Alternatives

While members' sensorial performances built collective bonds, members' appraisals of the organization's performance fostered alternative forms of participation within the APF and beyond. In discussing the APF's decline as a failure of performance, Buyisiwe highlighted the relevance of this concept as a category of appraisal. For Buyisiwe, the APF's performance involved its front-stage visibility in terms of political action and activity; he assessed it as "now low" (see chapter 4). The decline of visibility was due, according to Buyisiwe, to a backstage failure—a disconnect between the APF's leadership and its members. This disconnect constituted a failure of performance: the APF's constituent elements were not working in synchrony. As others made similar appraisals of the APF's activities, and of their experience within the organization, they created alternatives to the APF's main organization—most notably the women's forum, Remmoho. Remmoho's members criticized several elements of activist practice within the APF, including the erosion of community and the silencing of female members by the pervasive combativeness of meetings. In constituting their collectivity, Remmoho's founders chose to emphasize different modalities of activism, enacted through performance, including a focus on bodily wellness and care, attention to sensuality through the practice of ritual, and the nurturing of a sense of community through mutual investment in one another's lives.

Remmoho offered an alternative mode of participation in alliance with the APF, although the alliance was awkward. In other instances, critique led to disenchantment with and withdrawal from the APF. Tshepang followed this trajectory, along with others, choosing to focus on the needs of his community of residence rather than the APF's coalitional politics. Tshepang's reflections, which I discussed in chapter 6, are echoed in the explanation another activist, Richard Mokolo, gave for vacating his APF leadership position:

I realised that the focus of the affiliates of the Anti-Privatisation Forum is not on building the struggles, but it was only for personally building individuals. There is a lot of individualism in the APF whereby people are attending each and every meeting at the APF without having a constituency from where they come . . . when we attend the CC [Coordinating Committee], most of the time the discussions were around money, money, transport money, people were putting the requisition for money for projects that were not existing. Now I decided not to disturb or not to force people to change. Let me direct my energy to the community and then because Anti-Privatisation Forum is in my blood, I can work or I can do Anti-Privatisation work in the community.[7]

Mokolo's intentional vacation from his participation in the APF's broader forum captures an incongruence many APF members experienced, between the kinds of participation the APF's structure enabled and their priorities for collective activism. As I showed in chapter 4, the APF's organizational form belied the intentions of its founding organizers, who created the APF's structure with the intent of doing organizational work differently. Those founders, and those who guided the APF's later structural transformations, held lofty ideals, seeking to avoid the flaws they saw in past activist collectives, including the repression of contrary viewpoints and inattention to organizational sustainability. These intentions were partially realized; the APF's lifespan was among the longest of the new generation of social movements that emerged in the aftermath of the ANC's ascent to power in 1994. In critical ways, however, activists' lived experiences were incommensurate with the APF's structure and the modes of participation that flourished within its structure.

One of the unintended impacts of the APF's organizational form and its strategic emphasis on bureaucratic measures and transformation through legal instruments was a dissipation of collective energy and the atomization of resistance. Encountering a combative space dominated by individuals "playing politics"—maneuvering to secure individual financial gain by taking advantage of organizational procedures—many APF members found their core concerns unmet and sensed those needs would remain unmet. This realization often led activists to disengage from the main organization and direct their energies elsewhere, as Richard Mokolo and Tshepang did by shifting their focus to their own immediate communities rather than joining the fray within the APF's broader coalition. For Mokolo, the APF was "in my blood"; it constituted more than was contained in its problematic organizational structures. The APF was the work he pursued in his community outside of the coalitional structure that had lapsed into monetary disputes and individualism. Such appraisals remind us that, despite fervent intentions, movements are not inherently liberatory (Juris 2008a: 17). Members' critiques signaled alternate possibilities for the conduct of politics.

Performance is relevant to the dissipation and disenchantment that unfolded in at least two dimensions. First, the enactment of idealized intentions introduces unintended consequences, a key dynamic of performance. As practice itself, performance occupies the space between the idealized and the realized. Great intentions are often subverted, especially in the dynamic field of collective interdependence that makes up social movements. That distance, between the ideal and the real, should not be marked as a shortcoming; such a perspective would mean holding on to the immateriality of intentions, ever expectant of ideals that may never manifest. Rather, that distance should be held in tension, as an outcome—not a failure or absence—of performance. Readjusting perception in this way directs focus toward what did happen and how what happened yielded a particular effect, desired or undesired. Such reflection can clarify pathways forward and drive further action toward the transformation sought.

Second, cultural performances—the dynamically embodied expressions that fueled many members' activism—can attenuate the constraints of organizational structure. Given the multiple roles these performances played in the organization (fortification, identity building, collective bonding, commemoration, diagnosis), they could have provided an avenue to sustain the movement. More deliberate attention to ritual and cultural expression as movement-building platforms (an approach Remmoho and the Bophelong Community Service Forum [BOCOSFO] exemplified) might have deepened members' engagement, promoted horizontal collaboration, and strengthened the broader coalition.

However, these experiences of collectivity, whether they manifested in the immediacy of protest singing, unfolded over a longer duration in the rituals and routines of Remmoho, or emerged in the BOCOSFO's rehearsals, were momentary achievements. Protests ended, sometimes with brutal repression; factions broke off due to disagreement; people died because of the precarity of their conditions, providing powerful testimony to the severe social and political environments that activists navigated, against which performance must confront its limits. Even here, though, what remains is Ndumiso's observation: you can't go to war without song. In its manifestations in everyday life through song, movement, and ritual, cultural performance enabled marginalized communities to claim power and oppose a distribution of the sensible that would render them invisible or inaudible within the city and nation. Through performance tactics that facilitated collective protest, these communities sought to be seen, heard, and also heeded, their dignity recognized.

While these tactics were comprehensible in confrontation with external opposition, they were not suited to the APF's internal battles. That the internal workings of a social movement organization can become a battlefield is a well-recognized but also confounding truth: an organization built to cultivate unity can become a site for disunity, as the APF did. And yet, that disunity was generative, spurring the creation of alternative modes of participation in the collective. The APF's internal combativeness led to disengagement for many and to countermobilization in different spheres, on the basis of gender, youth, or location (exemplified in activists' redirection of energy away from the APF's collective and toward their immediate communities). These countermobilizations highlight how cultivated performance can enhance group cohesion and facilitate the internal processes of oppositional collectives; thus, they demonstrate the potential impact of similar interventions within the broader collective. APF affiliates like Remmoho, the BOCOSFO, and others offer important lessons for broad-based coalitions like the APF itself: the importance of humanizing activism, attending to individual experience within the varied stakes of daily struggle, and cultivating collective belonging through mutual care, manifested in quotidian interactions and modes of relationship that register sensorially and secure continued investment in the collective.

Throughout this book, I have sought to demonstrate how, through multiple manifestations in everyday life, performance constitutes and sustains activist community and mitigates its dissipation. A performance analysis draws into view marginalized individuals within the community, their experiences of participation, and the registered emotions, affective sensations, and senses of self that influenced their pursuit or abandonment of mobilization experiences. These performative outcomes can belie intention, yielding a gap (between idealized expectations and lived experiences of activism) that shapes organizational performance. Underserved activists in the APF (especially youth and women) responded to this gap through factional countermobilizations that drew on performance to emphasize different values and modes of relationship. Heeding the knowledge demonstrated by these countermobilizations highlights the significance of practices that enable inclusive political participation in ways that allow for the immediate experience of the benefits of participation. Such is the import of creative expression for collective activism.

While the APF has declined, some of its community-based affiliates remain active. And many members, like Ahmed Veriava, have expressed hope for its regeneration or continuation, even in a different guise. One activist offered a compelling reflection on the APF's demise and hope for its regeneration. Clarifying that attempts to address the divisiveness among APF's members needed to engage more than just the organizational structure, she acknowledged the absence of an intangible collective bond from the APF's latter engagements. That bond, she asserted, must be rediscovered: "There's something—if I was religious I would say a soul—or something that we need to find again, and it was there."[8]

In this estimation, the APF needed to rediscover its spirit and reconstitute a sense of community and ethical collectivity. This rediscovery would require drastic changes: "It does need a big shuffling, shaking up, and maybe if that shaking up is not possible, it will have to die. It will have to go through a process where things don't work out and you start fresh, sometimes that is also necessary." Such assessment extends an appreciation of the APF's decline beyond the disappointment of loss, seeing it as presenting the opportunity for new beginnings.

NOTES

1. Interview with Ahmed Veriava, conducted by Dale McKinley, February 19, 2010, Johannesburg, housed in the Anti-Privatisation Forum collection of the South African History Archive.

2. Interview with Lucien van der Walt, conducted by Dale McKinley, March 23, 2010, Johannesburg, housed in the Anti-Privatisation Forum collection of the South African History Archive.

3. Jon McKenzie notes of this ubiquity, "From annual performance reviews to high-performance missile systems—and yes, even to ritual and theatre— performance now gathers together a vast array of contemporary phenomena" (2003: 118).

4. Haugerud tempers this assertion with a consideration of Huizinga's thoughts on play: "If life, Huizinga says, is to be 'lived as play,' then that is to accept the wisdom of Plato 'when he called man the plaything of the gods' and to know deeply that 'none of our pronouncements is absolutely conclusive'" (Haugerud 2013: 196; quoting Huizinga 1955: 212).

5. Author's interview, March 18, 2010, Johannesburg. All of the quotes and comments from Charmaine in this section are from this interview.

6. Interview with Mashao Chauke, conducted by Dale McKinley, August 19, 2010. Johannesburg, housed in the Anti-Privatisation Forum collection of the South African History Archive.

7. Interview with Richard Mokolo, conducted by Dale McKinley, March 18, 2010, Johannesburg, housed in the Anti-Privatisation Forum collection of the South African History Archive.

8. Interview with Nina Benjamin, conducted by Dale McKinley, March 9, 2010, Johannesburg, housed in the Anti-Privatisation Forum collection of the South African History Archive.

—ɯ—

EPILOGUE

Wesley

IN 1957, WRESTLING WITH ADDICTION, John Coltrane locked himself in his room and went through withdrawal from heroin on his own, emerging two weeks later a transformed man. The experience of wrestling his demons we cannot know—it was his battle alone—but he shared his transformation with the world though transcendent musical output, including *A Love Supreme* and subsequent albums. I am transfixed by those two weeks; they evoke so many questions: How can a person be so broken that he can no longer continue as before? What must be endured alone? Where do we find the strength to endure alone in the face of uncertain outcomes? What emerges when we are stripped down to our essence? What is the role of others in the individual's quest for transformation? I imagine that Coltrane himself was transfixed; he could not move in any direction until his battle released him. His upstairs room, the upper room, contained the battle and the transformation. Even though I cannot possess his experience, I take refuge in Coltrane's room.

I begin with Coltrane to tell you about my friend Wesley. Hopefully by the end of this story, you will understand why. Evoking the essence of Wesley entails remembering May 1, 2010. Members of the Anti-Privatisation Forum (APF) were participating in a May Day march through Johannesburg's central business district to the Worker's Museum in Newtown. The route took the marchers straight through a busy street, disrupting the flow of cars down that road, although intersections were tricky. As I was wont to do during such marches, I went ahead, walking backward to face marchers as I recorded their movements, capturing the large, red cloth banner that constituted the front line of the march.

The marchers were singing and dancing forward. During one song, Wesley dove under the banner and emerged in front of it, dancing. He seemed moved by necessity, lost in his own world, the song demanding interpretation from his body, and he needed the space ahead, needed to be free of the constriction of the banner. He kicked gracefully and pulled back, drawing out through his movement interpretations of the song I had not previously considered. He placed rhythms in the song that had not been there before but that, with his movement, made perfect sense. His body became the melody, a visual counterpoint to the lyrics the others were singing. The moment stretched forward in time, an eternity that needed no end. That moment is Wesley, his genius, the essence of his being, to me.

Drawn by his talent, I sought him out for interviews. Along with his friend Matt, Wesley and I spent a number of afternoons at his apartment complex discussing the youth art group they had formed, the Immortal Art Group. I listened to their plans for growth, their hopes, and their frustrations. Despite the obstacles Wesley described, his talent gave me faith. And so, life continued routinely until one day, a mutual friend, perhaps it was Matt, informed me that Wesley had had an accident; he was in the hospital. He had fallen from the top floor of his apartment complex. Weeks of uncertainty passed. Slowly, the aftermath began to take shape. He was alive. His body was in dire condition, but he was alive and would continue to live.

The quality of my emotional proximity to Wesley, or, more precisely, the lack of such proximity, did not match the shock I felt from the tragedy. I did not know him well, but when I visited him in the hospital, he became dear to me. Commenting later on the visit, my friend said our connection seemed so intimate. Yet the connection she perceived was born of that visit. He was my life's love in the moment, when I saw him diminished in his hospital bed. I wanted so much for him to know that he was loved and that he could get through his pain.

That hospital was haunted by another. Months earlier, I had stood at the foot of Comrade Rose's bed, awkward and self-conscious. I had watched Nomvula stand by Rose's side with such love and tenderness in her eyes, uninhibited by Rose's condition. I had watched her care for Comrade Rose, feeding her water through the syringe, radiating only love. I did not know it then, but Nomvula was teaching me how to be with another person at their sick, possibly dying, bed. In Wesley's hospital ward, three of us were there to see him. I claimed his side, looking into his eyes; I was committed to seeing him through.

When I left the hospital, I did not know that I would not visit him there again. I had promised to bring him a book and continue our conversation about reconstituting a life. I had all the best intentions, but I did not follow through.

I ended my fieldwork and returned to the United States without seeing him again. I could say that I carried him with me, but I let go of his hand despite having promised to help pull him through. That was the end of 2010.

When I returned to South Africa in December 2013, Matt gave me Wesley's number. I called and arranged to meet him at his new place. As I waited at the security desk for Wesley to come down and let me in, I did not know how he would appear before me. I did not know what recovery he had made from the accident that had broken every bone in his body. Eventually, two men wheeled themselves from the elevators to the glass-door entrance of the building. One of them indicated that the security officer should let me in. By his face, I recognized Wesley, although he had thick shoulder-length locs, quite different from how he had kept his hair when I had last seen him.

As we settled into his flat, he told me about his first hospital days, how he could not move and could not see himself. The tears and other responses from his mother, family members, and friends at the sight of his body frightened him, suggesting the terribleness of the injuries he could not see for himself. He told me that he had been drunk and on an impetuous dare when he fell; as a result, he carried guilt about having brought his injury on himself. He did bring up my failure to visit him again, or to get in touch at all. I apologized and let him know the failure was not one of ill intent. I disconnected from him due to my own limitations.

We talked, then, about what pulled him through in those moments by himself on his hospital bed, when the responses of those around him only reminded him that he was truly lost. And we talked about how life was for him now, how he had come to survive. Wesley left the hospital having lost the use of his arms and legs and spent a period of time at a physical rehabilitation center. He was unaccepting of his condition, but through his friendship with the other person in the wheelchair who had come to meet me, he started to realize possibilities in his life again.

Engaging our imaginative capacity, fiction often powerfully prefigures real circumstances, offering pathways of connection before lived experience. Watching Jason Street's adjustments to paraplegia on *Friday Night Lights* had created a space within me to bear witness to Wesley's adjusted being-in-the-world. I knew to acknowledge my discomfort and awkwardness without letting them limit the possibility of connection. I was amazed and proud of what he had made of his life. He was working a good job, was in a relationship, and had secured his own place.

All that he had secured, though, was without my support, the support I had promised. But I reaffirmed that day my commitment to him and promised to keep in touch more regularly. If he needed me to, I told him, I could call on a weekly basis to check in. He told me he needed me to call, and I was so glad for the affirmation of interdependence. Because the truth is, I needed him too. Because I doubt my own life, but when I think about what he has made of his own, how he has rebuilt from broken bones, not to stand upright but to wheel himself forward, I am reminded that I, too, can live well. When I feel unrecognized, my worth unacknowledged, I know, through the friendship we have cultivated, that he sees me. I know through him that life has bigger stakes than the limitations of one particular person's vision. Despite any appearance of imbalance between us, I need him to survive.

He asked me to tell his story and carry it out into the world. I told him he would have to do that himself. That he had proven through his life that he was not limited. Like John Coltrane in his upper room, there are elements of what he has lived through that I cannot know, and yet I need to hear those things from him as a matter not just of survival but of transcendence.

I am transfixed by Wesley. He holds me in place. I grieve the loss of the use of his limbs. I grieve that he will not dance again or dare himself to greater heights in the ways that seemed so essential to his being. The loss is compelling, but it is not the end of his story. The melody that was his body lingers on, transformed but not constrained.

As I sit in a cold Cape Town flat, writing about him, I receive a text from Wesley, letting me know he had found me on a messaging app we discussed last week. "I was just about to call you," is the first thing I will tell him now.

Cape Town, June 2016

BIBLIOGRAPHY

Abu-Lughod, Lila. "Writing against Culture." In *Feminist Anthropology: A Reader*, edited by Ellen Lewin, 53–169. Oxford, UK: Blackwell, 2006 [1991].

African National Congress. *Reconstruction and Development Programme*. Policy document, South Africa, 1994.

Agawu, Kofi. *African Rhythm: A Northern Ewe Perspective*. Cambridge: Cambridge University Press, 1995.

———. *Representing African Music: Postcolonial Notes, Queries, Positions*. New York: Routledge, 2003.

Ahearn, Laura. *Living Language: An Introduction to Linguistic Anthropology*. Malden, MA: Wiley-Blackwell, 2012.

——— "'A Twisted Rope Binds My Waist': Locating Constraints on Meaning in a Tij Songfest." *Journal of Linguistic Anthropology* 8, no. 1 (1998): 60–86.

Ahmed, Sara. "Affective Economies." *Social Text* 22, no. 2 (2004): 117–39.

Alexander, Peter. "Rebellion of the Poor: South Africa's Service Delivery Protests—A Preliminary Response." *Review of African Political Economy* 37, no. 123 (2010): 25–40.

Allen, Lara. "Kwaito Versus Crossed-Over: Music and Identity during South Africa's Rainbow Years, 1994–1996." *Social Dynamics* 30, no. 2 (2004): 82–111.

Alvarez, Sonia E., Claudia de Lima Costa, Veronica Feliu, Rebecca Hester, Norma Klahn, and Millie Thayer, eds. *Translocalities/Translocalidades: Feminist Politics of Translation in the Latin/a Américas*. Durham, NC: Duke University Press, 2014.

Aminzade, Ronald, and Doug McAdam. "Emotions and Contentious Politics." In *Silence and Voice in the Study of Contentious Politics*, edited by Ronald Aminzade et al., 14–50. Cambridge: Cambridge University Press, 2001.

Ashforth, Adam. *Witchcraft, Violence, and Democracy in South Africa*. Chicago: University of Chicago Press, 2005.

Askew, Kelly M. *Performing the Nation: Swahili Music and Cultural Politics in Tanzania*. Chicago: Chicago University Press, 2002.

Austin, John Langshaw. *How to Do Things with Words*. Cambridge, MA: Harvard University Press, 1962 [1955].

———. "Performative Utterances." In *Philosophical Papers*. Oxford, UK: Oxford University Press, 1979.

Bakhtin, Mikhail. *Rabelais and His World*. Translated by H. Iswolsky. Bloomington: Indiana University Press, 1984.

Ballard, Richard, Adam Habib, and Imraan Valodia, eds. *Voices of Protest: Social Movements in Post-Apartheid South Africa*. Pietermaritzburg, South Africa: UKZN Press, 2006.

Bateson, Gregory. *Steps to an Ecology of Mind*. New York: Ballantine, 1972.

Bauman, Richard. "Verbal Art as Performance." *American Anthropologist* 77, no. 2 (1975): 290–311.

Beauregard, R., R. L. Bremner, X. Mngcu, and R. Tomlinson, eds. *Emerging Johannesburg*. New York: Routledge, 2003.

Bebey, Francis. *African Music: A People's Art*. Westport, CT: Lawrence Hill, 1975 [1969].

Becker, Heike. "South Africa's May 1968: Decolonising Institutions and Minds." *Review of African Political Economy* (blog), 2016. http://roape.net/2016/02/17 /south-africas-may-1968-decolonising-institutions-and-minds/ (accessed June 24, 2020).

Bernard, R. H. *Research Methods in Anthropology: Qualitative and Quantitative Approaches*. Lanham, MD: AltaMira, 2006.

Besteman, Catherine. *Transforming Cape Town*. Berkeley: University of California Press, 2008.

Biehl, João. *Vita: Life in a Zone of Social Abandonment*. Berkeley: University of California Press, 2005.

Black, Steve. "The Body in Sung Performance." *Anthropology News* 52, no. 1 (2011): 10.

———. "The Intersubjective Space–Time of a Zulu Choir/HIV Support Group in Global Perspective." *Social Semiotics* 24, no. 4 (2014): 381–401.

Black, Steven P. *Speech and Song at the Margins of Global Health: Zulu Tradition, HIV Stigma, and AIDS Activism in South Africa*. New Brunswick, NJ: Rutgers University Press, 2019.

Bond, Patrick. "Johannesburg's Resurgent Social Movements." In *Challenging Hegemony: Social Movements and the Quest for a New Humanism in Post-Apartheid South Africa*, edited by Nigel Gibson, 103–28. Trenton, NJ: Africa World, 2006.

Bonner, Philip, and Noor Nieftagodien. *Alexandra: A History*. Johannesburg, South Africa: Wits University Press, 2008.

Booysen, Susan. "Beyond the Ballot and the Brick: Continuous Dual Repertoires in the Politics of Attaining Service Delivery in South Africa." In *The Politics of Service Delivery*, edited by A. McLennan and B. Munslow, 104–36. Johannesburg, South Africa: Wits University Press, 2009.

———. "With the Ballot and the Brick: The Politics of Attaining Service Delivery." *Progress in Development Studies* 7, no. 1 (2007): 21–32.

Bourdieu, Pierre. *Pascalian Meditations*. Stanford, CA: Stanford University Press, 2000 [1997].

Bourgault, Louise M. *Playing for Life: Performance in Africa in the Age of AIDS*. Durham, NC: Carolina Academic Press, 2003.

Bourgois, Philippe. "The Power of Violence in War and Peace: Post-Cold War Lessons from El Salvador." *Ethnography* 2, no. 1 (2001): 5–34.

Bozzoli, Belinda. *Theatres of Struggle and the End of Apartheid*. Athens: Ohio University Press, 2004.

Brecht, Bertolt. *Poems 1913–1956*. New York: Methuen, 1987.

Brennan, Teresa. *The Transmission of Affect*. Ithaca, NY: Cornell University Press, 2004.

Bucholtz, Mary. "Youth and Cultural Practice." *Annual Review of Anthropology* 31 (2002): 525–52.

Budd, Malcolm. "The Intersubjective Validity of Aesthetic Judgements." *British Journal of Aesthetics* 47, no. 4 (2007): 333–71.

Buhlungu, Sakhela. "The Anti-Privatisation Forum: A Profile of a Post-Apartheid Social Movement." Unpublished case study, 2004.

———. "Upstarts or Bearers of Tradition? The Anti-Privatisation Forum of Gauteng." In *Voices of Protest*, edited by R. Ballard et al., 67–87. Pietermaritzburg, South Africa: UKZN Press, 2006.

Burdick, John. *The Color of Sound: Race, Religion, and Music in Brazil*. New York: New York University Press, 2013.

———. "Uniting Theory and Practice in the Ethnography of Social Movements: Notes toward a Hopeful Realism." *Dialectical Anthropology* 20 (1995): 361–85.

Butler, Judith. *Notes toward a Performative Theory of Assembly*. Cambridge, MA: Harvard University Press, 2015.

———. "Performative Acts and Gender Constitution: An Essay in Phenomenology and Feminist Theory." *Theatre Journal* 40, no. 4 (1988): 519–31.

Carlson, Marvin. *Performance: A Critical Introduction*. New York: Routledge, 2004.

Carrier-Moisan, Marie-Eve. "Saving Women? Awkward Alliances in the Public Spaces of Sex Tourism." In *Contesting Publics: Feminism, Activism, Ethnography*, edited by Lynne Phillips and Sally Cole, 48–75. London: Pluto, 2013.

Cavell, Marcia. *Becoming a Subject*. Oxford, UK: Oxford University Press, 2006.

Cell, J. *Segregation: The Highest Stage of White Supremacy*. Cambridge: Cambridge University Press, 1982.

Chance, Kerry Ryan. *Living Politics in South Africa's Urban Shacklands*. Chicago: University of Chicago Press, 2018.

Chau, Adam Yuet. "The Sensorial Production of the Social." *Ethnos* 73, no. 4 (2008): 485–504.

Chernoff, John Miller. *African Rhythm and African Sensibility: Aesthetics and Social Action in African Musical Idioms*. Chicago: University of Chicago Press, 1979.

Chikowero, Mhoze. *African Music, Power, and Being in Colonial Zimbabwe*. Bloomington: Indiana University Press, 2015.

Chomsky, Noam. *Aspects of the Theory of Syntax*. Cambridge, MA: MIT Press, 1965.

Christopher, A. J. *The Atlas of Apartheid*. London: Routledge, 1994.

City of Johannesburg. *City of Johannesburg: An African City in Change*. Johannesburg, South Africa: Zebra, 2001.

Clayton, Martin, Rebecca Sager, and Udo Will. "In Time with the Music: The Concept of Entrainment and Its Significance for Ethnomusicology." *ESEM Counterpoint* 11 (2005): 3–75.

Cohen-Cruz, Jan, ed. *Radical Street Performance*. New York: Routledge, 1998.

Cole, Catherine. *Performing South Africa's Truth Commission: Stages of Transition*. Bloomington: Indiana University Press, 2010.

Cole, Jennifer, and Deborah Durham. "Age, Regeneration, and the Intimate Politics of Globalization." In *Generation and Globalization: Youth, Age, and Family in the New World Economy*, edited by Jennifer Cole and Deborah Durham, 1–28. Bloomington: Indiana University Press, 2007.

Collins, Jane. "Theorizing Wisconsin's 2011 Protests: Community-Based Unionism Confronts Accumulation by Dispossession." *American Ethnologist* 39, no. 1 (2012): 6–20.

Comaroff, Jean, and John Comaroff. "Reflections on Youth, from the Past to the Postcolony." In *Frontiers of Capital: Ethnographic Reflections on the New Economy*, edited by Melissa Fisher and Greg Downey, 267–81. Durham, NC: Duke University Press, 2006.

Conquergood, Dwight. "Beyond the Text: Toward a Performative Cultural Politics." In *The Future of Performance Studies: Visions and Revisions*, edited by S. J. Dailey, 25–36. Washington, DC: National Communication Association, 1998.

———. "Health Theatre in a Hmong Refugee Camp: Performance, Communication, and Culture." *TDR* 32, no. 3 (1988): 174–208.

———. "Performance Studies: Interventions and Radical Research." In *The Performance Studies Reader*, edited by Henry Bial, 311–22. New York: Routledge, 2004.

———. "Rethinking Ethnography: Cultural Politics and Rhetorical Strategies." *Communication Monographs* 58 (1991): 179–94.

Coplan, David. "Fictions That Save: Migrants' Performance and Basotho National Culture." *Cultural Anthropology* 6, no. 2 (1991): 164–92.

———. "God Rock Africa: Thoughts on Politics in Popular Black Performance in South Africa." *African Studies* 64 (2005): 9–27.

———. *In Township Tonight! South Africa's Black City Music and Theatre.* 2d ed. Chicago: University of Chicago Press, 2008.

Cornell, Drucilla. *Between Women and Generations: Legacies of Dignity.* New York: Palgrave, 2002.

Corte, Ugo, and Bob Edwards. "White Power Music and the Mobilization of Racist Social Movements." *Music and Arts in Action* 1, no. 1 (2008): 4–20.

Coulter, Colin. "Introduction." In *The End of Irish History: Critical Reflections on the Celtic Tiger,* edited by Colin Coulter and Steve Coleman, 1–33. Manchester, UK: Manchester University Press, 2003.

Covington-Ward, Yolanda. *Gesture and Power: Religion, Nationalism, and Everyday Performance in Congo.* Durham, NC: Duke University Press, 2018.

Crapanzano, Vincent. "Hermes' Dilemma: The Making of Subversion in Ethnographic Description." In *Writing Culture,* edited by James Clifford and George Marcus, 51–76. Berkeley: University of California Press, 1986.

Craven, Christa, and Dana-Ain Davis. "Introduction: Feminist Activist Ethnography." In *Feminist Activist Ethnography: Counterpoints to Neoliberalism in North America,* 1–20. Lanham, MD: Lexington Books, 2013.

Csordas, Thomas J. "The Body's Career in Anthropology." In *Anthropological Theory Today,* edited by Henrietta L. Moore, 172–205. Cambridge: Polity, 1999.

———. "Introduction: The Body as Representation and Being in the World." In *Embodiment and Experience: The Existential Ground of Culture and Self,* edited by Thomas Csordas, 1–24. Cambridge: Cambridge University Press, 1994.

Currier, Ashley. *Out in Africa: LGBT Organizing in Namibia and South Africa.* Minneapolis: University of Minnesota Press, 2012.

Daniel, E. Valentine. "The Individual in Terror." In *Embodiment and Experience: The Existential Ground of Culture,* edited by Thomas J. Csordas, 229–47. Cambridge: Cambridge University Press, 1994.

Dave, Naisargi N. "Activism as Ethical Practice: Queer Politics in Contemporary India." *Cultural Dynamics* 23, no. 1 (2011): 3–20.

———. *Queer Activism in India: A Story in the Anthropology of Ethics.* Durham, NC: Duke University Press, 2012.

———. "To Render Real the Imagined: An Ethnographic History of Lesbian Community in India." *Signs: Journal of Women in Culture and Society* 35, no. 3 (2010): 595–620.

Dawson, Marcelle. "'Phansi Privatisation! Phansi!': The Anti-Privatisation Forum and Ideology in Social Movements." In *Popular Politics and Resistance Movements in South Africa*, edited by William Beinart and Marcelle Dawson, 266–85. Johannesburg, South Africa: Wits University Press, 2010.

de Lima Costa, Claudia. "Lost (and Found?) in Translation: Feminisms in Hemispheric Dialogue." *Latino Studies* 4, no. 1 (2006): 62–78.

Denisoff, R. S. *Sing a Song of Social Significance*. Bowling Green, OH: Bowling Green State University Popular Press, 1983.

Derrida, Jacques. *Speech and Phenomena*. Evanston, IL: Northwestern University Press, 1973.

Desai, Ashwin. *We Are the Poors*. New York: Monthly Review, 2002.

Diamond, Elin. "Introduction: Performance and Cultural Politics." In *Performance and Cultural Politics*, edited by Elin Diamond, 1–12. New York and London: Routledge, 1996.

Dillane, Aileen, Martin J. Power, Eoin Devereux, and Amanda Haynes, eds. *Songs of Social Protest: International Perspectives*, Lanham, MD: Rowman and Littlefield, 2018.

Dorsey, Margaret. "The Role of Music in Materializing Politics." *Political and Legal Anthropology Review* 27, no. 2 (2004): 61–94.

Downey, Greg. "Listening to Capoeira: Phenomenology, Embodiment, and the Materiality of Music." *Ethnomusicology* 46, no. 3 (2002): 487–509.

Drewal, Margaret Thompson. "The State of Research on Performance in Africa." *African Studies Review* 34, no. 3 (1991): 1–64.

Duncan, Jane. *Protest Nation: The Right to Protest in South Africa*. Pietermaritzburg, South Africa: UKZN Press, 2016.

———. "Thabo Mbeki and Dissent." In *Mbeki and After: Reflections on the Legacy of Thabo Mbeki*, edited by Daryl Glaser, 105–27. Johannesburg, South Africa: Wits University Press, 2010.

Durham, Deborah. "Youth and the Social Imagination in Africa." *Anthropological Quarterly* 73, no. 4 (2000): 113–20.

Durham, Deborah, and Frederick Klaits. "Funerals and the Public Space of Sentiment in Botswana." *Journal of Southern African Studies* 28, no. 4 (2002): 777–95.

Ebron, Paulla. *Performing Africa*. Princeton, NJ: Princeton University Press, 2002.

Eriksson, Åsa. *Empowering Women Activists: Creating a Monster—The Contentious Politics of Gender within Social Justice Activism*. Unpublished master's thesis, University of Cape Town, 2007.

Erlmann, Veit. *Nightsong: Performance, Power, and Practice in South Africa*. Chicago: University of Chicago Press, 1996.

Falola, Toyin, and Tyler Fleming, eds. *Music, Performance and African Identities*. New York: Routledge, 2012.

Fanon, Frantz. *Black Skin, White Masks*. New York: Grove, 1968.

Farmer, Paul. *Pathologies of Power: Health, Human Rights, and the New War on the Poor*. Berkeley: University of California Press, 2003.

Farnell, Brenda. "Ethno-Graphics and the Moving Body." *MAN* 29, no. 4 (1994): 929–97.

———. "Moving Bodies, Acting Selves." *Annual Review of Anthropology* 28 (1999): 341–73.

Fassin, Didier. *When Bodies Remember: Experiences and Politics of AIDS in South Africa*. Berkeley: University of California Press, 2007.

Faubion, James. "Toward an Anthropology of Ethics: Foucault and the Pedagogies of Autopoiesis." *Representations* 74, no. 1 (2001): 83–104.

Feld, Steven, et al. "Vocal Anthropology: From the Music of Language to the Language of Song." In *A Companion to Linguistic Anthropology*, edited by A. Duranti, 321–46. Malden, MA: Blackwell, 2004.

Ferguson, James. *The Anti-Politics Machine: 'Development', Depoliticization, and Bureaucratic Power in Lesotho*. Cambridge: Cambridge University Press, 1990.

Ferme, Mariane. "Staging *Politisi*: The Dialogics of Publicity and Secrecy in Sierra Leone." In *Civil Society and the Political Imagination in Africa*, edited by John L. and Jean Comaroff, 160–91. Chicago: University of Chicago Press, 1999.

———. *The Underneath of Things: Violence, History, and the Everyday in Sierra Leone*. Berkeley: University of California Press, 2001.

Foley, Ellen E. "Neoliberal Reform and Health Dilemmas: Social Hierarchy and Therapeutic Decision Making in Senegal." *Medical Anthropology Quarterly* 22, no. 3 (2008): 257–73.

Foster, Susan Leigh. "Choreographies of Protest." *Theatre Journal* 55, no. 3 (2003): 395–412.

Foucault, Michel. *Discipline and Punish: The Birth of the Prison*. Translated by Alan Sheridan. New York: Pantheon, 1977.

———. "Polemics, Politics, and Problematizations." In *Essential Works of Michel Foucault*, vol. 1, *Ethics: Subjectivity and Truth*, edited by Paul Rabinow, translated by Robert Hurley et al., 111–19. New York: New Press, 1997.

Franko, Mark. "Dance and the Political: States of Exception." *Dance Research Journal* 38, nos. 1/2 (2006): 3–18.

Freire, Paulo. *Pedagogy of the Oppressed*. Harmondsworth, UK: Penguin, 1972.

Gallie, W. B. *Philosophy and the Historical Understanding*. New York: Schocken, 1964.

Garner, Roberta. *Contemporary Movements and Ideologies*. New York: McGraw-Hill, 1996.

Gaunt, Kyra. *The Games Black Girls Play: Learning the Ropes from Double-Dutch to Hip-Hop*. New York: New York University Press, 2006.

Geertz, Clifford. "Common Sense as a Cultural System." In *Local Knowledge: Further Essays in Interpretive Anthropology*, 73–93. New York: Basic Books, 1983.

———. *The Interpretation of Cultures*. New York: Basic Books, 1973.

Geisler, Gisela. *Women and the Remaking of Politics in Southern Africa: Negotiating Autonomy, Incorporation and Representation*. Uppsala, Sweden: NAI, 2004.

Geurts, Kathryn. *Culture and the Senses: Bodily Ways of Knowing in an African Community*. Berkeley: University of California Press, 2002.

Gibson, Nigel, ed. *Challenging Hegemony: Social Movements in Post-Apartheid South Africa and the Quest for a New Humanity*. Trenton, NJ: Africa World, 2006.

Gikandi, Simon. "Race and the Idea of the Aesthetic." *Michigan Quarterly Review* 40, no. 2 (2001): 318–50.

Gilbert, Shirli. "Popular Music, Gender Equality and the Anti-Apartheid Struggle." In *Gender and Sexuality in South African Music*, edited by Chris Walton and Stephanus Muller, 11–18. Stellenbosch, South Africa: Sun ePress, 2005.

———. "Singing against Apartheid: ANC Cultural Groups and the International Anti-Apartheid Struggle." *Journal of Southern African Studies* 33, no. 2 (2007): 421–41.

Gill, Lesley. "The Limits of Solidarity: Labor and Transnational Organizing against Coca-Cola." *American Ethnologist* 36, no. 4 (2009): 667–80.

Gillespie, Kelly, and Leigh-Ann Naidoo. "Between the Cold War and the Fire: The Student Movement, Antiassimilation, and the Question of the Future in South Africa." *South Atlantic Quarterly* 118, no. 1 (2019): 226–39.

Gluckman, Max. "Papers in Honor of Melville J. Herskovits: Gossip and Scandal." *Current Anthropology* 4, no. 3 (1963): 307–16.

Goffman, Erving. *Frame Analysis*. New York: Harper Colophon, 1974.

———. *The Presentation of Self in Everyday Life*. Garden City, NY: Doubleday, 1959.

Goldstein, Daniel M. *The Spectacular City: Violence and Performance in Urban Bolivia*. Durham, NC: Duke University Press, 2004.

Goodwin, Jeff, James M. Jasper, and Francesca Polletta, eds. *Passionate Politics: Emotions and Social Movements*. Chicago: University of Chicago Press, 2001.

Gordillo, Gaston. "Resonance and the Egyptian Revolution." *Critical Legal Thinking* (blog). 2011. http://www.criticallegalthinking.com/?p=2318 (accessed May 5, 2016).

Gordillo, Gastón, and Silvia Hirsch. "Indigenous Struggles and Contested Identities in Argentina: Histories of Invisibilization and Reemergence." *Journal of Latin American Anthropology* 8, no. 3 (2003): 4–30.

Gould, Deborah B. *Moving Politics: Emotion and ACT UP's Fight against AIDS*. Chicago: University of Chicago Press, 2009.

Gouws, Amanda, ed. *(Un)thinking Citizenship: Feminist Debates in Contemporary South Africa*. Cape Town, South Africa: University of Cape Town Press, 2005.

Gray, Anne-Marie. *The Liberation Song: With Special Reference to Those Used by the African National Congress, the Inkatha Freedom Party and the Pan Africanist Congress*. Unpublished masters thesis, University of the Orange Free State, 1996.

Gunner, Liz. "Jacob Zuma, the Social Body and the Unruly Power of Song." *African Affairs* 108, no. 430 (2009): 27–48.

———. "Political Song in Africa." *Oxford Research Encyclopedia of Politics* 28. 2019. https://oxfordre.com/politics/view/10.1093/acrefore/9780190228637.001.0001 /acrefore-9780190228637-e-901 (accessed July 5, 2021).

———, ed. *Politics and Performance*. Johannesburg, South Africa: Wits University Press, 1994.

———. "Song, Identity and the State: Julius Malema's Dubul'ibhunu Song as Catalyst." *Journal of African Cultural Studies* 27, no. 3 (2015): 326–41.

Guss, David. *The Festive State: Race, Ethnicity, and Nationalism as Cultural Performance*. Berkeley: University of California Press, 2000.

Hamdy, Sherine F. "Strength and Vulnerability after Egypt's Arab Spring Uprisings." *American Ethnologist* 39, no. 1 (2012): 43–48.

Hamera, Judith, and Dwight Conquergood. "Performance and Politics: Themes and Arguments." In *The Sage Handbook of Performance Studies*, edited by J. Hamera and D. Soyini Madison, 419–25. Thousand Oaks, CA: Sage 2006.

Handelman, D. "Gossip in Encounters: The Transmission of Information in a Bounded Social Setting." *Man* 8, no. 2 (1973): 210–27.

Hanisch, Carol. "The Personal Is Political: The Women's Liberation Classic with a New Explanatory Introduction." 2006 [1969]. http://www.carolhanisch.org /CHwritings/PIP.html (accessed September 23, 2016).

Hart, Gillian. *Rethinking the South African Crisis: Nationalism, Populism, Hegemony*. Athens: University of Georgia Press, 2014.

Harvey, David. *A Brief History of Neoliberalism*. New York: Oxford University Press, 2005.

———. *Spaces of Global Capitalism*. New York: Verso, 2006.

Hassim, Shireen. *Women's Organizations and Democracy in South Africa: Contesting Authority*. Scottsville, South Africa: UKZN Press, 2006.

Haugerud, Angelique. *No Billionaire Left Behind: Satirical Activism in America Today*. Stanford, CA: Stanford University Press, 2013.

Hayem, Judith. "What Do We Call Post-Apartheid?" *Social Dynamics* 43, no. 3 (2017): 386–402.

Henry, Doug. "Violence and the Body: Somatic Expressions of Trauma and Vulnerability during War." *Medical Anthropology Quarterly* 20, no. 3 (2006): 379–98.

Heymann, P. *Towards Peaceful Protest in South Africa: Testimony of Multinational Panel Regarding Lawful Control of Demonstrations in the Republic of South Africa*. Pretoria, South Africa: HSRC, 1992.

Hirsch, Lee, dir. *Amandla! A Revolution in Four-Part Harmony*. DVD. Santa Monica, CA: Artisan, 2002.

Hobart, Angela, and Bruce Kapferer, eds. *Aesthetics in Performance: Formations of Symbolic Construction and Experience*. New York: Berghahn, 2005.

Hodgson, Dorothy L. *Gender, Justice, and the Problem of Culture: From Customary Law to Human Rights in Tanzania*. Bloomington: Indiana University Press, 2017.

Hodgson, Dorothy L., and Ethel Brooks, eds. *Activisms*. Special issue, *WSQ* [formerly *Women's Studies Quarterly*] 35, nos. 3/4 (2007).

Holmes, Seth. *Fresh Fruit, Broken Bodies: Migrant Farmworkers in the United States*. Berkeley: University of California Press, 2013.

Howes, David. *Sensual Relations: Engaging the Senses in Culture and Social Theory*. Ann Arbor: University of Michigan Press, 2003.

Huarcaya, Sergio Miguel. "Performativity, Performance, and Indigenous Activism in Ecuador and the Andes." *Comparative Studies in Society and History* 57, no. 3 (2015): 806–37.

Huizinga, Johan. *Homo Ludens: A Study of the Play-Element in Culture*. Boston: Beacon, 1955.

Hunter, Mark. *Love in the Time of AIDS: Inequality, Gender, and Rights in South Africa*. Bloomington: Indiana University Press, 2010.

Jackson, J. L. "An Ethnographic Filmflam: Giving Gifts, Doing Research, and Videotaping the Native Subject/Object." *American Anthropologist* 106 (2004): 32–42.

Jackson, John L. *Harlemworld: Doing Race and Class in Contemporary Black America*. Chicago: University of Chicago Press, 2001.

Jakobson, Roman. "Concluding Statement: Linguistics and Poetics." In *Style and Language*, edited by T. A. Sebeok, 350–77. Cambridge, MA: MIT, 1960.

———. *On Language*. Edited by Linda R. Waugh and Monique Monville-Burston. Cambridge, MA: Harvard University Press, 1990.

———. "Shifters, Verbal Categories, and the Russian Verb." In *Selected Writings of Roman Jakobson*. Vol. 2, 130–47. The Hague, Netherlands: Mouton, [1957] 1971.

James, Deborah. *Songs of the Women Migrants: Performance and Identity in South Africa*. Edinburgh, Scotland: Edinburgh University Press, 1999.

Jason, Stefanie. "Funda: Dark Days for Iconic Soweto Art School." *Mail & Guardian*, March 20, 2015. http://mg.co.za/article/2015-03-19-funda-dark-days-for-iconic-soweto-art-school (accessed December 17, 2021).

Jasper, James M. "The Emotions of Protest: Affective and Reactive Emotions in and around Social Movements." *Sociological Forum* 13, no. 3 (1998): 397–424.

Johnson, E. Patrick. *Appropriating Blackness: Performance and the Politics of Authenticity*. Durham, NC: Duke University Press, 2003.

Jolaosho, Omotayo. "Anti-Apartheid Freedom Songs Then and Now." *Smithsonian Folkways Magazine*, 2014. https://folkways.si.edu/magazine-spring-2014-anti-apartheid-freedom-songs-then-and-now/south-africa/music/article/smithsonian (accessed September 23, 2016).

———. "Awkward Activisms: Gender and Embodied Mobilization in a Postapartheid South African Social Movement." *Signs: Journal of Women in Culture and Society* 43, no. 2 (2018): 425–48.

———. "Cross-Circulations and Transnational Solidarity: Historicizing the US Anti-Apartheid Movement through Song." *Safundi* 13, nos. 3/4 (2012): 317–37.

———. "Political Aesthetics and Embodiment: Sung Protest in Post-Apartheid South Africa." *Journal of Material Culture* 20, no. 4 (2015): 443–58.

———. "Singing Politics: Freedom Songs and Collective Protest in Post-Apartheid South Africa." *African Studies Review* 62, no. 2 (2019): 6–29.

Jubasi, Mawande. Dancing in the Dark. [Johannesburg] *Sunday Times*, December 10, 2000.

Juris, Jeffrey S. *Networking Futures: The Movements against Corporate Globalization.* Durham, NC: Duke University Press, 2008a.

———. "Performing Politics: Image, Embodiment, and Affective Solidarity during Anti-Corporate Globalization Protests." *Ethnography* 9, no. 1 (2008b): 61–97.

———. "Reflections on #Occupy Everywhere: Social Media, Public Space, and Emerging Logics of Aggregation." *American Ethnologist* 39, no. 2 (2012): 259–79.

Kant, Immanuel. *Critique of Judgement.* Translated by J. H. Bernard. London: Macmillan, 1931.

Kaplan, Temma. *Crazy for Democracy: Women in Grassroots Movements.* New York and London: Routledge, 1997.

Klaits, Frederick. *Death in a Church of Life: Moral Passion during Botswana's Time of AIDS.* Berkeley: University of California Press, 2010.

Kompe, Lydia. "Trade Unionist—Not Tea Girl." In *South African Women on the Move*, edited by Jane Barrett et al, 97–109. London: Zed, 1985.

Kunene, D. P. "Language, Literature and the Struggle for Liberation in South Africa." *Staffrider* 6, no. 3 (1986): 36–47.

Latour, Bruno. *Reassembling the Social: An Introduction to Actor-Network-Theory.* Oxford, UK: Oxford University Press, 2005.

Lewis, Desiree. "The Politics of Feminism in South Africa." In *South African Feminisms: Writing, Theory, and Criticism, 1990–1994*, edited by M. J. Daymond, 91–106. New York: Garland, 1996.

Lieberman, Robbie. *"My Song Is My Weapon": People's Songs, American Communism, and the Politics of Culture 1930–1950.* Urbana: University of Illinois Press, 1995.

Livermon, Xavier. *Kwaito Bodies: Remastering Space and Subjectivity in Post-Apartheid South Africa.* Durham, NC: Duke University Press, 2020.

Livingston, Julie. *Improvising Medicine: An African Oncology Ward in an Emerging Cancer Epidemic.* Durham, NC: Duke University Press, 2012.

Lobelo, Donald. "Toilets Removed from Silver City." *Alex News*, May 27, 2010.

Lockard Craig. *Dance of Life—Popular Music and Politics in Southeast Asia.* Honolulu: University of Hawaii Press, 1998.

Lorde, Audre. *Sister Outsider: Essays and Speeches.* Trumansburg, NY: Crossing, 1984.

Lutz, Catherine. "Emotion, Thought, and Estrangement: Emotion as a Cultural Category." *Cultural Anthropology* 1 (1986): 287–309.

Mabin, A. "Origins of Segregatory Urban Planning in South Africa: 1900–1940." *Planning History* 13 (1991): 8–16.

———. "Struggle for the City: Urbanization and Political Strategies of the South African State." *Social Dynamics* 15 (1989): 1–28.

Madison, D. Soyini. *Acts of Activism: Human Rights as Radical Performance*. New York: Cambridge University Press, 2010.

———. *Critical Ethnography: Method, Ethics, and Performance*. Thousand Oaks, CA: Sage, 2005.

Makhulu, Anne-Maria. *Making Freedom: Apartheid, Squatter Politics, and the Struggle for Home*. Durham, NC: Duke University Press, 2015.

Mandela, Nelson. *Long Walk to Freedom: The Autobiography of Nelson Mandela*. Boston: Little, Brown, 1994.

Marks, Monique. *Young Warriors: Youth Politics, Identity and Violence in South Africa*. Johannesburg, South Africa: Wits University Press, 2001.

Martin, Randy. *Critical Moves: Dance Studies in Theory and Politics*. Durham, NC: Duke University Press, 1998.

Mascia-Lees, Frances E. "Aesthetic Embodiment and Commodity Culture." In *A Companion to the Anthropology of the Body and Embodiment*, edited by Fran E. Mascia-Lees, 3–23. Malden, MA: Wiley-Blackwell, 2011.

Massumi, Brian. *Parables for the Virtual: Movement, Affect, Sensation*. Durham, NC: Duke University Press, 2002.

Matolino, Bernard, and Wenceslaus Kwindingwi. "The End of Ubuntu." *South African Journal of Philosophy* 32, no. 2 (2013): 197–205.

Mavhunga, Clapperton Chakanetsa. *Transient Workspaces: Technologies of Everyday Innovation in Zimbabwe*. Cambridge, MA: MIT Press, 2014.

Mayr, E. *The Growth of Biological Thought: Diversity, Evolution, and Inheritance*. Cambridge, MA: Belknap, 1982.

Mbembe, Achille. *On the Postcolony*. Berkeley: University of California Press, 2001.

McAllister, Patrick. *Xhosa Beer Drinking Rituals: Power, Practice and Performance in the South African Rural Periphery*. Durham, NC: Carolina Academic Press, 2006.

McCallum, Cecilia. "The Body That Knows: From Cashinahua Epistemology to a Medical Anthropology of Lowland South America." *Medical Anthropology Quarterly* 10, no. 3 (1996): 347–72.

McDonald, D. "The Theory and Practice of Cost Recovery in South Africa." In *Cost Recovery and the Crisis of Service Delivery*, edited by D. McDonald and J. Pape. New York: Zed, 2002.

———. "Ubuntu Bashing: The Marketisation of 'African Values' in South Africa." *Review of African Political Economy* 37, no. 124 (2010): 139–52.

McElhinny B. "The Audacity of Affect: Gender, Race, and History in Linguistic Accounts of Legitimacy and Belonging." *Annual Review of Anthropology* 39 (2010): 309–28.

McKenzie, Jon. "Democracy's Performance." *The Drama Review* 47, no. 2 (2003): 117–28.

McKinley, Dale. *Transition's Child: The Anti-Privatisation Forum*. Johannesburg: South African History Archive, 2012.

McNeill, Fraser, and Deborah James. "Singing Songs of AIDS in Venda, South Africa: Performance, Pollution and Ethnomusicology in a 'Neo-Liberal' Setting." In *The Culture of AIDS: Hope and Healing through the Arts in Africa*, edited by Gregory Barz and Judah M. Cohen, 193–212. New York: Oxford University Press, 2011.

Meer, Shamim. "Experiences of Democracy in South Africa from a Feminist Perspective." *Development* 50, no. 1 (2007): 96–103.

Meillassoux C. *Maidens, Meal and Money: Capitalism and the Domestic Economy*. Cambridge: Cambridge University Press, 1981.

Mendoza, Zoila S. *Shaping Society through Dance: Mestizo Ritual Performance in the Peruvian Andes*. Chicago: University of Chicago Press, 2000.

Meyer, Birgit. "Aesthetics of Persuasion: Global Christianity and Pentecostalism's Sensational Forms." *South Atlantic Quarterly* 109, no. 4 (2010): 741–63.

Millar, Stephen. *Sounding Dissent: Rebel Songs, Resistance, and Irish Republicanism*. Ann Arbor: University of Michigan Press, 2020.

Mngxitama, Andile. "Xenophobia Is in Fact Afrophobia in Disguise." *Sowetan*, November 30, 2010. http://www.sowetanlive.co.za/columnists/2010/11/30/xenophobia-is-in-fact-afrophobia-in-disguise (accessed September 22, 2016).

Molyneaux, Maxine. "Mobilization without Emancipation? Women's Interests, the State, and Revolution in Nicaragua." *Feminist Studies* 11, no. 2 (1985): 227–54.

Mookherjee, Nayanika, and Chris Pinney. *Aesthetics of Nations: Anthropological and Historical Perspectives*. Special Issue of *Journal of Royal Anthropological Institute* 17 (2011): S1–S20.

Mosinki, D., and S. Moiloa. "From Apartheid to Democracy: Educating our Communities through Culture for the Liberation of our Nation." *Khanya: A Journal for Activists* 9 (2005): 30.

Mthembu, Aubrey Greyling. *Verbo-Motor Expression: Tradition in the Service of Liberation*. Unpublished thesis, University of KwaZulu-Natal, 1999.

Muñoz, José Esteban. "Feeling Brown, Feeling Down: Latina Affect, the Performativity of Race, and the Depressive Position." *Signs* 31, no. 3 (2006): 675–88.

Naidoo, P. *The Making of the Poor in Post-Apartheid South Africa: A Case Study of the City of Johannesburg and Orange Farm*. Unpublished PhD thesis, University of

KwaZulu Natal, 2010. https://researchspace.ukzn.ac.za/handle/10413
/5065 (accessed July 5, 2021).

Naidoo, P., and A. Veriava. "Re-Membering Movements: Trade Unions and Social
Movements in Neo-Liberal South Africa." Centre for Civil Society Research
Report 2005, Vol. 1, 2005.

Ngonyama, Percy. "The 2010 FIFA World Cup: Critical Voices from Below." *Soccer
& Society*, 11, nos. 1/2 (2010): 168–80.

Ngwane, Trevor. "Civil Society Protests in South Africa: The Need for a Vision of
Alternatives." Paper presented at a Centre for Civil Society seminar, Durban,
South Africa, March 9, 2010.

————. "Sparks in the Township." *New Left Review* 22 (2003): 36–56.

Ngwane, Trevor, and George Dor. "South Africa: IMF Can Only Bring Misery."
The Sowetan, Johannesburg, South Africa, July 12, 2000.

Nixon, Rob. *Slow Violence and the Environmentalism of the Poor*. Cambridge, MA:
Harvard University Press, 2011.

Njoya, Wairimu. "'Mindful of the Sacrifices Borne by Our Ancestors': Terror,
Historical Consciousness, and the Slave Sublime." *New Political Science* 32, no. 4
(2010): 575–91.

Nuttall, Sarah. "Stylizing the Self: The Y Generation in Rosebank, Johannesburg."
Public Culture 16, no. 3 (2004): 430–52.

Nxumalo, S'bu. [Liner notes]. In *Amandla! A Revolution in Four-Part Harmony
Original Soundtrack*. CD. New York: ATO Records, 2003.

Nyamnjoh, Francis B. *#RhodesMustFall: Nibbling at Resilient Colonialism in South
Africa*. Bamenda, Cameroon: Langaa Research & Publishing CIG, 2106.

Okigbo, Austin C. *Music, Culture, and the Politics of Health: Ethnography of a South
African AIDS Choir*. Lanham, MD: Lexington, 2016.

Opitz, Florian. *The Big Sellout*. DVD. Bavaria Media, 2006.

Ortner, Sherry. "Resistance and the Problem of Ethnographic Refusal."
Comparative Studies in Society and History 37, no. 1 (1995): 173–93.

Paine, Robert. "What Is Gossip About? An Alternative Hypothesis." *Man* 2, no. 2
(1967): 278–85.

Paley, Dawn. "Women Pushed Aside as Men Seek Power." Rabble.ca, 2004.
http://rabble.ca/news/women-pushed-aside-men-seek-power (accessed
January 21, 2013).

Palmer, Gary, and William Jankowiak. "Performance and Imagination: Toward an
Anthropology of the Spectacular and the Mundane." *Cultural Anthropology* 11,
no. 2 (1996): 225–58.

Panagia, David. *The Political Life of Sensation*. Durham, NC: Duke University
Press, 2009.

Parviainen, Jaana. "Choreographing Resistances: Spatial–Kinaesthetic
Intelligence and Bodily Knowledge as Political Tools in Activist Work."
Mobilities 5, no. 3 (2010): 311–29.

Perry, Keisha-Khan Y. *Black Women against the Land Grab: The Fight for Racial Justice in Brazil*. Minneapolis: University of Minnesota Press, 2013.

Peterson, Bhekizizwe. *Monarchs, Missionaries and African Intellectuals*. Trenton, NJ: Africa World, 2000.

Pineau, Elyse Lamm. "Re-Casting Rehearsal: Making a Case for Production as Research." *Journal of the Illinois Speech and Theatre Association* 46 (1995): 43–52.

Pithouse, Richard. "The Service Delivery Myth." *South African Civil Society Information Service* website, January 27, 2011. https://sacsis.org.za/s/story .php?s=500 (accessed May 5, 2020).

Pointer, Rebecca. "Questioning the Representation of South Africa's 'New Social Movements': A Case Study of the Mandela Park Anti-Eviction Campaign." *Journal of Asian and African Studies* 39, no. 4 (2004): 271–94.

Pollock, Della, ed. "Introduction: Remembering." In *Remembering: Oral History Performance*, 1–17. London: Palgrave Macmillan, 2005.

Rancière, Jacques. *Disagreement*. Translated by Julie Rose. Minneapolis: University of Minnesota Press, 1999.

———. *The Politics of Aesthetics: The Distribution of the Sensible*. Translated by Gabriel Rockhill. London and New York: Continuum, 2004.

Razsa, Maple, and Andrej Kurnik. "The Occupy Movement in Žižek's Hometown: Direct Democracy and a Politics of Becoming." *American Ethnologist* 39, no. 2 (2012): 238–58.

Redmond, Shana. *Anthem: Social Movements and the Sound of Solidarity in the African Diaspora*. New York: New York University Press, 2014.

Reynolds, Hilary, and Nancy Richards, eds. *Woman Today: A Celebration: Fifty Years of South African Women*. Cape Town, South Africa: Kwela, 2003.

Riley, Denise. *Impersonal Passion: Language as Affect*. Durham, NC: Duke University Press, 2005.

Robinson, J. *The Power of Apartheid: State, Power and Space in South African Cities*. Oxford, UK: Butterworth-Heinemann, 1996.

Rose, N. *Inventing Our Selves: Psychology, Power and Personhood*. Cambridge: Cambridge University Press, 1996.

Rose, Tricia. *Black Noise: Rap Music and Black Culture in Contemporary America*. Hanover, NH: Wesleyan University Press, 1994.

Ross, Fiona C. *Raw Life, New Hope: Decency, Housing and Everyday Life in a Post-Apartheid Community*. Cape Town, South Africa: University of Cape Town Press, 2010.

Routledge, Paul, and J. Simons. "Embodying Spirits of Resistance." *Environment and Planning D: Society and Space* 13, no. 4 (1995): 471–98.

Roy, Arundhati. "Public Power in the Age of Empire: Arundhati Roy on War, Resistance and the Presidency." Address to the American Sociological Association, San Francisco, August 23, 2004. http://www.democracynow.org /2004/8/23/public_power_in_the_age_of (accessed September 23, 2016).

Roy, William. *Reds, Whites, and Blues: Social Movements, Folk Music, and Race in the United States*. Princeton, NJ: Princeton University Press, 2010.

Runciman, Carin. "Questioning Resistance in Post-Apartheid South Africa: A Response to Luke Sinwell." *Review of African Political Economy* 38, no. 130 (2011): 607–14.

Samudra, Jaida K. "Memory in Our Body: Thick Participation and the Translation of Kinesthetic Experience." *American Ethnologist* 35 (2008): 665–81.

Scarry, Elaine. *The Body in Pain: The Making and Unmaking of the World*. Oxford, UK: Oxford University Press, 1985.

Schechner, Richard. *Between Theater and Anthropology*. Philadelphia: University of Pennsylvania Press, 1985.

———. *Performance Studies: An Introduction*. New York: Routledge, 2002.

Scheper-Hughes, Nancy. *Death without Weeping: The Violence of Everyday Life in Brazil*. Berkeley: University of California Press, 1992.

———. "The Rebel Body: The Subversive Meanings of Illness." *Traditional Acupuncture Society Journal* 10 (1994): 3–10.

Scheper-Hughes, Nancy, and Philippe Bourgois, eds. *Violence in War and Peace: An Anthology*. Malden, MA: Blackwell, 2003.

Scheper-Hughes, Nancy, and Margaret Lock. "The Mindful Body: A Prolegomenon to Future Work in Medical Anthropology." *Medical Anthropology Quarterly* 1, no. 1 (1987): 6–41.

Scott, James. *The Art of Not Being Governed: An Anarchist History of Upland Southeast Asia*. New Haven, CT: Yale University Press, 2009.

———. *Domination and the Arts of Resistance: Hidden Transcripts*. New Haven, CT: Yale University Press, 1990.

Searle, John. *Speech Acts: An Essay in the Philosophy of Language*. Cambridge: Cambridge University Press, 1969.

Seizer, Susan. "Jokes, Gender and Discursive Distance on Tamil Popular Stage." *American Ethnologist* 24, no. 1 (1997): 62–90.

Shouse, E. "Feeling, Emotion, Affect." *M/C Journal* 8, no. 6 (December 2005). https://doi.org/10.5204/mcj.2443 (accessed February 7, 2020).

Silverstein M. "Shifters, Linguistic Categories, and Cultural Description." In *Meaning in Anthropology*, edited by K. H. Basso and H. A. Selby, 11–55. Albuquerque: University of New Mexico Press, 1976.

Singer, Milton. "The Cultural Pattern of Indian Civilization: A Preliminary Report of a Methodological Field Study." *Far East Quarterly* 15, no. 1 (1955): 23–36.

———, ed. *Traditional India: Structure and Change*. Philadelphia: American Folklore Society, 1959.

Sinwell, Luke. *The Alexandra Renewal Project (ARP): A Case Study of Development and Participation in Alexandra*. MA thesis, Development Studies, University of the Witwatersrand, 2005.

Slovo, Gillian. "Mandela Did His Part. But Songs Saved South Africa." *The Observer* [cited December 14, 2003]. http://www.guardian.co.uk/film /2003/dec/14/features.southafrica (accessed September 26, 2016).

Small, Christopher. *Music, Society, Education: An Examination of the Function of Music in Western, Eastern and African Cultures with Its Impact on Society and Its Use on Education.* New York: Schirmer, 1977.

Smith, Christen A. *Afro-Paradise: Blackness, Violence, and Performance in Brazil.* Champaign: University of Illinois Press, 2016.

Smith, Constance. "Collapse: Fake Buildings and Gray Development in Nairobi." *Focaal* 86 (2020): 11–23.

Smith, D. M., ed. *The Apartheid City and Beyond: Urbanization and Social Change in South Africa.* London: Routledge, 1992.

Snead, James A. "On Repetition in Black Culture." *Black American Literature Forum* 15, no. 4 (1981): 146–54.

Spry, Tami. "'A Performative-I' Copresence: Embodying the Ethnographic Turn in Performance and the Performative Turn in Ethnography." *Text & Performance Quarterly* 26 (2006): 339–46.

Steingo, Gavin. "The Politicization of 'Kwaito': From the 'Party Politic' to Party Politics." *Black Music Research Journal* 27, no. 1 (2007): 23–44.

———. "South African Music after Apartheid: Kwaito, the 'Party Politic,' and the Appropriation of Gold as a Sign of Success." *Popular Music and Society* 23, no. 3 (2005): 333–57.

Stoller, Paul, ed. "Prologue: The Scholars Body." In *Sensuous Scholarship,* ix–xviii. Philadelphia: University of Pennsylvania Press, 1997.

Stone, Ruth M., and Verlon L. Stone. "Events, Feedback, and Analysis: Research Media in the Study of Music Events." *Ethnomusicology* 25, no. 2 (1981): 215–25.

Strathern, Marilyn. "An Awkward Relationship: The Case of Feminism and Anthropology." *Signs* 12, no. 2 (1987): 276–92.

Strine, Mary S., Beverly Whitaker Long, and Mary Frances Hopkins. "Research in Interpretation and Performance Studies: Trends, Issues, Priorities." In *Speech Communication: Essays to Commemorate the Seventy-Fifth Anniversary of the Speech Communications Association,* edited by Gerald Phillips and Julia Woods, 181–93. Carbondale: Southern Illinois University Press, 1990.

Taussig, Michael. "Culture of Terror—Space of Death. Roger Casement's Putumayo Report and the Explanation of Torture." *Comparative Studies in Society and History* 26, no. 3 (1984): 467–97.

———. "Terror as Usual: Walter Benjamin's Theory of History as a State of Siege." *Social Text* 23 (1989): 3–20.

Taylor, T. *Global Pop.* New York: Routledge, 1997.

Taylor, Verta, and Nella Van Dyke. "'Get Up, Stand Up': Tactical Repertoires of Social Movements." In *The Blackwell Companion to Social Movements,* edited by David A. Snow, Sarah A. Soule, and Hanspeter Kriesi, 262–93. Oxford, UK: Blackwell, 2004.

Teitelbaum, Benjamin R. *Lions of the North: Sounds of the New Nordic Radical Nationalism.* Oxford: Oxford University Press, 2017.

Thayer, Millie. "Translations and Refusals: Resignifying Meanings as Feminist Political Practice." *Feminist Studies* 36, no. 1 (2010): 200–30.

Thrift, Nigel. "Intensities of Feeling: Towards a Spatial Politics of Affect." *Geografiska Annaler: Series B, Human Geography* 86, no. 1 (2004): 57–78.

The Times. "Half of SA Youth Unemployed." January 31, 2011. https://www .timeslive.co.za/news/south-africa/2011-01-31-half-of-sa-youth-unemployed/ (accessed December 18, 2021).

Tsing, Anna. *Friction: An Ethnography of Global Connections.* Princeton, NJ: Princeton University Press, 2005.

Turino, Thomas. *Music as Social Life.* Chicago: University of Chicago Press, 2008.

Turner, Victor. *The Anthropology of Performance.* New York: PAJ, 1986.

———. *From Ritual to Theatre: The Human Seriousness of Play.* New York: Performing Arts Journal, 1982.

Vail, Leroy, and Landeg White. *Power and the Praise Poem.* Charlottesville: University Press of Virginia, 1991.

Van der Walt, Lucien, David Mokoena, and Sakhile Shange. "Cleaned Out: Outsourcing at Wits University." *South African Labour Bulletin* 25, no. 4 (August 2001): 54–58.

Van Wolputte, Steven. "Hang On to Your Self: Of Bodies, Embodiment, and Selves." *Annual Review of Anthropology* 33 (2004): 251–69.

Veriava, Ahmed. "Review of Voices of Protest: Social Movements in Post-Apartheid South Africa." *Journal of Asian and African Studies* 43 (2008): 482–88.

von Schnitzler, Antina. "Performing Dignity: Human Rights, Citizenship, and the Techno-Politics of Law in South Africa." *American Ethnologist* 41, no. 2 (2014): 336–50.

Waterman, Christopher. "The Uneven Development of Africanist Ethnomusicology: Three Issues and a Critique." In *Comparative Musicology and Anthropology of Music: Essays on the History of Ethnomusicology,* edited by Bruno Nettl and Philip Bohlman, 169–86. Chicago: University of Chicago Press, 1991.

Weiss, Meira. *The Chosen Body: The Politics of the Body in Israeli Society.* Stanford: Stanford University Press, 2002.

West, Cornel. "Celebrating Tikkun and Tragicomic Hope." *Tikkun* 19, no. 6 (2004): 53–54.

White, Luise. *Speaking with Vampires: Rumor and History in Colonial Africa.* Berkeley: University of California Press, 2000.

Wickstrom, Maurya. *Performance in the Blockades of Neoliberalism: Thinking the Political Anew.* Basingstoke, UK: Palgrave Macmillan, 2012.

Williams, Raymond. *Marxism and Literature*. London: Oxford University Press, 1977.

Wilson, Elizabeth. "The Brain in the Gut." In *Psychosomatic: Feminism and the Neurological Body*, 31–48. Durham, NC: Duke University Press, 2004.

Wittgenstein, Ludwig. *Philosophical Investigations*. Translated by G. E. M. Anscombe. Oxford, UK: Blackwell, 1953.

Wolfe, Katharine. "From Aesthetics to Politics: Rancière, Kant and Deleuze." *Journal of Contemporary Aesthetics* 4 (2006). http://www.contempaesthetics.org /newvolume/pages/article.php?articleID=382 (accessed September 22, 2016).

Wolpe, H. "Capitalism and Cheap Labour Power in South Africa: From Segregation to Apartheid." *Economy and Society* 1 (1972): 425–56.

Wood, Leslie. *Direct Action, Deliberation, and Diffusion: Collective Action after the WTO Protests in Seattle*. Cambridge: Cambridge University Press, 2012.

Xali, M. et al. "The New Social Movements: Women's Participation and Women's Leadership." Centre for Civil Society Grant Report, 2005.

Xulu, M. "Music and Power in Traditional Zulu Society: The Social Role of Amahubo Songs. In *Afro-Christianity at the Grassroots: Its Dynamics and Strategies*, edited by G. C. Oosthuizen, M. C. Kitshoff, and S. W. D. Dube, 97–104. Leiden, Netherlands: E. J. Brill, 1994.

Yang, G. "Achieving Emotions in Collective Action." *The Sociological Quarterly* 41, no. 4 (2000): 593–614.

Zhang, Sarah. "Yes, That's a Huge Floating Mass of Live Fire Ants in Texas." *The Atlantic*, August 29, 2017. https://www.theatlantic.com/science/archive/2017/08 /fire-ants-flooding-hurricane-harvey/538365/ (accessed December 18, 2021).

INDEX

accountability, 84, 156, 157–58, 188

activist networks of Johannesburg, 41–43

activist portraits: individual experience and organizational issues in, 26–27; Kanelo, 99–106, 145–46, 151; Lebo, 124, 127–28, 136–43; Ma Patrycja, 19, 26–27, 35–40, 121–22, 175–76, 192, 201–2; Wesley, 253–56; Willeen, 172–76, 191–92, 193–94, 202, 246

aesthetics: in creative expression, 111, 112, 115–16, 120, 131; political, 10–17, 18, 21, 26, 31–32n12, 112, 215–16, 246; of relationships, 9, 16, 19, 28–29, 213, 216, 218–26, 230–32

affirmation, 44, 45, 91, 129–30, 194, 205

African National Congress (ANC): and APF, 46, 50–51, 59–61, 64–65, 70, 243; favoritism in housing and employment by, 137; neoliberal policies of, 13–15, 41–42, 65; in routinization of dissent, 80–84; in state violence and marginalization, 13–14; and women's countermobilization, 178–79; youth in, 213–14, 215–16

African National Congress Youth League, 213–14

aftermath of struggle, 238–40

Agawu, Kofi, 118–19

Ahmed, Sara, 134n24

Alexandra Township, 70–71, 81–82, 84–90, 92–93, 94

alignment/misalignment, 42, 43, 55, 56–57, 60, 148–49, 226

ambivalence, 52–53, 58, 59–60, 178, 214–15, 238–39

Amina (Remmoho facilitator), 190–91, 192–95, 199–200, 202–3

Aminzade, Ronald, 31–32n12

"Angeke sizwe ngabo" (song), 93

anger, 35–39, 69–70, 126, 157, 174–76, 205

anti-apartheid organizations/activism: change of ANC from, into neoliberalism, 13–14, 41–42, 65; creative expression in, 108–11, 122, 123, 131; in emergence of APF, 41–42, 45–49, 50–51, 65; gender parity in, 178, 179; strategies of, in APF's practices, 3, 81, 85–86; youth in, 212, 213–16

Anti-iGoli Forum, 52–53, 54–55

antiphony (call-and-response), 108–9, 112–17, 120

Anti-Privatisation Forum (APF): bureaucratization of, 62–63, 72, 150, 249; constitution of, 61–65; decline of, 4, 9, 129–32, 162–66; feminist critiques of, 179–80; fieldwork on, 21–26; gendered interventions attempted by, 186–98; naming of, 54–55, 58–59; neoliberalism in emergence of, 3, 13–15, 41–44, 51–54, 57–58, 65; normalization of, 15, 45, 59–65, 70–71, 96–97, 181–82; performative geography by, 71–80; political aesthetics of performance by, 12–14; in the postapartheid political landscape, 243–44; World Cup march as

Anti-Privatisation (*Cont.*)
  failure of, 144–46; youth engagement in, 212, 216–18, 232–35. *See also* emergence of APF; routinization; ruptures in APF
apartheid, 38, 39–40, 71, 73–74, 80–81, 108, 131–32
apathy, 130–31, 215
Appolis, John (founding member), 48–49, 59, 61–62
appraisal. *See* evaluation
Ashforth, Adam, 192–93
Askew, Kelly, 7–8
Austin, J. L., 6–7
autonomy, 36–39, 61, 184–85, 199, 200–201, 217
Ayize (activist), 128–29, 131–32

Bauman, Richard, 10, 30n3
Bebey, Francis, 118–19
belonging, 55–56, 73, 197, 217–18, 219, 223, 235–36, 250–51
Besteman, Catherine, 214
Biehl, João, 32nn14–15
Black Economic Empowerment programs, 13–14
bodies. *See* embodiment
Boipelo (organizer), 20–21, 83–84, 145–46
bonds, interpersonal and collective, 148, 156–57, 163, 167–69, 195, 197–98, 217–18, 222–23
Bophelong Community Service Forum (BOCOSFO), 227–30, 236–38, 250–51
Bourdieu, Pierre, 197–98
boycotts, 14–15, 50–51, 213
Bozzoli, Belinda, 81
Brecht, Bertolt: "A Worker's Speech to a Doctor," 89
"briefcase comrades," 153–58
Bundy, Colin, 42–44, 66–67n1
burdens/unburdening, 20, 122, 174–76, 178–79, 197–203, 208n27
Butler, Judith, 7, 31n9, 67n2, 198
Buyisiwe (activist), 4–6, 9, 83–84, 149, 220, 222–24, 230–32, 248

Calata, Nomonde, 134n22
Campaign Against Neoliberalism in South Africa (CANSA), 52–53

capability/capabilities: disruptive action in enjoyment of, 247; in emergence of APF, 55–56; personal, in transcendence, 93–94; in women's countermobilization, 205–6; in youth engagement, 212, 221, 223, 240
Capacitar, 189–90, 191, 207–8n23
capacities, 16, 21, 215–16, 221, 222–23, 255–56
care: bodily, 18, 19; in ruptures, 169; in women's countermobilization, 177–78, 189–90, 195–98, 200–201, 203, 205–6, 245–46, 248
Cartesian gap/duality, 16–17, 218
Castro, Nancy, 181–86
Cavel, Marcia, 222
centralization/decentralization, 62–63, 70–80, 91, 96–97, 146–47
Ceruti, Claire (APF founding member), 46–48, 61, 63–64, 158–59
Charmaine (activist), 195–96, 219–20, 224, 227–29, 246–48
choirs, 228–29, 233–34, 241
class, socioeconomic. *See* status, socioeconomic
cognition, 16–17, 185–86
cohesion, group: cohesive sociality, 19; creative expression in, 245–46; in emergence, 48, 56, 65; performance enhancing, 250–51; in ruptures, 151–52; in women's countermobilization, 190, 195–98
collaboration, 56, 183–84, 202, 228–30, 250
collectivity: activist, contestations in, 4–10; alignment of individuals into, 55; durability of, 13; ethical, 94, 148–49, 150–51, 163, 244; experiences of, 250; in performance of freedom songs, 108–9; political aesthetics of, 14, 15, 31–32n12; ritual in, 20–21; variations within, 28; and women's countermobilization, 195–98; in youth engagement, 213
colonialism, 13, 92–93, 108, 208n27
combativeness: in anti-apartheid activism, 50–51; in appraisal and the search for alternatives, 250–51; effects of, 4; in performance and collective politics, 244, 246, 248, 249; in ruptures, 160–61, 166, 167–69; in women's countermobilization, 181–83

commitment: of APF to the working
class, 63–64; creative expression in,
28, 107, 111–12; embodied, in exposure,
91, 95; in emergence of APF, 47–49,
55–56; to home, 35, 39–40; performance
and collective politics in, 246; in
ruptures, 148, 153–54, 156; in women's
countermobilization, 178, 179, 191, 203; of
youth, 29, 219, 222–23, 246
community-based groups and struggle: in
emergence of APF, 46–47, 49–50, 51–52,
60, 62–63; post-APF activism of, 251–52;
in routinization, 78; in ruptures, 146–47,
153–54; in women's countermobilization,
187–88, 189; in youth engagement, 229
Concerned Learners Committee, 228
Congress of South African Trade Unions
(COSATU), 48–49, 59–61
Conquergood, Dwight, 32–33n15, 86–87
contestation, 4–10, 63, 69–70, 72, 74, 81,
179–80
convergence, 45, 49–54, 55, 107, 131, 168–69,
192
Coplan, David, 215
copresence/co-performative witnessing,
26, 91
corruption, 112–13, 161–62
cost-recovery approach to service provision,
48–49, 51–53
countermobilization, women's: appraisal
and the search for alternatives in, 250–51;
backlash from, 203–6; bodily health in,
198–203; creative expression in, 245–46;
Gender Reference Group in, 180–86; need
for, 177–80; Remmoho in, 186–98. See also
Remmoho women's group
Covington-Ware, Yolanda, 17–18
creativity/creative expression: and APF,
62, 129–32, 244; dignity and deprivation
in, 170n8; embodiment in, 2–4, 19–20,
106–7; musical structure in, 111–20; in
performance and collective politics,
245–48, 250, 251; in singing dynamics at
protests, 120–29; in social movements,
27–28; in South African protest singing,
108–11, 132n2; in youth engagement,
229–30

cultural performance: aesthetics of
collective power in, 12–13; in appraisal and
the search for alternatives, 250; creative
expression in, 113–14; in emergence of
APF, 43; as presentation of society to
itself, 29–30n2; in youth engagement,
211–12, 226–32

dance/dances, 17, 20–21, 112–14, 118–19, 120,
123, 211–12, 230–31. See also toyi-toyi dance
Dave, Naisargi, 68n16
death: of activists in youth engagement,
211–12, 213–14, 220–21, 222–23, 236–38; in
creative expression, 128–29; in protests,
146–47; and remembrance, 169–71
demobilization, 28–29, 46, 67n4, 149, 163
democracy, 48–49, 63, 65–66
demonstrations. See marches, protest;
protests
dependence/independence: of APF, on
affluent members, 160–61; housing in,
38, 39–40; of perspective, in women's
countermobilization, 185; of Remmoho,
177, 178, 186–87; routinization of
exposure in, 89–90; of youth, 217. See also
interdependence
depression, 191, 193–94, 198, 199–200, 201
Desai, Ashwin, 33n19
dignity: in activism, 2–3, 148–49; in
contemporary social movement
scholarship, 33n19; and deprivation
in creativity, 170n8; in everyday life,
70–71; in Ma Patrycja's story, 35–40;
in mourning, 167–68; in the political
aesthetics of collective power, 15–16; and
routinization of the APF, 70–71, 84–88,
91–94, 95; and ruptures, 28, 148–52,
153–54, 155–57, 162–63, 166–68, 169; in
social movement scholarship, 33n19;
song in reclamation of, 104; women's
countermobilization in, 196–97, 201
Dike, Fatimah, 108
direct action, 41, 55–56, 65, 107, 146–47, 212
Disebo (activist), 225, 227, 228–29, 236,
238–39
disillusionment, 15, 47–49, 213, 235–40
displacement, 85–90, 137

displays, collective: bodily enactment as, 20–21; creative and artistic, 2–4, 5–7, 9, 112–13, 245–46; ephemera in, 75–77; of militancy, in emergence of APF, 61–62; as spatial disruptions, 69; in youth engagement, 233–35

disruption: of alienation, in women's countermobilization, 184–85, 206; in community-level insurgence, 146–47; in enjoyment of capabilities, 247; militant, in emergence of APF, 41–44, 56, 57–58, 60–61; as political aesthetics, 12, 13–14, 15; and routinization, 69–70, 80–81, 82–84, 95–96; of social order, 6, 30n4; in youth engagement, 212

dissent: bodily engagement in expression of, 104; cultural performance in displaying, 6, 12–13; routinization of, 71, 76, 80–84, 95, 96–97; stifled, in emergence of APF, 48–49, 56–57, 65

distribution of the sensible, 11–12, 13–14, 43–44, 104, 106–7, 250

diversity: in creative expression, 107; in emergence of APF, 27, 41–42, 65; in ruptures, 153–54, 157–58; tactical, 245–46; in women's countermobilization, 187; and youth engagement, 212

drama, 94, 228–29, 244

dramatization. See staging of protest

Drewal, Margaret Thompson, 25, 30n4

Duncan, Jane, 82–83

dynamics: gendered, 156–57, 158–59, 177, 184–85, 197–98; intergenerational, 210–12, 218–19, 223, 228, 229–30, 239, 240; internal, 21, 27, 29, 64, 115, 181–82, 193, 204–5 (See also ruptures in APF); of singing at protests, 120–29

education, 142–43, 210–11, 224–25, 228, 229–30, 243–44

efficacy, 5, 6–7, 112, 128–29, 247–48

efflorescence. See creativity/creative expression

electricity. See services, basic/service delivery

embodiment: of burdens in women's health, 198–203, 208n27; in co-performative

witnessing, 91; in creative expression, 106–7, 109–10, 118–20, 122–23, 128, 130–31, 134n22; of destruction, in youth disillusionment, 239; of living conditions, 88–90; performativity in, 8–9; in political mobilization, 1–3, 16–21; of protest, in emergence of APF, 43–44, 53–54; in women's countermobilization, 177–78, 179–80, 181, 183–84, 189–95, 196–97, 198–203, 206

emergence of APF: convergence of movements in, 49–54; formalization in, 61–62, 64, 66; formation stage in, 45, 49–50, 54–59; neoliberalism in, 3, 13–15, 41–44, 51–54, 57–58, 65; normalization process in, 59–65; organizational constitution in, 61–65; political sensibilities in shaping of, 244; post-apartheid oppositional void in, 45–49

emotion: confrontation in, 100; and creative expression, 107, 112, 117–18, 120, 122–24, 127, 130–31; embodiment of, 19–20; in emergence of APF, 43–44, 45, 55–56; in the political aesthetics of collective power, 10–16, 31–32n12; song in transmission of, 85–86; in transcending routinization, 96–97; in women's countermobilization, 185–86, 191–92, 204–6; in youth engagement, 219, 220, 226, 230–32, 234–35

energy: creative expression in, 109, 117, 119–20; in emergence of APF, 57–58, 65–66; in mobilization, 18–19; protest singing in, 103–4, 109; ruptures in dissipation of, 139–40, 165, 249–50; in women's adaptive performance techniques, 185–86, 189–90, 193–94, 202; and youth engagement, 215–16, 229–31, 236

engagement, activist: degeneration of, in ruptures, 163; performance and collective politics in, 245–46; performing arts in, 213, 229, 232–35; response to song in measuring, 130–31; and women's countermobilization, 182–83, 190–92. See also youth and youth engagement

enjoyment, politics of, 215–16, 240, 247

equality and equity: in emergence of APF, 49–51, 53–54; neoliberal economics in,

13–15; and selective invisibility, 90–91; in women's countermobilization, 178–79, 180–81, 183, 197–201, 203, 204–5

Eriksson, Åsa, 186

evaluation: of activist engagement through song, 130–31; antiphony and repetition in, 114–15, 117; of expectations and outcomes, 9, 244–45; organizational, in outcomes, 165–66; and the search for alternatives, 248–52; standards in, 5–6, 9–10

everyday life/lived experience: in activist collectivity, 8–10; APF's incompatibility with, 248–49; embodiment of, 17–18, 88–90; in emergence of APF, 43, 45, 48–51, 54, 57–58, 61–62, 63, 64–65, 66; language in sharing of, 34n25, 201–2; mediation of, 3–4, 120–23, 126–27, 134n24; in mobilization, 16–21, 35–40, 153–54; as performance, 5, 6–8, 31n9, 244, 250, 251; in performative geography, 74, 79–80; in the political aesthetics of collective power, 10, 11–12, 13–14, 16; protest singing as, 107, 109, 117–18, 120–22, 123–24, 128–29; in Quagga Estates, 101–3; routinization of poverty in, 74, 94, 95–96; in routinization of space, 27, 70–71, 83–84, 85–86, 91, 92–96; in ruptures, 149, 151, 156, 157–58, 170n4; in women's countermobilization, 175–76, 177–80, 181–86, 189–92, 193, 198–204, 205–6, 208–9n30; in youth engagement, 219, 226. See also embodiment; senses/sensation/sensory experience

exercise, 3–4, 18–19, 189–90, 191–92, 197–98, 202, 207–8n23. See also movement practices

Farnell, Brenda, 22n20, 33n20

feminism/feminist approaches, 11, 178, 179–80, 182–84, 199–202, 203–5. See also countermobilization, women's

fieldwork, 21–26

Foley, Ellen, 89–90

forgiveness, 174–75

form, organizational: in conflict with collective spirit, 4; gap between intention and reality in, 249; in normalization, 61–62, 64–65; political sensibilities in shaping

of, 244; in ruptures, 154–55, 157–58; in women's countermobilization, 181, 204–5

Foster, Susan Leigh, 33–34n21

Freedom of Expression Institute protest, 106–7

freedom songs/singing: in creation of space and resistance to routinization, 83–84; as creative expression, 28, 106–7, 108–11, 114–15, 116–17, 119, 128–29, 131–32; cross-geographical connections of, 30–31n5, 106–7; in emergence of APF, 61; memory of, 118, 120, 121–22; in transmission of sentiment, 19–20; and youth aesthetics, 231–32

Freire, Paulo, 202

Funda Center, 210–11

funding, 60, 158–59, 160–61, 188, 239

Gatsha (protester), 119

gender: in anti-apartheid activism, 178, 179; in anti-Black state constitution, 33n17; in hypermarginality, 13, 15; opposition to gendered mobilization, 203–6; in performance, 28, 245–46; as performative act, 7, 31n9; in ruptures, 156–57, 158–59. See also countermobilization, women's

"Gender and Neoliberalism and the Social Movements" workshop, 180–81

Gender at Work, 3–4, 5–6, 19, 189–91

Gender Reference Group, 180–86, 203

generations/generational distinctions: aesthetics of relationships between, 218–26; intergenerational dynamics, 210–12, 217–20, 223, 228, 229–32, 239, 240; in performance and collective politics, 245–46; and South Africa's transition, 213–18. See also youth and youth engagement

geography: and the Alexandra Renewal Project, 89–90, 91; in emergence of APF, 45, 49–50, 54; freedom songs in connections across, 30–31n5, 106–7; performative, 27, 71–80, 82; protest songs in continuities across, 112–13; in ruptures, 153–54

Ghanda Center, 88

Gibson, Nigel, 33n19

globalization, 56–58. See also neoliberalism

Goffman, Erving, 31n9
Goldstein, Daniel, 29–30n2
Goldstone Commission of Enquiry, 97–98n6
gossip, 149–50, 156–58, 167–69, 203, 239
Gould, Deborah, 19
grassroots struggle, 46, 48–49, 61–62, 84–90
Greater Johannesburg Metropolitan
    Council, 52, 56
Growth, Employment and Redistribution
    Strategy (GEAR), 41–42, 46, 57

Haugerud, Angelique, 245–46
health/healing: creative expression in, 245–46;
    embodied mobilization in, 18–19; in
    emotional ideology, 134n22; routinization
    of exposure in, 88–90; in women's
    countermobilization, 179–80, 189–90,
    192–97, 198–203. See also wellness/
    well-being
hierarchy, 63, 65–66, 152–53, 188
HIV/AIDS, 233–34, 236–38, 241–42n14,
    241n3
Holmes, Seth, 198–99
home and housing, 35–40, 72–73, 84–90, 94,
    95–96, 101–5, 136–38
humanity: in political aesthetics of power,
    14–16; recognition of, in ruptures, 148–49,
    152, 153–54, 155–56, 167; shared, visibility
    of, 88, 91–92; song in reclamation of, 104–5;
    in women's countermobilization, 186
hymns, 108, 195–96
hypermarginality/hypermarginalization.
    See marginality/marginalization

ideals, activist, 9–10, 13–14, 41–42, 149,
    249–50
ideology, 46–48, 54, 63–64, 111–12, 134n22,
    138, 153–54, 185
iGoli 2002 plan, 51–53
Immortal Art Group, 145, 235
improvisation, 43–44, 108–9, 115–16, 123,
    127–28, 131–32
inclusion/exclusion: in collective power, 15;
    and creative expression, 27–28, 123–24,
    132n2; dynamics of, in fieldwork, 23; in
    emergence of APF, 43–44, 53, 55, 63–64;
    neoliberalism in, 13–14; ritual in, 20–21;

spatial, in anti-apartheid protests, 81; in
    women's countermobilization, 182–83,
    203–4; in youth engagement, 214
independence. See dependence/
    independence; interdependence
individualism, 128–29, 160, 203, 248–49
"Ingculaza (HIV/AIDS)" (poem), 237–38
innovation, 125, 178, 212, 215–16, 229
Intabazwe Townships, 146–47
intentions: disruption of neoliberalism as,
    13–14; in emergence of APF, 27, 63;
    individual, in ruptures, 158–60, 169; and
    outcomes, 9–10, 63, 146, 149–50, 163, 248–49,
    251; and practice, 10, 163–64, 244; in
    women's countermobilization, 194, 200–201
interconnections/interconnectedness: in
    emergence of APF, 45, 61; of performance
    and politics, 245; of public sphere and
    home, 84–85; of stratification and rupture,
    152–53; in women's countermobilization,
    192, 193, 197, 206n3; in youth engagement,
    163, 216, 219
interdependence, 13, 14–16, 39–40, 51–52,
    114, 168, 218–19. See also dependence/
    independence
International Socialists of South Africa
    (ISSA), 46–48
interpersonal abuse, in ruptures, 155–57
intersubjectivity, 91–92, 123, 127, 201–2, 218,
    220, 222–23, 226–27. See also subjectivities
interviews, fieldwork, 23–24, 26
Ireland, performative geography in, 72–73
Iscor iron and steel company, 101–2

Jim Crow laws, United States, 73
Johannesburg Metropolitan Municipality,
    51–53
justice, 2–3, 55, 92, 94, 167, 169, 239

Kanana Community Development Forum
    (KCDF), 51, 54
Kanelo (activist), 99–106, 145–46, 151
Keep Left, 47–48, 64
Khabane (activist), 93–94, 220–23, 224–25,
    231–32, 238–39
Khanya College, 60, 70, 71–80, 180–86,
    233–35

Khanyisa (activist), 109–10, 117–18, 119, 128, 129–31
kinesthetics, 17, 76–77
kinetics, 53–54, 139–40
Klaits, Frederick, 220
Kunene, D. P., 124
Kungawo (activist), 139
kwaito, 215–16, 240–41n2

Landless People's Movement (LPM), 124, 127–28, 136, 137–38
language, 6–7, 34n25, 63, 92, 108–9, 124, 125–26, 201–2
leadership: activism in training, 138; appraisal of, 248–49; and creative expression, 107, 114–15; in emergence of APF, 42–43, 55; and rupture, 149, 161–63, 167–69; in women's countermobilization, 179, 181, 187, 188, 204–6; in youth disillusionment, 212, 235–36
Lebo (activist), 124, 127–28, 136–43
legitimacy/legitimation, 63–64, 93, 154–55, 158–59
Library Gardens/Department of Housing march, 164–66
living conditions, 39, 65, 84–91, 93–94, 95, 136–38, 150–51, 184
Lubisi, Bongani, 211
lyrics: in claiming dignity, 93–94, 104; in creative expression, 110–12, 116, 117–18, 125–27, 129–30, 247; gesture paired with, 140–41; in youth engagement, 213, 231, 237–38

Madison, D. Soyini, 91
Makarube, Peter, 108–9
Ma Lindi (activist), 1–4, 5–6, 8–9, 18–19, 20
Mandela, Nelson, 213
Mandela Park Anti-Eviction Campaign, 206–7n5
Ma Patrycja (activist), 19, 35–40, 121–22, 175–76, 192, 201–2
marches, protest, 60–62, 74, 80–84, 112–14, 115–16, 144–46, 149, 163–66. See also under name of march
marginality/marginalization: and creative expression, 132n2; in formation of social

movements, 55; in performance and collective politics, 244–45, 250, 251; performative geography in, 73–74, 80; and the political aesthetics of collective power, 12–14, 15–16; in ruptures, 156–58, 168–69; in women's countermobilization, 177, 179–80, 182–83, 198–99, 208n27; of youth within APF, 212
Marikana massacre, 13, 15
Marlboro Transit Camp, 87–88
Martin, Randy, 16–17
Masekela, Hugh, 108
Matt (activist), 231–32
May Day observances, Khanya College, 233–35
McAdam, Doug, 31–32n12
McKinley, Dale (founding member), 24, 48–50, 154
media, 20–21, 94, 147
Media for Justice, 100
melody, 125, 133n12, 237–38
membership, APF: alienation of, in ruptures, 149–50, 157–58, 162, 163, 166–69, 244; alienation of, in women's countermobilization, 179, 181–83, 184–85, 187–88, 203–4, 206; in emergence, 53–54, 62–63; structure of, 62–63, 244; visibility of, to APF, 70–71, 90–92, 96, 138
memory, 81–82, 117–18, 166–67, 169, 172–74, 186, 210–11
mental illness, 172, 173–74, 191, 193–94, 198, 199
mentors/mentoring, 220–21, 223, 236
militancy, 41–44, 48–49, 56, 57–58, 60–62, 76
Mini, Vuyisile, 132n5
Mngxitama, Andile, 25
mobility, 53–54, 74, 80, 181–82, 184–85
Mokolo, Richard, 248–49
money: in appraisals of APF, 248–49; in ruptures, 142, 155–56, 158–59, 160–62, 167–68; and youth engagement, 224–26, 239, 248–49
motivation: conflicting, in ruptures of APF, 28; divergence of, in ruptures, 153–54; home life and domestic situations in, 35–40; overcoming fear and timidity in, 103–5; in women's countermobilization, 179–80; for youth engagement, 216, 240
Motlanthe, Kgalema, 211–12

mourning, 166–69, 195–98
movement practices, 12–13, 96–97, 106–7,
    118–19, 198–203, 230–32. *See also* exercise
Mtukudzi, Oliver, 126
Mum Alice (APF organizer), 88–90, 91

Naidoo, Leigh-Ann, 56–57
National Youth Act of 1996, 216–17
National Youth Day, 213–14
Ndlovu, Duma, 108
Ndumiso (activist), 109, 113–14, 120–21
Nenze (apartheid-era activist), 131
neoliberalism: in the ACR protest, 84–90;
    creative expression in opposition to, 110;
    in emergence of APF, 3, 13–15, 41–44, 51–54,
    57–58, 65; in performative geography,
    72–73; and women's countermobilization,
    178–79, 197–98, 200–201; in youth
    engagement, 214
Ngema, Mbongeni: "Safa Saphel' Isizwe,"
    237–38
Ngwane, Trevor (founding member), 48–49,
    52–55
Nomvula (activist), 18–19, 79–80, 184–85,
    192–93, 194–99, 205, 254
Ntuli, Sifiso, 85–86
Nxumalo, S'bu, 115

opportunities: for protest singing and songs,
    108–9, 114, 117–18; transformation from
    apartheid in, 46–48; in youth engagement,
    214, 215–16, 223–25, 240
oppositional social movements, 45–49, 67n2,
    70–71, 213–18
Orange Farm Water Crisis Committee, 39,
    95–96, 161
Orlando East march, 112–14, 115–16
Orlando Residents Association, 10
outcomes: backstage performance in, 148,
    149–50; and intention, 9–10, 63, 146, 149–50,
    163, 248–50, 251; organizational reflection
    in, 165–66; of privatization, 69–70
outsourcing, 51–52, 53, 56–57, 212

Paballo (activist), 166–69, 208n24
pain: and creative expression, 121–23, 127,
    129–30; embodiment of emotion in,

174–76; and embodiment of freedom
    songs, 19–20, 231; in intergenerational
    bonds, 217–18, 219, 231–32; routinization
    of exposure in, 88–90; in South African
    emotional ideology, 132n22; and women's
    countermobilization, 186, 196; in youth
    engagement, 221–22
patriarchy, 178, 179, 181–82, 184–85, 187,
    197–98, 199, 203
"people's inspection" at Alexandria, 84–90,
    91, 92–93, 94–95
perception: of intentions and outcomes,
    249–50; and political aesthetics, 12, 32n13,
    32n15; rhythmic, 119; in rupture, 151, 168;
    and women's countermobilization, 178,
    179–80, 185, 197; in youth engagement, 213,
    218–19. *See also* senses/sensation/sensory
    experience
performance: in the aesthetics of collective
    power, 10–16; and collective politics,
    244–52; dimensions of, 3–4; embodiment
    in, 16–21; as essential contestation, 4–10;
    as a motivator for activism, 2–3; and
    organizational decline, 162–66; in youth
    engagement, 226–32, 235–40, 246. *See also*
    creativity/creative expression; cultural
    performance
performativity: in the constitution of
    community, 6–9; in emergence of APF,
    43, 44–45, 54, 64–65; performative
    geography, 27, 71–80, 82; resonances of,
    206; in ruptures, 28, 163–64; transience
    in, 67n2
placemaking, citational, 74–77
poetry, 107, 233–35, 236–39
police: cooperation with, in protest
    planning, 82–83; creative expression in
    resisting, 121–22, 124–26; in dispossession,
    100, 104–5; violence by, 13, 97–98n6,
    121–23, 146–47; and the World Cup march,
    144, 145–46, 164–65; youth activist poem
    on, 234–35
political organizations/parties, 51, 63–64. *See
    also* African National Congress
politics: critical practice of, 59; internal,
    in ruptures, 158–62; internal, in youth
    disillusionment, 240; material, in

Alexandra's "people's inspection," 84–85; oppositional, 60, 65

politics, collective: aesthetics of, 10–17, 18, 21, 26, 112, 215–16, 246; bodily labor in, 1–2; performance in, 2–3, 4, 244–52; volunteering as alternative to, 239; women's emphasis on the personal in, 190–92

polyrhythmic layering, 119

postapartheid period: APF in political landscape of, 243–44; continuities of structural violence in, 13–15, 198–99; creative expression in, 110–11, 125; in emergence of APF, 45–49, 62; socioeconomic inequities in, 178–79; use of term, 33n18

poverty: of APF's members, 79, 90–91, 94, 95–96, 148–49, 156, 160–61; in backlash against Remmoho, 203–4; and creative expression, 110–11, 129–30; in emergence of APF, 42–43; in living conditions, 136–43; routinization of, 74, 79, 84–91, 94–96; in ruptures, 146–47, 148–49, 156, 160–61, 170n8; in women's countermobilization, 185–86, 198–99; in youth engagement, 214, 239

power/empowerment: collective, 10–16, 32–33n16, 57–58; in creative expression, 115, 117–18, 140–41; in emergence of APF, 49; in generational dynamics, 217–18; in ruptures, 149–50, 153, 156–57, 160, 244; song in reclamation of, 104–5; in women's countermobilization, 172, 177–78, 182–84, 187; of youth mobilization, 215–16

Prince Shapiro: "I attack" (poem), 233–34

privatization of basic services: in emergence of APF, 41–44, 51–54, 56–58, 65; outcomes of, 69–70; in women's countermobilization, 178–79; in youth engagement, 212, 225–26, 230

procedures, organizational, 10–11, 63, 64–65, 90–91, 144, 155, 163–66, 181–82

Protea South, 127–28, 136–37, 138–39, 141–42, 151

protests: emotion in aesthetics of, 10–16; public, in fieldwork, 25–26; singing dynamics at, 120–29; spatial access and routinization in conditioning, 80–84; success of, in emergence of APF, 65–66

Prudence (activist), 4, 151–52, 158–59, 163–64

Quagga evictions, 99–105

race: in backlash against Remmoho, 203–4; in hypermarginality, 13, 15; in ruptures, 155–58, 162

Rancière, Jacques, 11–13, 16–17, 59

reciprocity, 66, 74, 86, 91, 96, 220

reclamation, 58, 69–70, 72–77, 104, 179–80, 185–86, 202–4

Reconstruction and Development Programme (RDP), 46, 101–2

Redemption (activist), 232–35, 240, 247–48

Redmond, Shana, 132n2

refugees, economic, 86–90

Regulation of Gatherings Act of 1993, 82–84, 97–98n6

relationships: aesthetic of, 16, 19, 28–29, 213, 216, 218–26, 230–32; in appraisals and seeking alternatives, 250–51; elements of freedom songs in, 112, 115, 120; embodied, 18, 20; in emergence of APF, 54, 65–66; intimate, in building a home, 98n9; in townships, 39–40; in ubuntu, 91–92; uneven, in ruptures, 151, 153–55; in women's countermobilization, 190, 196, 199–200, 201–2, 203–4; in youth engagement, 28–29, 213, 216, 218–27, 230–32, 235–36, 240

religion, 108, 121, 123–24. See also spirituality

Remmoho women's group: as alternative channel of communication, 156–57; alternative modes of engagement in, 245–46; as alternative to APF, 248–49, 250–51; APF backlash to gendered mobilization by, 203–6; gendered approaches to performance in, 28; in helping women, 175–76; methodologies of, 177–78; and routinization of space, 95; transformation in workshops by, 35–39; in women's countermobilization, 177–78, 179–80, 186–98. See also countermobilization, women's

repetition in musical structure, 115–18

representation: in emergence of APF, 21–22, 49–50, 59–60, 62–64; performance in, 20–21; in women's countermobilization, 179 resources: in emergence of APF, 54, 63; in performative geography, 75, 80; in ruptures, 154–56, 157–58, 160–63; and women's countermobilization, 188; in youth disillusionment, 238–39

restructuring, municipal and university, 51–54

Rethabile (activist), 205

rhythms, 53–54, 66, 118–20, 128, 230–32

Riley, Denise, 201–2

rituals, 2–3, 20–21, 77–78, 107, 185–86, 189, 246, 250

"rona reakena" (song), 125

Rose (activist), 192–93, 195–98, 220–23, 254

Ross, Fiona, 157

routines, quotidian, 2–4, 6–7, 17–19, 20, 77–78. See also everyday life/lived experience

routinization: of dissent, 71, 76, 80–84, 95, 96–97; of exposure and the Alexandra renewal project, 84–90; and performative geography, 27, 71–80; of protest through spatial access, 80–84; in selective invisibility, 90–92, 95; spatial negotiations in, 69–71

Runciman, Carin, 183

ruptures in APF: community-based groups and struggle in, 146–47, 153–54; divisiveness in, 21, 95–96, 153–58, 245–46, 251–52; in organizational efficacy, 28; performative geography in, 71; race, class, and internal politics in, 150–62; reconsidering performance in, 162–66; self-interest in, 143; in youth disillusionment, 235–36

Scheper-Hughes, Nancy, 198

security/insecurity: economic and material, 136–37, 168–69, 192–93, 196, 216, 224; embodied, 208n27; in housing, 101–5; spiritual, 168–69, 192–93. See also poverty

Sedibeng Committed Artists (SCA), 227–28

segregation, 80, 81, 90–91. See also apartheid

self-construction, singing in, 128–31

self-sovereignty, 92–94, 104

senses/sensation/sensory experience: in claiming dignity, 91–94; embodiment in, 16–18, 20–21, 32n13; in emergence of APF,

44, 45; in performance and collective politics, 2–4, 246; in the political aesthetics of collective power, 10–13, 15–16; singing dynamics in, 120–21; song in transmission of, 85–86; in women's countermobilization, 185, 190–92, 205; in youth aesthetics, 218–19, 230–32. See also perception

services, basic/service delivery: in the Alexandria Renewal Project, 86–88, 94; in creative expression at collective protests, 107, 110–11, 112–13; in emergence of APF, 48–49, 50–53, 58, 65–66; in performative geography, 75–76; in post-apartheid neoliberalism, 13–15; in Protea South, 136, 137–38, 141–43; "service delivery protests," 146–47, 170n4; in women's countermobilization, 178–79, 185–86; in youth engagement, 211, 217–18, 228

sexuality, 182–83, 184–85

shack dwellers, 39–40, 98n9, 122–23, 136–43, 151

silence in protest, 106–7, 115

Silindiwe (regional organizer), 79

Silver Town Transit Camp, 86–87, 90

"Sizolala" (song), 104

Sizwe (activist), 115

Slovo, Gillian, 123, 127

Small, Christopher, 117

Small Farm Crisis Committee, 232, 233–35

"sobashiy' abazal' ekhaya" (song), 213–14

social body/"body politic" model, 89–90

sociality: in claiming justice, 94; embodiment in, 122–23; form of, 68n16; in women's countermobilization, 178, 189–90, 191, 193, 194–95, 197–98, 200–202; in youth engagement, 218–19

sociopolitics, 17–18, 45, 111–12, 116–17, 198, 200, 245

solidarity: of APF, 60, 244; education in, 142–43; embodied performance in, 21; intergenerational, in youth engagement, 240; material and spiritual insecurity in, 192–93; in performance and collective politics, 246; reciprocity in, 86; sonic, 124; spatial routinization in, 69, 71, 95–96

songs: anti-apartheid, APF adaptations of, 3; embodiment of, in protest, 106–7;

as manifestations of performance, 5–6; in motivation, 103–5; in the political aesthetics of collective power, 12–13; of resistance, in dignity, 92–94; subversive content of, 111–12. *See also* freedom songs/singing; *song titles*

Songs of the Working Class Volume 1 (APF), 111, 145

sonics, 43, 61, 112–17, 120, 124–28, 139–40, 197

South Africa Communist Party (SACP), 47–48, 59–60

South African History Archives, 24

South African Municipal Workers Union, 52

Soweto Electricity Crisis Committee (SECC), 58, 142, 210–11, 223–24, 225–26

Soweto Heroes Day, 210–11

space: activist, ruptures in, 150–62; claiming of, 43, 44, 61, 72, 97n2; domestic, in the formation of social movements, 1–2; in emergence of APF, 43, 44, 52; in routinization of APF, 69–71, 72–75, 80–84, 96–97; in women's countermobilization, 177, 202–3

speech. *See* voice/voicing

spirit, collective, 4, 5, 146, 202

spirituality, 19, 121, 168–69, 183, 192–93, 196, 197. *See also* religion

spontaneity, 10–11, 65, 82–83, 104, 147

staging of protest, 32–33n16, 80–84, 94

status, socioeconomic: in backlash against Remmoho, 203–4; over ideology, in emergence of APF, 63; in the political aesthetics of collective power, 16; in ruptures, 150, 151, 152–58; and women's countermobilization, 178–79, 198–99; in youth engagement, 215, 216–17, 231–32

Steingo, Gavin, 215

Strathern, Marilyn, 204

"street comrades," 153–58

stress, 4, 89, 102, 172, 192, 198–202

structure: of APF, 39, 44, 59, 61–65, 66, 154, 159, 244; musical, 108–9, 111–20; societal, 198–200

struggle fatigue, 47–48, 56–57, 61–62, 67n6

students, 55–56, 131, 212, 215–16, 231

subjectivities, 32n15, 72–73, 82, 122–23, 127, 212–13, 216–19

subordination, 74, 115, 178–79, 217–18

subversion/subversiveness, 30n4, 81, 111–12, 125–27, 200–201, 240–41n2

suffering. *See* pain

surveillance, 72, 87–88, 115

suspicion, 29, 155–56, 158–59, 160–61, 166, 167–68, 235–36, 239. *See also* trust/distrust

sustainability, organizational, 15, 44, 45, 61–62, 64–66, 249

synchrony, 9, 114, 145, 248

tactics: as APF legacy, 244; in community division, 142; in emergence of APF, 43–44, 48–49, 58; freedom songs as, 108; internal, in ruptures, 160–61; in performance and collective politics, 245–46, 247–48, 250; and reality, 103; of youth, 213

Talent (activist), 193, 194

tempo, 139–40, 230–32

temporality: in creative expression, 106–7, 111–12, 117–18, 120; in emergence of APF, 44, 66; in routinization, 70–71, 72, 77–78, 79, 97n2

"That's Why I'm a Socialist" (song), 129–31

Thembelihle Crisis Committee (TCC), 60

"thina senza nje" (song), 140–41

Thokozani (activist), 223, 225–26, 239

Thulani (activist), 50–52, 53–54, 161–62, 232–33

toyi-toyi dance, 42–43, 53–54, 123–24, 145. *See also* dance/dances

trade unions, 42–43, 48–49, 52–53, 55–56, 57–58, 59–60

transcendence, 20–21, 32–33n16, 83–84, 85–86, 92–94, 96–97, 122–23, 253–56

transformation: organizational, 59, 61–62, 63–64, 204–5; personal, 1–2, 4, 8, 25–26, 35–36, 184–85, 189–90, 243–44; political, 17–18, 201–2

transgression, 12–13, 15, 32–33n16, 244–45

transition, political, of South Africa: in conditioning protest, 80–84, 97–98n6; in emergence of APF, 3, 13–14, 45–49, 50–51, 65; generational dynamics in, 213–18; in Ma Patrycja's story, 26–27 transmission: of emotion, 85–86, 107; intergenerational, of activism, 210–12, 222–23; of sentiment through performance, 19–21

transparency, organizational, 155, 156, 162

trauma, 89–90, 133n17, 203–4

troupes, performance, 145, 226–28

trust/distrust: of APF comrades, in ruptures, 29, 152–53, 155–56, 158–63, 166, 167–69; of APF leaders, and youth engagement, 235–36, 239; of neighbors, 192–94, 208n25; and women's countermobilization, 182–83, 192–94, 195

Tseliso (activist), 163–65

Tshepang (activist), 4, 225, 236–37, 238, 239, 248–49

Tsibo, 228, 236

Turner, Victor, 29–30n2

ubuntu ethical philosophy, 14–16, 51–52, 91–92

Umkhonto we Sizwe, 213–14

unity/disunity, 53–54, 63–64, 119, 143, 148, 250–51. See also ruptures in APF

Urban Futures Conference, 2000, 42–44, 56–58, 69–70

Vaal Triangle land invasion, 49–51

van der Walt, Lucien (activist), 170–71n11, 243–44

Veriava, Ahmed (activist), 24, 53, 55–58, 243

violence: domestic, 36–39, 175–76, 199; in evolution of township protests, 81; in the Regulation of Gatherings Act, 97–98n6; retaliatory, against activists, 141–42; in ruptures, 146–47, 150; sexual, 75, 78–79, 88, 139, 172–76, 199, 204; state, in marginalization, 13–14; structural, 95, 150, 179, 198–200, 211–12; and women's countermobilization, 188–89, 197–200, 201; xenophobic, 24–25

visibility/invisibility: of APF, 90–92, 101–3, 130–31, 147–48, 243–44, 248; in APF's break with ANC, 60; of members, to APF, 70–71, 90–92, 96, 138; in the political aesthetics of collective power, 11–12, 13,

32nn15–16; routinization in, 74, 80, 81, 90–92, 96; and ruptures, 151–52, 163; in women's countermobilization, 190–91

voice/voicing: of dissent, in emergence of APF, 48–49, 56–57, 61; power of, in youth engagement, 220, 221–22; representation of, in APF, 64; in ruptures, 154–55, 156–57, 158, 168; of trauma, 173–76; in women's countermobilization, 180, 181–82, 185, 188–89, 191–92, 197–98, 199–200, 201–2, 203–6

vulgarity, 124–25, 126, 247

vulnerability: of activists, 29, 120; of home life, 35–40; to neoliberalism, 15, 52–53; routinization of exposure in, 86–90; in ruptures, 142–43, 151; in selective invisibility, 91; to sexual violence, 176; song in confrontation of, 104, 120, 124–25; of women, in countermobilization, 178–79, 181–82, 186, 191, 196

Vuyiswa (activist), 110–11

water. See services, basic/service delivery

weaponry, song as, 123–27

wellness/well-being: creative expression in, 245–46; loss of, in ruptures, 168, 169; performance of, 2–3; routines in, 20–21; in women's countermobilization, 23, 28, 177–78, 189–90, 194–95, 200–203, 205–6, 245–46, 248. See also health/healing

Wesley (activist), 253–56

Wickstrom, Maurya, 72–73

Willeen (activist), 172–76, 191–92, 193–94, 202, 246

Williams, Raymond, 46

Winter School 2005 Reference Group, 181. See also Gender Reference Group

Wits University, 42–44, 53–54, 56–57, 69–70

Wits University Crisis Committee, 53–55

Working Class Crisis Committee (WCCC), 219, 227–28

World Cup (2010) protest march, 74, 81–82, 144–46, 149, 163–66

World Summit on Sustainable Development (WSSD) 2002 conference, 60–62, 81–82

xenophobia, 24–25

youth and youth engagement: aftermath of struggle in disillusionment, 235–40; alternative creative expression by, 245–46; in APF, 212, 216–18, 232–35; apolitical culture of, 28–29, 215–16, 240–41n2; challenges in, 223–26; employment in, 214–15, 216, 223–24, 225, 229–30, 240; intergenerational dynamics in activism of, 210–12, 218–19, 228, 229–30, 240; performance in, 226–32, 235–40, 246; political subjectivities in, 212–13; relationships in, 28–29, 213, 216, 218–26, 230–32, 235–36, 240; in South Africa's transition, 213–18; at the World Cup march, 145; youth choirs, 228–29, 233–34, 241. *See also* engagement, activist

Zabalaza Anarchist Communist Front, 136, 138

OMOTAYO JOLAOSHO (*they, them, their[s]*) (1985–2021) was a cultural anthropologist with a background in performance and integrated arts. They were an Assistant Professor of Africana Studies in the School of Interdisciplinary Global Studies at the University of South Florida. Their previous publications include the transnational anthology *African Women Writing Resistance: Contemporary Voices*.

www.ingramcontent.com/pod-product-compliance
Lightning Source LLC
Chambersburg PA
CBHW031351290326
41932CB00044B/953